INSTANT RELIEF:
The Encyclopedia of Self-Help

INSTANT RELIEF

The Encyclopedia of Self-Help

TOM GREENING, Ph.D. and DICK HOBSON

Raachel Jurovics, Ph.D.
Associate Editor

WIDEVIEW
BOOKS

MANUFACTURED IN THE UNITED STATES OF AMERICA

Second Printing

Library of Congress Cataloging in Publication Data

Main entry under title:

Instant relief.
    Includes bibliographies. Index.
        1. Conduct of life—Dictionaries.   2. Phychology, Pathological—Dictionaries.   I. Greening, Thomas C., 1930-   II. Hobson, Dick.
BF637.C5157   158′.1′03   79-11255
ISBN 0-87223-571-8

Contents

An Introduction
to Self-Help Psychology

Research shows that quick cures seldom last. Deep changes take time and effort. And yet you *can* experience rapid reduction in anxiety and depression when you are guided into taking some initial steps to work on your personal problems and when you are shown a way of seeing your problems that gives you hope.

Doctors estimate that about 60 percent of office visits are made by patients suffering from psychological rather than medical problems. This is a waste of doctors' time and patients' money. We need simpler ways to help people become more capable of self-care for emotional upsets and long-term stress reactions.

Overdependency on expensive experts to cure you by doing something to your head can be replaced by strengthening your own independent capacity to solve your problems of living. Just knowing that this is possible can be a great source of "relief." And learning specific first steps to take can reduce the anxiety that otherwise keeps you stuck in your problem.

You may have great energy and courage and yet remain confused and depressed by disabling myths and draining dependencies that rob you of your power. Once you grasp the fact that the way you see yourself and the world, and the ways you act, are *learned* rather than caused by mysterious forces changeable only by medical experts, you can begin to learn new ways: There is indeed "instant relief" in knowing that you can learn, and in having concrete help to begin that learning.

The purpose of this book is to help you set yourself free. It is a guidebook to assist you in finding your way out of psychological hangups that form the emotional chains and situational prisons that keep you from the full and free use of your human potential. The psychological self-help approach involves five basic strategies:

Strategy 1: Deepen your insight into the causes of your problem. This is sometimes decisive, especially if you have not had much experience in looking into your internal processes ("what makes you tick") or into the external forces that have shaped your character and personality.

Sometimes just tracing the sequence of events that produced your problem can help you step out of that sequence the next time it starts to happen. A car salesman realized that he was easily triggered into arguing with any male customer who claimed to know a lot about cars. He traced this back to his anger at his domineering father, who scoffed at his son's efforts to fix the family car. The salesman gained insight into this repetitive pattern from the past and saw that restaging old battles with his father was interfering with his present wish to earn a living. His new awareness was sufficient to release him.

Unfortunately, a theory that merely explains why you have a problem may actually work to keep you stuck in the problem. Thousands of people have spent millions of dollars and hours, if not years, of their time on the couch plumbing the depths of their psyches, emerging with profound insights—and making few changes except to grow older and poorer. It's a reminder of the persistent human tendency to avoid risks, to go through just the motions of change, or to blame external factors for our problems. Insight is valuable, but we need other strategies too.

Strategy 2: Recognize the secret payoffs that bribe you into holding on to your problem. A housewife whose children had grown to the age where they required much less of her time complained that she could not find a meaningful part-time job. Through self-examination she came to see that she was very comfortable staying at home and was dependent on the familiar household routines she'd said were boring.

Avoidance of risks is a frequent and powerful payoff. When we are smuggling bootleg rewards into our lives, we try our best not to get caught—even by ourselves. Much well-advertised suffering and pseudo-seeking of help is a smokescreen to cover up the fact that the sufferer is deriving some benefit from the symptom.

Actually, that is what symptoms are for: to *solve* problems. The fact that they are costly, inefficient solutions does not negate their usefulness. Nor does it mean that a suffering person is faking or malingering. Beneath the symptoms lie greater pain, anxiety, depression.

Instant relief and long-term growth often necessitate recognizing the cause and function of a nagging symptom, letting go of its secret payoffs, and working through the deeper problem you have been avoiding. When you finally do that, you will be surprised at the relief and progress that occur, just when you thought you were going to feel worse forever.

Strategy 3: Activate your willingness to take responsibility for changing. When you gain insight into the causes of a problem and admit the secret payoffs that have helped sustain it, you are ready to take charge of overcoming it. This sense of responsibility is not the same as guilt, which is immobilizing and useless. Nor is it the same as old-fashioned willpower, which is often an attempt to conquer your problems with force rather than to understand their causes and face up to the incentives that prolong them.

A true desire to change is expressed as a natural, integrated willingness (not a strained willfulness) and determination to be responsible for being the guiding source of your own life. It is the clear recognition that change must come from within, even if the remedial action involves attack on the external world. It is not self-blame or tortured faultfinding; those reactions just waste energy and divert you from constructive action.

As Ezra Pound said, "A slave is one who waits for someone else to come and free him." Our focus is on how you can set yourself free.

Strategy 4: Open up your awareness of new ways of thinking, feeling, and acting. Increase your capacity to experience what is going on in your life. Relief from your problems can result from loosening up the way you look at and carry around whatever bothers you. Much pain comes from tightness—not just muscle tightness in the body, but a "tight" way of viewing life. Learn to release buried feelings, invent creative fantasies, explore alternate ways of thinking, and try experimental actions.

Strategy 5: Raise your sights to aim at growth and self-actualization. Most problems of living contain the seeds of growth and personal development. Often a problem occurs because an important aspect of your inner nature is being denied fulfillment. The challenge presented by the problem contains the potential for the deepening and expansion of your core self.

A real estate developer went to see a biofeedback expert for relief of his headaches. As he learned to relax the muscles that caused the headaches, he was flooded with new feelings, some scary but many of them warm and enthusiastic. He changed his whole approach to real estate development, generated projects that better satisfied his aesthetic and community-service needs, and became friends with his partner for the first time in many years. He realized that he had been stuck at the threshold of change, holding on to his old ways of operating because they "worked." His headaches "woke him up" and gave him the incentive and opportunity to embark on a change process, one that opened up far more horizons than he had envisioned the day he walked in for his first biofeedback session.

Self-actualization is not a luxury or a far-out hobby for psychology faddists. It is a fundamental human drive, and it sometimes first emerges in the form of pain and distress. Although cancer, for example, is a physical illness, it generates severe emotional problems in many of its

victims and their relatives. Being ill with cancer can be turned into an
opportunity for growth precisely because it forces you to face the reality
of death. There are patients for whom falling ill with cancer can be the
start of rising up to new levels of living. (In Chinese the word for "crisis"
is composed of the characters for "danger" and "opportunity.")

Several streams of psychology flow together into this encyclopedia.
Psychoanalysis, behavior therapy, inspirational approaches—all bring
something of value.

Psychoanalysis has provided great wisdom about the roles of the
unconscious, dreams, fantasies, resistance to change, and early-childhood
learning. The powerful drives of sex and aggression are seen by psychoanalysts as presenting people with basic problems in living comfortably
in organized society. Physical and emotional symptoms result from
desperate, compromise attempts to balance needs, values, and the
limitations of the real world. Self-help psychology has benefited greatly
from the insights of psychoanalysis as a theory, even though the treatment is contrary to the self-help approach due to its expense and
reliance on the "expert" doctors treating the "sick" patient. Also,
psychoanalysis tends to be rather pessimistic regarding the capacity for
change toward happiness and fulfillment. At best, said Freud, you can
hope to exchange deep, disabling neuroses for the ordinary neuroses
of daily existence. Too strict an application of Freudian theory can
lead to creativity being explained away in oversimplified terms. There
is a tendency in psychoanalysis to dwell on the "sick" side of the self.
Assertive, exploratory action gets labeled "acting out" if it is less than
perfectly free of neurotic and defensive motives.

Behavior therapy attempts to apply practical, effective techniques to
change behavior. It aims at concrete, immediate results rather than insight and overall lifestyle modification. Behavior therapists have devised
some dramatically effective methods to relieve symptoms. Critics of
behavior therapy argue, however, that if you treat people like machines,
you may succeed in "fixing" the malfunctioning "machine" at the cost
of depersonalizing the human being. There is also some disagreement
about how long behavioral changes last if they are not backed up by
deeper changes in the person.

Positive thinking is advocated by many self-help books. Some include
a religious emphasis on faith in God's benign will and belief that we can
be "saved from sin" (or unhappiness or neurosis) by spiritual means.
Religious faith and spiritual practice can be powerful resources for
changing one's life if not used naively. Unfortunately, positive thinking,
with or without a religious component, often glosses over the stubborn
underlying roots of problems, such as secret payoffs or unconscious guilt.

Self-critical or guilt-ridden people may try positive thinking, fail to get instant relief, and end up thinking even more negatively about themselves. Religion is sometimes misused in ways that aggravate guilt and suppress feelings that need to be experienced openly before change can occur. It is important to distill for yourself the essence of the formal religions and the personal spiritual approaches available to you. Experiences of peace, wholeness, harmony, and love can provide you with marvelous relief and long-term growth.

Existential humanistic psychology makes use of the various other methods and theories when appropriate, but includes them as part of a special way of being in the world and regarding existence. It takes into account our psychological complexity, is optimistic regarding our human potential, and is profoundly challenging regarding the steps necessary to fulfill that potential. The drive for self-actualization is seen as a core part of human nature, crusted over though it may be by defenses and ordinary survival drives.

People yearn for self-expression, closeness, and a sense of meaning in their lives, even in the midst of their despair and sabotage. But such affirmation in the face of life as we know it requires risk, commitment, and responsibility, and this is where existentialism comes in.

Existential philosophy asserts that you are constantly in the process of choosing and creating who you are. That process can stir up feelings of dread and nausea, as well as joy and exhilaration. Your job is to go through whatever you must in order to claim and use your freedom. You are not who you were, even a moment ago. That is your past, your history, your "soap opera script."

You can avoid existential anxiety (or plain old responsibility) by moaning that you are a helpless pawn at the mercy of your childhood traumas, your conditioned behavior, malevolent social forces, or God's mysterious will. There is always lots of evidence to "prove" that you are helpless. But even if external events do seem to render you helpless in one sense, you always have the option of struggling to alter the future course of events or, more significantly, to alter the way you interpret and experience those events.

Really choosing what you choose or are stuck with is the great unsung art. Some very common people are masters at this uncommon skill. Once in a while, for example, you may see a waiter totally absorbed in serving a bowl of soup, dedicated to that act as a way of creating a moment of enlivening contact with a customer. Once in a while you may see an old couple who have truly chosen each other for life.

Much of the time, however, we hold on to our pseudo-freedom, hold back from full presence in the immediate situation, and create distress for ourselves and others through our unwillingness to risk, through our reluctance to surrender ourselves to the intensity and vulnerability of all-out commitment to a course of action or a relationship.

War and high-risk sports catch some people up in this way; living at the edge of death can pull us into total involvement. Gambling can be used defensively to create an illusion of intense participation in life. Such contrived situations are usually artificial substitutes for sustained commitment to life.

The real heroes are those who doggedly and joyfully work at becoming more loving and self-actualizing in ordinary life. They know that every personal advance is purchased with effort and forgone choices, that there are no uncomplicated relationships or easy triumphs, and that it is still possible to create happiness and fulfillment out of hurt and loss.

Creative, venturesome risking can be done only from a secure base. You can endure suspense, anxiety, vulnerability, and the possibility of defeat only if you know that you have a core within you that will remain whole and undamaged. The motto for gamblers—"Never gamble more than you can afford to lose"—applies to life outside the casinos as well. You must know and value who you are underneath the problems, joys, vanities, ambitions, worries, successes, and crutches that form the outer layers of your personality. If you have a solid place to stand, you can move adventurously into growth and change.

Why not become your own guru? If you have a problem, it makes sense to hire an expert who really cares and who really knows what's going on—*you*. You care more about your suffering than anyone else does.

Potentially, you are the best consultant, guru, psychotherapist, or just plain friend for yourself that you can find. Consider the Goodwill Industries slogan: "Hire the Handicapped—It's Good Business." After all, we are all handicapped by our past conditioning, by the limitations of our backgrounds. So do what you'd do for any handicapped person— hug yourself with compassion, assess your strengths and weaknesses, give yourself some encouragement, and get to work.

There are times, of course, when professional medical, psychological, financial, legal, or spiritual help may be your best resource. When in doubt, don't endanger yourself by neglecting to make use of experts. Just remember, you remain responsible for how you go about choosing the experts and how you use what they have to offer.

Sigmund Freud started one revolution when he got us to face the power of unconscious motives and sexuality. The behaviorists started another revolution when they showed how behavior can be shaped and controlled by manipulation of rewards and punishments. We are calling for another revolution, one that raises our vision of what we can become and strengthens our competence to fulfill that vision. *Psychological self-help,* in the hands of ordinary citizens, can transform individual lives and our whole society.

The psychological self-help movement views people as desiring fulfilling work as naturally as they seek play or rest. They want to develop and exercise their competence for the pleasure of it, as well as the rewards it brings. Thus, externally imposed control and coercion are not the best ways to get results. Nor is internal control and coercion that takes the form of nagging, self-attack, hurtful comparisons, or Prussian willpower. Not just on the job, but in "working" on ourselves, we have a great capacity, often untapped and undirected, to exercise self-control and self-direction. We want to enrich our lives, and we will voluntarily take on responsibility and make commitments as part of a plan we believe in.

Instant Relief is an alphabetized household manual for psychological self-help. But beyond this simplicity and practicality, it is enriched by an affirmative humanistic vision of the capacity for self-directed growth inherent in all people. Even when you are struggling with what may be labeled a mundane problem or pathological symptom, at another level you are also working on meaningful issues of awareness, dignity, freedom, and self-actualization.

This encyclopedia can help you solve your personal problems at the level of relief from suffering. In addition, it can help you experience your exciting potential for making deeper changes and for creatively turning your problems into challenges and opportunities.

INSTANT RELIEF:
The Encyclopedia of Self-Help

ABORTION

"I'm pregnant!" This realization can be the happiest, most thrilling moment of your life—or the most terrifying.

Pregnancy can be a feared and desperate situation, especially if you are young and unmarried, or married and very poor or very ill, or you already have more children than you can cope with. It can be a terrible problem if you are a career woman on the way up, or a woman on the verge of divorce, or if you and your husband have planned a life together that does not include the burden or responsibility of children.

In the United States, every year nearly two million women decide on abortion.

If you are pregnant with an unwanted child, you may be filled with guilt and shame, or feel simply trapped and desperate. You may be angry at God or the world or your husband or lover. But all your regrets and anger cannot change the fact that you now have a decision to make. For some women, the answer to "Shall I have the baby?" is clear-cut. But perhaps you truly don't know what to do. You are wavering back and forth between one decision and another. Other people are pushing you in some direction that you're not sure you want to go.

Why did this happen to you? Sometimes reliable contraception methods fail. Many women become pregnant out of ignorance about birth control, or from carelessness. Sometimes "carelessness" means that, whether you realize it or not, the act of getting pregnant is an affirmation of your creativity, fertility, womanhood, sexuality. Or perhaps it means that your parents or some social agency will take care of you, and you won't have to be responsible for taking care of yourself. This is often true of young women who become pregnant repeatedly. Understanding the reasons for your pregnancy can help you make a decision about what to do.

Your task now is to face yourself and your problem clearly and take responsibility for finding the best possible solution for *you*. From this effort you can gain a new self-awareness and inner strength. You can also build closer relationships with those you love, if you allow them to share this experience with you. Turn this crisis into a time of growth and personal rewards.

Start your decision-making process right away. Otherwise, you may find that nature has made the decision for you.

• First, take a pregnancy test to be sure your diagnosis is correct. Go to your doctor or to a state-licensed clinic that gives the simple test free. Menstrual periods can be delayed for reasons other than pregnancy. Stress, some kinds of drugs, illness, and even changes of climate can stall your period's arrival. Symptoms like morning nausea can also stem from other causes. If you find you really are pregnant, obtain the best care possible from your doctor or the clinic.

• Get counseling. Talk to your parents, your doctor, a religious counselor, your husband or lover, or another close friend. Keep in mind that each of them may have a personal bias and may lecture you or try to coerce you in some direction. Contact an organization like Planned Parenthood Federation of America or National Clergy Consultation Service on Abortion. Their services are free, and the advice is likely to be objective, understanding, and nonmoralistic. Remember that this is *your* decision. Listen to all of the advice and input that you can get. Sift it thoughtfully. Ask yourself how it really fits with the way you feel.

• Get a current book on abortion that includes this information: how to locate reputable agencies that can help you, explanations of abortion procedures, what to do if you want to have the baby, information on giving your child up for adoption, considerations about raising your child yourself, and how to keep from becoming pregnant again until you are really ready to. Set up a timetable for decision making. Different stages of pregnancy call for different procedures. As pregnancy continues, the risks and costs of abortion increase—and many states and hospitals have set "cut-off points" beyond which women seeking abortions are turned away.

• Start your self-exploration. If you became pregnant through ignorance or negligence, think about the reasons you neglected to get information or thought you would be safe without precautions. Think about whether being pregnant makes you feel somehow more creative or fulfilled or feminine. Ask yourself whether you want your parents to pay attention to you as an adult, or want other people to take care of you, or want to find out whether your boyfriend really loves you.

• Put all the information about yourself, and all the information from your reading and counseling, into your self-computer. Whatever the reasons for your pregnancy, accept them as being okay for you at that time and in that place. If you were affirming yourself as a woman or as an adult, enjoy that affirmation. Determine, however, to find less costly ways to fulfill your very real, legitimate needs.

• If you are single, consider the alternative of marrying the baby's father—but recognize that instead of solving your problem, marriage can create even bigger problems. Be sure that you and your boyfriend are truly ready and willing to marry each other and to become parents. Think what changes in your lives, especially in your plans for the future, this would mean for each of you.

• Consider having the baby without getting married. Find out about medical care and places you can live until you have the baby, if you can't live at home. Find out about adoption procedures in case you should decide to give your baby up. Think about what would happen if you decided to raise the baby yourself. For each of these alternatives, find out about the costs involved. Ask yourself who would pay them. Ask yourself what your life would be like in each circumstance.

• If you aren't sure what being a mother would be like, find out by talking to mothers about their lives. Take care of someone else's small child for a while. Spend time working with a group of children.

• Look at your fantasy (if you have one) that the baby will be a little pet with whom you will create a loving, warm relationship in the desert of human coldness. Ask yourself whether you have the inner resources, the child-rearing skills, and the finances to do it. If you don't, then recognize that you may be using the baby in a naive, selfish, and potentially destructive way. Remember that your prime consideration should be what you can give to this baby as another human being.

• If you decide to keep the baby, don't feel guilty that you once considered aborting it. Recognize that many women have these doubts initially. And don't panic if you don't love your baby at first sight. Trust that your feelings will grow as the relationship between you develops.

• Make your decision. If you decide to have the baby, set those plans in motion. Remember that you do not have to make a final decision about adoption until after your baby is born.

• If you decide to have an abortion, go to a legitimate, state-licensed facility, where you can have both medical care and counseling. Don't delay. Find out when is the best time to have your abortion, from a medical standpoint, and schedule it.

• Don't go to a commercial abortion-referral agency. They are sometimes rackets and can refer you to a quack. Don't try "home remedies" to get rid of the baby—pills, exercises, medicines, instruments such as knitting needles. They can cause you great injury and even result in death.

• Don't kid yourself about the emotional impact of having an abortion. Recognize that you will probably have a sense of sadness, guilt, or loss. Recognize that abortion is the ending of a life process, and make sure that you understand all of your feelings about it.

• Make a list of questions to ask the hospital or agency about the abortion: exactly what procedure will be done, how long it takes, the cost, whether any pain is involved, what aftercare is necessary, what its consequences may be. Find out exactly what to expect before you go for the abortion.

• After you have the abortion, take positive steps to rebuild and renew yourself. Remember that you have released yourself from a burden and responsibility that you weren't ready to carry. Use that liberation to do something that feels creative for yourself or others. If you have other children, help them to grow and be creative. Participate in the life process, as a balance to the abortion process you have experienced.

• Expect and accept any feelings of loss or grief. Try to discover if they recall other losses or partings you have had in the past, and accept those feelings too. If you feel guilt, ask yourself whether it is your own guilt or it is being put on you by others. Recognize that some of your feelings, even wide swings of mood, may be from temporary hormonal changes. If your feelings are too difficult to deal with, get counseling help.

• Remember that it is possible to become pregnant again immediately after an abortion. While you are at the hospital or clinic, arrange for and *take with you* whatever contraception you have decided on.

• Think about what you have gained from this experience. Use your new knowledge about yourself to build a creative, joyful life. Enjoy your strengths and potentials. Try to reshape the parts of yourself that give you difficulty. If you need help to do this, get it.

• If you are the parent of a teenager who is pregnant, help her through her decision-making time. Do not moralize or blame her for what has already happened. Do not try to coerce her into having an abortion to "save the family reputation," or ask her to have the baby because you would feel guilty if she didn't or because you regret an earlier abortion of your own. Try to understand what your daughter may be saying to you by her pregnancy. Respect her needs. Try to use this time to build a closer relationship between the two of you as adults.

• If you are the husband or lover of the woman, share your feelings about the pregnancy. Express your opinion about what you would like her to do, but remember that it is her body. Recognize that this may be a time of crisis in your relationship. Give her your love and support through whatever decision she makes. If you need to, seek counseling for yourself, to help you confront and resolve your own feelings.

• If you are the woman's parent or her husband or lover, after the abortion you may feel relief, sadness, anger, and shame all at the same time. Accept each of these feelings. Do not blame anyone for what has happened. You, too, should take positive steps to renew yourself.

SUGGESTED READING:

Arnstein, Helene S. *What Every Woman Needs to Know About Abortion.* New York: Scribner's, 1973.

Planned Parenthood of New York City. *Abortion: A Woman's Guide.* New York: Abelard-Schuman, 1973.

Skowronski, Marjory. *Abortion and Alternatives.* Milbrae, California: Les Femmes Publications, 1977.

See also: ANXIETY, CHILDBIRTH, FEAR OF SICKNESS, PRE-MARITAL SEX, SINGLE PARENTING, STERILIZATION, TEEN-AGE SEX

AGING

We begin aging as soon as we are born. Unless we die young, we will all experience old age, regardless of our education, job, or socioeconomic status. There are 31 million Americans who are sixty or older, constituting 14.7 percent of our population. By 1980, the total U.S. population since 1900 will have tripled, while the number of people sixty-five or older will have increased an astounding eight times. Clearly, older people are becoming a substantially larger part of our nation.

Yet, in a culture where so many people live to a ripe old age, we still find that aging is often looked upon negatively. There are too few images of aging that are positive, creative, and dignified. Instead, old age is often viewed as a life stage somehow separate from the rest of one's life; a time of decreased social worth and involvement; a period of loss and degeneration leading to loneliness and helplessness; and a time of gradual physical deterioration and accompanying loss of beauty and health. People frequently feel that life is fun and rewarding only while there is youth and vigor. When this vitality wanes, life is viewed as a downhill slide. Aging is seen as a never-ending battle against the forces of loss, anxiety, depression, loneliness, and sickness. These negative cultural images affect all of us even while we are young, for they instill in us the fear that when we lose our youth, physical power, and economic productiveness, we will be neglected and eventually discarded. Even when young, we suffer from not having an inspiring vision of old age as a time for wisdom, love, reflection, spirituality, and leisurely service to the young.

However, as more is learned about aging and the forces and potentials that contribute to this developmental process, we discover that growing older doesn't have to be considered a negative experience. With the right attitude, attention, and preparation, aging can be experienced as a full and meaningful maturation process, like the ripening of a fine wine or a musical instrument. Many people discover that the golden years of life offer greater freedom from economic competition, social striving, child-rearing burdens, and job hassles. This can be the perfect time to develop self-awareness, cultivate special interests, begin new hobbies and leisure activities, and deepen friendships. It can also be a unique opportunity to reflect on the experiences and trials of a lifetime in such a way as to develop the kind of wisdom and caring for people that comes only from having lived a long and full life.

In recent years, increasing numbers of people have begun to recognize the fact that they can actively shape their lives. Aided by the developing fields of humanistic psychology and holistic health and the revolution in physical fitness, self-improvement, and human potential, millions of Americans are taking fuller responsibility for their own health, well-being, and aging, and by so doing have begun to generate new and positive images of aging and activities for the aged. In turn, as more and more older people become healthier, more confident, and more aware, they begin to serve as much-needed positive role models for others involved in similar situations. This positive or "growth" orientation toward living and aging has generated a variety of techniques, programs, and attitudes about aging that offer worthwhile suggestions to all of us involved in the process of growing older.

• Recognize that "old age" is not a life stage separate from the rest of our experience. Rather, old age is a natural extension and reflection of our earlier life activities. People who lead a rich, full, healthy life have a better chance of enjoying a rich, full, and healthy old age.

• Decide that your old age is definitely something you can prepare for by taking care of your health, maintaining close friendships, and keeping a positive attitude about living.

• Stop seeing yourself as a victim of the aging process or as an innocent bystander in your life. Instead, realize that you are the "source" of much of your life and can therefore be responsible for influencing your health, vitality, relationships, and well-being.

• Practice being more appreciative and less critical of yourself. By seeing yourself in terms of your potentials and special talents rather than focusing primarily on your weaknesses and problems, you allow yourself a greater sense of personal involvement and "empowerment" in the daily challenges and activities of your life.

• Aging is an honest teacher. Remember that life is a continual learning process. Learn from your mistakes and take advantage of the many lessons you have experienced throughout your life. The wisdom that comes from experience is a great treasure. Appreciate your years for having allowed you the opportunity to participate deeply in life's adventures.

• Select some people, living or dead, who can serve you as positive models of aging. Who aged in ways you admire? Albert Einstein? Mae West? Jack Benny? Eleanor Roosevelt? Methuselah? Think about your various heroes and favorites. Read their autobiographies or books about them. What qualities did they develop that you can emulate—childlike curiosity, unique style, humor, dignity? Learn from your seniors, and in turn set an example for the younger people who will look to you for guidance.

• Go beyond mere positive thinking. No matter what your predicament, there are things you can do to improve your situation.

• Make friends with and care for your body. Find a group, setting, or activity that will allow you to stretch, breathe, and carefully exert yourself. Regular exercise is an excellent way to maintain vitality, reduce stress, and simply have fun. In addition to swimming, walking, bicycle riding, and golf, there are a variety of less traditional activities, such as yoga, meditation, tai chi, Feldenkrais exercises, and relaxation techniques, that are well suited for older people in that they gently allow you to rebuild muscles, release tension, and improve respiratory, cardiovascular, and neuromuscular functioning.

• Take responsibility for your health. Rather than putting up with accumulating physical problems and ailments, see what changes you can make in your life to alleviate many of the causes of the problem. Poor diet, lack of exercise, overmedication, and stressful living habits cause many of the symptoms that the doctors treat. Work toward making your whole life "healthy," and realize that every improvement you make in a healthful direction will probably brighten your day and add years to your life. And remember to view your doctor as an educational resource and friend rather than as a body mechanic or pill dispenser.

• Develop relationships that have meaning for you and in which you can honestly share your feelings and concerns with people who care and understand. Unfortunately, as people age, close friends often move or die. Yet you can always find new friends, acquaintances, and lovers.

This may mean finding new groups and settings to replace those relationships that are no longer available. Fortunately, the number of programs focusing on the special social needs of the elderly are rapidly growing, and most churches, YMCAs, colleges, community centers, senior centers, senior residences, and social halls now have special activities for the elderly. Take a risk and attend some of these events. Meet new people. Realize that they may be just as anxious or shy as you are. Be open to people different from yourself. Don't get stuck in the past; allow yourself to begin new adventures, relationships, and dialogues with others. Enjoy yourself.

• Keep your mind active and continue to learn. In addition to informal opportunities available through conversation, reading, movies, and television, the formal educational opportunities open to the elderly are quickly expanding throughout the country. Numerous high schools, colleges, universities, churches, and senior residences offer "continuing education" or "lifelong learning" programs open to older people. In addition, some colleges and universities have developed special "emeritus"-type programs that allow elders to attend courses, receive degrees, and even live in the dormitories right along with the younger students. You may wish to take courses specifically on issues related to aging, or perhaps to study something completely new. Whatever you choose, be sure to take advantage of the interesting programs and courses available to you in your community. Classes and courses are also an excellent way to meet people of all ages.

• If you like, continue working. One in four men past sixty-five still works. Older workers have less absenteeism and fewer accidents than young workers! Work can be a place to maintain friendships and a sense of worth and meaning. There are many jobs that older people can do as well as or better than younger people and that especially utilize maturity and wisdom. Also, if you have free time you might like to volunteer your services and talents as a business consultant, a clerk, or a foster grandparent. Realize that there are numerous ways in which you can be of service and assistance to others. Older people, with their years of experience dealing with other people, can be especially good at the human-relations side of work.

• If you like, stop working. You might be the kind of person who feels that you have worked long and hard enough and now you would like some time for yourself. If this is the case, give yourself permission to enjoy whatever leisure activities you choose to pursue. Remind yourself to have fun. You deserve it, and it will make you a more pleasant person to be around.

• Don't allow yourself to become a professional "taker." Wherever possible, be a giver. Turn your years of experience and your new free time into a resource to help others. Avoid self-pity. As you reach out to other people, you will find your days brighten considerably. There are numerous hospitals, child-care centers, nursery schools, day camps, high schools, businesses, parks, nursing homes, army bases, and orphanages that are desperately in need of the kind of sensitivity and mature care that you may be able to offer. Realize that each generation can always find ways to be of assistance to the others.

• Don't let yourself become sedentary or cooped up in your house. Whenever possible, plan to move about and leave your house for short walks, visits, shopping trips, or just a friendly adventure around your neighborhood. Stimulate yourself frequently with activity and your mind and body will remain healthy and alert.

• Travel if you can. Many travel agencies, bus companies, and senior-citizen groups offer inexpensive travel packages to interesting and exciting locations. The later years of life can be the perfect time to embark on new sightseeing adventures. If you live alone and are afraid to travel alone, you will be pleased to discover that there are many other people just like yourself looking for travel companions. Explore new places, taste new foods, meet new people.

• Discover all the large and small activities that give you pleasure, and do them. Don't settle for withdrawal, isolation, apathy, dependency, and passivity. Find ways to spark your spirit, and work toward having your life be as meaningful and joyous as possible.

• Write to the National Association for Humanistic Gerontology (NAHG) for information about programs and services throughout the country related to healthy and positive approaches to aging: NAHG, Claremont Office Park, 41 Tunnel Road, Berkeley, California 94705. The National Council on the Aging (1828 L Street, NW, Washington, D.C. 20036) also serves as a central resource for older people, as does the American Association of Retired Persons, 215 Long Beach Boulevard, Long Beach, California 90802.

• Contact the Gray Panthers, 3700 Chestnut Street, Philadelphia, Pennsylvania 19104.

SUGGESTED READING:

Beauvoir, Simone de. *Coming of Age*. New York: G. P. Putnam's, 1972.

Comfort, Alex. *A Good Age*. New York: Crown Publishers, 1976.

Geba, Bruno. *Vitality Training for Older Adults*. New York: Random House, 1975.

Luce, Gay. *Your Second Life*. New York: Delacorte, 1979.

See also: BOREDOM, DEPRESSION, FEAR OF DEATH, FEAR OF

SICKNESS, HYPOCHONDRIA, LONELINESS, LOSS OF LOVE, MENOPAUSE, MID-LIFE CRISIS, RETIREMENT, SEX IN LATER LIFE

AGORAPHOBIA

Do you always choose an aisle seat in movie theaters and a table near the door in restaurants? Do you feel uneasy—even panicky—standing in line at the supermarket? Do you avoid walking alongside tall buildings? These are all symptoms of mild agoraphobia.

Literally, "agoraphobia" means fear of the marketplace or assembly hall. The term is generally applied to the fear of being in crowds or traveling alone. It also encompasses fears of open fields, lakes or oceans, or city streets, or of being lost. In the fearful situation, the victim is overcome by sudden panic. He or she may faint or experience heart palpitations, dizziness, trembling, nausea, breathing difficulties.

A recent survey revealed that 2.5 million Americans suffer from this problem. Not all are able to retreat successfully from the world as Howard Hughes did. Most are housewives in their twenties and thirties. They try to hide their problem by staying in the house until a child or friend can accompany them out. Or they go places where they can remain in the car, which provides some of the safety of home.

Agoraphobes live with the constant fear that "something terrible" will happen. Most are plagued with continual anxieties. Women, in particular, fear being alone in the house, death, childbirth, illness and accidents, harming another person. They lack confidence and feel depressed, worthless, and insecure. Male agoraphobes worry about having heart attacks, not being able to cope at work, being lonely.

Frequently agoraphobia develops when an individual is recovering from surgery and stamina is particularly low. It can also be brought on by domestic strain, bereavement, work difficulties, depression, living with domineering parents. Its victims see the world as a huge, noisy, chaotic place. They think, "I will get lost or swallowed up out there. I feel uncertain. I can't make choices. I don't know who I am." They project their inner fears outward onto the world. They may claim they fear "forces" out there are going to get them; they actually fear what they themselves might do if they went out. They may be suppressing unacceptable sexual or aggressive impulses.

The agoraphobic condition is self-perpetuating. After an individual experiences an anxiety attack away from home, he or she fears it will happen again. An agoraphobe has only to think fear to feel fear. The nervous apprehension of going into a panic can trigger the attack. Ultimately, it is the terror of panicking and appearing foolish or disabled in public which keeps the sufferer home, not the fear of any specific danger outside. People with this problem feel so bewildered by it that they think they must be crazy.

Agoraphobia is a strong signal from your mind that you need to confront what is really going on inside you. Don't judge yourself for having this problem. Take advantage of it. Discover your inner fears, and use this opportunity to work at eliminating them.

• Understand that no outside force is making you agoraphobic. Your body is simply responding to the way you're thinking. Learn to cope with your nervous symptoms as well as with the situations you fear.

• Face your panic and accept it for what it is. Don't try to explain it as a physical rather than a nervous reaction. Accepting your panic as a real problem is different from "putting up" with it, which usually results in limiting your activities.

• Remember that panic comes in a wave and will subside. Sit. Take a deep breath and let it out slowly. Be tolerant of your inner trembling. Float with the panic. Wait it out.

• List the physical symptoms which accompany your panic attack. Evaluate them. Remember that panic is a stage of physical shock. Blood vessels may dilate or constrict drastically; your brain may be deprived of blood, and faintness may result. Realize your body is functioning normally in the circumstances of fear and tension you are creating for it. If you have palpitations, remember that the heart is perfectly able to compensate for temporary upsets in timing. It cannot burst. If you gasp for air, remind yourself that your body regulates breathing according to the amount of carbon dioxide in the blood. Experiment now with holding your breath. Notice that you're soon forced to breathe. In a panic attack, your lungs will regulate themselves no matter what you do.

• Avoid taking drugs. They provide a false sense of relaxation and foster dependency.

• Recall the circumstances of your first panic attack. Were you over-stressed by work, money worries, family tensions? Could there have been a physical contribution to your vulnerability to panic at that time, such as fatigue or low blood sugar? Skipping breakfast or lunch could lower your blood sugar level and cause dizziness. A stress you could normally handle could then overwhelm you and send you into an attack of agoraphobia.

• Visualize yourself outside your home, faced with social interactions as well as new places. What disturbs you? Examine your feelings about talking to strangers. Are you afraid to assert yourself? Do you fear personal criticism; do you feel you lack social graces? Think of the groups you've felt comfortable in before—perhaps school or church.

Consider taking a class or joining a church in your neighborhood. Choose small, safe steps.

• Fantasize going out. If you cannot do this by yourself, talk it out with a friend or counselor. Visualize a place you'd like to go. Describe what you think you'll encounter, step by step. As you approach each feared event, experience it wholly. Give yourself the freedom to retreat, to go back and forth flexibly in this fantasy. Reward yourself for your imaginary courage.

• Plan a short, safe outing. Put yourself in a relaxed mood with a pleasant fantasy beforehand. Now take an actual step outside. Pause to determine how nervous you are when you step out the door, then again when you are in front of the house, across the street, several blocks away, and so on. Expect and allow the fear to come. Remember that you are practicing, not testing yourself. Nervous symptoms will cease to come only when their coming no longer matters.

• Practice going out. Go into the frightening situation for at least four hours at a time. (Eight hours gives best results; under four appears ineffective.) Make a commitment to yourself that no matter what happens, you will not give up until the appointed time to return home. If you cannot face a four-hour session, go only as far away as you can without feeling anxious, then return home. As soon as you feel better, head back out again. Repeat this procedure for the four hours.

• Travel with a friend for your first outing if you'll feel more comfortable having company. Visit places which pique your interest, such as a concert hall, museum, or park. Plan to visit at least three places, and set up several tasks to do, such as getting a schedule of events or an application for membership. Have a few backup tasks in case you finish before the time is up.

• Bring along candy or nuts. Nibbling will give your body something to deal with other than anxiety. Take along a walking stick, umbrella, or piece of luggage to help focus your concentration away from yourself.

• Plan mental tasks as well as physical ones. You can take along your bank statement and checkbook and reconcile them in a restaurant or a crowded hotel lobby. Gradually discontinue these aids as you progress.

• Give your body some physical problems to deal with. Prior to your outing, spend thirty minutes exercising. Let your strained muscles cool down and become slightly stiff before you set out. Wear tight, uncomfortable clothes. Learned anxieties will be reduced when your muscles are sore and tired and can't fight back.

• Realize that each person recovers in his or her own time. Don't regard any halts in your progress as setbacks. Accept them. Expect to have a few "flashbacks" to your old fears.

• Realize that the "well" you will be an unfamiliar self at first. Life itself may seem different—perhaps blander than you'd expected—as the agoraphobic state is one of continual agitation and drama.

• Consider whether this is a time in your life when you may *need* to withdraw and retreat. This problem could be a signal that your personal world—your job and your friends—is not right for you. Maybe you need to find a new world to go into. Look for the inner wisdom in your symptoms.

• Many medical facilities offer programs to cure agoraphobia. One of these may be close to you: the Phobia Clinic of the Long Island Jewish Hillside Medical Center (New Hyde Park, New York), White Plains Hospital and Roosevelt Hospital (New York), Butler Hospital (Providence, Rhode Island), University of Mississippi Medical Center (Jackson), University of Utah (Salt Lake City), Veterans Hospital (Palo Alto, California; Miami, Florida), Temple University School of Medicine (Philadelphia, Pennsylvania).

• If you know someone suffering from agoraphobia, be sympathetic about his or her fears even though they may be difficult for you to comprehend. Realize that saying "straighten up" won't help. Encourage and support any moves to remedy the problem.

SUGGESTED READING:

Smith, Manuel J. *Kicking the Fear Habit: Using Your Automatic Orienting Reflex to Unlearn Your Anxieties, Fears, and Phobias.* New York: Dial Press, 1977.

Weekes, Claire. *Simple Effective Treatment of Agoraphobia.* New York: Bantam Books, 1979. (Dr. Weekes's self-help program is also available on cassette tapes. For information, write to Galahad Productions, P.O. Box 5893, Lake Charles, Louisiana 70601.)

See also: ANXIETY, DEPRESSION, FEAR OF FLYING, FEAR OF HEIGHTS, JOB DISSATISFACTION, LONELINESS, MID-LIFE CRISIS, PARANOIA, PASSIVITY, SHYNESS, STRESS

ALCOHOLISM

Alcohol abuse is the number one public health problem and the number one drug problem in America today. It is now the number three killer disease, behind cancer and cardiovascular disease. There are about 10 million alcoholics in the U.S., and they die fifteen years sooner than average. One out of every fourteen people who drinks is an alcoholic.

Of the patients admitted to city, county, and large metropolitan hospitals, 50 percent suffer from alcoholism and alcohol-related diseases. Alcohol is involved in 50 percent of highway fatalities, 55 percent of murders, 45 percent of suicides, and 55 percent of all felonies.

Old myths die slowly, and many clichés about alcoholism persist: "I can't be an alcoholic because I clean the house, take care of the kids, and prepare all the meals." "I don't drink in the morning, so I'm not an alcoholic." "I only drink on weekends, so I can't be an alcoholic." "I only have a few drinks after work and stop." "I only drink beer or a few glasses of wine, therefore I can't be an alcoholic." All of the above quotes are untrue. Less than 4 percent of the alcoholic population is on skid row, and more than 70 percent work. The American housewife is the largest group with problem drinking. It is a serious problem with the aged, and a new epidemic among teenagers.

Dr. Melvin Knisely, using a microscope to observe the capillaries in the white of the eye, proved that alcohol causes clumping of red blood cells starting with one drink. The more alcohol ingested, the more the clumping. Capillaries carry red blood cells single file to the body cells, delivering oxygen and vital nutrients. A large amount of clumping from several drinks leads to cellular damage and cellular death. If the cellular death occurs in the brain, no regeneration takes place. Because we have around 18 billion brain cells, it may take years to become aware of the cumulative damage from alcohol.

Alcohol passes from a pregnant woman's bloodstream into her fetus's. A pregnant woman who drinks more than two ounces of 80-proof alcohol, more than two twelve-ounce cans of beer, or more than two eight-ounce glasses of wine a day risks a probability that her baby will be born with abnormalities such as facial and head malformations and mental and physical retardation of varying degrees. A man who impregnates a woman within six weeks of any one heavy bout of alcohol ingestion runs the risk of transferring defective genes during conception.

Recent evidence shows that even with the best nutritional intake the alcoholic will still develop cirrhosis of the liver and many other alcohol-related conditions.

How does a drinker know if she or he is an alcoholic? Answer the following questions as honestly as you can.

1. Do you lose time from work due to drinking?
2. Is drinking making your home life unhappy?
3. Do you drink because you are shy with other people?
4. Is drinking affecting your reputation?
5. Have you ever felt remorse after drinking?
6. Have you gotten into financial difficulties as a result of drinking?
7. Do you turn to self-destructive companions and unhealthy situations when drinking?
8. Does your drinking make you careless of your family's welfare?

9. Has your ambition decreased since drinking?
10. Do you crave a drink at a definite time each day?
11. Do you want a drink the next morning?
12. Does drinking cause you to have difficulty sleeping?
13. Has your efficiency decreased since drinking?
14. Is drinking jeopardizing your job or business?
15. Do you drink to escape from worries or trouble?
16. Do you drink alone?
17. Have you ever had a complete loss of memory as a result of drinking?
18. Has your physician ever treated you for drinking?
19. Do you drink to build up your self-confidence?
20. Have you ever been to a hospital or institution on account of drinking?

If you answered yes to any one of the questions, you may be an alcoholic.

If you answered yes to any two questions, you probably are an alcoholic.

If you answered yes to three or more, you are definitely an alcoholic.

(These questions are used by Johns Hopkins University Hospital in deciding whether a person is alcoholic.)

To overcome alcoholism, an alcoholic must undergo a basic change of attitude and lifestyle. This means dropping defensiveness, because it prevents self-treatment.

• If you have a drinking problem and want to change, open yourself up to the information presented here. Problem drinkers find it difficult to look inward and admit their bondage to alcohol, and their deeper problems of pride, selfishness, self-deception, insecurity, and distrust. People who recover from alcoholism have faced these aspects of themselves. Are you willing to?

• Own up to your psychological addiction to self-deception. Alcoholism is a disease of self-deception. That is the prime reason it takes an average of thirteen years for an alcoholic to reach out for treatment to a hospital, doctor, psychotherapist, or Alcoholics Anonymous. Learn about the ways your self-deception is reinforced by society, which avoids facing the magnitude of the problem. The government receives $10 billion in taxes from the liquor industry each year and gives only about 1 percent of that for treatment of alcoholism. Is your problem made worse by the glorification of the drinking person and the American drinking cult through massive advertising? Look at how others profit from your self-destructiveness.

• Face the fact that you have a complex problem that is a disease, a way of life, and a game with payoffs. Recognize that you need a three-pronged attack: physical, emotional, and spiritual.

• Consult a physician trained in the treatment of alcoholism. Especially if you have a history of delirium tremens (shakes, rapid heartbeat, profuse sweating, mental disorientation, and hallucinations), severe liver decompensation (jaundice, mental confusion and memory loss, tremor, etc.), pancreatitis, withdrawal seizures, heart condition, or kidney failure, you will definitely need medical advice.

Begin a program to detoxify yourself. To stay with a regimen that will cleanse and nurture your body requires great honesty with yourself, determination, and a comprehensive program of good diet, food supplements such as vitamins, and exercise. A malnourished state occurs with moderate to heavy drinking. Just four to six drinks cause small hemorrhages of the gastrointestinal tract. Protein assimilation and digestion are drastically decreased, as is absorption of B-complex vitamins, vitamin A, and ascorbic acid (vitamin C). Alcohol increases blood pressure, decreases the amount of oxygen delivered to tissues, and increases blood cholesterol.

Nutrition is not emphasized by most MDs, and many people treated for alcoholism leave the hospital too nutritionally deficient to maintain sobriety. Some medical alcoholism specialists have been able to help 70 to 80 percent of their patients stay sober using a vitamin-and-mineral regimen that includes the following:

high-potency multiple vitamin, one a day
B-complex 100, one a day
niacin or niacinamide, 1000 mg., one, three times a day (Niacin may cause an uncomfortable flush and prickly feeling in a few people. Taking it on a full stomach or with a glass of milk usually prevents this.)
vitamin E, 400 IU, one, two times a day
vitamin A, 25,000 units a day
zinc tablets, approximately 25 mg. per tablet, one a day
calcium-magnesium supplement
foods: whole-grain cereals, whole-grain breads, foods with no refined sugar. Natural foods when available. High natural carbohydrates like seeds, nuts, grains, fruits, vegetables, and low animal protein. Seventy-five percent vegetable and 25 percent animal protein, about 1½ ounces per day.

• If you have decided to stop drinking, take Antabuse (disulfiram). Antabuse is the only substance known that is insurance against being able to drink alcohol, due to its toxic interaction. A small amount of ingested alcohol can set off the Antabuse-alcohol reaction. When mixed with alcohol, Antabuse causes acetaldehyde to build up in the blood-stream and cause an adverse body reaction: pounding headache, rapid heartbeat, labored respirations, nausea, and at times vomiting. A physician must prescribe Antabuse, so you need to call on an alcoholism specialist to discuss taking it. Many alcoholics have been thankful to have been on Antabuse while they worked through a crisis, had sudden urges to drink, or felt depressed and wanted to drink.

• Include exercise as a vital part of your program. Get Dr. Kenneth H. Cooper's book *New Aerobics* (New York: Bantam Books, 1970), a useful guide with instructions for different age groups covering four areas: jogging, running, bicycling, swimming. Time your pulse as you increase your exercise, and stop if the pulse reaches the rate listed for your age. If you work up to Dr. Cooper's "excellent" level, you will be ten to fifteen years younger in the cardiovascular and respiratory systems than a person your age who doesn't exercise.

• To gain a vivid picture of how alcohol weakens the body, have someone muscle-test you with pressure downward on your outstretched arm held parallel to the ground. Put a few drops of booze under the tongue and have yourself muscle-tested again. The almost instantaneous weakness is because of the toxic effect of alcohol relayed to the entire body.

• Join Alcoholics Anonymous. Of all the resources available to an alcoholic, none surpasses Alcoholics Anonymous. It is probably the most effective self-help organization in the world, and serves over a million American members. At AA you will get kindness, understanding, support, honesty, confrontation, practical assistance, horror stories, laughs, spiritual enrichment, and a new social life. You may have to "shop around" a little to find the AA group where you feel most at home. People who think they can beat alcoholism without AA usually pay a high price in terms of suffering and financial expense. If you think you don't need AA, make sure you have an alternative plan that is as carefully designed and as likely to succeed.

• Learn all about "games alcoholics play." You can learn them at AA, from reviewing your own life history, from asking people close to you (although they may be conspirators in the games), and from reading *Games Alcoholics Play* by Claude Steiner. The secret payoffs for alcoholism are numerous in these games. Are you "Drunk and Proud," taking hidden delight in your skill at frustrating "persecutors" trying to reform you? Or do you avoid the risks of an adult search for love and sex by soothing the pain of your loneliness with alcohol and enticing "rescuers" to give you a substitute form of love?

• Stop trying to use willpower. Your addiction to alcohol is too powerful to be kicked by yourself with willpower. Alexander the Great, conqueror of the world, was conquered by alcohol at age thirty-three. You need help from as many sources as you can get. AA includes a strong emphasis on spiritual help from a "higher power" or God or whatever source you conceive of. If you are religious in a formal or informal way, deepen and practice your faith.

• Give extensive thought and planning to what you are going to do instead of drinking. How else are you going to overcome your shyness? How are you going to make new friends who won't urge you to drink? Resolve to fill up your life with meaningful involvements that bring you genuinely close to people, so that you won't need to fill up your inner void with alcohol and buffer yourself against people.

• Admit to yourself first and eventually to your loved ones that you are an alcoholic and unable to cope with drinking. Drop your false pride and your delusion that you can handle alcohol. Reach out for help to AA and to medical experts trained in alcoholism treatment. Enjoy how relaxing humility and honesty can be once you get used to them.

• Reduce your guilt and low self-esteem by accepting treatment. Acknowledge when you have made a mess of things, and clean them up as best you can without making them worse. Forgive yourself for your past and concentrate on the present. Select supportive people in AA and elsewhere who can help you overcome your negative thinking and celebrate your gains in sobriety.

• If you have an alcoholic friend or relative, do not get stuck in repetitive attempts to accuse, blame, help, advise, defend, cover up, protect, comfort, argue, plead, and rescue. Until an alcoholic faces the consequences of drinking and decides to seek help, efforts by others mostly waste time, stir up resistance, and make things worse. Learn to take care of yourself without depending on the alcoholic to reform, and make it clear that this is your plan. Join Al-Anon or Al-Ateen, groups that help relatives of alcoholics kick their addiction to such relationships. You will become more informed about the disease of alcoholism, and learn to outgrow the destructive patterns of relating between family members.

• Other helpful groups are Women for Sobriety, 344 Franklin Street, Quakertown, Pennsylvania 18951, and CareUnit Program, call tollfree (800) 422-4143.

SUGGESTED READING:

Steiner, Claude. *Games Alcoholics Play.* New York: Grove Press, 1971.

Twelve Steps and Twelve Traditions. AA Publishing, Inc., 1952.

Weston, Drake. *Guidebook for Alcoholics.* Hicksville, N.Y.: Exposition Press, 1964.

See also: ANXIETY, DEPENDENCY, DEPRESSION, LONELINESS, SHYNESS

ANGER

Anger itself is not a problem. How we express or suppress it is what counts. For most of us, it is very difficult to find appropriate, effective, self-affirming ways to express our angry feelings.

Too often, we vent our anger in ways that serve no real purpose, or hold it inside, where it festers. When we dump our anger out on others, it generally has destructive effects on them and on ourselves. Angry explosions tend to be short-lived power trips that take us nowhere. And virtuous efforts to deny our angry feelings can store up inner tension that pops up later in the form of headaches, depression, irrational grudges, etc.

Our culture gives us mixed messages about anger. Sometimes a soft answer does turn away wrath; sometimes it invites it by making us look like an easy target for hostility. If we value meekness (in hopes of inheriting the earth) and turn the other cheek (in hopes of encouraging mildness and love), we may find ourselves feeling guilty about our hidden, pent-up anger. If we mimic the counterculture and strive to "let it all hang out" in a simplistic and aggressive openness, we may find ourselves struggling with constant conflict and irritation. But overcontrol of natural, legitimate needs and emotions may result in unexpected outbursts of misplaced "justifiable" anger. Dwelling moralistically on our "right to be angry," we try to make up for all the hurts and injustices we absorbed in the past.

Answer the following questions when you feel anger surging up inside you. They will help you sort out your feelings and needs so that you can express them constructively and satisfyingly.

• What do you really want from this person? What do you want to achieve with your anger? Don't get so caught up in justifying your anger to yourself and others that you lose sight of what you really feel. Look behind your anger for unfulfilled positive wishes. If you snap at someone you want as a friend because you think he or she is putting you down, you lose an opportunity for closeness. Instead, say what you really feel: "I value our friendship and am upset that something is happening between us to threaten it. Let's talk and try to solve this conflict."

• Are you really angry at this person? Are you really angry for the reasons you're giving yourself and others? Are you perhaps misdirecting your anger because it's safe to be angry at this person for this reason?

Picking on an easy target as a scapegoat won't solve anything, and has the danger of blinding you to the real cause of your anger.

• How much of your anger is really hurt and frustration arising from the inevitable difficulties of human life and from all the suppressing of your feelings and needs that you have been required to do? Are you trying to make individuals pay for your anger at the cosmos? Are you blaming some person or situation for deeper feelings of hurt and help-lessness? Do you feel unloved and unnurtured? Do you feel raw and alone in the world? Do you need more pleasure and caring in your life? If this is the case, the solution lies in obtaining more pleasure and emotional support for yourself. That will soothe the anger away. Thrashing around aggressively just makes your "wounds" worse.

• Is your so-called anger a smokescreen to hide hurt pride? Is your survival as a human being really threatened, in which case anger is a natural and often effective reaction—or has your vanity merely been stung? How much is it worth to you to fight for your image? Lives have been lost defending a position that was not really essential for anyone's survival.

• If you feel you are being victimized or being made the target of someone else's anger, ask yourself, "Do I have to take this personally? Do I have to feel hurt by this?" Other people are just as capable as you are of picking on a scapegoat. Don't volunteer to be a scapegoat, and if someone chooses you anyway, duck out of the role. Don't get hooked into a fight that has nothing to do with you and that you can't win.

• Take responsibility for your angry feelings and for expressing them constructively regardless of what triggered them. Go beyond the old cycle of righteous indignation, blaming, lashing out, and moralistic justifications of your temper outbursts. You need to understand the true nature of your anger and communicate your needs in ways that get you what you want from people, not just empty victories.

• Many times our anger and hostility cover up our feelings of inferiority and insecurity. Expressing anger *constructively* does increase our self-esteem, and enables us to fight when it is necessary for what we need in life. Learn to deliver understandable, effective messages. Clear the air of poor communication so that you can work out satisfying solutions with people.

• Pay attention to your anger and learn from it. Learn the difference between anger, which is of limited duration, and sustained, long-term hostility or hatred. Note the differences in intensity of anger in various circumstances or toward various people. Identify the different kinds of anger you can feel. This will help you make better decisions about when and how to express it.

• Don't be afraid of your anger. Think back to the last time you expressed intense anger. Did the world end? Angry feelings by themselves do no harm: Your anger won't kill anyone, nor will someone else's angry feelings kill you. Serious trouble occurs only when we stubbornly or impulsively insist on expressing anger in some particular way that may be dangerously excessive or unworkable in a particular situation.

• Anger doesn't exclude love, gratitude, and other positive emotions. You can care about someone deeply, feel anger toward him or her, and still continue to care deeply. In fact, the anger may occur *because* you care so much, and it may even be a way of showing that you care.

• Express your anger honestly and responsibly, without physical or emotional violence. Telling others what angers or hurts you—telling them what you really want—helps them see you clearly as the individual, special person that you are.

• Don't pretend to feel no anger. Don't deaden yourself by denying your anger. There are undesirable side effects both to bottling up anger and to dumping it impulsively. Neither tactic gets you what you want, and both can burden you with frustration and guilt.

• Emotional or physical violence only generates further anger, hurt, and revenge. Any erupting into actual aggression tends to increase the tendency toward aggression in the future. Aggressive acts, whether verbal or physical, do not purge anger. Verbal attacks on people are not the same thing as talking out your feelings. You can learn to express your anger without attacking the annoying person. There is an important difference between saying "I'm angry because what happened really threatens me" and "I hate you for being such a rat." Attack the problem, not the person.

• We all do carry some amount of unexpressed anger and so need some outlets for the stifled energy. Release it in some physical activity: walk fast, run, jog, play handball, bicycle, hit your bed with a rolled-up towel, yell in your closed car. These outlets can help free you to think constructively and calmly about your anger without its explosive charge.

• After blowing off the steam in some nondestructive way, try to understand what you're really angry about, and communicate it. First tell yourself. Then tell someone who is not the object of your anger. Sometimes a neutral listener can help you sort out your feelings satisfactorily. You may discover you're not really angry at the person or circumstance you were blaming—and save yourself the embarrassment of venting anger at the wrong target. Last, when you understand why you're angry and what you really want from the object of your anger, tell him or her in a positive, nonviolent way.

• Come to value the expression and release of your anger as something separate from attacking another person. Transform anger into effective action. Focus on the future instead of dwelling on blame for past injustices. Work on changing your relationships in the present.

• Don't turn anger and blame on yourself if you do blow up sometimes. Don't wrap yourself in guilt or self-righteousness. Apologize.

• Avoid predictable annoyances: Take a book along if you have to stand in line; use the time you "gain" in a traffic jam—over which you have absolutely no control—to relax and daydream a little.

• Use some old-fashioned delaying tactics to give yourself time to understand angry feelings: Count to ten, put yourself in the other person's shoes, walk around the block. Give yourself a chance to regain perspective and a sense of humor. Talk to a neutral party and express your irritation.

• Use the energy anger provides to write a letter to the editor or to a politician. Or write a detailed, angry, specific letter to the person you are mad at. Put it away until the next day. Reread it. After twenty-four hours you'll have a pretty good idea of what is worth mentioning to the person who angered you and what deserves to be discarded.

• Anger is an opportunity to learn more about ourselves and how to act assertively. By looking honestly at what really makes us angry and what we really need to do about it, we can grow beyond immature spinal-reflex reactions into powerful, constructive assertiveness. Anger is energy. Learning to channel it can provide great satisfaction, turning a problem into a solution.

SUGGESTED READING:

Ellis, Albert. *How to Live With—and Without Anger.* New York: Thomas Y. Crowell, 1977.

Hauck, Paul A. *Overcoming Frustration and Anger.* Philadelphia: Westminster Press, 1977.

Layden, Milton. *Escaping the Hostility Trap.* Englewood Cliffs, N.J.: Prentice-Hall, 1977.

Rubin, Theodore Isaac. *The Angry Book.* New York: Macmillan, 1969.

See also: CHILD ABUSE, HYPERTENSION, MARITAL QUARREL-ING, SADISM, SPOUSE BEATING, STRESS, TEENAGE REBEL-LION

ANXIETY

Anxiety stirs up powerful physical and mental symptoms: shortness of breath, pounding heart, sweating, fidgeting, rapid (even irregular) pulse, headache, stomach upset (such as those well-known butterflies), dizziness, faintness, and a sense of intense foreboding ("When is the ax going to fall?").

An anxious person may also experience disturbing dreams, insomnia, or sexual dysfunction. His or her life may be disrupted by countless disquieting worries: "Did I leave the gas on?" "Maybe there'll be an earthquake today." "What if my car breaks down on the freeway?" "Will they like me?"

Regardless of the physical symptoms and disquieting thoughts that beset us when we're anxious, the basic underlying experience of anxiety is that of a diffuse, free-floating dread. It is very hard to confront it in this form; it surrounds us like a fog and seems to offer no target for attack or action.

To escape this formless terror, we may focus on some specific situation, object, person, or animal as the supposed cause of our anxiety. For example, we may develop an intense fear of flying as a psychological hook on which to hang our otherwise free-floating fearfulness toward life. A fear of something that can be named and avoided—dogs, spiders, heights, airplanes, elevators, crowds, buses, social gatherings—can be used as a solution to general anxiety. It can focus our attention on something more definable and manageable than an anxious fog.

Anxiety frequently takes the form of panic—an intense fear of losing control of ourselves. There is a saying that "the fear conceals the wish." This means that anxiety is often the result of, and a cover for, repressed impulses. We may feel anxious when we are threatened with a breakthrough into consciousness or action of some repressed wish or need—when we come close to feeling or doing something that will get us in trouble with our conscience or with the outside world. We fear that if we express even part of what we feel, we won't be able to stop and will overdo it.

Anxiety can result from stirring up repressed wishes to express sexuality, anger, sadness, or even joy. We may get anxious when we feel turned on in a situation where sex is forbidden. An explosive surge of anger toward a tyrannical boss may send us into a panic. A wave of sadness can make us feel anxious if we don't feel free to let our tears flow. And a surge of exuberant joy can cause anxiety if we find ourselves in a setting where frivolity is frowned on.

Because it can come on us so fast and without our being aware of the cause, anxiety can be paralyzing. It can cut us off from our inner awareness, from people close to us, and from life itself. We can expend enormous physical and emotional energy trying to control our anxiety and the impulses beneath it (which is why we sometimes shake with the effort). Unlike stress, which has to do with our reaction to outside stimulus, anxiety has to do with trying to keep the lid on what's stirred up inside us.

Underneath the specific fears that can mask general anxiety lies a deeper fear about our place in the world. Many of us live all the time expecting disapproval. We don't feel we belong. We don't understand why we question our place in the world in which we live, but we're sure we're not quite good enough to be in it.

Some psychologists, such as Rollo May, see positive value in anxiety. They suggest that learning to recognize the nature of our anxiety and to identify the fears about ourselves that generate it can help us become more alive and creative. When we learn that there is more to gain by suffering through anxiety and conquering it than by surrendering to it or medicating it away, we also learn a valuable lesson about our own survival strength and capacity to profit from adversity.

The following suggestions and questions can help you learn to live with and grow from your encounters with anxiety.

• What is it about you that makes you worry about your place in the world? Basically, how do you see yourself in this life? Do you think your feelings, wishes, impulses, or viewpoints mark you as a misfit? Do you feel set apart from your friends or family as a bad or inferior person? Do you worry that others will discover your sins or inadequacies and reject you? Are you afraid of being left alone to hate yourself for what you are? If you're left alone, do you feel you'll just die?

• Remember that we all have a wide range of feelings and impulses, including most of the "evil" or antisocial ones.

• Admit your feared, repressed needs, feelings, and impulses to yourself. Follow your anxious thoughts and identify them. Accept them as part of your internal experience. Don't hide them from yourself—you don't have to act on them.

• Don't pretend not to have strong feelings. This sort of pretending actually makes you more vulnerable to their sneaking up on you unexpectedly, and ties up your energy in trying to suppress feelings. If you pretend that you're never angered, you won't be prepared for inevitable, normal, appropriate human feelings of anger when they do occur. Feelings don't have to have dangerous consequences; saying to yourself "I am angry/hurt/afraid/happy/in love/excited/joyful" will not destroy your place in the world.

• Go even further than just accepting what comes up spontaneously inside you—go on to practice thinking up and accepting a wide range of "bad" wishes and fantasies. Rehearse them in your mind, and even enjoy them. Explore all the satisfactions and disasters that might happen.

• Ask yourself what would be some of the worst possible things you could do. By letting these things into your consciousness you will gradually decondition yourself against the anxiety they stir up when you are trying to push them away.

• Make very clear to yourself that there is a vast difference between imagining doing something and actually doing it. Even the least violent among us can imagine getting back at someone by pushing him or her off a cliff—without needing to act on this fantasy. Remind yourself that you know the difference between a wish and an action. If, for example, you are angry at someone and he or she does have an accident, don't blame yourself for having wished it into happening. Remember all the times you had socially unacceptable impulses and were able to stop them. Give yourself credit for the inner controls you do have, and develop trust in yourself as someone who can entertain all sorts of wild ideas but still keep out of serious trouble.

• Look at whether your anxiety comes from a deep sense of being adrift in life, without meaningful connections.

• Ask yourself if you are free-floating. Do you have roots in loving, secure relationships? Are you afraid of falling off into empty space emotionally? Have you created a dimension of significance and purpose through your commitments? Do you share values with family, friends, and community? Are you paying a self-denying price for the connections you do have because you must repress too much of yourself? Do you seek approval at the price of pretending to be other than who you really are? Have you given up freedom and growth to keep this approval?

• Take inventory of yourself. Who are you? What really matters to you? What social, personal, and religious values or observances carrry meaning for you? What can you do to act on your values that will bring greater meaning and connection to your life? How can you reach out toward and with other people in pursuit of these values? What are the suppressed parts of you that are clamoring for expression, and causing anxiety when blocked?

• Take a good look at your current ways of connecting with other people. Are they working or are they empty, lifeless, formal? Do your relationships have external form without emotional and spiritual substance? When you do the "right thing" without your heart in it or because you think you're tough and cynical, you may be ignoring your need for warmth and for positive, loving connections. This too can leave you feeling stranded or adrift, and generate anxiety.

• Don't confuse keeping busy with making progress. Don't tire yourself out with activity that doesn't bring you closer to understanding and resolving your anxiety. Busy-ness and competition may take your mind off your anxiety for a while, but they won't help you get close to yourself. Sometimes you can calm anxiety with quiet, either alone or in the company of an accepting friend—someone with whom you can just be.

• Don't look for an escape from anxiety in liquor, overeating, smoking, or drugs. People gobble tons of useless tranquilizers and drink oceans of alcohol without making lasting changes in their anxious state. Moving into and then through anxiety teaches you to live with it and use it. Escape imprisons you.

• Be realistic in your efforts to reduce anxiety. Don't seek to eliminate it entirely. Life will always contain a large amount of uncertainty and danger. We need to be alert for genuine threats to our emotional and physical well-being. Anxiety and the tension it brings can be part of our creativity, originality, and intelligence. It can stimulate us out of inactivity and boredom, spur us to solve problems. Emotional discomfort can carry an important survival message. Think of anxiety, up to a point, as being a form of super-vigilance and preparedness.

• Learn the difference between a genuine danger alert and a paralyzing anxiety fog. Don't magnify dangers out of proportion. Things can go wrong in small ways; not all setbacks turn into disasters. Try to get some distance when you need it. Step back from your anxiety and give your subconscious time to sort out your feelings. Suppose you are driving alone and hear a funny noise under the hood. Are you just concerned about a mechanical problem with your car, or does the mysterious noise remind you that you feel basically unsafe any time you're alone?

• Pay attention to your anxious thoughts. Keep track of them. Make a list of them. How often do they occur? Which ones occur most often? Which ones are really important? Try to gain some perspective on the kinds of worries you have. See if you can reduce the hold of anxiety on your life by putting off anxious thoughts until a scheduled "worry time." When you reach this scheduled time each day, you may be better able to tell the difference between a little worry and one that requires attention. You may have already moved through some of the experiences you started to worry about and have learned that they are manageable and survivable.

• Exercise. Addict yourself to a healthful activity. Spend about an hour a day on yourself: Practice yoga, work out in a gym, run or jog, work in the garden, ride a bike. If possible, do something that totally and rhythmically engages your whole body. Let it work in a smooth, full way. Keep your mind turned off or involved only in your physical activity, but not in an evaluating or competing way. Play. Fool around. Anxiety feeds on itself. Its symptoms can make you think you're sick. Worrying about your health can contribute to anxiety. Break this cycle with physical and mental relaxation.

• Learn a meditation technique. Learn to relax your mind as well as your body. Some relaxation exercises combine mental and physical relief from stress and anxiety. Do these exercises while lying in bed when you wake up and before going to sleep:

1. Stretch your legs until all the muscles from thigh to toes feel tense. Hold for a few seconds and release. Enjoy the feeling of relaxation. Repeat this sequence in the other muscle groups: abdomen and back, chest, arms, neck and face.

2. Inhale deeply and hold to the slow count of ten. Exhale slowly, letting go of tension and anxiety. Repeat for a total of three inhalation-exhalations.

3. Imagine a scene that you find pleasant and soothing, perhaps a beautiful natural environment that you've visited or that you create in your mind. While your body is relaxed from the tensing exercises, let this tranquil scene relax your mind. Explore the scene with your mind's eye. Tell yourself over and over, "I feel calm. I am relaxed."

SUGGESTED READING:

Geba, Bruno H. *Breathe Away Your Tension*. New York: Random House, 1973.

Rathus, Spencer A., and Jeffrey S. Nevid. *BT: Behavior Therapy*. New York: The New American Library, 1978.

Walker, Eugene C. *Learn to Relax*. Englewood Cliffs, N.J.: Prentice-Hall, 1975.

See also: ANGER, BOREDOM, COMPULSIONS, DEPRESSION, GUILT, HYPERTENSION, HYPOCHONDRIA, LONELINESS, NIGHTMARES, OBSESSIONS, PAIN, PSYCHOSOMATIC ILLNESS, SELF-HATE, SEXUAL DYSFUNCTION, SHYNESS, SLEEP DISORDERS, STRESS, SUICIDE

BOREDOM

At first thought, boredom may not seem like a serious problem. Some psychologists, however, emphasize the dangers of chronic boredom. If no steps are taken to reduce it, such generalized boredom becomes psychologically unhealthy, taxing us similarly to depression or procrastination.

Boredom may be characterized as a "substitute" problem. Very often it represents an avoidance of something other than the immediate "boring" situation or task. Many times it offers a way to avoid active wishes we're afraid to risk in the real world, over which we have no control. Sometimes it allows us to escape wishes which frighten or shame us.

Boredom's discomfort comes not so much from the absence of excitement as from the irritation of an unconscious drive. A bored person seems to look for entertaining distractions. Yet no distraction is ever really sufficient to relieve the underlying feeling of boredom; nothing the bored person can imagine doing feels adequate to relieve the hidden inner tension.

Frequently boredom is a form of anger without enthusiasm. It appears to be a passive state, yet something active and intense is going on internally. This boredom is an overcontrolled, constricted, barely voiced protest. As such, it is easily overlooked—and this can only increase the anger and frustration it covers.

There are, of course, secret payoffs for expressing our boredom. We get to complain about something without having to do anything about it—a put-down without responsibility. We get to hold on to a job, a relationship, or an obligation (and to whatever security it provides for us), grumbling all the while, without taking the risks of change. We can blame our discomfort on other people who failed to spark our interest or engage our enthusiasm. (Here we glimpse the covert hostility and passive protest that underlie so much boredom.)

Such payoffs exact costs, though (a form of psychological kickback, so to speak). Left to itself, boredom tends to get worse. It leads to tiredness and draws us away from our active, creative energies. It appears to be a safe way to express hostility, yet it has a corrosive effect on our self-esteem. It is a nonsolution, like going on a sitdown strike in quicksand.

If you keep in mind boredom's role as a substitute problem, you can learn to use it as an informative signal about your internal self. Take a look at the signal:

Is something fundamental missing in your life? Does boredom reflect fear or reluctance to involve yourself deeply in life, to invest part of yourself in relationships with others?

Have you cut yourself off from lively people, from a stimulating career, from arts, nature, changes, risk?

Do you use boredom to control impulses that seem frightening or dangerous? This sort of control deprives you of freedom, eats up all your energy in trying to hold yourself together. You need to work at understanding the thoughts that frighten you. Sometimes what we really fear is not that we might hurt someone but that we might be punished for expressing our feelings of anger or frustration.

Do you use boredom to avoid frustration, guilt, or risk? Such avoidance only feeds itself; boredom begets ever more boredom.

You can bring an end to boredom by activating your own strengths. Bolster your sense of self-worth by doing something that has meaning for you and enhances your good feelings about yourself. In a sense, you cure yourself of boredom by unbalancing your life. Give up the security of the way things are for a chance at increasing your sense of wholeness. Accomplish this by a creative act. Begin with something you can handle, and avoid hiding out with drugs or alcohol or plunging into dangerous excitement, such as reckless driving.

If you find it necessary to deal with a bored person, try making a friendly but firm, clear statement that you don't have (nor have you contracted to supply) a solution to his or her boredom. Your blunt confrontation may jar your bored friend into action. Refuse to be bored yourself; don't let others draw you into their boredom.

- Take action against your boredom. Be determined to accept risks.
- Start by concentrating on the present. Decide to live just a few moments at a time. Choose to use up your present time in personally fulfilling ways. You do count.
- If your boredom covers anger toward someone, try to talk about it. Your openness may encourage your friend, spouse, parent, co-worker, neighbor, or lover to work with you to improve your relationship.
- Novelty is less dangerous than sameness. Try something at random: Vary your eating or recreation habits, check out new activities, stimulate your mind with new interests. Accept challenges.
- Examine your health. Get a medical checkup. Sometimes boredom is the result of poor physical condition, inadequate diet, or lack of exercise. A stultified mental state can sometimes be dispelled by physical action. If your health permits it, try anything that requires intense attention and moves rapidly with a few breaks—that could be Ping-Pong or a high-risk sport such as skiing. Active physical sports probably do the best job of fully absorbing our minds. Dancing, or walking in lovely natural settings, can have a similar effect.
- Do something for others. Do three good deeds in secret. Become a volunteer for a service organization. Help a friend pack for a move. Visit someone who is stuck at home or in the hospital.
- Do something for yourself or your environment that gives you sensual, physical stimulus-intensity. Polish all your shoes (no, not the tennies). Wax your car. Make something for your home.
- Take responsibility for shifting your attention from something that bores you to something more engaging. Use your memory to re-enjoy pleasant or stimulating past events. Undertake an internal dialogue with yourself—work on a life problem and try to puzzle out a solution. If you anticipate spending time in an unstimulating way, such as waiting in a long line, plan ahead: Take along a book, crossword puzzles, some needlepoint, a packet of travel folders to help you plan your next vacation.
- Think about what you really want to do. Boredom sometimes

signals an important life transition. It may be a resistance to a scary emotional upheaval resulting from needing and trying to undertake a major change. Look inside, try to clarify your present needs and wants, set goals that will help you achieve them. Follow your fantasies, looking for hints about the way you'd really like to live your life.

• Set goals and pursue them, whether that means learning a new craft skill or completing your education or beginning a reeducation. Participation in a learning process, getting somewhere, reduces feelings of stagnation and boredom.

• Along with trying more spontaneity, also try more planning. To create space in which to have fun and be spontaneous, you may need to plan ahead so as to protect yourself from boring demands and routines that tend to fill up life. Keep alert to ways you can prevent an over-load of responsibility from stifling you, and insist on time for fun.

• Involve yourself with yourself and with others. Congratulate your-self for your efforts. Share your feelings with friends and family. Talk over your strategy for energizing your life, for eliminating boredom. Celebrate things: Create and enjoy ceremonies at home for big and small occasions (birthdays, nonbirthdays, holidays, the end of your first Spanish course).

• Remember that overcoming boredom means learning to take risks —basically, the risk of feeling the full range of human emotions. Your first success will convince you that the reward far exceeds the effort and risk.

SUGGESTED READING:

Bach, George R., and Herb Goldberg. *Creative Aggression: The Art of Assertive Living.* New York: Avon Books, 1974.

Cohen, Stanley, and Laurie Taylor. *Escape Attempts: The Theory and Practice of Resistance to Everyday Life.* New York: Penguin Books, 1976.

See also: ANGER, ANXIETY, DEPRESSION, FEAR OF FAILURE, FEAR OF SUCCESS, GUILT, LONELINESS, MID-LIFE CRISIS, PROCRASTINATION, TIME-WASTING

CANCER

It has long been considered possible that there is a relationship be-tween individual psychology and contracting cancer. Certain ancient Greek physicians thought they perceived such a connection, as did many other medical observers throughout the intervening centuries. In our own time, the emphasis on treatment—on fixing rather than on causation—has obscured this possibility. The increased power of medical technology to repair the body has taken up most of our attention.

In the past, it was a medical commonplace that the condition of the mind had much to do with the condition of the body. We ourselves are comfortable blaming ulcers on stress, headaches on tension, heart attacks on anxiety. Most of us have heard enough about psychosomatic illness to joke about catching the flu in order to get out of a tough spot at work. Cancer, however, is a particularly frightening and intimidating disease, and it is very scary for some of us to imagine that we could have anything to do with inflicting it on ourselves.

Twentieth-century research has begun to rediscover and confirm some of our predecessors' theories, though. The issue is a very complex and controversial one, with serious implications for health care and medical practice. Those who see a psychological connection to the onset of cancer do not seek to blame the patient, as some of their critics have suggested. Rather than reducing sympathy or diminishing help for those suffering from so catastrophic a set of diseases, they point to the healing value of taking responsibility for oneself.

By the same token, interest in the psychology of cancer does not imply reduced concern for the dangers of an environment polluted by countless carcinogens (cancer-causing agents). If our air, water, food, and work places are filled with hazardous substances, if we persist in polluting ourselves with drugs or cigarettes, we are no less at risk because we can point to an important psychological component in falling ill. Even if future research should prove the psychological component the most important one, environmental carcinogens pose a serious threat to all of us. Psychology may determine who can best resist environmental threats, but, psychology or not, these pollutants constantly menace all of us—waiting for whatever can lower our resistance to disease.

Psychologically oriented medical researchers are increasingly convinced of the existence of a relationship between mental outlook and contracting cancer, and then succumbing to or surviving it. Continuing studies and controlled experiments seem to validate this conclusion. Individuals who have already contracted cancer apparently share certain psychological characteristics, enabling us to sketch a profile of the cancer-prone personality. Until they worked at confronting themselves, the patients studied showed a marked lack of awareness concerning the wishes and needs they had been denying. (This profile may reflect increased probability, but it does not predict inevitably that persons with any, some, or all of these characteristics will develop cancer.)

Cancer patients often exhibit a kind of emotional constriction, tend-ing to resist expressing emotions such as anxiety, depression, anger, and guilt. They often report that their parents treated them coldly. They may hide a deep need for affection behind a mask of strength and self-control. Such behavior has been found to have physical effects. Bottling up one's emotions increases the body's production of the so-called stress hormones, and these have a suppressive effect on the body's immune system. They lower the body's defensive barrier against infection and disease.

Other commonly shared characteristics of cancer patients include a low self-image, resentfulness, and a tendency toward self-pity. They may have difficulties developing and maintaining long-term close relationships, and seem unforgiving of past hurts. Circumstantially, they have often experienced the recent loss of a serious love relationship or a needed occupation.

Lawrence LeShan, a psychotherapist who has long worked with cancer patients, places great emphasis on the impact of childhood experiences. Many cancer patients seem to see their illness as the culmination of their life history, almost as if they expected it and were not really surprised by it. The patterns of how an individual copes with stress become established in childhood. Many eventual cancer patients share childhood experiences of loss, experiences that taught them to associate emotional attachment with pain. Perhaps a parent or sibling died, and the uncomprehending child came to blame himself and hide his burden of guilt. For whatever reason, the child concludes that loneliness is the inescapable condition of his life. Loss of another love object in adult life only confirms this. Feelings of inadequacy and hopelessness take over, and the person despairs of ever achieving any real feelings of joy or meaning in life.

Recent studies, by LeShan and others, show cancer patients torn between the fear of death and the sometimes greater fear of life. If, however, the mind can make the body receptive to disease, the mind can also lead the struggle back to health. This has been the experience of Dr. O. Carl Simonton, who, with his wife, psychotherapist Stephanie Matthews-Simonton, treats cancer patients at the Cancer Counseling and Research Center in Forth Worth, Texas. Not only does Dr. Simonton find it possible that cancer can be willed into manifesting itself, he also finds strong evidence to suggest that cancer patients have the power to "image away" their illness. Like LeShan, Simonton finds a direct correlation between a patient's attitude and the response of the patient's cancer to therapy.

Cancer cells are by nature weak and vulnerable, defeated most of the time by the body's immune mechanism. This being the case, Simonton asks those whose systems have not resisted these weak, vacillating cells to ask themselves: "What is my cancer doing for me? Why did I need this disease?" It is very difficult to accept responsibility for one's own illness, and many of Simonton's patients prefer to rely on surgery, radiation, or chemotherapy exclusively, rather than confront their own emotional involvement in the disease.

Responsibility is not the same thing as blame. We all have avoided emotional conflict by becoming ill at one time or another; it's not uncommon to get sick during periods of unusual stress or depression. If we hide from our real emotional needs—as does a personality like the one in the cancer-prone profile—our lives lose meaning and we may begin to seek our death.

In combination with radiation and other conventional medical therapies, Simonton has very successfully helped patients attack cancer with a meditation technique that combines relaxation and visualization, and with group psychotherapy that joins patient, family, and sometimes friends in a supportive network. This set of methods reduces the psychological isolation typical of catastrophically ill people and helps cancer patients fight for their lives.

Cancer patients, like others faced with serious illness or sudden loss, tend to act like helpless children at first, relegating all decisions to doctors and family. They need to learn that (1) they can take responsibility for themselves and use their own will to fight back and (2) they are not prisoners of the past. They can change their lives. Illness can provide a startling opportunity for enrichment.

At Simonton's Center, patients enhance their medical treatment with psychotherapy and with a meditative technique in which they relax, mentally picture their disease, and then visualize their immune system attacking it. The meditation process begins when the patients relax with the help of a tape recording and physical relaxation techniques. After visualizing a peaceful natural setting, the patients are taught to image their cancer being vigorously and successfully attacked by an army of white blood cells. Before ending the meditation period, the patients visualize themselves as well and strong. To bolster the effects of this procedure, Simonton's patients are provided with detailed information about their illness and about the positive results of the treatment program they have chosen.

Patients and their physicians are proving the strength of the long-observed link between mind and body. "The search for one's own being, the discovery of the life one needs to live, can be one of the strongest weapons against disease," according to Lawrence LeShan. As patients examine their lives, identify the emotional needs they have left untended, and reactivate their will to live and to change, they often find themselves regaining physical well-being.

• Cancer is a choice point, providing an opportunity to exert your will to live. It demands a transformation of the self: You have to move to a new level of commitment to life or die.

• Cancer doesn't just challenge your physical health. It comes as a severe test of your whole support system: physical, social, emotional, intellectual, spiritual. You may find you need the help of religious faith, psychological counseling, meditative techniques, as well as a different diet, medical attention, and perhaps alternative therapies. You will need nurturance of all kinds from yourself and your family and friends.

• It is not uncommon to feel your judgment paralyzed. The responsibility for choice truly remains yours, however, as you seek the real goals of maintaining dignity and infusing your life with meaning. In the face of a bombardment of terror—crazy cells, radiation, surgery, chemotherapy—your survival may hinge on not delegating responsibility to others. You can't simultaneously turn over responsibility to your physician or family and foster your own inner resources.

• There is no clear right or wrong in cancer treatment. It's very starkly your body, your life. A patient needs—and should demand— access to information and choice rather than relying strictly on the unverified advice of a single physician or on the possibly inaccurate scattered ideas about cancer he or she has gleaned from the media over the years.

• If you suspect you have cancer, get a diagnosis immediately. If your suspicions are confirmed, begin to fight back right away. Cancer does not mean death; both medically and psychologically, it is important to begin your fight as soon as possible.

• Don't be immobilized by statistics. Many people have lived well beyond medically predicted survival dates. You can investigate and make choices relative to your medical and emotional needs. Based on individual risk preferences, some choices of treatment include (singly or perhaps in combination): (1) the familiar conventional methods, (2) participation in developmental (experimental) programs, (3) participation in controlled clinical trials of advanced techniques—something between the conventional and the experimental—and (4) alternative therapies, such as diet, megavitamin, or oxygen treatments. Don't assume that the truth is totally in either the medical or antimedical camp. For you, it may be found in some combination of traditional medicine and psychological or alternative approaches.

• You are a source of strength to yourself, not someone who needs to be totally looked after. *Fight back.* You are not to blame for creating a disease. Your responsibility lies in trying to identify the emotional needs that have not been filled in your life, the needs that make illness seem like an escape or a solution.

• Help is available. Contact the American Cancer Society or the Leukemia Society of America. For alternative therapies, consult the Cancer Control Society. Locally you may find such groups as the Los Angeles Center for the Healing Arts or Dr. Simonton's Fort Worth Cancer Counseling and Research Center.

• Knowledge is power. Many people have successfully overcome cancer by combining their inner resources with medical and psychological treatment, by searching for their individual human identity, by laying claim to their own life. Consider, for one, Laurel Lee, author of *Walking Through the Fire: A Hospital Journal,* who has chronicled her fight to defeat cancer. Her struggle shows us what it means for each of us to declare that our life matters to us, that it is worth saving—if only for ourselves—and that it can be saved.

SUGGESTED READING:

Achterberg, Jeanne, and G. Frank Lawlis. *Imagery of Cancer.* Institute for Personality and Ability Testing, 1602 Coronado Drive, Champaign, Illinois 61802, 1978.

Goodfield, June. *The Siege of Cancer.* New York: Dell, 1975.

Lee, Laurel. *Walking Through the Fire: A Hospital Journal.* New York: E. P. Dutton, 1977.

Simonton, O. Carl, Stephanie Matthews-Simonton, and James Creighton. *Getting Well Again: A Step-by-Step, Self-Guide to Overcoming Cancer for Patients and Their Families.* Los Angeles: J. P. Tarcher, Inc., 1978.

See also: FEAR OF DEATH, FEAR OF SICKNESS, MASTECTOMY, PAIN, PSYCHOSOMATIC ILLNESS

CHILD ABUSE

The heartbreaking reality of child abuse touches families in all walks of life, rich and poor, educated and not. An estimated one million children suffer from abuse each year, and at least two thousand die of it. Far too often the abuse continues undetected because the parents feel too guilty and afraid to seek help. Even doctors who treat children for what looks suspiciously like abuse are reluctant to report it or to open up discussion with the parents. Sometimes a child's scars are emotional, from violent verbal abuse. Sometimes the abuse is purely neglect, and the child is emaciated and filthy.

Parents abuse their children because they feel desperately aggravated or frustrated by them in some way. The children seem too dumb, too active, too smart, too ugly, too stubborn, too different, too troublesome. But most often it is the crying, demanding, complaining child who is abused. The harassed parent hears the crying as an accusation: "You're a bad parent, you don't love me enough, you're a failure." In desperation, the parent strikes out at the child, to silence that terrible sound of crying. The parent wants silence and obedience from the child, not accusations and demands. Such parents' own lives are often emotionally empty and unfulfilled. They need the child to be a source of love and approval, not one more person to make them feel inadequate or bad. Parents who abuse their children often were themselves abused as children. As adults they suffer deep feelings of helplessness, vulnerability, and uncertainty about their own self-worth. They want to be good parents, but the stresses of child-rearing drive them beyond their limits of control. Unfortunately, the children they abuse will very likely grow up to do the same thing to their own children.

Maybe you are the parent of a seemingly impossible child. You sometimes lose control and punish him or her too severely. You are ashamed of your behavior but afraid to ask for help. But help is available, if you can ask. There are also self-searching steps you can take by yourself, to help relieve your frightening situation. You have an opportunity not only to solve your immediate problem, but also to build a more loving, rewarding life for both you and your child.

• Try to discover what events seem to trigger your feelings of helplessness and rage. Consider what other stresses you feel at the same time, especially if the triggering event seems insignificant as you look back on it. Recognize that you are mistreating your child because of some frustration in your life, such as your work or family situation.

• Ask yourself whether your current life is fulfilling—whether you have other people with whom you can give and receive affection and warmth. If you do not, then resolve to build a more nourishing lifestyle for yourself.

• Think about whether annoying things your child does remind you of yourself or someone in your family. Recognize that you may be punishing your child for some quality you dislike in yourself or someone else.

• Think back to your own childhood and your relationships with your parents. Ask yourself whether you received love and emotional support from them. Determine to give yourself any caring and warmth that they denied you. Try to give your own child the same love that you need.

• Learn to see your child as a separate, unique person, with both good and bad points. Appreciate your child's individuality and try to help him or her develop as a warm, loving person. And remember that your child is only a child and cannot behave like an adult, no matter how hard he or she tries.

• Learn to express your disappointments and anger verbally, directly, to the person who angers or disappoints you. Recognize that you may be taking your problems out on your child because that seems safer than confronting another adult, especially your spouse.

• If you have a job that requires you to be very aggressive or stirs up anger in you, don't carry those feelings home with you. Let them melt away. Refresh yourself by accepting whatever warmth and comfort your family has to give. Hug your children.

• Recognize that despite "bad" things you may have done, either now or in the past, you are as worthwhile and deserving of love as any other person. Try to feel warm and accepting about yourself. Praise yourself for things you do well. And ask yourself if you need to spend more time caring for yourself, not just others.

• Seek help from a crisis referral service or an organization such as Parents Anonymous. Contact the National Committee for Prevention of Child Abuse (111 East Wacker Drive #510, Chicago, Illinois 60601) for a list of services and organizations in your community. Take advantage of the personal relief and rewards that come from sharing your problems with other parents who have the same feelings you do. Also, use the practical information they can give you on parenting skills, emergency medical services, and where to turn in time of crisis.

• Subscribe to the newsletter *Caring*, published by the National Committee for Prevention of Child Abuse. Send for free publications from both state and community organizations.

• If you know of a child who is being abused, report the situation to a social agency so that the family can get help. Remember that an abused child sometimes turns to delinquency, drugs, crime, and, in later life, child abuse. Help break the chain of suffering.

SUGGESTED READING:

Department of Health, Education and Welfare. *Child Abuse and Neglect—The Problem and Its Management*. Washington, D.C.: HEW, Publication No. OH 75-30073, 1975.

Fontana, Dr. Vincent J. *Somewhere a Child Is Crying*. New York: Mentor, New American Library, 1973.

Soman, Shirley Camper. *Let's Stop Destroying Our Children*. New York: Hawthorn, 1974.

See also: ANGER, INCEST, SADISM

CHILDBIRTH

Being pregnant and giving birth can be beautiful, natural, fulfilling experiences when all goes well. In most cases women's bodies are marvelously designed to have babies. In fact, some doctors claim that, due to the nature of female physiology, being pregnant or nursing is the most healthy and appropriate condition for women during their twenties and early thirties. In these days of women's liberation and zero population growth, such views are not likely to be popular, and certainly many women lead creative, healthy lives without having any children at all. Nevertheless, childbirth is always going to be a basic part of the human experience, and we will all benefit if it can be made as safe and happy an event as possible.

Thus, it need not be a "problem." Modern medical science has made great contributions toward reducing problem pregnancies, mother and infant mortality, birth defects, and pain. Antiseptics prevent fatal infections, anesthetics reduce labor pains, fetal monitors alert obstetricians to complications, cesarean deliveries release stuck babies, some drugs prevent hemorrhaging, and other drugs induce labor when necessary. These methods have saved women's lives and brought babies into the world who would never have made it otherwise. If you are pregnant or helping someone who is, learn all you can about what conventional medicine offers. Scientific obstetrics as practiced in approved hospitals may be your best bet. But know what you are getting, and what you aren't.

Debate rages over the advantages and disadvantages of hospital deliveries, especially those that include drugs, fetal monitoring, separation of father and mother, and separation of mother and baby after birth. For example, some critics claim that fetal monitoring causes more problems (such as increased numbers of cesareans) than it prevents. The monitors are expensive technological marvels. Doctors feel pressure to use them to "keep up" with scientific progress and the community standard of practice so as to avoid malpractice suits. The reliability of the monitors and of doctors' and nurses' interpretation of their data output has not been adequately demonstrated, however.

Similarly, drugs once thought safe have been shown to infiltrate the baby's bloodstream. Success in reducing pain and infection turns out to have costly side effects. Babies born to drugged or unconscious mothers may have minimal brain damage due to oxygen deprivation. Scared women cut off from emotional support tighten up and have labor complications.

After you have found out what your doctor and hospital offer, learn what critics say about the conventional birth experience available to you. Read the books listed under Suggested Reading, for example.

More and more prospective parents are deciding they want their children to start life as naturally and lovingly as possible. For them this may mean one or more of the following: no drugs, an awake and joyfully participating mother, a trained and loving labor coach (husband, lover, relative, friend), a peaceful birth environment, a cozy home birth, a "birthday" party, a spiritual ceremony of welcome and thanks. Obstetricians and hospitals are aware of these trends and take varying positions regarding them. Think over what you want, talk it over with everyone you can find who has actual experience or training, weigh the trade-offs, and decide what you want. Then talk tactfully but frankly with your obstetrician to see if he or she will cooperate.

• When you learn what your doctor proposes, find out from him or her and other sources the answers to these questions:

Why do you need each drug or procedure?
Will your baby and you be healthier as a result of using the drug or procedure? Or are they for the physician's convenience or part of a routine?
What are the known side effects and liabilities?
Will the benefits outweigh the side effects?
What are the risks to you and your baby if you don't have the drug or procedure?
• Women are often conditioned to believe childbirth is painful, when in fact it need not be. Much pain is the result of a vicious circle of ignorance, anxiety, and physical tension. That sequence can be prevented. One reason the normal processes of pregnancy, childbirth, and nursing become problems is the lack of training and experience on the part of new parents. As recently as 1971, only one out of five first-time mothers had even touched a baby, and only one in ten had ever seen a baby breast-fed. This situation is improving rapidly, but the need for childbirth education continues to be great.
• Regardless of how much you think you know, attend childbirth classes. For information, write to the American Academy of Husband-Coached Childbirth, P.O. Box 5224, Sherman Oaks, California 91413; American Society for Psycho-prophylaxis in Obstetrics, 7 West 96th Street, New York, New York 10025; or the International Childbirth Education Association, 208 Ditty Building, Bellevue, Washington 98004. Even if you decide not to have a natural childbirth, the classes will make you better prepared for a medicated birth, reduce your anxiety, and lessen the chance of complications.

• Go to La Leche League meetings and read *The Womanly Art of Breastfeeding,* published by the League. (See phone book listing or write La Leche League, Franklin Park, Illinois 60131.) La Leche League teaches mothers all about breast-feeding and infant care. Even if you decide not to breast-feed, you will gain invaluable information about mothering.

• One of the wonderful bonuses many couples derive from attending classes and working together for a prepared natural childbirth is a deepening of their relationship. Many a man who was afraid he would feel squeamish has discovered that being an effective, educated participant at his child's birth brought him closer to his wife and baby, and gave him a new sense of masculine pride. Mothers and fathers can take active responsibility for giving birth to their babies, rather than submitting in passivity and anxiety while the baby is "delivered." Childbirth is too complex, demanding, and important an event to rely on someone else to do it for you. As in many areas of life, awareness, choice, and decisive action have great rewards.

• Books have been written about the "birth trauma" and its consequences for subsequent personality development. Dr. Leboyer's nonviolent birth procedures apply the principles of involved, knowledgeable, loving participation to the period right after birth. Here also, rather than allowing the baby to be whisked off to the care of "experts," mother and father take careful, gradual steps to introduce their baby into the world.

• If you have decided on a hospital birth, visit the hospital to become familiar with the physical layout and the sequence of events you will go through. Take care of any paperwork and financial arrangements you can ahead of time.

• In childbirth classes you will learn about proper diet, exercises to prepare for effective labor, breathing, and relaxation. Some expectant mothers worry excessively about gaining too much weight. As a result, they may not eat sufficient protein, and then their doctors may prescribe diuretic pills to reduce water retention. Research by Dr. Tom Brewer and others has demonstrated the crucial importance of good nutrition during pregnancy, and the dangers of diuretics.

• Research has also revealed the vital role of early mother-child bonding through immediate and sustained contact. Be sure you know what you want and how to get it in that regard also. Don't accept separation from your newborn baby unless you are convinced it is medically required. The American Medical Association has adopted a formal statement supporting the immediate bonding of mothers with their newborn babies. Be sure your doctor knows this.

Dr. Robert Bradley, the originator of husband-coached natural childbirth, likes to emphasize that normal childbirth is more like an athletic event than a medical problem. Consequently, the "athlete" needs to be in good physical condition and specially trained, and needs to be guided and supported by an expert labor "coach." When these conditions are met, childbirth can indeed be one of life's most fulfilling experiences.

SUGGESTED READING:

Boston Women's Health Book Collective. *Our Bodies, Ourselves*, rev. 2nd ed. New York: Simon & Schuster, 1976.
Bradley, Dr. Robert. *Husband-Coached Childbirth*. New York: Harper & Row, 1974.
Karmel, Majorie. *Thank You, Doctor Lamaze*. New York: Doubleday.
Leboyer, Dr. Frederick. *Birth Without Violence*. New York: Alfred A. Knopf, 1975.

See also: FEAR OF SICKNESS, PAIN

CHILDREN OF DIVORCE

The children of divorcing parents suffer emotional stresses that take a long time to heal. They are torn by a variety of fears, sadness, anger, grief, panic, self-doubt, and guilt. A child often thinks, "If I had been good, this wouldn't have happened," or "My daddy doesn't love me or he wouldn't have gone away. I'm bad."

The most potentially damaging element to a child is the hostility between the parents, not only after the divorce but while the parents are still together. For this reason, most psychologists and social scientists agree that children often are better off living with a divorced parent than in an intact home filled with conflict.

The way in which you as parents handle your relationship with each other and with your children (or child) has a great effect on how soon and successfully they can resume a relatively happy, normal life after the divorce. Despite the many negative aspects of divorce, it also presents opportunities for growth. Out of the change and upheaval you can achieve a sense of mastery and creative control of your life. Even though you leave your home and children, or live as a single parent, you can become an even better parent than before. Finding ways to help your children recover from the family rupture can not only make them happier, but provide all of you with a new sense of closeness and achievement.

Here are some suggestions to help you reach this goal.

• If you are only considering getting a divorce, don't inflict your conflict and indecision on the children or involve them in helping you decide.

• If possible, consult a professional divorce counselor, preferably one who also specializes in helping couples make decisions about the children's welfare.

• Agree with your spouse about what, when, and how to tell the children about the divorce. Do this together if you can. If not, be sure both of you talk to them. Tell them a few days in advance of the actual split, rather than having one parent just disappear. This allows a time of family normalcy during which they can assimilate the facts and ask questions.

• Be clear with the children about what is happening. Don't blame your spouse or go into detail about your difficulties. Say that the two of you are very unhappy living together and so one of you is going to be living somewhere else. Be clear about the permanency of the split, to keep from stirring up their hopes about a reconciliation.

• Assure the children that you still love them and always will, and that you will always be their parent. If it is appropriate, say you're sorry you weren't always a good parent, but now you will be happier and things will be better. This may be reassuring to the children, who probably anticipate that things will get worse.

• Be specific about what happens next. For example, say that Daddy is going to be living at an apartment and will come to take them to dinner next Saturday. The more specific you can be, the more secure they will feel.

• Be clear to yourself about what constructive actions you will now take with your children. Recognize the part of yourself that doesn't want to make the extra effort, or may want to use them as a weapon against your spouse. Be on guard against blaming them for the divorce, or resenting the economic burden they pose. Accept your negative feelings as natural, but try to give your children all the love and care your positive feelings will allow.

• Ask yourself whether there is anything in particular in your relationship with your children that now needs special attention. If you feel guilty about the divorce's effect on them, let that motivate you to spend more time talking through difficult feelings or doing special things together.

• Be prepared to help your children experience and work through their emotions. The most common are anger, guilt, grief, depression, and hopes for the parents' reconciliation. A child may fear being abandoned or may deny what is happening. He or she may regress into babyish or immature behavior, or may appear super-mature and unaffected. Recognize these as natural reactions to the divorce, and help your child talk about the feelings going on inside. Be accepting of them, even if they upset you.

• Your child may try to test your love by expressing anger or blame at you. Don't be triggered into an angry self-justification. Keep reassuring the child that he or she is loved and will be taken care of. Say that this is a difficult time but you will all do what you can to get through it and find the good parts.

• Make it very clear to the children that the divorce is not their fault. Children often believe they are to blame and feel they must somehow "undo" the divorce. Reducing blame helps relieve this anxiety and the accompanying unrealistic hopes.

• Be on the watch for prolonged, intense grief in a child, or other excessive feelings, as a signal that the divorce may have brought to the surface deeper insecurities that have existed all along. Try to help the child talk about negative self-feelings. Consider offering your child the opportunity to talk to a professional counselor.

• A child may feel like running away, so put extra effort into keeping the bond between you strong. If you and your spouse are still in open conflict, this may be an additional reason for the child to want to get away. Try to shield the child from painful scenes.

• Offer support and affection to your children, but give them freedom to control the degree of closeness. Don't push, but try to be responsively available when needed. If a child creates too much distance, talk it over and try to learn why this is happening. Do the same if your child becomes anxiously clinging. In either case, try to express in a nonjudgmental way how you would like the relationship to be. If you are a mother with a teenage son, he may especially need some distance and autonomy. Too much closeness can create an intensity that will cause him to withdraw in self-protection.

• Tell your children's teachers about the divorce, but don't make a big deal out of it.

• If a child begins to have trouble at school, with friends, or in being responsible and obedient, consider whether these problems may be signs of emotional distress. Be supportive and firm in dealing with symptoms, and keep looking to see if there are deeper causes.

• After the breakup, if at first you cannot cope with the strain of handling the children, have them taken care of by your family or a community agency. Ask for help. Don't let yourself get so desperate or angry that you punish or abandon a child.

• Don't use your children for approval or solace, and don't allow them to side with you against their other parent. Don't criticize your ex-spouse to them. If you and your ex disagree on something, deal directly with each other. If necessary, explain to the children that you and your ex disagree on certain issues. Clarify your values and standards, but emphasize that even well-intentioned people often differ about how to live. Just because they disagree does not mean that one is right and the other wrong.

• If your ex-spouse abandons the children, tell them that their other parent still loves them down deep. Explain that sometimes it's hard to love others even though we want to, and that their parent is doing the best he or she can right now.

• Consider getting a Big Brother or Big Sister for a child (see your telephone directory or write 220 Suburban Station Boulevard, Philadelphia, Pennsylvania 19103). A relative may also be able to provide warmth and companionship in place of a missing parent.

• If your ex-spouse has custody, have visitation rights spelled out in the agreement. A regular schedule gives security to your children. If possible, get permission from the court for reasonable spontaneous visits also. Try to see your children separately as well as together.

• Always keep your appointments with your children, or explain in advance that you cannot, and the reason why.

• If your first visits seem difficult, consider scheduling shorter, more frequent visits, to let you both adjust to the new situation. Plan in advance what you are going to do, at least in general. An activity such as dinner helps structure an evening and gives you time for relating. When it is practical, let the children help plan their visit.

• If you have trouble talking with your children, make it easier by talking while you do something simple together, such as walking, sewing, cooking, or fishing. Also, talking about your own childhood may stimulate your children to talk about theirs.

• Take your children to your new home, for an overnight stay if possible. Give them a drawer or closet for their things, to make it seem like their home too.

• Don't let guilt make you afraid to discipline your children. And don't get overinvolved in elaborate activities that do not leave enough time for simple, relaxed ways of being together.

• Phone or write short notes to your children occasionally. Encourage them to call you, too, so they can continue to feel connected.

• Expect your children to have activities that occasionally interfere with your visiting schedule. Try to be flexible and not be hurt when this happens. If one of your children wants a friend to come along on a visit with you, consider it a compliment, whether you like it or not. Try to be flexible in matching your children's preferred activities to your own.

• Clarify with your children that you may be dating, and talk about it with them. Don't spring a new person on them abruptly. Give them all the time they need to be wary and to get acquainted at their own pace.

• If you remarry, recognize that this ends your children's reconciliation hopes. They may also fear that you will disappear if you remarry. Reassure them that you will continue to love them. Don't push them into closeness with your new spouse—allow adjustment time.

• The remarriage of you or your ex-spouse offers your children the benefits of an expanded family. Talk about the new relatives. Make a family tree. Get pictures, write letters, and make vacation visits. Recognize that this new situation may be much more beneficial for your children than before the divorce, when you lived together as an intact but unhappy family.

SUGGESTED READING:

Dodson, Fitzhugh. *How to Father*. New York: Signet, New American Library, 1974.

Gardner, Richard A. *The Boys' and Girls' Book About Divorce*. New York: Bantam Books, 1970.

Tessman, Lora. *Children of Parting Parents*. New York: Aronson, 1978.

See also: DEPRESSION, DIVORCE, GUILT, SINGLE PARENTING, STEPPARENTING

COMMUNICATION BLOCKS

Clear communication is essential to sustain satisfying and effective relationships in all areas of life—personal, business, and social. We need to be able to say what we mean in a way that gets results. But most of us sometimes have trouble getting across what we really want to say to other people. We may wish to give or request advice, information, or instructions, or share a feeling, offer sympathy, or express a need. But blocks get in the way. Sometimes people don't hear us the way we want to be heard. Sometimes we can't get through because we don't have effective communication skills for a particular situation. Business partners split up, employees get fired, husbands and wives divorce, children run away from home, doctors get sued for malpractice, and the waitress forgets to bring you coffee because communication breaks down.

Actually, you are always communicating *something*, but it may not be what you want to communicate. Or it may be received by the other person differently from the way you intended. Communication involves a sender and a receiver. However, all too often the message sent is not the same as the message received. For good communication, both people must be good senders and receivers. It takes two to tango. It takes two to argue. It takes two to keep an angry silence going. The point is, communication is a shared problem. Either person can take steps to improve it.

• Don't withdraw into discouragement or righteousness when you have communication blocks. You *can* do something. Blaming yourself or the other person won't help, but taking a new approach may, even if you have to do all the work in the beginning. Good communication skills tend to bring out the best in other people. Your partner can learn from you, even when not aware of the change that is happening.

• Try being more specific and personal in what you say. Speak for yourself; don't use vague generalizations about people in general.

• Pay attention to what is happening in the present moment within yourself, in the other person, and between the two of you. Do this even if the topic concerns the past, the future, or other people. Pay special attention to *feelings*—when they are overridden they cause serious communication blocks.

• Be sparing in making moralistic or evaluative judgments. Use them only when you really want and need to, because they can turn your partner off even if they aren't aimed at him or her. Everyone has insecurities and guilts, and no one needs more judges and critics. If you do have criticisms to make, remember that to be effective you first have to get yourself taken seriously as an expert or trusted friend, and that takes communication.

• People usually want support, approval, and agreement. Be as generous with these as you can. Even if a person is determined to be pessimistic and self-critical, he or she may at least want some agreement, rather than opposition in the form of a pep talk. Don't become a yes-man, but don't neglect to give affirmation whenever you honestly can. It will make people open up to you and be more receptive to what you have to say.

• Take time and effort to know what you want to communicate. "Do not operate mouth until brain is in gear." Spontaneous, unrehearsed communication is a natural, necessary, and enjoyable part of daily life. But there are also times when you will do better if you dig deeper into yourself in privacy to discover what you want to convey. Particularly if people don't seem to understand you or take you seriously, you might consider whether you are speaking with conviction in a way that commands interest and respect.

• Give your partner time and "space" in which to communicate. Don't interrupt or complete his or her sentences. Make it clear that your intention is to communicate, not to make a speech, conduct a monologue, or win a debate. That takes real listening.

• Remember that feelings are facts. Your partner may feel differently from you because he or she sees things differently. You won't get anywhere arguing that the feelings are wrong, because the person is directly experiencing the reality of those feelings. Let your partner know you hear the feelings being expressed. Then go on to explore the causes of your different views and reactions, and to look for areas of agreement or compromise.

• Face the fact that the message you think you are receiving is not always the message sent. Repeat your partner's message back to him or her in your own words and ask if you've heard it correctly. This will clear up distortions, show that you are really trying to hear, and keep you from tuning out in order to prepare your rebuttal before the other person has finished talking.

• Ask yourself if your goal is to communicate or to win. Are you willing to put yourself out there as clearly as you can, let the other people respond, and hear them nondefensively? Or do you want to control, dominate, and manipulate? There may be times when you prefer to do these things for noble or ignoble reasons, but at least don't confuse them with communication. True communication involves the capacity to be open and effectively expressive of your feelings, ideas, values, wants, intentions, and requirements without the use of "managed news" or force to get your way. If people seem to resist you or to hold back from communicating, you might do well to explore whether they see you as trying to win at their expense.

• Look at what you might be trying to win. It isn't just the actions of others that we try to control. Often we try to win a virtue contest. The relationship becomes a courtroom complete with judge, jury, prosecutor, defense attorney, witnesses, and evidence. Confessions must be extracted, guilt must be proven, and self-worth must be weighed. Unfortunately, with this approach, if one person wins, the other loses, and the relationship fails.

• Watch out for anger and covert resentment as barriers to communication. Silence often occurs because a person is afraid to erupt into anger or to risk triggering it. Shouting and threats of physical violence can easily overload a relationship—avoid them if you can. But that doesn't mean you should suppress anger altogether. You may need to clear the air by venting some anger, or allowing some to be blasted at you. Overprotectiveness of yourself or your partner can dam up the flow of expression to the point where you also can't say positive things.

• When you are in the process of getting anger out in the open, in a quarrel or a blunt confrontation, remember that anger also conceals vulnerability, fear, and hurt. Try to listen for those feelings too, in yourself and in the other. Shift over to a compassionate concern for the feelings when the timing seems right. Think of a raging lion with a thorn in its foot and look for the thorn.

• If you feel courageous and can find people you trust enough to play rough with, try this method: Agree that for a specified period of time you are going to suspend the normal rules of politeness, tact, consideration, fairness, and even truth. Say whatever you want, no matter how exaggerated, distorted, unfair, insulting, or inflammatory. Let it all hang out. Do this only if you have confidence that you and whomever you do it with will be able to take it in the spirit of a constructive exercise, rather than carrying it on into "real life" with hurt feelings and grudges. This kind of experiment can open up issues that can later be explored more sanely.

• Own up to the secret payoffs you may be getting by not communicating clearly. Maybe you feel you have more to lose than to gain by opening up. "Better to keep one's mouth shut and be thought a fool than to open it and remove all doubt." Perhaps you remain distant and aloof to maintain a sense of your superiority. Perhaps you fear the consequences of getting close to someone.

• Don't give mixed messages, at least not if you expect to be understood. Contradictory messages can be confusing and even demoralizing to other people. Of course, we always communicate in several different ways at different levels. There is more going on than the literal meaning of our words. Along with the message, there is a message about the message. The second message can be conveyed by tone of voice, facial expression, or body language. Usually this message fits, is congruent with the literal message. Other times it is incongruent— for example, "I am not angry," said with gritted teeth, or "Okay, have it your way," said sarcastically. These messages put the receiver in a conflict. To which message should you respond? What can you do? If you are getting a double message, point out both messages. If you are giving a message, make your implicit message explicit.

• Be clear about limits and requirements, and the consequences if they are not met. Don't work at being nice, nondirective, sympathetic, or tolerant when what you really need to do is set someone straight about your true feelings and intentions. It is not fair or effective to lull people into a false impression of you as a mouse and then suddenly roar at them like a lion. Parents sometimes have this trouble in disciplining children, and people raised in a strict religious environment sometimes also have difficulty being appropriately tough. You don't have to become a monster—just an honest person who bends only so far. Give people a fair warning of your limits, and be consistent about your requirements so they can learn what you are like.

• Take a course or a home-study program in communications skills. Join a group like Toastmasters where you will be able to practice public speaking in a supportive setting. The Dale Carnegie course has been popular for many years and has been continually updated with modern training methods. Find a congenial discussion group on a topic that interests you. Set aside time with someone close to you during which you agree to work conscientiously on deepening your communication and providing each other with feedback.

• Take a look at the "response modes" you use and the results they produce for you. Professor Gerald Goodman at UCLA has developed a way of looking at communication that focuses on six response modes, or what he calls various kinds of "helping-talk": questions, advisement, spacing, reflection of feelings, interpretation, and self-disclosure. Become aware of what these ways of talking are, when you use them, and how they affect the conversation.

Questions. Closed-ended questions ("What time is it?") are useful for getting specific information. In helping communication, open-ended questions ("How was your day?") are usually more useful. Questions are often used to disguise a command or piece of advice ("Don't you think the door needs closing?" instead of "Please close the door"). If you are overusing questions and obscuring what you really mean, try sending more direct messages.

Advisement. When people ask for help, they usually expect advice. But advice is often rejected. Receiving advice makes some people feel put down. So be cautious if you do give advice. Make sure you really understand the other's concern. Reflect their feelings back to them. Ask yourself if you are really competent to give advice. If you give advice, give clear support for it and avoid focusing on the other's personality. Most people can choose their own solutions.

Spacing. Silence can be golden. Give your partner time to pause and think. Verbal crowding and interrupting are two of the worst causes of problems in communication. They are small behaviors that eventually produce big difficulties.

Reflection of feelings. This is the most underused but probably the most helpful aid to communication. Reflect feelings back by stating in your own words the essence of the feeling in the other's message. For example, someone might say to you, "I don't know what to do. Whichever way I go could be disastrous." You could say, "I guess you're feeling cornered." Reflections make people feel understood. Make your reflections crisp and concise. Sometimes people repeat their message over and over again, getting louder each time. This means that they don't feel their message is getting through to you. Reflect their feelings. They will feel understood and go on to say something new.

Interpretation. This classifies or explains behavior. It is usually overused. Focus on understanding the other person, rather than giving explanations. Do not label or pigeonhole.

Self-disclosure. Use "me-too" disclosures to convey empathy: "Hey, I had that feeling too when I . . ." Self-disclosures are about immediate here-and-now experiences; they are very useful for solving communication difficulties. If you are confused, for example, tell your partner. If what he or she says touches you deeply, share that.

Use this framework to see communication more clearly and give yourself more options to choose from.

The cassette-tape training package designed and researched by Professor Gerald Goodman and his colleagues is available from UCLA Extension, Department of Human Development, Los Angeles, California 90024. It is called "SASHAtapes" and consists of six tapes that will direct you and a friend or a small group in carefully organized training sessions. Each session is led by the tape and includes group exercises, examples, mini-lectures, and time for discussion.

SUGGESTED READING:

Carkhuff, R. *Helping and Human Relations.* Volumes I and II. New York: Holt, Rinehart and Winston, 1969.

Goodman, Gerald. *SASHAtapes User's Manual.* Los Angeles: UCLA Extension, 1979.

Guerney, B. *Relationship Enhancement: Skill Training Programs for Therapy, Problem Prevention and Enhancement.* San Francisco: Jossey-Bass, 1977.

Van der Veen, Ferdinand. *Dialoguing: A way of learning to relate constructively in close relationships.* Institute for Juvenile Research (1140 South Paulina Street, Chicago, Illinois 60612), 1977.

Walters, Barbara. *How to Talk with Practically Anybody About Practically Anything.* New York: Dell, 1976.

Wassmen, Arthur C. *Making Contact.* New York: Dial Press, 1978.

Zimbardo, Philip. *Shyness: What It Is—What to Do About It.* Reading, Mass.: Addison-Wesley, 1977.

See also: ANGER, SHYNESS, STAGE FRIGHT, STUTTERING

COMPETITIVENESS

Our society values and rewards competitiveness. We're used to evaluating the worth of individuals according to how well they succeed in competition with their peers. Many of us base our sense of self-esteem on our ability to compete successfully and to accumulate the tangible rewards of winning.

Competitiveness can be a healthy motivation for action. Often it contributes to the fun of a game, to the excitement of learning, to the thrill of achievement. It can help children and adults strain for excellence and develop their talents fully. A young musician who strives to match the accomplishment of a Rubinstein sets before himself or herself a shining example to follow and a rigorous standard of achievement to match.

The value of competitiveness can easily be overemphasized, however. Both Little League and the Olympics offer familiar examples of competitive situations in which the celebration of excellence frequently gives way to excessive and unhealthy personal or international rivalry. The concern for genuine individual improvement is lost in the scramble for prestige, success, and even commercial reward.

If not handled carefully, individual competition can take on the aspect of warfare. Highly competitive people often display hostile aggressiveness in their dealings with others. In their high-pressure struggle to do more and more in less and less time—even at someone else's expense —they are irritable and easily moved to anger.

External standards of worth and achievement can be valuable markers and reference points for us. Problems arise, however, when our *only* standards are external ones. Sometimes the standards learned from a particular family or social environment do not fit the way we really feel internally, and are not appropriate for our personal needs and abilities.

There is some danger in clinging to these external measures of worth. First, we risk measuring ourselves by inappropriate standards, such as wealth, appearance, or popularity. Second, we may come to define ourselves only as the sum of our acts or products—the total of what we do and make, not of what we are. Highly competitive people are often very insecure. They lack personal, internal standards by which to measure their worth to their own satisfaction. They depend on external validation of their worth. No amount of success ever seems sufficient to soothe their discontent.

In addition to the damage excessive competitiveness can cause to personal relationships and to one's own emotions, it can also threaten physical health. There is a significant correlation between the highly competitive, time-pressured, aggressive personality and the risk of coronary disease.

It is not necessary to give up competition altogether in order to maintain your mental and physical health, however. You can learn to strike a balance. Your competitive drive can become a source of confidence and security instead of remaining an irritating goad. If you learn to work without agitation, to your internal satisfaction, you will not sacrifice success. Indeed, recent studies show that a willingness to work hard and to accept challenging tasks has more to do with success than competition does with others.

Answer the following questions, then try out some of the suggestions to reduce excessive competitiveness.

• Do you truly enjoy competition and the benefits it wins you? Or are you hooked on getting rather than living? Are you able to savor the rewards of competition? Or do you plunge on compulsively, barely pausing to notice the victories and their cost?

• Do you compete for your own sake or to satisfy someone else's ambitions for you? Are you a competitive puppet, with someone else pulling your strings? Do you really think you can ever earn enough love and respect to satisfy you that way?

• Who is in control, you or your competitive drive? Can you honestly claim that you are in charge, and that your drive to win is something you can turn on and off?

• Does competition carry over into your private life? Do you feel you're in competition for personal rewards, too—love, support, attention? Think back—did you spend your childhood competing with your siblings or others for your parents' attention and approval?

• Do you define yourself only in relation to others? Do you try to seek your own values and make your own choices, or do external considerations determine your course?

• What are you trying to prove . . . and disprove? Competitiveness often covers a sense of inferiority or shame, sometimes based on past incidents of no real significance today. Don't let yourself be run by your history. Wipe the slate clean and decide what forms of self-actualization really feel good now for their own sake.

• What are the qualities, achievements, experiences, and talents that you value in yourself? Are you developing yourself to the fullest? Have you set your own goals? If not, why not?

• Do you create pressure where there is none? Can you see a task through to completion without deciding in advance that it must be finished by a certain time or in a certain way?

• Do you try to do everything for everyone? Can you let someone you think is less competent than you finish a task at his or her own rate without impatiently taking over? Must you dominate every situation?

• Are you caught in a numbers game, counting money, trophies, degrees, sales, lovers, friends, trips? Are you convinced that more is always better? Could you stop competing if you reached some special number? Try setting a reachable goal and really relaxing once you reach it.

• Accept the fact that no one is ever really "number one." There are so many worthwhile things to do in life. Even if you do some of them very well, there will be lots you do poorly or not at all.

• Try to work with others instead of alone and competitively. Give yourself a chance to experience the pleasures and powers of teamwork. You can develop your own strengths without trying to undercut someone else's. Your career may move along much faster with the support and cooperation of your peers than it could move on your competitive drive alone.

• Repeat this slogan to yourself frequently: "To err is human." Human beings make mistakes. They are imperfect by nature. You have a right to make mistakes, even to fail outright. Wins and losses are both temporary and incomplete. Learn from success and failure. Gain strength from varied experience.

• Compete with excellence, not with other people. You will not be able to build an enduring sense of self-worth on cutthroat interpersonal competition. Winning cannot be all. Try to do something well, something that matters to you alone. Enjoy your sense of accomplishment. Do not compare your accomplishment favorably or unfavorably to anyone else's. Get used to pleasing yourself, to meeting your personal standards.

• Slow down. You may have succeeded up to now in spite of your excessive competitiveness. Do not exaggerate time pressure. Good work does not always come out of being pressured. It's more likely that you will do excellent work slowly and carefully.

• Take stock of your abilities and qualities honestly. Compare yourself to others only insofar as the comparison helps you appraise your true self. When you have put together an unbiased picture of yourself, you can begin working on what's really there, not on what you or others think *should* be there. Value your weaknesses and vulnerabilities as well as your strengths. Value your individuality. As you work on developing your true self, you will become less dependent on the views of others. You will be able to choose what you really want to do and be in life.

• Set private goals for your life, as well as public, professional ones. Ask yourself what you really need for a satisfactory life. Try to achieve a life of quality, not quantity.

• Don't try to do it all. Learn to distinguish between essential and nonessential tasks. Learn to delegate responsibility and to share work. Give others an opportunity to learn new skills by working with you. (See TIME-WASTING to help you organize your work time efficiently and in an unpressured way.)

• Allow yourself time for the noncompetitive things you want to do. Work steadily and efficiently, but provide time for the rest of living: family, friends, relaxation, recreation, reading, music, walking in the woods. Pause. Listen to yourself. Learn to be alone to restore yourself.

• Work on diminishing your hostility and aggressiveness. Learn a meditation or progressive relaxation technique and practice it daily. (See ANGER. Also, the entry on PASSIVITY may help you learn the difference between aggression and assertiveness.)

• Let yourself laugh—even at yourself or at your mistakes. Don't take the competitive parts of your life so seriously that you miss all the fun. Smile—even at people who have given up expecting you to be good-natured.

• Don't limit your socializing to equally competitive individuals or go-getters. Nurture friendship and caring in your life. Develop a supportive system of friends and family. Try to develop a sense of tradition and ritual that you can share; enjoy personal, social, and religious occasions in the company of loving people.

• When you do compete, do it fairly. Don't sacrifice your sense of what's right to gain some competitive goal. If you do, when you win you'll have lost.

• Don't compete through your kids. Don't use them to feed your ego. Emphasize fairness, skill, and enjoyment rather than winning. Your children will develop confidence best in an atmosphere of encouragement and praise. If winning is the only goal, your child will be upset by losing and miss the pride of having tried his or her best. Concentrate on being a model of good sportsmanship.

• Focus your attention on enhancing the quality of each day as it comes. The best way to be a winner in the long run is to live lovingly and creatively in the present.

SUGGESTED READING:

Aberti, Robert E., and Michael L. Emmons. *Your Perfect Right: A Guide to Assertive Behavior*. San Luis Obispo: Impact, 1974.

See also: ENVY, GREED, NARCISSISM, PERFECTIONISM, SIBLING RIVALRY

COMPULSIONS

Sometimes we get on our own nerves. We suddenly realize that for the fiftieth time in three hours we've taken off our glasses to chew on the earpiece. Why? How did we ever develop such a useless, repetitive, uncontrolled gesture?

Habitual actions or sequences of actions can come to take on compulsive significance in our lives. Some of us go back to check the front door repeatedly before finally leaving for work. Others can't stand to let the dinner dishes wait for even a few minutes—what is dirty must be cleaned up immediately. Millions of us smoke. Uncounted numbers of us chew our nails. An unspeakable number of us punctuate every sentence with "y'know."

These compulsive habits can reflect unconscious efforts to resolve inner conflicts. Habit can be a way to handle anxiety, fears, guilt, anger, terror. Habit can give us a rigid, yet very protective, shield against inner problems. Habit can help us manage our emotions or defend ourselves against an unpredictable world. "If I check the door just one more time, my life will be safe from all threats." "If I keep everything in order, I'll never be punished for all the naughty things I did as a child."

Compulsive habits can take many forms. They tend to reflect conflicts concerning aggressiveness and submissiveness, cruelty and gentleness, dirtiness and cleanliness, disorder and order. They may show up in any aspect of our behavior: eating, lying, stealing, smoking, drinking, grooming, housekeeping.

When is a habit a bad habit? Who decides? It's largely a matter of degree. If habitual behavior becomes overdeveloped, overemphasized, you may begin to feel that it is getting in the way of your life. The habit may show itself as counterproductive. It may cut you off from people or activities you want and need in your life. Overeating, for example, can develop as a habitual response to a problem you cannot easily solve: loneliness, sexual anxiety, fearfulness. Eventually, however, the overeating habit itself monopolizes your attention, because obesity becomes the most apparent—though not necessarily the most pressing—problem in your life.

You yourself need to decide how much is enough. You alone can accurately judge how much a particular habit is interfering with your life experience as a whole. You alone know if your habit really is antisocial, if it really lets you avoid important life tasks, if it really soothes your fears of risk, change, challenge, or intimacy, for example. You may practice guitar five hours a day because you're trying to break into pop music. You may also practice to use up the free time that might otherwise be spent with people or in activities that made you feel inadequate.

• If you're troubled by a particular habit, try to discover what sort of a need it fills for you. How does it keep you busy? How might it block you from doing, or saying, or even thinking something you're afraid of—such as expressing anger, shame, dissatisfaction, love? Do you see a way in which your habit keeps you from doing something else, something you might feel is worse? Do you have that second martini in order to control your urge to tell off your boss?

• Recognize the way in which a habit can cover intense internal activity. Some privately developed ritual behavior is a way of creatively approaching inner pain. Study your compulsive habits for the clues they give you to your true interior life. Are you always washing or cleaning something? Does that make you feel good or bad? What is it you're really hoping to clean? It may be that indulging yourself in this symbolic cleansing may lead you to recognize and resolve a long-hidden need to clean up a problem, or fear, or guilt.

• If you decide to break a habit, first list all the reasons why you have chosen to give it up. Why is it a bad habit? Then make another list of what you'll gain by giving up your bad habit. Now you can concentrate on the rewards for successfully changing your behavior patterns.

• If you need to reinforce your will to attack an unattractive habit, such as nail-biting or chewing on a braid or cracking your knuckles, spend a few minutes twice a day in front of a mirror doing what you want to stop. This will give you an idea of what others see—and will help you strengthen your willpower.

• Behavior therapy proposes ending undesirable habits by removing the rewards they provide. If there is nothing to be gained by keeping the habit, or, worse yet, if there is a punishment attached, no matter what the reason for developing the habit, it becomes too painful to continue it. Aversive therapy (punishment therapy) is a powerful, proven technique for stopping bad habits. You might consider aversive therapy for a costly, dangerous, disabling habit. (See SMOKING.)

• If you want to take a behavior-therapy approach to your own bad habit, begin by identifying the circumstances under which the unwanted behavior occurs and recognizing the immediate results of the unwanted behavior. When do you do it and what do you get out of it? Without trying to control your bad habit, take a couple of weeks to keep track honestly (on a chart) of *when* you do it, *where, how* you are feeling at the time, *what* happened as a consequence of your unwanted action. For example: You note that at 9:30 P.M. on Tuesday you were bored, watching TV with your spouse in the living room, and began chewing your nails, and he or she didn't even notice. You might record that at another time, at work, a co-worker did notice and asked you to stop.

• Knowing when and where and for what reward you do something will help you change the environment and the behavior. Chart your progress daily. Post your chart so you can praise yourself for your progress and so others can offer their praise. Be specific about what you want to change. "I want to be more attractive to others" is too broad; "I want to stop pulling on my ear" is manageable.

• There are many ways to reduce the reward for a bad habit. If it's something you do in many places, prohibit yourself from doing it except in a single, confined place. If you have to get up and go into the bathroom every time you insist on chewing your nails, the cost exceeds the reward. At the same time, you're reducing the strong association between most of your environment and the unwanted habit.

• Stay away from situations that trigger your problem habit. If you can't watch TV without eating, cut out the viewing until you're more in control of your dietary pattern. (See OBESITY.)

• Set up a positive behavior in competition with the unwanted one. If you go for a brisk walk around the block when tempted to wolf down a pastry, you put off the opportunity to eat unnecessary calories and give yourself a chance to overcome the negative impulse. Exercise diminishes appetite, as does the time to reflect on how you look now as opposed to how you want to look.

• Reward yourself immediately for good behavior. Give yourself points, for example, each time you refrain from doing something you want to stop, or do something you want to increase. Give yourself a treat for earning a certain number of points. If you want to read more, but find yourself tempted by TV, give yourself a half hour of TV time for every fifty pages you read in excess of your base reading rate.

• Imagine yourself behaving the way you want to behave. Imagine your friends, co-workers, family, acquaintances noticing your behavior and praising you for it. This is called "covert reinforcement." It will help you carry out your intentions to change your behavior. It will help prepare you to transfer your improved behavior into the world at large.

• If your goal is a complex one, break it down into smaller goals. Reward yourself more and more at each level. For example, if you want to cut 3,500 calories a week from your diet, reduce your calorie allowance by 750 calories a week for the first two weeks, by 1,000 calories a week for the next two weeks. Increase the reward for achieving each new level. Continue to reward yourself for meeting your weekly goal.

• If you have a friend, child, spouse, acquaintance, or co-worker who exhibits a compulsive bad habit, try not to pounce on him or her with criticism. Try to see the need this behavior fills, the value it has for the other person. Don't judge from the outside; do make yourself available to praise and reinforce someone else's efforts to change.

SUGGESTED READING:

Cammer, Leonard. *Freedom from Compulsion.* New York: Pocket Books, 1977.

Robbins, Jhan, and Dave Fisher. *How to Make and Break Habits.* New York: Peter H. Wyden, 1973.

See also: ANXIETY, OBSESSIONS, PERFECTIONISM

DELAYED EJACULATION

Although it is more common for men to have problems relating to coming too quickly (premature ejaculation), some men find they have trouble coming as quickly as they would like. If you have this problem, you may find that intercourse goes on so long before you ejaculate that it may actually become uncomfortable or painful for you. Or your partner may become uncomfortable or tired, and you may have to stop intercourse before you come. Or, even more complicated, your partner may like extended intercourse but you feel physically or otherwise uncomfortable with it. However you experience this problem, the main thing is that you want to learn how to come more quickly or how to have more choice about when you come.

• There are several things that often cause men to have trouble ejaculating, and it may help for you to examine your sexual attitudes for these pitfalls. Do you turn yourself off sexually during intercourse? Do you think about other things or fence out your partner? Are you afraid of letting go or being vulnerable with your partner? Why? How do you imagine you look and sound when you are having an orgasm? Does this embarrass you? Sometimes men unconsciously hold back ejaculation because of the sounds or faces that they make when coming. Also, some men believe that the man who "lasts longest" is the best lover (not so!), and they try to learn to turn off their excitement to keep from coming. Have you done this? In any case, the key to working on this problem is to get you back in touch with your sexual feelings.

• Do the exercises recommended under SEXUAL DYSFUNCTION and place special emphasis on exploring your body and penis on your own, without a partner. Focus especially on what feels good or sexually exciting to you. What part of your penis is most sensitive? What speed or pressure feels best? Try using nonirritating body lotions or creams on your penis. How do they feel to you? Vary your self-stimulation in as many ways as you can think of; focus on the things that feel good and exciting, but don't narrow down too quickly. Try doing an exercise in the bathtub, or standing up, or in rhythm to music. Try different fantasies: Be a seducer or the seduced, in bed or in public. (You may want to look at Thom Anicar's book, *Secret Sex,* a collection of men's sexual fantasies.) Discover what turns you on.

• In doing one of these exercises, it's best if you don't come, though it does not spoil the exercise if you do. Be sure not to make orgasm the aim of the exercise, however—exploration, not orgasm, is the goal.

• When you are comfortable with your own masturbation and have discovered what most excites you, you may want to introduce your partner to your discoveries. Initially, let her explore you on her own—she may discover some new things. Later, gently guide her and teach her the ways of touching you that you've found most exciting. Your hand is better for this than words—put your hand over hers and *show* her what you like. Again, it is best if you don't come during these exercises, but okay if you do. As you make more and more discoveries about what you like and start to get more and more excited, it will usually be hard to stop yourself from coming when the excitement gets very intense. Don't worry about this.

• When your partner has learned to do the things you like with her hand or mouth—and you have learned to relax and enjoy them—you may be ready to move on to the next phase, which involves having your penis in her vagina. At first, have her lie fairly quietly after she has inserted your penis. She should then *slowly* start to try out different ways of moving. Let her control the movement and explore the possibilities. After a few sessions, you may want to begin to let her know what is most exciting for you. Use a minimum of words; this will keep you from making things too complicated. Feel free to try to engage in fantasy while with your partner—she may be willing to play a role in your fantasy, or you may just want to fantasize privately.

• With time, you and your partner will find those activities that most excite you. Begin to concentrate on these. Again, make enjoyment your goal, rather than orgasm. As you begin to let yourself indulge more in the pleasure and excitement of sex, you'll probably find that you don't have to try to come—it comes naturally!

SUGGESTED READING:

Anicar, Thom. *Secret Sex*. New York: Signet, New American Library, 1976.

Kaplan, Helen S. *The New Sex Therapy*. New York: Quadrangle, 1974.

See also: MASTURBATION, PREMATURE EJACULATION

DELUSIONS

Delusions are ideas or beliefs that do not agree with what other people define as "reality." Other people will tell you that you are deluded if you believe something they do not believe, and if they do not like what you believe. If they like what you believe, even though it is different, they will call you "inspired" or "visionary" or "imaginative." Thus, having what are called "delusions" is a social problem—you run the risk of being labeled and rejected.

Delusions can also jeopardize physical survival. If you believe you can fly, you may try, and crash. If you believe you are Jesus and can walk on water, you may drown. Of course Jesus thought he was the Son of God, was accused of being deluded, and was killed. Years later a lot of people believe that he was right and his persecutors were deluded.

The point is that arguments about reality can get very fierce, complex, and prolonged. Stay out of them if you can.

• If your beliefs work for you, hold on to them. But you may not always want to advertise them, especially around people who believe differently and like to win.

• If your beliefs are *not* working well, review them systematically. Write down what you actually believe to be true about yourself and the world. Become an amateur scientist—check out your beliefs systematically against what actually happens. But be fair—don't select the evidence to support what you want to prove. Pay equal attention to contradictory evidence. Keep an open mind. Learn to consider several different viewpoints at the same time.

• If you don't have to decide on a belief, remain flexible for a while. Don't worry too much about whether it is a delusion.

• Decide which beliefs are so important to you that you really must assert their "truth" even if that gets you persecuted. But don't get into hassles about nonessential beliefs.

• If someone says you are deluded, explore what you can learn from that person. Maybe he or she has your welfare at heart and is trying to help you. Maybe he or she knows something you don't know, from life experience, education, or a more objective perspective.

• On the other hand, you may need to be self-protective and skeptical about the accusation that you are delusional. Consider the source. Does the other person have something to gain by persuading you that you are having delusions? Why does he or she care what you think? Are the other people really concerned about your welfare, or about their own selfish interests and their need to bolster their own grasp on "reality"?

• If you worry that you are having delusions, or have been told that you are, a trusted friend or an independent professional counselor can be a great help. Talk over your beliefs and see what feedback you get. A truly helpful person will hear you out without attacking, labeling, or trying to change you. Such people won't try to sell you on their own beliefs. If they believe something different from what you believe, they will offer it to you to consider, and help you with your process of deciding what feels right for you.

• Delusions will usually have some value or truth to them, even if they turn out to be mostly misguided thoughts. Try to retain the valuable part while you correct the error. For example, a man developed the delusion that he was a great artist and should quit his job as a postal clerk to paint full time. It turned out that other people did not agree that his art was worth buying, and he finally had to get a job again. His delusion got punctured, but the true part was that he really wanted to paint and really benefited from putting out on canvas some of his inner struggle. He was a "great" artist when it came to satisfying his own need to develop his expressiveness. Look to see what the delusion may be saying about you that needs to be attended to.

• Remember that reality is hard to grasp and keeps changing. Today's delusion may be tomorrow's inspiration. Study your mind and learn how it works. It will play tricks on you—learn to catch it when it does. But also learn to exercise, trust, and respect your mind and its capacity to conceive of alternate interpretations of events and new possibilities.

SUGGESTED READING:

Fadiman, James, and Donald Kewman, eds. *Exploring Madness.* Monterey, Calif.: Books/Cole, 1973.

Laing, R. D. *The Politics of Experience.* New York: Ballantine Books, 1967.

See also: ANXIETY, HALLUCINATIONS, OBSESSIONS

DEPENDENCY

We are all dependent creatures. Our dependency becomes a problem when we feel we cannot act or maybe even survive without the support, encouragement, approval, or love of another person. Dependency is also a problem when we believe that we cannot function or be happy without the help of substances like drugs, alcohol, or food, which stimulate us or give us at least a temporary feeling of being comforted, turned on, or "filled up."

When feelings of dependency prevent us from being self-reliant, from doing the things we enjoy, and from contributing creatively to our families, friends, and work, then they are destructive, hurtful feelings which need to be understood and changed.

How can you tell if you are an overly dependent person? Answer some of these questions: Do you find it hard to make your wishes known? Do you hate saying no to someone whose love or support you want? Do you have to have someone else's approval for what you do? Do you often have a lonely or empty feeling? Do you have trouble making decisions by yourself? Do you avoid taking on independent responsibilities?

There are many reasons why a person may be overly dependent. Some people had overprotective parents who prevented them from developing self-confidence. Such people still expect someone who they think is stronger or wiser to act or make decisions for them. Other people may not have had sufficient parenting when they were young, so now they try to make up for their earlier loss by expecting their spouse, their friends, or even their children to take over the protective role. Some people were taught to be dependent. They were told by their parents that their future spouse would always look after them, or that if they found the right job they would always have security. When they find that their expectations and reality do not match, they become angry and resentful, and then often feel guilty for having these feelings.

Sometimes we continue to act in a dependent manner because we get an emotional or even a material reward. We may feel safe or protected because we don't have to work, or we may be afraid of taking on responsibility, finding it easier to let someone else make decisions for us, even if we don't like those decisions.

Some of us are afraid of being alone, so we accept a dependent role just to ward off a feeling of loneliness; and we try to make other people dependent on *us* to hide from ourselves that we really need them. We may try to make our children overly reliant on us because we are dependent on their love, or we may try to be indispensable to our friends, our spouse, or our boss because our own feelings of dependency make us feel terrified that they could get along without us. Here are some ways to cope with excessive dependency.

• Recognize that, regardless of the cause, it is first of all important to accept your feeling of dependency without feeling guilty. We all experience ourselves as dependent at some times. Growing up consists of progressing through gradual steps from the complete dependency of early childhood to the greater emotional and physical self-reliance of a mature adulthood. A healthy adult has learned to establish workable mutual dependencies with reliable people:

• Be alert to the changes in life that can bring an increase in feelings of dependency. The loss of a loved person, an illness, the birth of a baby, a forced change of residence or job, or advancing age may all tend to increase your feeling of needing support from someone or something other than yourself. If you recognize this need you will be better able to seek appropriate sources of comfort and support which will help you back to self-reliance.

• Review your life and your choices. Keep in mind that becoming independent is not always easy, but that if you learn to take responsibility for yourself you are really learning to behave as an adult rather than as a child. You will find after a while that you are treated with the respect and consideration which you have seen accorded other people but had missed out on for yourself.

• Try to understand that feelings of dependency are hard for us to overcome because they are naturally so much a part of our lives. It is important to remember, however, that if we choose to we can grow and learn all the days of our lives. Life is a process of continual change, which, if we make the effort, can lead to always greater maturity. Keep working on moving through the various dependencies that arise as you move from one developmental stage to the next.

• Look for appropriate sources of support, but beware of exaggerated expectations focused on the wrong people. A spouse, for example, is not a parent and should not be expected to act as one. If you recognize that, and if you can realize that you are no longer a young child needing frequent help and reassurance, you might feel less angry and resentful and consequently offer more positive aspects of yourself in your marriage.

• Reassure yourself that other people also feel dependent. You are not unique in having this problem, even though other people may show it in different ways. If you can turn your need into an asset, you can help other people as you yourself would like to be helped. For example, one young mother felt hopeless because the husband on whom she had been completely dependent had run off and left her with two infants. She found several other women in the same situation, started a group which met regularly, and found that not only did she get a great deal of support from the other members of the group, but she was also able to help them. Her self-esteem rose, she learned to make decisions for herself and her family, and she found that her relationships with other people were more satisfying because they were more genuinely reciprocal.

• Note that feelings of dependency usually go along with feelings of inadequacy. You may think you cannot handle a certain task or a certain situation, so you don't even try. It is often helpful to make a list of what you can do and what you really cannot do, so that you can learn to ask for help appropriately, and only in those areas in which you really need it.

• Begin by doing a little at a time. If you always expect your children to invite you to visit on the weekend, make alternate plans with a friend, and don't wait for your children's invitation. If you want to see a movie, don't wait for someone to ask you: Take the first step and find someone to go with you. Focus on specific ways in which you can act independently, and choose small steps that will increase your independence.

• Learn to expect different things from different people. No one person can give you everything. Your friends may be interested in areas of your life which do not interest your family. Add up the satisfactions you can get from your work. Can you take on more responsibility and get rewarded for it? Use some of the extra money you make to indulge yourself. Learn to enjoy the alternation between pushing yourself to develop independent strengths and rewarding yourself. Your self-image will improve as other people value what you do and pay you for it. Having your own income, even if it is small, will greatly increase your sense of independence and self-reliance. In the eyes of a child, it is always the grown-ups who work and earn money. If you are working and earning money, you will find that you have "grown up" in your own eyes. You can also find non-paid ways of contributing to society and raising your self-esteem.

• Venture forth in carefully selected activities that increase your feelings of self-confidence. Take small risks. Try doing something you have always wanted to do. But remember that most skills take time to learn, and that no one becomes an expert overnight. Children believe that changes happen magically, but adults learn slowly and painfully that most worthwhile achievements take time and effort.

• Look to see if you are allowing someone else to control and direct your life. Then think through what you really want to do with your life. Remember that what you want to do is at least as important as what someone else wants you to do. Sometimes it is helpful to consult a career counselor. A specially trained counselor can help you clarify your interests and discover activities for which you may have particular aptitude or talent. Seek out friends and other people with whom you can talk freely without having their values imposed on you.

• If you feel dependent on someone's love, define what positive qualities of yours attracted that person to you. Then develop those qualities further, to make the most of what you already are. The better you feel about yourself, the less you will need reassurance from someone else.

• When you feel you cannot act independently, think back to people in your childhood who encouraged you and thought you could function well on your own. If negative memories creep in, tell yourself that you are no longer the child your parents or other insensitive adults used to criticize. You can learn to be your own good parent. Think of anyone who admired or valued you for what you could do: your teachers, your pastor, your brothers or sisters, or your friends. You will find that those positive memories will help you in the present. Develop a sense of loyalty to those people who have had faith in you, and show that faith in yourself.

• Remember that in our society independence and self-reliance are valued, but so are group activities. If you feel you need some external support, join an organization. A church group or a political group, for example, may give you a feeling of belonging, and may allow you to grow and feel more self-confident within the security of a formal organization.

• If your dependency is on drugs, alcohol, or food, you might find it helpful to get together with other people who have the same difficulties. In helping one another, in learning to depend on one another, and in getting emotional support from one another, you may find that you are becoming more self-affirming and productive, so that your dependency on an impersonal source of solace is reduced. Self-help groups are one of the most powerful resources available in our culture.

• Feelings of dependency sometimes stem from a fear of being separate from another person. You may fear that if you are separate you will feel intolerably lonely and won't be able to function or perhaps even survive. You might find it useful, as a first step, to rehearse in fantasy what it would be like to be alone and act independently. You can sometimes practice in your imagination what you are not ready to do in real life. Perhaps the fear of being alone will be overwhelming at first, but gradually pleasant fantasies may emerge. You may start thinking of doing things alone or with people with whom you are not involved on a daily basis. The feeling of separateness can be very frightening, but it can also be very exciting.

• For the very dependent person, the first movement toward self-reliance can be equated with a child's learning to walk. At first the child walks a few steps alone, then returns to its mother. Later, with greater courage and skill, the distances get greater and the length of time away from mother longer. Anyone who has observed young children will remember the tremendous pleasure and satisfaction they express when they can first move independently. That same pleasure can come to the dependent person who gradually learns to be self-reliant.

• Take an honest inventory of your dependencies. If you avoid recognizing your dependency, you trap yourself in a prison of your own making. You fail to grow, and you allow your life to be controlled by your needs and by those who would exploit those needs.

• Don't let yourself be crippled by knowing that you feel dependent. Clarify what you want, from whom you want it, and whether you can realistically expect to get it. Sometimes it also is a question of being able to wait. Unlike the infant, who cannot tolerate much frustration and must be fed and loved frequently and regularly in order to thrive, an adult can learn to postpone gratification of his or her wishes.

• Nurture yourself. The greater your inner strength and resources, the more sensitive you can be to other people's needs, and the more friends and the more genuinely reciprocal relationships you will have.

• Remember always that the feeling of dependency is part of our heritage as feeling human beings. If we are too dependent it means only that for some reason we have stopped growing in that particular area of our emotional development, and that, like all real growth, it may take some effort and some pain to achieve. The effort is worthwhile, however, when it leads to a fuller, happier, and more productive life. Remember that an internal feeling of security and self-confidence is a more reliable source of well-being than any external support or approval.

SUGGESTED READING:

Galassi, Merna Dee and John P. *Assert Yourself: How to Be Your Own Person.* New York: Human Sciences Press, 1977.

Newman, Mildred, and Bernard Berkowitz. *How to Take Charge of Your Life.* New York: Bantam Books, 1977.

See also: ANXIETY, LONELINESS, LOVE ADDICTION, PASSIVITY, SHYNESS

DEPRESSION

Nearly everyone feels depressed sometimes. We all know the mental and physical symptoms: tiredness, indecision, poor concentration, disturbed sleep or eating patterns, a sense of hopelessness. Depression has many possible causes. Some researchers think it is hereditary, some trace it to biochemical origins, some look to personality to explain it.

Quite often, we become depressed in reaction to something outside ourselves, something we cannot control. An unexpected reward as well as an unexpected failure may provoke a depression. So, too, can tension, anxiety, or stress, including the stress of social or self-imposed pressures.

Physical changes, including life crises such as aging, illness, and injury, are also numbered among causes of depression. Feelings of helplessness can depress people. Someone who thinks nothing he or she does makes any difference is likely to pay for this lack of self-esteem in hopelessness, in the despair that things will never be better. As a result, a depressed person, feeling unworthy and burdensome, may retreat from those very relationships that could help him or her relieve the pain.

Within reason, depression is "normal" to the human condition. It can even be thought of as a natural defense gone awry, a kind of detour away from a struggle against seemingly overwhelming odds. Under sufficient strain, almost anyone can slip into a depressed state. While you may not decide by free choice to be depressed, you can help yourself out of mild or even moderate depression.

• Depression signals to you that your life is out of balance. The challenge is in finding the source of the signal. The chief danger of depression is that it can immobilize you. To overcome this, recognize depression as an opportunity to learn, grow, and heal. Feel the pain it brings; let it alert you to the real problem. Depression can be the motivating force to revise your life.

• Ask yourself whether your depression is a wise and a necessary withdrawal from having pushed yourself into too much striving and stimulation. Perhaps you have worn yourself out in activities and relationships that were not sufficiently nourishing. This can be a time for reassessment of what you really value in life.

• Remember that most depressions leave even without help: Time can be a cure, especially if you use it to be good to yourself in ways you've been neglecting.

• Sometimes depression is caused by the loss of a relationship or a personal defeat that stirs up old bad feelings about yourself that go far deeper than the immediate situation. If your depression hangs on, explore whether you are reliving an old trauma in which you learned to dislike yourself. This can be your chance to face that buried hurt and build a stronger self.

• If you discover that your depression is caused by some error you have committed or by your dissatisfaction with something you have done, avoid self-blame. Self-blame is worse than the error you regret. Admit the guilt you are feeling—after all, to err is notoriously human— but try to learn from the mistake how to avoid repeating it. Sometimes you can gain relief from a trapped, immobile state by expressing your feelings of guilt or anger. Remember to direct your anger at the appropriate target, however. If you blame the wrong person or circumstance, you may only feel guilty and even more depressed.

• Ask yourself whether you are harboring secret resentments. Depression can be caused by bottled-up anger we feel toward people we are supposed to love. We "solve" the problem of having unacceptable anger by turning it inward. Give yourself permission to feel anger. Express it out loud to yourself. Indulge in angry fantasies. If you can find safe

and constructive ways to express your anger to the target of it, do so.
If you can't, do so in your imagination.

• Take inventory of yourself when feeling depressed. Write out how
you see yourself and how you would like to see yourself. In a realistic
way, decide what differences you would like to create, and put your
energy into acting out those differences. Acting *as if* you were content
can help you come to feel content.

• Recognize that you are not helpless to do or to act or to change.
What you do does make a difference to your life and to the lives of
others. Do things that remind you that you can affect your environment.
Volunteer time to help people worse off than yourself. Finish a household task you've been avoiding. Plunge back into a hobby or craft you've
neglected. Reach out to old or new friends. Make a long-distance call
to someone you've drifted out of touch with.

• Choose to do something you know you can complete. This reduces
your problem only to starting. Don't tax yourself. Avoid difficult jobs
for a while. Failing at a big job will only enhance your feelings of inef-
fectiveness.

• Undertake tasks you can do to your own satisfaction easily, things
that will give you a sense of accomplishment without requiring too much
mental or physical skill.

• Reward yourself for what you do, not for how well you do it.
Congratulate yourself for finishing any project, without telling yourself
how much better it might have been done.

• Take care of yourself. Concentrate on the positive things that you
do or that happen to you every day. Few things are more depressing
than believing that nothing good ever happens in your life.

• Have a medical checkup. Find out if there is a medical cause for
your depression. Learn which medications aggravate depression and
which relieve it for you. Explore with your doctor ways you can take
better care of yourself, such as improving your diet or getting more exercise. Tell him or her you are depressed and enlist his or her support
as an ally, not just a doctor whom you hire to treat you.

• Pay special attention to your appearance. Looking good and attracting a compliment or two will help relieve depressed feelings. Also,
when you're feeling low, treat yourself to something out of the ordinary
that you really enjoy. Play hooky and take yourself out to a matinee. An
unscheduled lark—even an unplanned vacation, if possible—can help
restore your balance and renew your energies.

• Vigorous physical exercise, within safe limits dictated by your health,
often helps shake depression. Exertion changes your blood chemistry and
nervous system in ways that seem to relieve depression. Physical motion
also gives you a basic sense of being alive. It puts you in touch with

your life force and energy again. It will also help you sleep more soundly.

• Believe in your own worth. Making your own decisions, rather than passively waiting for other people or outside events to make them for you, will reduce the likelihood of depression. Do what you want to for others, but don't unquestioningly put everyone else's needs first: Your needs count too.

• Recognize those things you cannot change and work at ignoring unavoidable irritants. If you really cannot leave a job you dislike, for example, you'll need to commit yourself to coping with its problems in order to keep your dissatisfaction from leading to recurrent depression.

• Refuse to use alcohol, food, or sleeping pills to get you through a depression. Alcohol is itself a depressant, fat will only depress you further, and pills can be dangerous and addictive. You can live through some sleepless nights or times when you resist urges to take refuge in food or drink.

• Remind yourself that some clichés carry a truth. Time does heal most of our depressive wounds. Most of us do tend to feel better as time passes. Depression is not an illness; certainly it is not terminal. Rather, it is an opportunity for account-taking and reevaluating, for looking inside and learning.

• Don't expect your progress up from depression to be steady with no backsliding. Don't overreact to times when you feel down again. They don't mean all is lost. It is normal to have periods of discouragement in the process of general improvement.

• Believing that depression can be turned into a growth opportunity can help you deal with a friend or loved one who is depressed. Listen to a depressed person without offering judgment or criticism, without interrupting the person's efforts to define and analyze his or her feelings.

• Helping someone else to express feelings and gain enough perspective to admit to being depressed and identify the sources of self-rejection that often cause depression requires you to offer companionship and support. It does not require you to sympathize—that can sometimes reinforce a depressed person's conviction that he or she should be depressed. Instead, empathize. Show that you understand how the other feels, even if you don't express the very same reactions.

• Your understanding, your letting a depressed person tell what's wrong in his or her own way and time without intruding your own reactions, can lead your friend or loved one to self-analysis and to the end of immobility and hopelessness.

• For your own sake, when dealing with someone else's depression, avoid making commitments you can't handle. Try to steer anything too severe for friendly help to a professional counselor.

SUGGESTED READING:

Cammer, Leonard. *Up from Depression.* New York: Pocket Books, 1976.

Flach, Frederic F. *The Secret Strength of Depression.* New York: Bantam Books, 1974.

Hauck, Paul A. *Overcoming Depression.* Philadelphia: Westminster Press, 1973.

See also: ANXIETY, BOREDOM, FEAR OF DEATH, GRIEF, GUILT, LONELINESS, LOSS OF LOVE, SELF-HATE, SUICIDE

DIVORCE

Most of us who marry do so for a mixture of healthy and unhealthy reasons. Sometimes—all too frequently, it seems—married couples come to realize that they can no longer live together without doing serious psychological (and sometimes physical) damage to each other and perhaps to their children. That doesn't necessarily mean that the marriage was all bad or a total failure. Even if a marriage must end for the good of the individuals involved, it may be that at an earlier life stage it was a good relationship. In fact, one of the reasons it is so painful and difficult to end a marriage is often because there was and even still is some real good in it.

In spite of the pain, divorce can be faced as a challenge and an opportunity rather than just as a problem. For each separating partner the divorce provides a chance to work on independence, to discover his or her own special self. This is particularly important if the marriage has been one in which one or both partners have been too dependent, or if the marriage was used as a way to hide from the demands of the adult world.

The task of creating our own selves is never completed. It takes lifelong attention and effort to develop and maintain a self-supporting sense of worth and individuality. For whatever reason you chose to end your marriage, seize the opportunity offered by divorce to learn more about yourself: your needs, your strengths and weaknesses, your values, your hopes, fears, and fantasies. If you tackle the work of change honestly and learn from it, you will be better able to share your life with the important people in it, now and in the future.

• Don't rush into divorce. If you're thinking about it as a solution to your marriage problems, don't pressure yourself to make a decision. If your relationship is going through a difficult time, recognize that. Try to identify the causes of conflict and search for alternatives to separation. Do you understand your own role in the problems that are destroying your marriage? Can you see no other way of resolving these problems? Look for acceptable compromises. Divorce is not the only solution to marital problems. Maybe together you'll work out another solution; maybe not. Whatever the outcome, you'll do well to give yourself the opportunity to define and understand the situation and its possible solutions.

• Imagine the future without your spouse. How will you (and your children, if any) react to living without him or her? Can you cope with the loneliness ahead? Are you already trying to find someone new to love? Do you worry about no longer being lovable? Are you prepared to announce this major change in your life to your family—parents, children, brothers and sisters, your maiden aunt in Detroit—and to friends, co-workers, fellow church members?

• Consider seeing a marriage counselor with your spouse. Or see if the court or a mental health center offers a reconciliation service. Try to learn whether divorce will be a positive, growthful move out of an unhealthy relationship. Use a marriage counselor's help to discover whether you're mistakenly seeking divorce as a solution to some internal problem you find it too painful to face. Give yourself and your spouse a chance to learn *why* you can no longer go on together—if in fact you can't.

• Once you've decided on divorce, consider seeking the help of a divorce counselor. Some family therapists and other helping professionals have begun to work with people during the process of divorce. Divorce therapy can make it easier to get out of your marriage in a nondestructive way, leaving you and your spouse (and children) emotionally strong enough to adjust to your new freedom and to the possibility of new relationships.

• Learn everything you can about why your marriage failed. Do this in a nonpunishing way: A relationship with one other person did not work out, but that doesn't mark you or your spouse as a failed or unlovable individual. Avoid the extremes of self-blame and self-pity. Accept the fact that you—like everyone else who goes through a divorce —will struggle with bitterness, blame, guilt, anger, self-justification, a sense of failure, and many other turbulent emotions. Try to achieve a clear understanding of what went wrong. What did you do that contributed to the problems? How did you choose your partner in the first place? What traits did you look for? What traits made him or her hard to live with? Why didn't your needs and feelings function well together?

• Prepare yourself for the crucial step of making your decision public. Divorcing (and divorced) people still face some social disapproval. Your married friends may suddenly see you as a threat to their sense of marital security. You may be surprised at the judgmental attitudes you encounter and at the discrimination you may confront at work, in getting a bank loan, in joining a social club. Expect a period of family confusion—your parents, siblings, in-laws, and children need to adjust to the idea of divorce, just as you do. Expect to feel uprooted from familiar surroundings, social patterns, friendships, habits, and financial arrangements. Very little in your life will escape the influence of divorce.

• Stay in control of the dissolution of your marriage. With your spouse, identify areas of mutual concern: child care, finances (including support payments, if any), life and medical insurance, wills, real estate, automobiles, other possessions, education expenses for yourselves or your children, child custody and visitation, even pet custody. Recognize that the nature of our legal system very often makes divorce into an adversary confrontation. It introduces competition into arrangements that could usually be made cooperatively. Try to agree on a mutually acceptable settlement before going to a lawyer, but be sure not to agree to anything you may regret later, because you will have weakened your bargaining power. Inform yourself concerning the legal and financial implications of divorce. Even if you don't "do it yourself," try to find a simple, understandable explanation of your state's divorce laws; a book like *Compatible Divorce,* by Robert Veit Sherwin, might be useful.

• Freedom can be scary. It's not easy to dissolve a relationship and then renew your sense of self-worth and self-sufficiency, especially if you were very dependent on your spouse. Resume dating carefully; don't hurry into a new involvement or marriage just because you miss the "safe," familiar role of wife or husband. Concentrate on seeing yourself as a separate person of positive, individual worth. Give yourself gentle encouragement to try new things. Let yourself learn and change. Put energy and effort into your job, your relationship with your kids, your recreational interests. Take up a new sport or hobby. Reward yourself for being adventurous and taking even a small risk, like enrolling in an evening class.

• If you did not want the divorce but your spouse did, you will need to work on your feelings of rejection, abandonment, and diminished worth. Even if you sincerely wanted to end your marriage, divorce is a trying and difficult change. Divorcing people are particularly subject to depression, alcoholism, guilt, severe anxiety, loneliness, illness, accidents, even suicide. Expect to go through a mourning process.

Don't be surprised that you miss someone you can't stand—you probably have a lot invested in each other in spite of your need to separate. Dependency dies hard.

• Don't hang on to hate. You won't be free of each other so long as you're bound together by the intensity of anger or the desire for revenge.

• Help your children adjust to the divorce. Work on developing the new ways you will need to relate to your kids. Investigate Parents Without Partners, a group that can help you cope with the difficulties both you and your children now face. Recognize that you have to continue some sort of a cooperative relationship with your ex-spouse in order to handle your kids' needs and problems. (See CHILDREN OF DIVORCE.)

• Accept your fragility and vulnerability. Ending a relationship, even an unsatisfactory one, is quite painful. Resist the urge to hide from your feelings—be careful about drugs, alcohol, and overeating. Expect to find it hard to go on sometimes. Don't be surprised if you just can't make it to work some days or if you lose your touch as a cook. Be patient. Time does heal. You'll feel better, worse, and better again in stages. Don't fight it—accept your feelings and give yourself time to heal. Don't be frightened by the intensity of your anger, loneliness, bitterness, anxiety, or disappointment. These are common, perhaps necessary reactions, and you will live through them. Work hardest on overcoming your self-doubt. You are still a lovable, special, needed person. You have not failed as a human being.

• Let yourself convalesce. You're most susceptible to sorrow, fear, self-pity, and despair when you're exhausted. Rest. Pamper yourself. Take long hot baths. Work out your tensions physically with jogging, yoga, or some other regular exercise. Begin slowly and become addicted to some daily bodily activity. Eat well, but not too much (you don't want to add obesity to your other difficulties). Getting enough protein, B vitamins, and vitamin C will help you cope with stress and anxiety.

• Trust yourself. Accept the end of this part of your life and reach out to the new experiences ahead. You can make it.

SUGGESTED READING:

Krantzler, Mel. *Creative Divorce*. New York: Signet, New American Library, 1975.

Sheresky, Norman, and Marya Mannes. *Uncoupling: The Art of Coming Apart (A Guide to Sane Divorce)*. New York: Dell, 1973.

Sherwin, Robert Veit. *Compatible Divorce*. New York: Universal Publishing, 1970.

See also: ANGER, ANXIETY, COMMUNICATION BLOCKS, DE-
PENDENCY, DEPRESSION, GRIEF, GUILT, LONELINESS, LOSS
OF LOVE, LOVE ADDICTION, MARITAL QUARRELING, MID-
LIFE CRISIS, SINGLE PARENTING, STRESS

DRUG ABUSE

Drug abuse can mean anything from a minor nuisance to a major
tragedy. Almost everyone in the United States uses drugs of one kind
or another, ranging from the caffeine in morning coffee, nicotine in
cigarettes, cold remedies, and aspirin to prescription drugs, alcohol, and
marijuana to illegal narcotics. In 1978 more than 250 million prescrip-
tions were written for psychoactive drugs.

It's hard to say when drug *use* becomes drug *abuse*. To a large extent,
this is for you to decide. When your use of drugs becomes a problem *for
you* (or for someone close to you), you are involved in drug abuse. This
might be true even though you are taking a drug prescribed by a doctor
or bought in a pharmacy. Answer these questions: Does your drug-
taking interfere with other activities in your life? Do you spend more
money or time getting or taking drugs than you think you should? Is
your drug-taking harming your health? Does your drug-taking harm
your family or friends? (Ask *them*, too!) Do you wish you could stop
taking a drug, but you find this too difficult or you always put it off
until tomorrow? A yes answer to any of these questions may indicate
that you have a drug-abuse problem. If you can admit this to yourself,
there are steps you can take to relieve the problem. This section is
meant to help you do this, so it will focus on drug problems and solutions. That is not to say that drugs do not have useful or pleasant effects
—if you are a drug user, you know about these already. If you are
also a drug abuser, however, you may need help confronting the negative effects or "costs" of drug use, which this section will focus on.
So don't be moralistic about your drug use; just realistically consider its
benefits and costs and make a decision about its value for you. If you
decide the costs outweigh the benefits, *take action.*

Almost anything you take into your body can be considered a drug,
so it's not possible to deal with all of the drugs which might cause problems. Fortunately, drug-abuse problems have enough in common so
that some general principles can be applied to most of them. This section will deal with drug-abuse problems *in general.* In addition, you will
find separate sections below dealing with the drugs which most often are
abused: stimulants (amphetamines, speed); cocaine; LSD and other
psychedelics; PCP (angel dust); marijuana and hashish; barbiturates

and tranquilizers. (Also see ALCOHOLISM.) It's not unusual for people to have a problem with more than one drug, so you may need to use more than one section to work on your problem. One more thing: In addition to dealing with how to stop using or abusing each drug, each section will also help you deal with acute or temporary problems, such as "bummers" or overdoses.

Generally, drugs artificially imitate or mimic something that the body can usually do on its own. The body is like a piano—you can't play a note that's not there to start with. Drugs taken in from outside are much more crude than the body's own systems—like playing the piano with a baseball bat. As a result, besides doing what they're designed to do, they have side effects. For example, alcohol not only relaxes the drinker, it also kills cells in the liver and brain and causes hangovers. Harmful side effects make drugs a costly and inefficient way to achieve whatever effect you're seeking.

• A good way to begin working on your drug-abuse problem is to examine just what it is you get out of taking the drug(s) and why you need the drug. What does the drug do for you? Have you ever experienced any similar feelings without drugs? When? Is there something missing in your life that drugs supply? What is it—excitement, peace of mind, imagination? Is there something in your life that the drug protects you from—boredom, anxiety, your own shyness or uptightness? Honestly exploring these questions will teach you a lot about your drug use and about your life.

• A very important aid for self-examination is a diary. Keep a diary that focuses on your drug use. Write down what time of day you took the drug and how much you took. How were you feeling when you took the drug? Who was with you when you took it? What were you doing? How did the drug affect you? What did you do when the effect wore off? What other important things happened that day, before or after you took the drug? Sometimes you can learn surprising things by keeping such a diary. You may be shocked at how much you use the drug. Or you may discover that you use the drug only when things have not gone well at work or at home. Perhaps you use it only when you're feeling anxious or angry, or only when you're with certain friends.

• You may discover problems that you have been hiding from by using drugs. If you do, try confronting these problems, facing them squarely, and doing something about them. If you have been using a drug to blot out your feelings of depression, for example, you might want to work directly on being less depressed. (See DEPRESSION.) In any case, determine what you want from drugs and what this says about your life.

Here are some general guidelines for what to do when you want to start using a drug less. It's a good idea to get medical help in getting off some drugs, especially "downs" or sleeping pills. You should see a doctor and tell him or her about your problem. This book provides well-researched advice but is not a substitute for professional treatment.

• With many drugs, it will be easier to cut down gradually rather than stop abruptly. This prevents the change from being too much of a shock to your system. The difficulty with cutting down is that it's very easy to fool yourself and make endless excuses.

• It is helpful to make a specific, written plan or program and then follow it to the letter. Use your diary to determine just how much of the drug you are using and then make a specific calendar showing how you will cut down. Reduce the amount of the drug you take each time; take the drug less often; introduce drug-free days (for example, *No drugs on Tuesdays*). And no cheating! It can be helpful to get someone's co-operation in this—someone to act as a secretary to remind you what the plan calls for.

• You may also find it helpful to make deliberate attempts to act in ways which make you need or want the drug less. For example, if you smoke marijuana because it helps you feel sexy, work on other ways to feel sexy—using sexual fantasies, for example. (See SEXUAL DYS-FUNCTION.)

• Be careful about substituting other drugs for your "problem drug." This can sometimes be helpful, but also has dangers: You may end up with more of a problem than you started with. Taking Valium (diazepam), for example, *may* help you stop drinking, but could also lead to abuse of Valium. Even worse would be taking downs or sleeping pills, a habit which can be very hard to kick.

• A change of scene can be important—break your routine. This is especially important if a setting or a person is related to your drug use. If you take cocaine with a particular group of people, stay away from them for a while; they will only encourage you to continue your drug use. If you use drugs mainly at parties, avoid parties until you've successfully mastered your drug problem. Find out how your surroundings affect your drug abuse and then use this information to help you control it.

• A caution: Once your body has gotten used to coping with the drug(s) you've been putting into it, it may be a shock to your system when you stop taking it. This can be true even though the drug is actually harming your body. Specifically, you may have uncomfortable physical or emotional reactions, which are called "withdrawal symptoms." These vary from drug to drug, but are usually part of what keeps you using the drug over and over again, because it feels unpleasant to stop.

If you examine your behavior, it may be that you're taking the drug just to keep from experiencing these withdrawal symptoms. If so, you're on an endless treadmill. The key to getting off some drugs is to deal with your body's reaction to the withdrawal. An important first step is to recognize the symptoms (this book will help) and remind yourself that they will go away if you stay off the drug. Taking more drugs to get relief just puts you back on the treadmill.

The second thing to do about withdrawal symptoms is to slowly cut down on your drug use, rather than stopping abruptly. This makes withdrawal less of a shock to your system.

A third solution is to learn to cope with your withdrawal symptoms. For example, irritability is a common withdrawal symptom, which can be dealt with by learning to relax and cope with irritation and annoyance. (See ANGER.) However, keep in mind that if your body's reaction to stopping a drug becomes severe, you may need to seek medical help.

• To restate: Explore your drug abuse and your motivations for it, formulate a specific plan, and be prepared to deal with the discomforts of withdrawal. Finally, don't rest too easy once you have stopped taking the drug: You need to keep your guard up to make sure you *stay* off. Keep a chart on which you make a mark for every day you go without the drug; this will remind you of your goal. Also, put energy into working on the life problems that led you into drug abuse in the first place. You'll live longer and more happily as a result.

Many organizations offer information and support in dealing with a drug-abuse problem, among them: Addicts Anonymous (P.O. Box 2000, Lexington, Kentucky 41001), Narcotics Anonymous (P.O. Box 622, Sun Valley, California 91352), and Pills Anonymous (184 East 76th Street, New York, New York 10021). Families Anonymous (P.O. Box 344, Torrance, California 90508) holds group meetings for relatives and friends of people with drug-related problems.

Stimulants

A stimulant (amphetamines, speed, ups, bennies, Ritalin, diet pills) is an energy-producing drug. It can be taken in pills, through the nose by "snorting," or, most dangerously, by injection. The attraction of this drug is that it gives the user a "lift" of energy. People who use speed say they like the feeling of energy and well-being that they get when they take it. It also enables the user to be awake and alert for a long time, and suppresses the appetite. Many "speed freaks" first started using speed to help them study for exams, keep them awake while driving, or lose weight.

The important thing to understand about speed is that the energy it gives you is not "free." It's not a gift but a loan, to be repaid with interest. This means that a speed "high" uses up your body's store of energy very quickly. As a result, when you come off the high you're likely to feel very "down" and depressed. If you stop using speed after you've been using a lot of it for a long time, this depression can last for a long time, making it tempting to use more speed. Instead, deal with the depression directly—be active and get exercise, but be sure to get enough sleep (you'll need a lot of it). If you were taking speed because of boredom and lethargy, do something to make your life more exciting. (See DEPRESSION and BOREDOM.)

Speed *can* cause bummers or unpleasant experiences, particularly when a person takes more than he or she is used to. A person in such a state will be very suspicious and paranoid. In really severe cases, a person may see, feel, or smell things that aren't there; feeling bugs on the skin is especially common, and the person also may have "religious" or "profound" experiences which are hard to explain. When in this condition, the speed user needs to be in a quiet place and to get lots of reassurance. In severe cases, he or she should be brought to the hospital.

Cocaine

Cocaine (coke, snow, lady) is usually a fine white powder taken by inhaling through the nose (snorting). Although many users are unaware of this, cocaine works very much like speed, and has many of the same problems. One difference between the two is that coke is often used to heighten sexual excitement or feeling. If you use coke for this purpose, ask yourself: How do you feel about sex without cocaine? What is missing? How can you improve your sex without drugs? See section on stimulants for more information.

Psychedelics and Hallucinogens

Psychedelic drugs (LSD, peyote, psilocybin, mescaline, DMT, STP) are taken because they change the user's perception of the world, making things look, feel, or sound different. Colors may seem brighter or may shimmer; tingling feelings may be felt on the skin; objects may seem to move. A major danger of using these drugs is not due to the drugs themselves, but to their distribution via the illegal "street market." Most of the time, when you think you're buying these drugs you will be getting something else. (LSD is an exception.) Most often you will get PCP (see below) and/or speed, a dangerous combination. So even though some of these drugs may be fairly safe, street versions of them are likely to be quite dangerous.

Most people who develop a drug-abuse problem with psychedelics are seeking an exciting escape from their lives, which they find depressing, boring, or frightening. Often they feel that their lives are meaningless and they try to get meaning from their drug experiences. What are the sources of meaning in your life? Do you feel connected with people or distant from them? Do you seek psychedelic experience because it helps you break down the barriers you set up between yourself and others? If so, you may need to work directly on becoming more connected to other people. Share your perceptions and emotional experiences with them, and listen openly when they share with you.

Psychedelics have no withdrawal effects, so cutting down is easy—you must simply decide to do it and then follow through. On occasion, you may feel "spacy" or high after you stop, but this usually doesn't last long.

Bummers or bad experiences are not uncommon with psychedelics, especially when you get the drugs on the street. They occur more often if you are feeling bad or worried about something when you take the drug, so be careful of trying to run away from your troubles by using psychedelics. People on bummers are usually very frightened and sometimes paranoid; they may cry or scream, and may see or hear frightening things. If you get on a bummer, find a very quiet place to be where there aren't too many things going on. Taking something to calm you can sometimes help (for example, Valium or an over-the-counter cold medicine called Ny-Quil). It may also help to remind yourself that your experience is due to the drug and that it will stop when your body washes the drug out. Do what you can to relax and wait for it to pass.

PCP

PCP (angel dust, hog, mist, crystal, rocket fuel) is a psychedelic drug which is usually a pill or a white powder that is snorted or smoked in marijuana joints or tobacco cigarettes. Unfortunately, it is often sold to unwitting buyers, misrepresented as mescaline, psilocybin, or THC (a concentrated form of marijuana). Users of PCP may first feel somewhat drunk, but later (especially if a large dose is taken) may become very confused, frightened, and even violent. In this condition, the user may see things, have trouble walking, and act bizarrely, even walking nude in the street, for example. Resting in a quiet place can be helpful if this happens, as can *small* doses of Valium. Unlike the other psychedelics, PCP is dangerous and harms your nervous system, especially memory. Stopping PCP does not produce withdrawal problems.

Marijuana

Marijuana (grass, pot, often just "dope"; hashish is a concentrated form) is a psychedelic drug which is usually smoked, although it may also be eaten. Most users report that this drug heightens their sensations and gives them a pleasant feeling. Although many people have tried marijuana or smoke it regularly with no problems, some people do develop abuse problems with the drug. Usually, this happens when the drug is overused. Ask yourself: Are you almost always high? Is your thinking seldom clear? If so, you may be overusing marijuana.

If you are a heavy user, you may feel restless and irritable when you try to stop. You also may sweat a lot and have trouble sleeping. Cutting down on your use instead of stopping abruptly will usually minimize these problems. Don't fool yourself into putting it off, however.

Barbiturates and Tranquilizers

Barbiturates and tranquilizers (downs, sleeping pills, reds, Valium [diazepam], Librium [chlordiazepoxide]) are drugs which cause the body to shut down and are therefore sometimes used by doctors to help people sleep or to relieve anxiety. Many people who are given these drugs by their doctors become abusers; abuse of downs is among the most common drug-abuse problems.

Usually, downs are abused by people who have had thoughts or feelings they want to turn off or block out. Is there something you are trying to escape by getting high? What is it? If it is a feeling, is there some other way to cope with it? If it's an external situation, can you change it? These drugs can turn off the signals your body gives you that tell you there is something wrong, and thus keep you from doing anything about it. Decide to stop escaping and face your problems.

Some of these drugs are *extremely* addicting. This means that you may begin to take more and more of them as their effect seems to become weaker. Also, you may feel uncomforable or even sick if you don't take them. If this description fits you, you have a serious and dangerous drug-abuse problem. These drugs are dangerous in several ways. They are harmful to your mind and body. Also, because they make you drowsy, they can cause accidents, especially if you drive while high. One kind of accident which is often fatal occurs when a user takes one of these drugs and drinks alcohol at the same time. This can cause such a powerful drowsiness and confusion that the user forgets how many pills he or she has taken and may take more, causing an overdose. *An overdose of some of these drugs can be fatal.* If an overdose has been taken and the user is awake, he or she should be kept walking until the drug wears off. Also, try to induce vomiting by sticking a finger down his or her throat. If the user can't be kept awake, get him or her to the hospital emergency room immediately!

Downs are also very dangerous because your body reacts very strongly when you stop taking them. *Do not stop these drugs abruptly.* This can lead to weakness, tremor, nausea, vomiting, and even to seizures. Use of these drugs should be reduced gradually, preferably under a physician's care. Don't wait until it's too late—start a program to reduce your drug use *now*.

SUGGESTED READING:

Brecher, E. M., and the Editors of Consumer Reports. *Licit and Illicit Drugs*. Boston: Little, Brown, 1972.

Lingeman, Richard R. *Drugs from A to Z: A Dictionary*. New York: McGraw-Hill, 1974.

See also: ALCOHOLISM, ANXIETY, DEPENDENCY, DEPRES-SION

ENVY

Envy is an attitude and emotion easily stirred up in a competitive, materialistic society like ours. On TV and all around us we see a vast array of things that represent "the good life." And we see people who have acquired the wealth and power to own and enjoy these possessions. The possessions take on importance above and beyond their actual usefulness and beauty. They become symbols of achieved happiness, not just the means to attain happiness.

A Mercedes, when it is not in the repair shop, can be a truly delightful and secure car to drive. It provides great safety, comfort, and driving pleasure. Is that why people buy a Mercedes, or envy others who own them? Only partially. The Mercedes has become a symbol of success and alleged happiness. Thus, many of the people who pay extravagant amounts of money to buy these cars and keep them running do so because of their value as status symbols, rather than for the tangible advantages they provide.

Per dollar of cost and per hour of hassle about servicing, a Mercedes will probably not get you from one place to another any faster, safer, or more happily than many other cars. But if you believe in it as a symbol of having "made it," owning one will give you a satisfied feeling of being part of an elite group. And if you believe all this and *don't* own one, you will envy people who do.

Envy is a problem because it is a destructive, self-devaluing emotion. It negates who you are and what you have accomplished. It focuses instead on what you lack and how you have failed. Your energy is wasted making comparisons between yourself and others, comparisons that result in your feeling inferior. Envy leads to begrudging others their achievements, and builds barriers between you and them. Coveting what others possess blocks you from caring about them as persons, and also blocks you from caring about yourself.

Some religions see wanting and desiring as the source of all pain and unhappiness. Such teachings seem to go against our American spirit of ambition, hard work, and the pursuit of happiness. That is not necessarily true. Here are some ways to rid yourself of envy while keeping your drive to improve yourself and your standard of living.

• Study carefully the people you envy and the possessions or advantages for which you envy them. Look at what this tells you about yourself: your values, your aspirations, your negative self-concept. Use your envy as a mirror in which to see yourself more clearly.

• Ask yourself if there is a deeper, more positive drive beneath the specific focus of your envy. You may be using a symbol, such as a Mercedes, to express more important self-actualizing motives of which you are unaware and which gain expression only in this culturally stereotyped way. For example, you may be longing to assert yourself in a stylish and powerful way, but not yet have chosen a means to develop this capacity.

• Daydream about having what you envy. Enjoy your daydream. But don't stop there—daydream about having these things day after day, and ask if they would really satisfy you. Would merely having and using *things* be enough for you? Or are you looking for something more, such as loving relationships with people? Does your envy bring you any closer to that goal?

• Envy is a passive, cop-out stance. It burns up energy just looking, not in moving, doing, or creating. Face the fact that when you indulge in envy you are abandoning yourself. In effect, you are making a passive, futile appeal or protest to "fate" or "Uncle Sam" or some power you wish would dole out the goodies more fairly and generously. "The system" is unfair—but did someone promise you it would be fair? Why make it worse by being unfair to yourself? That is what you do when you waste your precious time and energy envying others.

• To shake yourself out of an envious mood, put your energy into action. When you are absorbed in doing something as best you can, you won't have time to envy someone else. And if you keep doing things you care about as best you can, you will get results and feel proud of yourself. Eventually you will be the kind of person whom others envy. But you will be so busy doing what you really like and do well that your pleasure will come from being who you are, not from being the focus of envy. And you will see the irony in the fact that you, who were once so envious, have now become the object of envy.

• Right now, take stock of your assets. Are you a person who complains that his or her glass is half empty, when someone else would see that it is half full? For one thing, you are alive, which gives you a decided advantage over a lot of people who were born the same day you were. Also, you can read. What other assets and skills do you have? Watch out for your tendency to say "Yes, but . . ." Don't let that voice cancel your affirmation of the positive parts of your life. Practice countering each envious thought with a specific affirmation of yourself.

• Envy is often a twin problem to jealousy. Jealousy focuses on personal relationships, especially loving and sexual ones. Examine whether your envy also contains elements of jealousy. (If so, see JEALOUSY.)

• Woody Allen concluded his autobiography with the statement "My only regret is that I was not someone else." His humor carries envy to its ridiculous extreme, and thus exposes its fundamentally self-negating quality. Try the same thing for yourself. Do you really want to have and be all the things you envy? What are the unique aspects of your own life that you cherish, even with its struggles and deficiencies? Other people have paid a price for the things that you envy them for. Are you willing to pay that price? What if it meant giving up who you are? Take pride in making the most of what you have. No one else on earth has the particular challenge you have: to make a good life out of the unique combination of positive and negative ingredients you have to work with.

SUGGESTED READING:

Goldberg, Herb, and Robert T. Lewis. *Money Madness: The Psychology of Saving, Spending, Loving, and Hating Money.* New York: William Morrow, 1978.

See also: COMPETITIVENESS, GREED, JEALOUSY, MONEY WORRIES, SELF-HATE, SIBLING RIVALRY

EXHIBITIONISM

Exhibitionism is the desire to show off in order to get attention from others. Harmless, socially approved forms of exhibitionism include all sorts of public performances and displays: singing, dancing, acting, sports, flirting, taking public pride in one's clothes, car, boat, or house.

Everyone has exhibitionistic wishes, and gratifying them can be a pleasant part of social life. Watch how young babies enjoy performing and delight in the reactions they get from grown-ups.

Unfortunately, some people in growing up are deprived of rewarding opportunities to show off their positive qualities and to learn that they are pleasing to other people. Children who are not praised and complimented for the way they look and act may develop inferiority feelings and a craving to be seen and admired. When these feelings and wishes become too strong, they may seek expression in strained and inappropriate ways. The person may become obnoxiously attention-seeking, insensitive to the actual feelings of other people and excessive in the demand for approval.

A further step into an abnormal form of exhibitionism is when the person becomes aggressive, provocative, and socially defiant. Such a person seeks more to shock and upset than to impress, entertain, or gain approval. Some educated people do this with argumentative, pompous proclamations that disrupt congenial conversation. They are more interested in parading their brilliance and putting down their opponents than they are in communicating or contributing to enlightening conversation.

Sex is sometimes selected by exhibitionists for its special capacity to elicit responses. Obviously, healthy exhibitionism plays a large and lovely role in sexual relations. But people with a problem about valuing their bodies, their sexual impulses, and their wishes for sexual attention may overuse or misuse sexual exhibitionism.

Often the word "exhibitionist" is used to refer specifically to persons who display their genitals to people who aren't expecting them to do so. The purpose is more aggressive than sexual—it is to shock, embarrass, and upset the unwilling viewer. Reacting with indignation and distress gives the exhibitionist what he or she wants and encourages repetition of the behavior. For example, a simple acknowledgment that a male exhibitionist does in fact have a penis but that it is no cause for hysterics may put an end to the scene in the calmest, most efficient way. Thus, a woman confronted by a strange man unexpectedly exposing his penis to her might keep the incident from being upsetting by simply saying, "Very nice, but cover yourself up before you catch a chill." The man gets the satisfaction of a response, but not the drama he had hoped for. The woman makes it clear that she is not willing to play his game by acting the role of "outraged lady." She also spares herself the awkwardness of pretending nothing has happened.

Beneath the antisocial aspects of the exhibitionists' behavior is the poignantly human wish to be noticed and to be accepted as attractive.

• If you are troubled by exhibitionistic impulses, sexual or otherwise, face the fact that you have an intense, natural need that has been blocked from normal expression.

• Accept your need, even if you do not accept the form of expression it may take.

• Look for more frequent and conventional ways to get attention so that your need doesn't get too frustrated.

• Review your life to see how you learned to doubt your attractiveness or inhibit your search for recognition.

• Ask yourself whether you have internalized certain critics and judges who tell you not to be sexual, not to be a show-off, not to enjoy the spotlight. Don't let these critics ruin your life, either by suppressing you or by driving you into senseless exhibitionistic rebellion.

• The cure for exhibitionism is not shame and modesty—it is the creative channeling of the need for attention into truly rewarding, socially acceptable channels. That doesn't mean dull conformity. The aggressive, provocative aspect of exhibitionism can be channeled into creative behavior that plays with conventions, tests and extends the limits of what is acceptable, and makes a social contribution by loosening people up.

A shy young attorney avoided trial work because he felt awkward speaking in front of older men. This awkwardness stemmed from a childhood incident when he'd been caught and shamed by his grandfather for masturbating with another boy. When he went to college, in an attempt to overcome his shyness he developed a talent for doing impersonations of politicians. But he would do his impersonations only for close friends after he'd had a few drinks. After graduation, with his friends' encouragement, he gained more confidence and put together a comedy act that he performed at a local nightclub. Gradually he saw that he did not need to be so earnest and serious when appearing in court. He took to dressing flamboyantly and began to enjoy being the focus of attention.

• Some families, social groups, and work groups are not very generous with recognition and praise, particularly of members' physical appearance. That kind of deprivation could aggravate a person's exhibitionistic longings. Maybe a new, more appreciative audience is the answer. Seek out people who do pay attention to style and looks.

• Get help from experts: a voice coach, a charm school, a public-speaking class, an acting workshop, a friend with good taste in clothes.

• Spend more time in places where people enjoy looking and being looked at.

• Take some tips from nature. Visit a zoo and marvel at the way peacocks, monkeys, tigers, and tropical fish join in the world's great costume party.

• Remember, exhibitionism is a basic human trait. It becomes a problem only when thwarted and misdirected. Learn to cultivate it and enjoy it. By giving and receiving direct physical attention, you will connect in exciting, enriching ways with the dance of life.

• If you have a friend or relative whose exhibitionism bothers you, don't play into it by making a big fuss over it. Simply give the person honest feedback about what you like and don't like about his or her behavior, and point out how your relationship could be more comfortable and fulfilling if the exhibitionistic provocation and demands were toned down.

• Help your friend or relative rechannel the need for attention into activities he or she is truly good at and that are actually valued by you and others.

See also: COMPULSIONS, SEXUAL PERVERSIONS, SHYNESS, VOYEURISM

EXTRAMARITAL SEX

It's not at all uncommon for one or both partners in a marriage to try some extramarital sex. Most extramarital sex, however, is casual and without commitment. Most affairs are short-lived and unpremeditated, and do not break up the marriage.

Extramarital sex sometimes helps married partners discover how to revive a fading relationship that they both value and wish to continue. Often people "stumble" into an unplanned sexual adventure only out of curiosity. A simple desire for variety combined with an unexpected opportunity may spark an affair that is not meant to deflect affection, caring, and love away from one's spouse.

This is not always the case, of course. People enter into extramarital sexual relationships for many reasons, some less constructive than others. Some people seek escape from various sexual problems. Others worry about their sexual adequacy and feel a need to prove their virility or attractiveness. Some are suffering from boredom or depression and think sexual activity will bring relief. Others are committed to marriages that satisfy important needs but do not provide sexual fulfillment. We could think of dozens of possible explanations; the point is that every case of extramarital sexual involvement occurs in different circumstances, with different consequences, in different lives.

Even though the marriage agreement seems outdated and unimportant to many, we have all grown up in a culture that puts tremendous value on that agreement. It's very hard for most of us to shake off the feeling that sharing sex with someone other than a legal spouse is more serious than having more than one lover while still unmarried. Many unmarried people find it possible to allow themselves and their primary lover the option of having other sexual relationships. Marriage tends to have more overall life significance for us than an affair does. We tend to have a much greater emotional stake in keeping it going.

• Extramarital sex can be quite complicated. If you're thinking about it or if you're already involved in it, don't underestimate the complexity and intensity of such an adventure.

• Make a careful review of your own values and standards, your feelings toward your spouse and your shared way of life, and your capacity to cope with moral and emotional conflict.

• Do you understand that your spouse may not accept your behavior because it breaks a promise, involves deception, or threatens his or her basic security and self-esteem needs? Are you willing to inflict emotional pain on your spouse?

• Do you accept your behavior or do you feel guilty about it? Do you believe that sexual faithfulness is a moral duty? What are your feelings and your spouse's feelings about adultery? Do you both have the same understanding of marital responsibility? Is your marriage based on a religious or moral commitment? Do you feel that you are cheating? Have you promised to be sexually faithful in marriage? Have you and your spouse discussed the underlying beliefs you each have about your marriage? Would extramarital sex fit in with these beliefs, or would one or both of you need to change? This is an opportunity to clarify where you stand, with yourself and with your spouse.

• If you practice a religion that forbids adultery, face up to the religious or moral problems connected with extramarital sex. Matters of faith are not easily skipped over; they carry deep emotional force in our lives.

• If you are troubled by the possibility of violating your religious beliefs but feel that you are likely to do so, seek counseling to help clarify your feelings. Talk to a sympathetic friend who understands the importance of religion in your life or to a professional counselor or a member of the clergy.

• Remember that people have strong pro and con feelings about extramarital sex and that a friend or religious professional may not give you the unbiased help in exploring your feelings that you need. Look for support and nonjudgmental counseling. Don't expect someone else to give you permission, rules, or explicit directions that will fit your needs and your life. The decisions and risks and consequences are yours. Good counseling can help you achieve a more solid direction in your life, regardless of what you decide to do about an affair.

• Take stock of the degree to which you may be influenced by the attitudes of people around you. Your circle of friends, relatives, and associates may or may not share our culture's generally negative view of extramarital sex. Be aware of the signals being sent to you. Does your circle accept "wandering husbands" but condemn "unfaithful wives"? Are there social rewards for being liberated—swinging or sharing mates, perhaps? Are there social penalties for seeking sex outside of marriage? Do your friends romanticize seduction? Is sexual variety an important goal for them, or do they express approval only for developing sexual fulfillment in marriage? How much do your friends influence your thinking about what is acceptable for you and your spouse? Be sure you are making your own choices, not just going along with the crowd.

• Ask yourself if your marriage can tolerate the stress of an extramarital affair. Do you really want your marriage to be subjected to this sort of strain?

• How do you feel about your spouse having sexual independence too? Can you handle a relationship in which you each have lovers and are open and honest about that fact? Can you work together to develop a relationship in which each of you has free time to fill responsibly in any way desired—but without sharing the nature of the activity chosen for that time? Many otherwise satisfactory marriages leave important needs unfilled, not just sexual needs. If you can accept non-sexual outside involvements for yourself and your spouse as growth-enhancing, you may also be able to work out a similar understanding to fill your separate sexual needs.

• Do you think your marriage is stable but not very fulfilling? Extramarital sex may appear to be a step toward solving this problem, but maybe it's the wrong step. Have you talked to your partner? Are you sure that you have to go outside marriage to satisfy your sexual and affectional needs, or do you just assume that your spouse won't understand and give what you want? Can you work together to improve your sexual life, and to add variety, romance, and adventure to your marriage in other ways too?

• Are you really deprived of sex and love? Due to unfortunate circumstances, some people really are trapped in unsatisfactory relationships and need another outlet for their sexuality. Couples may stay together for child-rearing, economic, religious, social, or health reasons. Is this your situation? Or are you possibly depressed and focusing on your love life as the problem? Are you trying to use extramarital sex to cope with feelings of loss and deprivation?

• Consider the possibility that extramarital sex provides a diversion from something else in your life that needs to be faced: loneliness, depression, fear of intimacy, sexual dysfunction, mid-life crisis.

• How much hostility is involved in defying society or your spouse? Are you on a power trip, racking up conquests in the name of love? Are you trying to prove something or to dominate someone? Do you use sex to seek revenge?

• Consider whether your involvement in an affair is a true movement toward sexual and emotional liberation or a way of avoiding real intimacy and commitment. Are you really drawn to love another person or to live out your belief in sexual freedom, or are you just caught up in the excitement of a secret game?

• Are you getting as much fulfillment from two part-time relationships as you could get if you concentrated on one? Can you deal with the fragmentation an affair brings to your life? Can you divide your attention and affection satisfactorily?

• Is extramarital sex good enough? Is it the best you can do, better than what you've got or could develop in your marriage?

• Can you face having to make a choice if and when it comes to that? If you value your primary, marital relationship and don't want to end it, do you get enough from the extramarital relationship to make the risk worth it? Are you willing to pay the hidden cost—the hurt and anger and loss that may result if your spouse discovers your affair and doesn't share your view of it as harmless?

• Are you a jealous person? Is your spouse? For some couples extramarital sex is enriching and accepted. Many people who have tried it, however, have found it difficult to manage being married, having a lover, and dealing with jealous feelings about their spouse's affairs.

• If you learn that your partner is having an affair and you both want to keep your marriage going, try to solve this shared problem by working together. Suspend judgment for a while and listen to your spouse's explanation of why he or she sought extramarital sex. Discuss the outside relationship and the needs it fills—but not while you're angry. Be patient. Give yourself time to think about each other's feelings and needs. If your goal is to stay together, don't separate. Don't make a big righteous uproar about having been betrayed if you hope to rebuild your trust in each other. Try to listen without defensiveness to your spouse's explanation of the needs filled by extramarital sex. Try to express your own needs and feelings about loyalty and sex without defensiveness. You each have to learn what the other wants. Do not involve your relatives, children, or friends in these matters. Work on enhancing your own sexual satisfaction together.

SUGGESTED READING:

Bartuses, Mary Ann. *Every Other Man.* New York: E. P. Dutton, 1978.

Myers, Lonny, and Hunter Leggitt. *Adultery and Other Private Matters—Your Right to Personal Freedom in Marriage*. Chicago: Nelson-Hall, 1975.

Smith, James, and Lynn Smith (eds.). *Beyond Monogamy: Recent Studies of Sexual Alternatives in Marriage*. Baltimore: Johns Hopkins University Press, 1974.

See also: DEPRESSION, GUILT, JEALOUSY, LONELINESS, LOVE ADDICTION, MID-LIFE CRISIS, SEXUAL DYSFUNCTION

FEAR OF DEATH

Most of us are afraid of dying. It is natural to be frightened at the thought of being separated from loved ones and ceasing to exist. It is natural to fear a painful death, or an illness that weakens us until we can no longer function by ourselves. It is natural to feel pain and fear at the thought of being struck down prematurely, in the bloom of life, leaving unfinished work and responsibilities. When we view death only as a final and horrible end, cutting us off from everything dear to us, annihilating us as persons, it is natural to fear it a great deal.

Because we are frightened, most of us avoid even thinking about death. We feel almost superstitious about it, as if just hearing the word or reading about it might cause it to happen. We put off going to the doctor, for fear of discovering that we have something terribly wrong with us. We avoid scenes of accidents, or else seek them out with morbid fascination, because the sight of a dead or injured body threatens us. Some people have trouble getting to sleep because somewhere inside they feel that surrendering to sleep is like dying.

We play games with words to avoid speaking bluntly of death. A person "passes away." The "dear one" is "prepared" at the mortuary and placed in a "sleep room," then "interred" in a "final resting place."

Many years ago people lived in large family groups, where the elderly spent their last years, eventually dying, while new children were periodically born into the family. Now we shut old and terminally ill people away, so that we cannot see them die. This puts us out of touch with death and makes us feel that it is strange and horrible. We also try to deny the inevitability of death by keeping a person "alive" with the wonder machines of medical science, even after the person has ceased to be alive in any real sense.

Some people are so frightened of death that even though they are not sick or in danger, they imagine they are going to die soon and become very panicky and disoriented.

The person who is terminally ill is also frightened of death. But many dying people, because they now know that the end is near and in-evitable, have learned how to make this phase of their life profoundly satisfying and meaningful. We can learn from them. As Goethe said, "Death is nature's expert advice—to get plenty of Life."

In the past few years there has been a lot of attention paid to the experience of death. Several fine books have been written about it, such as Dr. Kübler-Ross's *On Death and Dying*. Death is finally becoming less of a taboo subject. This is fortunate, because the more we avoid the idea of it, the more frightened of it we are. Our problem is that we have lost sight of the fact that death is part of the natural process of living—as winter is a natural part of the changing seasons and the end of the year.

A person's fear of death is sometimes intensified by a fear of living, or the fear that he or she has never really been alive. Fear of dying can be especially intense if your life lacks real meaning and motivation. Your feeling of fear can be a substitute for other forbidden feelings, such as hate or anger. If you feel responsibility for another person's death, you may fear that you will die as retribution.

In other words, an excessive fear of death can mean that you are not facing some of your problems in living. You can even use your fear of death as an excuse for not living fully—for becoming withdrawn and lonely and disappointed at the futility and barrenness of your life.

Whether your fear is intense or mild, whether you have a terminal illness or only are aware that because you are alive you must someday die, your awareness of death can be made into an opportunity. You can use it to do more and be more, to feel more intensely, to connect with the people you care about, to appreciate every moment of your day.

• Ask yourself if you are really alive now and relating to other people. Ask yourself if you are carrying around some unexpressed feel-ings or some deadness inside you, perhaps even a wish for death and its release and peace. Fear often conceals a wish. Thus, fear of death may conceal a wish for death as an escape and a "solution." Do some-thing about making your life more meaningful by seeking solutions in fuller living, not withdrawal. Savor every precious moment. Live fully and appreciatively. Let living become an enthusiastic, joyous experience.

• Don't hide from the idea of death. Read some of the fascinating books on death that are now available. Once you are familiar with the subject and used to hearing about it, it will frighten you less.

• Try to think of death as a natural process, a part of life. When the blossom dies, the fruit appears; when the fruit falls, the seed enters the ground and sprouts into new life. Recognize death as part of the continuity of nature. Feel that you are in tune with the rhythm of nature.

• Make a point of relating to older people and ill people instead of pushing them out of your mind. Become accustomed to all portions of life's cycle.

•Take comfort in your immortality through your children and through your work, especially in the good you have done for others.

• Take comfort in religious beliefs, if you hold them. Remind yourself that at the moment of death you will not be alone. Feel your link with the infinite.

• Remember that belief in a life after death is no longer limited to religious people. Death can be a tranquil or even happy experience. Several studies report that shortly before death some people become cheerful and elated, or serene and calm. People also report visions of loved ones coming to help them make the transition from this life into the next. Others, who have come near to or "returned from" death, report experiences of an unbelievably beautiful and loving existence, or "life," at the end of life.

• If you are very ill, share your fears about your death with those near you. Let them comfort you. Be close to them. Feel your love for them and the love they return. At the same time, experience the beauty of the world around you. Savor every moment. Recognize that you, in your special situation, can fully appreciate the preciousness of life. This is a gift that has been given you now.

• If you are terminally ill, take advantage of community resources. Some cities provide a hot-line service to give you counseling and comfort. Some hospitals have a hospice service, to help you and your family to face this time of your life together as a family unit, sometimes in your home environment rather than the hospital.

• If you are close to someone who is dying, help him or her prepare to die. Do not shut him or her out of your life. Try to make these last weeks or months the most meaningful of all, for both of you. The end of life is a profound, vital phase in which both of you have much to give and receive.

• If it is appropriate to your situation, join a mutual-support group of individuals who have encountered a life-threatening illness—either personally or as a concerned family member or friend—such as a local chapter of Make Today Count (national headquarters: P.O. Box 303, Burlington, Iowa 52601).

SUGGESTED READING:

Kübler-Ross, Elisabeth. *On Death and Dying*. New York: Macmillan, 1970.

Lifton, Robert Jay, and Eric Olson. *Living and Dying.* New York: Bantam Books, 1974.

Moody, Raymond A., Jr. *Life After Life.* New York: Bantam Books, 1974.

Osis, Karlis, and Erlendur Haraldsson. *At the Hour of Death.* New York: Avon Books, 1977.

See also: AGING, CANCER, DEPRESSION, GRIEF, MID-LIFE CRISIS, PAIN

FEAR OF FAILURE

The powerful ways our society rewards success and punishes failure make it difficult to take a balanced view of the true importance of these familiar and inevitable life experiences. Children learn to be ashamed of failure—even in games—and they carry this lesson into adulthood. People who experience failure too early or too often come to expect it. They become obsessed with their fear of failing again. Still others, carrying around some secret guilt, fear failure because they see it as a punishment that will expose their unworthiness.

No one really wants to fail, even people who sabotage themselves. They arrange to fail in order to get it over with, and to avoid some imagined worse consequence of succeeding. It is reasonable to want to avoid failure, given the amount of disapproval and deprivation it can bring. You don't have to remain scared of failing, however. And you don't have to run away from it by constant striving for success.

The judgment that we have failed often comes from outside ourselves. Other people, applying their standards, tell us that we are not successful. Even in those cases where we judge ourselves to have failed, the pain comes from taking those external standards inside ourselves and equating failure to have achieved some goal with failure as a person.

Fear of failure grows out of this equation of ourselves with our actions. Every effort that meets with less than complete external approval reinforces it. Fearing disapproval (because his or her sense of self-worth depends on external support), the failure-fearing person wallows in self-rejection and anxiety.

If you are afraid to fail, you may become afraid of acting. You may drop out. After all, if you don't act, your actions can't be judged wrong or inadequate. Your fear may cause you to avoid risks or new situations —anything that doesn't remind you of a past success. When you are worried about failure you may become defensive about everything you do. You may get into boasting, exaggerating minor achievements, putting other people down, or lying to yourself and others about what really counts as success for you.

The same success-obsessed social environment that encourages competitiveness and perfectionism makes fear of failure seem like a natural part of life. But it doesn't have to be. You don't have to accept the pressure to succeed as an appropriate way to feel. When striving and winning are too highly rewarded, you may get caught up in a way of life where fear of failure gets expressed as the determination to succeed at all costs. You must learn to allow yourself to fail, and to see that the problem is not failing but the inability to accept it as part of life.

Here are strategies for dealing with the fear of failure:

• Take a close look at how you learned to fear failure. Who taught it to you? What were the crucial lessons? Look at your family, work, and social environments. Are the people around you overly judgmental or perfectionistic? Does someone else have a stake in your failing or in your being afraid to fail? Are you letting someone push you to succeed in ways that just aren't right for you, so that your fear of failure is realistic?

• Are you setting appropriate goals for yourself? Are your standards the right ones for your life? Are they really your standards? If you are trying to do too much, you have good reason to fear failure. Give yourself a chance to grow and develop in ability. Don't take on excessive tasks or aim for unreachable achievements; go step by step.

• Also look for the opposite manifestation of fear of failure—are your standards set so low that you can't fail? Give yourself a chance to improve. Try something new, something a little harder than what you've done before. Allow yourself positive learning experiences.

• Keep in constant touch with what makes you feel good about yourself. Savor all the small pleasures and successes that come your way. List the ways you naturally succeed in living a satisfying life even in humble and inconspicuous ways. You are doing the best you can so far, given what you know about yourself and life.

• Beware of defining yourself only as the sum of your achievements. You are more than what you do or make. You are more than the money you earn—or the trips, clothes, friends, or possessions you accumulate. You are a growing person who can learn from all the experiences of your life, even the unpleasant ones.

• Think back to a "failure." What did you learn from it then? What more can you learn from it now? Accept failure as a normal part of living. View it as part of the process of exploring your world; make note of its lessons and move on. Often the lessons of a past failure make possible a future success. A famous skier skied too fast in races and kept falling down and losing. He continued to ski fast, but analyzed each fall and made corrections. One day he stopped falling, and was unbeatable.

• Don't overrate the value of worldly success. Don't let the pursuit of success replace more important goals such as developing loving and supportive personal relationships, gradually improving your skills and abilities, learning to try new—and therefore risky—ventures.

• Don't repeat a worn-out formula that brought you success in the past. It can lead to stagnation and eventual failure. Look what happened to the Edsel when the Ford Motor Company did that.

• Free yourself of the enslaving myth that you have to be *the best* to be acceptable to yourself and/or others. Is anything less than perfection a failure? What would happen if you just did something for the joy of doing it—not to "do your best"? Learn to play. Provide yourself with stimulating but noncompetitive experiences. Discover the delight of exploring and trying new things. Take risks, small ones at first— you'll soon learn there's nothing to fear. Change and discovery can be energizing if you free yourself from the fear that any change brings an added risk of failing.

• Review those times when you really did fail. What happened? How did others react? Was the worst part the actual consequences, other people's disapproval, or your own self-attack? Did failing mean the end of love and support from your friends or family? Did you lose the respect of others or of yourself? Did you learn something valuable and find ways to keep going or shift to better strategies and goals?

• Accept the possibility of failure as part of the human condition. You have a human right to make mistakes, to try and not succeed, to fail outright. Wins and losses are both temporary. Your value as a person does not rest on your success at any one thing; failing at a task does not mean you've failed as a person.

• Make a list of what you actually get when you succeed and what you actually lose when you fail. Notice that failure does not always cut off the opportunity to try again.

• Fantasize about things you'd like to try. What risks do you fear? Imagine failing. Imagine succeeding. Imagine the absolute worst happening. Imagine yourself surviving that and trying again. Visualize succeeding beyond your wildest dreams.

• Stop keeping score on yourself. Don't dwell on the discrepancy between your achievements and goals. The only constant in life is change. Ride out life's ups and downs. Periodic failures do not mark you as a failure at living, only as a normal, fallible, striving human being.

• Don't try to compensate yourself for low self-esteem by never failing. Focus on the task, not on yourself.

SUGGESTED READING:

Korda, Michael. *Success: How Every Man and Woman Can Achieve It.* New York: Random House, 1977.
Viscott, David. *Risking.* New York: Dell, 1977.

See also: COMPETITIVENESS, GUILT, OBSESSIONS, PERFEC-TIONISM, PROCRASTINATION

FEAR OF FLYING

In some situations a certain amount of fear is a natural and adaptive reaction. Fear is healthy when it alerts us to danger, heightens our awareness, and motivates us to be careful. But given the safety of modern commercial air travel, fear of flying is not an adaptive reaction. Planes do crash, but so do cars, buses, trains, and bicycles. Statistics show that you are safer on a plane. Nevertheless, large numbers of people are afraid of flying. Some fly anyway, but suffer. Others don't fly, and miss out on pleasure trips, visits with friends and relatives, and business opportunities.

Why all this fear of flying? Leaving solid ground scares us. To fly we must accept our lack of control and the necessity to trust the pilot, control-tower personnel, and a strange machine. If you don't feel emotionally supported or on solid ground in your daily life, you may overreact to the predicament of being suspended in midair in a metal box, helplessly dependent on the sanity and goodwill of others.

The very situations that frighten us, however, can be sources of fun and exhilaration once we master them. Many people have conquered their fear of flying and discovered how easy and delightful flying can be. They have also learned more about themselves in the process.

Gaining the necessary trust and confidence takes repeated positive experiences and concerted effort. Flying fears often have straightforward causes. One is direct experience—that is, having a "bad flight." People also learn inappropriate fears from other sources, such as a relative who won't fly, a friend who had a scary experience, or an exaggerated movie. Dwelling on the causes of your fear, however, may only serve to heighten and reinforce it. What you need, very directly, is to understand and systematically overcome your reactions.

Extreme fears or phobias consist of three elements: emotions (the way we feel), cognitions (the way we think), and behaviors (the way we act). All three aspects, although interrelated, must be understood and dealt with separately.

Overcoming Emotional Obstacles

"When I get on a plane, I panic; it's like I'm going to die." "I'm afraid I'll just break down and make a fool of myself." Such reactions can include feelings of rapid heartbeat, stomach cramps, dizziness, headache, and nausea. They have a common cause: increasingly rapid breathing (hyperventilation). In extreme cases, such overbreathing leads to feelings of choking or dying. It is crucial to realize that such breathing is *under your control.* You can accelerate it—leading to feelings of increased fright and eventual panic—or decelerate it—leading to feelings of greater control and calm.

• Try an experiment.* Practice holding your breath or breathing into a paper bag. Then force yourself to hyperventilate by breathing rapidly. At the point of panic, immediately hold your breath (or breathe into the bag). The symptoms will cease. They are under your direct control.
• Learn one of the highly effective methods of deep muscle relaxation that involves the systematic tensing and relaxing of various muscle groups. *Progressive Relaxation Training: A Manual for the Helping Professions*, by Douglas Bernstein and Thomas Borkovec (Champaign, Ill.: Research Press, 1973), presents an excellent guide to this method.
• Practice deep-breathing exercises. Practice inhaling *slowly* to the count of 15, then exhaling *slowly* to the same count. Do this several times daily, until you can do it without the need to concentrate. Try out the method in a variety of anxiety-arousing situations, moving gradually from those of low arousal to those of high arousal.
• Use systematic desensitization. Think of ten flight-related situations, ranging from those with low arousal ("It's two days before my flight" or "Seeing a picture of an airplane in a magazine") to those of high arousal ("The plane is taxiing down the runway" or "We are bouncing in the plane due to turbulence"). Rank the items from least threatening to most threatening. Beginning with the least threatening, imagine each scene over and over until it no longer bothers you. This method can be quite effective when combined with relaxation techniques.
• Use emotive imagery. Combine each of the above scenes with two or three images that would be pleasurable and gratifying. For example:

* Before following these suggestions, get your physician's approval. These symptoms may have direct physical causes which require medical attention. This is rarely the case, however.

"You are relaxing in your bedroom, thumbing through a magazine with pictures of airplanes in it. The bed feels soft and cozy, birds are chirping outside, and you feel the warmth of your spouse/lover beside you." "You are relaxing comfortably in the soft seat of the plane. You have just finished a fine meal and are talking animatedly to a friend about your mutual destination."

• Another emotional obstacle may be a secret payoff. Ask yourself what you *gain* by being afraid to fly. Beneath the "problem" and the complaining you do about it, is there some hidden reward? Consider these possibilities: You get to focus your fears on flying in airplanes, and thus can avoid seeing what else you may be afraid of. Perhaps you really don't want to go on a plane trip because you don't want to do whatever will be expected of you when you arrive. Maybe you don't want to deal with certain people or tackle certain responsibilities. One woman was not afraid to fly from her home city to a vacation resort, but she panicked when it came time to board the return flight. She discovered that she didn't want to face all the pressures and responsibilities awaiting her at home.

• Press yourself to explore in depth the question "Where do I really want to go in my life, and does this plane trip fit in with that goal?" If it does not, your fear of flying may be a wise rebellion against pressure to go against your true nature. For example, a scientist developed an acute fear of flying when he began working on a military project that violated his values and took him away from his basic research. His fear cleared up after he took time out to review his life goals and announced that he was withdrawing from the project to concentrate on work that he really cared about.

Overcoming Cognitive Obstacles

"A wing fell off." "An engine will fail." "I don't care about statistics. My flight will be the one that crashes." These types of cognitions or "catastrophic" thoughts are actually voluntary and self-taught. You have a choice: You can actively continue saying such statements to yourself—leading to increased physical discomfort and avoidance—or you can choose to combat and stop them—leading to peace of mind and the enjoyment of flying.

Successful methods of voluntary thought control include information seeking, thought stopping, and thought transformation.

• *Information seeking.* Many fears are based on "what ifs" or fear of the unknown. Sit down now and write out every fear you have regarding flying. Then thoroughly research each area so as to become a knowledgeable and expert passenger. Contact local airlines for seminars. Talk with airline personnel. Find out why airplanes won't crash if an engine fails and how modern aircraft avoid storm areas and can fly as easily at night as by day. Read books like *Flying,* by Barry Schiff.

• *Thought stopping.* Each time you say to yourself some fear-arousing statement, eliminate it by shouting "Stop!" to yourself and snapping a rubber band around your wrist. With enough practice and repetition, these thoughts will disappear.

• *Thought transformation.* Counter *every* fear-arousing cognition with an alternate positive statement. For example: "Flying—I hate it!" becomes "Flying—I enjoy it!" "The plane will crash" becomes "My flight will be a safe one." Again, perseverance by repetition with every thought is the key.

Overcoming Behavioral Obstacles

"When it's time to board, I turn around and go home." "I want to—I just can't!" Extreme fear, as previously mentioned, is self-perpetuating. No matter how you first learn to feel uneasy in a situation, if you run away from it and subsequently avoid it, a full-blown phobia is in the making. The longer your avoidance, the more severe your phobia will become. Conversely, by exposing yourself to feared situations and making yourself remain in them (no matter how bad you feel initially), you will eventually become calm and overcome your fears. It is that simple—and one of the best-documented of psychological principles.

• First with a friend or loved one, then by yourself, seek out and overcome the various situations which make you uneasy. Visit airports. Read aviation magazines. Tour a control tower. Seek permission to board airplanes and strap on seat belts. Take not just one flight but many flights. While in the air, if you fear looking out the window, look out the window. If you fear moving or "rocking the boat," walk up and down the aisles.

• As you do so, practice your relaxation. If you begin to hyperventilate, hold your breath or use any procedure that works for you. Tell yourself, "Let the fear come. I can handle it and I don't care. I'll do my damnedest to prove that nothing is going to happen." And do it! Remain in the situation until you become calm (usually ten to fifteen minutes *at most* is required). Every time you force yourself through such a situation, your fear will diminish.

• Savor each triumph, no matter how small. Tell your friends; brag a little. Become smug. You are meeting a personal challenge and conquering it.

• Most important, realize that in *all* these circumstances you are in charge. You are not the victim of mysterious and uncontrollable forces; at each point you have a choice and can choose your reactions to specific situations. It is understandably difficult at first. Don't be discouraged. Plan ahead. Use determination. And enjoy the results.

Some final tips when taking a flight:
• Prepare ahead to minimize a stressful journey. Get plenty of sleep the night before. Plan to arrive at least forty-five minutes before departure. Avoid heavy meals, alcohol, and sedatives before boarding. Take along items that will make your flight more enjoyable: high-interest books and magazines, crossword puzzles, needlework, a deck of cards.
• Before and during takeoff, practice your relaxing and breathing exercises. Hold hands with a friend. Wiggle your toes and fingers. Don't fight the thrust of takeoff; sink back into your seat. Rest your head on a pillow.
• During the flight, look around. Notice people. Be curious and examine your surroundings. Walk around. If you hear a strange noise or experience an unfamiliar movement, ring for the cabin attendant and ask about it. Alternately, check one of your aircraft manuals. Everything has an understandable cause—find out about it. Be in control. This is your opportunity to meet a challenge and master it. The rewards can be exhilarating.
• If you want more information, contact Dr. Stephen Alkus, Psychology Clinic, University of California, Los Angeles, California 90024. He is a consultant to SAFE, a special seminar for fearful fliers. Or write Jay Beau-Seigneur, Director of Fearful Flyers Seminars, Pan American World Airways, 30 South Michigan Ave., Chicago, Illinois 60603.

SUGGESTED READING:

Ellis, Albert. *How to Master Your Fear of Flying.* New York: Institute for Living, 1977.

"How to Fly: Getting the Most Out of Air Travel" (brochure). Air Transportation Association of America, 1709 New York Avenue, N.W., Washington, D.C. 20006.

Schiff, Barry. *Flying: A Guide to Principles and Practice.* New York: Western Publishing Co., 1971.

Smith, Manuel J. *Kicking the Fear Habit.* New York: Dial Press, 1977.

See also: AGORAPHOBIA, ANXIETY

FEAR OF HEIGHTS

A young executive whom we'll call Dan began sharing his coffee break with Corine, a very pleasant woman working in the same office. After a few months of getting acquainted this way, he took her out to lunch. She reciprocated by inviting him to her home for dinner. Dan was delighted to accept her invitation, and wrote down her address. But when he arrived at the building he discovered that it was a high-rise and that Corine's apartment was on the seventh floor. Dan immediately tensed up, and it was with an ever-increasing sense of dread that he rode up in the elevator and went to her door. By the time Corine answered his knock, his heart was pounding; he was shaking, sweating, breathing heavily, and feeling faint. By no means was this passion. Dan suffered from acrophobia: fear of heights. Unable to control his embarrassment and fear, Dan gave the excuse of feeling suddenly ill, apologized, and went home.

Numerous people who are terrified by height share these symptoms, as well as others, such as paralysis of movement, feelings of weakness or numbness in the extremities, muscular tension, even the urgent need to go to the bathroom. They also suffer from the added distress of feeling that no one else can understand their fear. They carry it around like a secret vice, and their fear drastically restricts their lives.

Height phobics can fear anything from a curb to the roof of the Empire State Building: planes, steep stairs, ladders, bridges, anywhere they lose contact with their sense of being "well grounded."

Phobias of all kinds are irrational uncontrollable fears of ordinary situations, objects, animals—of anything, in fact—that overcome us even when there is no likelihood of harm. It doesn't matter to someone who fears flying that air travel is safer than driving to the airport. Similarly, the height phobic is sure that he or she *will fall,* even though there is no actual reason for believing that any danger of falling exists. No railing can be secure enough, no window sufficient protection against the dreaded plunge.

Like obsessions and compulsions, phobias can serve as defenses against anxiety, ways to deal with situations in which a person feels he or she may lose self-control. Phobias are often symbolic of other fears: fears of success, intimacy, independence, or of one's own self-destructive tendencies. A phobia can be a way of asking for a riskless life of guaranteed safety and security.

A fear of heights may reflect a lack of trust in your own internal controls and in your will to live. That fear can conceal a wish to let go, to surrender to events, to get out, to be free of the boundaries of your life. Sometimes height phobics feel drawn to the very edge that they fear. One height phobic on vacation had the fantasy that he could fly from his hotel balcony to the beach, thereby avoiding the elevators and crowded lobby. Moving to the balcony railing, he rapidly backed off. He didn't trust his ability to distinguish fantasy from reality, and as a result felt acutely anxious until he had put a safe distance between himself and the railing.

• In order not to fear heights, you have to be able to depend on your own sense of control, balance, and orientation. You have to be a sort of psychological roly-poly toy, the kind that rights itself after tipping over. You need to be enough in touch with your body to know when you are upright and when you are leaning. It's as if your kinesthetic awareness and controls—your body sense of orientation—were symbolic of your psychological stance. Ask yourself: "Where do I stand? How firmly do I stand here? How do I handle the conflicting forces in my life? Where is my center of gravity? What keeps me in balance?"

• When you first become aware of a phobic attack, try to pin down exactly what you are feeling and doing. Try to identify and define your emotional state. What else are you thinking of as you become fearful? What do you expect to happen? Why do you expect it to happen to you especially? Are you reminded of anxieties that also appear in nonphobic situations?

• You can learn that there is no cause for your fear of heights. You can retrain yourself. Phobias are rarely the outgrowth of valid natural caution, or an appropriate fear acquired from a specific frightening incident. You may find, therefore, that in retraining yourself not to fear heights you begin to see the connections to the true fear you're struggling with—and can begin to deal directly with that.

• If there is a physical reason for you to avoid stress, such as a heart problem or high blood pressure, consult your physician before beginning your retraining program. He or she may have some suggestions that will help you modify it to suit your special needs.

• One method used by behavior therapists to treat fear of heights and other phobias is called the "threshold" method. First, establish a goal, such as being able to work comfortably in a tenth-floor office. Next, *gradually* expose yourself to increasingly fearful situations that are similar to the goal. For example, begin on the first floor of a building at which you start to feel anxious. Stay on that floor doing some kind of eye-hand–coordinated task for as long as you comfortably can. When the anxiety gets too high, leave. Keep returning to the same place, and do things such as drawing the scene from the window, counting all the blue automobiles below, watching for a pedestrian in a hat, or whatever distracting task you wish (that still involves you in your environment), until you no longer feel fearful there. Then move on to the next level. Repeat this until you have retrained yourself to be comfortable in your goal situation. Try to exceed your goal in practice sessions if possible, but don't push yourself. You don't want to scare yourself while you're learning gradually to reduce fear.

• Another behavior-modification method teaches you that your distress can be temporary. As described by Spencer A. Rathus, Ph.D., and Jeffrey S. Nevid, Ph.D., in their book *BT: Behavior Therapy,* this is a method in which you purposely expose yourself for gradually increasing periods of time to the feared situation you wish to master. So long as you can stand some exposure to the feared high environment and you can completely control when you leave, this method may work for you. Go to your target location and stay for as long as your discomfort is bearable. Leave when it becomes intolerable. As soon as you've regained your calm, return to the place, and gradually increase the time during which you can tolerate being there. You will soon learn that you can stay without being overcome by fear. Each small success will help you on to the next. You will be able to reassure yourself as you go that your previous accomplishments prove the safety and tolerability of high places.

• Don't berate yourself for any relapses, even if you have to do a step or two of your program over again. As you continue working on your problem, it will become more manageable. It is easier to retrain yourself the second time than the first, so don't be discouraged if after some time away from your target environment you have to return to retraining for a while.

• If you are forced into your phobic situation—if you have no choice but to stay and deal with your fear—you will probably find that after a while your physical sensations of fear will exhaust themselves and end. Unless you are extremely depressed or agitated, you are likely to learn the limit of your fear and that the situation is, after all, tolerable.

• Keep reminding yourself that your fear of heights is an opportunity concealed in a problem. This is your chance to develop more self-respect by overcoming a hangup. By working steadily and patiently on your fear of heights, you will strengthen your confidence not only in high places but out there in life generally. You will also learn more about yourself, especially about how you really view yourself and the pressures—including gravity—that threaten you. Fear of heights is your signal that you are not solidly "grounded" and harmoniously "balanced." Let your fear be your teacher, not an enemy. Learn to listen more deeply to the part of yourself that is afraid, and to the part of you that guides you toward safety and confidence. It may help to give these parts of yourself voices and have them conduct a discussion, or argument. But remember, they are just parts of you. You may have to remind them that you are still the boss, and that you want creative solutions, not just an argument. If you hang in there and confront your fear, the solutions will emerge.

SUGGESTED READING:

Fensterheim, Herbert, and Jean Baer. *Stop Running Scared*. New York: Rawson Associates, 1978.
Smith, Manuel. *Kicking the Fear Habit*. New York: Dial Press, 1977.

See also: ANXIETY, AGORAPHOBIA, FEAR OF FLYING

FEAR OF SICKNESS

It's difficult to be either a patient or a physician in the United States today. Physicians are burdened by a kind of split image as either all-knowing, magical healers or money-grubbing, heartless bumblers. Patients are intimidated by their own fears of disease and death, by the increasing complexity and cost of medical care, and by anxiety about becoming another malpractice victim.

It benefits both you and the medical professionals trying to help you when you take as much responsibility as you can for understanding your medical problems and their treatment. Participating intelligently in the decision-making process will add to your peace of mind and commitment to your health-care program.

• Many of us find it easy to dump our medical needs on our physician's doorstep. We don't like to go in for routine checkups. We're afraid we'll discover a problem. Our fear makes it tempting to behave in a childish way, turning over responsibility to a parent figure. This dependent approach deprives us of an important medical resource: ourselves. We are closest to our own bodies. We know when we hurt or feel something wrong. We can often be the first to notice a medical problem. Unfortunately, we often ignore what we know and delay acting on our knowledge.

• One way to overcome this tendency is to work out a mutually cooperative and supportive relationship with your physician—*before* a medical crisis occurs. Be interested in yourself and your needs. If possible, do your medical "shopping" while in good health. If you are not comfortable, confident, and in good communication with your physician, find someone else.

• To be an active, intelligent medical consumer, you may have to train your doctor to work with you the way you want him or her to. Many fine physicians have been educated to take an authoritarian, all-knowing approach to their patients. They have been trained to take charge and make all the decisions without patients' interference. Some physicians are so attached to this role that they take advantage of it to dominate patients and run their practices in a simplified, assembly-line manner. Such a physician may, in effect, say, "Trust me, these matters are beyond your comprehension." Or he or she may punish you for your appropriate curiosity by giving out exaggerated warnings detailing extreme and scary possibilities, in effect saying, "If you really want to know I'll tell you, but you'll be sorry you asked." Medical treatment often involves risk, and some aspects of treatment are hard to explain to laypersons. There is, however, a middle ground on which patient and physician can meet to discuss risks and benefits in a balanced and mutually nonthreatening manner.

• You are, of course, responsible for developing good habits to help prevent illness or injury. This does not mean you are "guilty" of becoming ill, however. Needing medical care is not something to be ashamed of or to avoid. Demanding and receiving respectful and considerate care is your right.

• You are entitled to your dignity and have every reason to expect a physician's manner to foster—rather than undermine—your confidence. Speak up if you don't understand a medical term used by your physician or anyone else connected with your treatment. Speak up if you don't understand the treatment itself. Speak up if you are frightened, if you're confused, if you want to raise an objection. You are right to worry about yourself. It is reasonable and normal to ask questions at every stage of your interaction with medical personnel.

• Seek out independent consultation if you face a serious medical problem. No responsible physician will discourage this. Your health plan, the county medical association, or a reference such as the *Directory of Medical Specialists* (often available at public libraries) can help you choose a reliable consultant. Specialists tend to see things in terms of their own specialty—don't be surprised if a surgeon recommends surgery. Verify the need for an operation by getting a second opinion from a surgeon who understands that he or she will not be engaged to perform it.

• Stay out of the hospital unless you really need to be there. Hospitals are complex bureaucracies, often too unwieldy to give you personalized care. One doctor, Robert Mendelsohn of Atlanta, actually warns us, "Going into the hospital is like going to war. You should try not to get into it. If you have to go, go with maximum force, never go alone, and get out as soon as you can. . . . If you have a bunch of tough-looking relatives take one with you."

• Throughout your lifelong relationship with the medical profession, make it your responsibility to demand the facts you need to understand yourself physically. You can't give informed consent for medical procedures unless you are truly informed. Ask for explanations of the diagnosis, the treatment, possible side effects and risks, and the expected outcome of treatment, in words you understand.

• Don't be afraid to ask about long-term effects. Don't be ashamed to reveal concern about how you'll feel—physically and emotionally—after treatment. Don't try to control your fears by hiding them. You may have questions such as: Will I be in pain? Will this affect my looks? When can I go back to work? When can I resume sexual intercourse? These are all important questions. Ask them. Don't make important medical decisions until you feel satisfied with your knowledge of the situation. Always ask about and discuss alternatives.

• About those hospital consent forms—don't let them intimidate you. You can't sign away your rights. You can't really relieve your medical personnel of their obligations to give quality care or to be attentive to critical details by signing a waiver in advance. Also, the American Hospital Association recognizes the patient's right to refuse treatment within certain legal conditions and to be informed of the medical consequences of refusal.

• Be aware of the common emotional reactions to entering a hospital. In unfamiliar and vaguely threatening surroundings, it is usual to feel suddenly powerless and scared. Fears of the unknown, of pain or disfigurement or dependence or death, can assault you. You may feel lonely and alienated from your usual support system of family, work, and friends. It can be hard to protect your fragile sense of identity. Hospital routine can sometimes make you feel more like "the gallbladder in 402" than the individual you were when you checked in. Fear and discomfort invite feelings of childish dependence, which can increase anxiety. Pain can increase irritability, and under the best of conditions your anxiety has probably already made you oversensitive to every word and action around you. You may be worried about embarrassment or about looking undignified or laughable. You may not know what to expect after treatment. You may forget that your concerns are normal, temporary, and predictable.

• You can help yourself deal with these feelings by confronting them, acknowledging them, and seeking answers to the questions they raise. Inform yourself about your condition and its treatment. Ask about the relationship between the various health-care professionals you meet. Ask the staff to explain the hospital rules and practices that apply to you.

• Even in the best-run hospital, the potential for error is large. For example, many errors in medication occur in the chain that runs from prescribing physician to pharmacy to nurse to you. Identify yourself to your nurse before accepting medication. Talk to your physician; be aware of what has been prescribed for you. Ask technicians to double-check your identity and the physician's orders before undertaking a procedure. Help the staff prevent mistakes.

• Finances can be a source of difficulty and anxiety. If you must pay your own expenses, you will want to discuss ways to reduce cost and yet be responsible and thorough. Even if your medical care is covered by a health plan or insurance, you should receive a copy and explanation of your bill. Feel free to ask in advance, "What will this actually cost?" "Who will be receiving payment?" Errors are common in the government-administered health plans, such as Medicare and Medicaid. Always double-check the statements you get.

• Additional patient rights recognized by the American Hospital Association include the right to expect a hospital to respond to your reasonable requests for service and to inform you if you will be part of any sort of research or experiment during your treatment.

• You can prepare yourself to talk intelligently to your physician; you can educate yourself about medications you take and procedures you follow. You can learn to use references such as the *Merck Manual* or the *Physician's Desk Reference*—not to second-guess or compete with your physician, but to help you ask intelligent questions about your health care, to understand your doctor's answers, and to participate responsibly in your recovery process.

SUGGESTED READING:

Department of Health, Education and Welfare. *Surgery*. Washington, D.C.: HEW, 1978.

Gots, Ronald, and Arthur Kaufman. *The People's Hospital Book*. New York: Crown, 1978.

Taylor, Dr. Robert B. *Doctor Taylor's Self-Help Medical Guide*. New York: Signet, New American Library, 1977.

See also: ANXIETY, CANCER, FEAR OF DEATH, HYPOCHON-DRIA, PSYCHOSOMATIC ILLNESS

FEAR OF SUCCESS

If your accomplishments lag behind your ambitions and you often seem to lose out at the last minute after a promising start, you may be one of the many men and women who struggle with fear of success.

If you carry around a nagging sense of failure and inadequacy in spite of all you have achieved, or if you cannot enjoy the fruits of your achievements, you may be afraid of success.

This fear is really a very common one. Most people have some misgivings about the changes success would bring into their lives. Some people, however, are so uncomfortable with their success or even with the possibility of success that they sabotage their own efforts and unconsciously try to fail.

A full-blown fear of success can be paralyzing: It can make it impossible for you to take necessary risks and accept rewarding challenges. Underlying such fear is the internalized conviction that any success you achieve is really undeserved, that you are really a fraud—and will be exposed as such by the rest of the world.

For all the emphasis placed on "making it" in our society, there is also a very strong antisuccess mythology. It teaches us that it is better to be one of the honest poor, to be safely inconspicuous. Money corrupts, says the myth, and the rich pay for their wealth in deserved personal suffering. (For example, many people hold the view that the Kennedy wealth and ambition somehow caused or attracted the family's tragedies.) The antisuccess myth drums into us how dangerous it is to be singled out, much less to soar above the masses. Many of us have accepted this superstitious fearfulness, and anticipate that misfortune will follow on the heels of victory.

Guilt can keep you from attaining or enjoying success. If you are afraid to rival certain important people—a competitive parent, for example—you may prevent yourself from succeeding. If you feel your desire to get attention and recognition is unacceptable to someone else you depend on, you may feel too much guilt over your "impure motivation" to allow yourself to achieve anything. Unconsciously you may be convinced that such unacceptable ambition will bring upon you a well-deserved punishment.

Some people cannot stand to succeed because they feel worthless and inadequate. If you are trying to succeed in order to deny your feeling of being no good, you probably still secretly believe you don't deserve to succeed. No wonder you fear success: It would only whitewash your evil or inferior self. Until your self-esteem catches up with your abilities and ambitions, you'll never really let yourself achieve your goals.

A common cause for fearing success is anxiety about change. Achievement often does bring added demands and expectations. Each goal accomplished moves us ahead to a place where the next goal may be too difficult and threatening. You may not think success is worth it; it can be so lonely at the top that you prefer to stay safely at the bottom. Studies of auto accidents suggest that some people become dangerously accident-prone when they feel overwhelmed by the demands and pressures of a new position. Perhaps in some less dramatic way you are trying to avoid achieving at a level that would subject you to further high expectations.

You can learn to prevent internal sabotage and to let yourself succeed. Use the following questions and recommendations to help you discover what you really want, what you think you really deserve, and what you are willing to let yourself accomplish.

• Recognize the roles anxiety and superstition play in your fear of success. Watch for that telltale feeling that "something terrible is about to happen" as you get close to succeeding. Look out for the ways anxiety can lead you to sabotage your own efforts. Pay attention to what you do and say: Catch on to your own negativism, to your tendency to put yourself down or diminish the importance of your achievement. Keep track of your self-inflicted put-downs—count them. Become aware of your self-punishing behavior.

• Define success for yourself. What achievements are truly important to you? Are you pursuing your own goals or trying to fulfill someone else's definition of success? Take stock of your talents, abilities, ambitions, dreams. Try to establish your own realistic goals and act to accomplish them. Be specific; take one step at a time.

• What levels of success in which areas of life are you comfortable with? Be selective. You can't do everything. Concentrate on succeeding at projects where you have a fighting chance and where you will feel okay about being a winner. Be honest with yourself: If you don't want some particular kind of success—monetary, career, family, artistic, athletic—admit it to yourself, and go after what you do want.

• Set your aspirations at a reasonable level, not so high as to guarantee failure nor so low as to be unchallenging.

• Recognize the complexity of your problem: Fear of success is not just a wish to fail. You may genuinely want to achieve success and avoid failure but be crippled by an unconscious need to escape the very success you seek. Open up your awareness to all the mixed, contradictory feelings you have about success. Only then can you begin to sort them out.

• Survey your attitudes about yourself. How do you react to praise? Can you take a compliment? Do you acknowledge deserved recognition with pleasure? Are you proud of yourself, or do you think you're really a phony? Do you give yourself honest credit for your skills and abilities, or do you belittle them? Does the prospect of succeeding at something make you anxious and fearful? Do you try to get out of succeeding by shifting the reward to someone else or by actually sabotaging your own efforts?

• Reward yourself for turning off your internal critic. Try to look at yourself from the outside: If you were someone else, would you take such a negative view of your personality and achievements?

• Does someone else have a stake in your being a failure? Are you getting subtle messages not to expect too much of yourself, or to underestimate your chances? Are people close to you making it easy for you not to succeed, soothing your sense of failure without encouraging you to do better? Maybe they fear your success would go to your head and cause you to leave them behind. Enlist the support of your family and friends. Ask them to be supportive of you, to bolster your feelings of being a potential success. Share your ambitions and goals, and then work toward them with the important people in your life so that your success will include them, not separate you from them or threaten their sense of being important to you.

• As you work toward a goal, try to anticipate the possible changes success might bring. List for yourself the "dangers" of success: increased responsibility, rivalry from co-workers, envy, resentment, increased competition and expectations, change from your present role to a new and unfamiliar one. Bring your fear of success out into the open. After you identify the risks, try to gauge your willingness to take them. Separate the real risks from the imaginary ones, however. Fearing some stresses that success will bring is realistic; fearing punishment because you guiltily feel you don't deserve the success you have worked for reflects an inner problem, not an external reality.

• Watch out for addiction to the security and familiarity that failure provides. You can stay put and avoid the discomforts of change. If you're caught in a pattern of failure, try to analyze what you do to contribute to it and the payoffs you get. Look for evidence that you are willing to sabotage success in order to stay in familiar surroundings. Do you collect excuses and rationalizations for your failures? Maybe your greatest successes consist of justifying your failures.

• Are you ashamed of succeeding, especially of making money? It is not dishonorable to set goals, even purely monetary goals, and to go about accomplishing them responsibly and honestly. It is not shameful to do well whatever it is you do. Keep in mind, though, that success isn't exclusively a question of money. Take pride in your accomplishments, however they can be measured. If you have trouble with guilt, commit yourself to a plan for sharing your success with friends and relatives. Give generous credit to people who help you succeed. Give to charity. Help others succeed.

• Call to mind a past success. What was your state of mind? How did it feel to let yourself achieve something? Transfer that state of mind to your present efforts. Feed your self-confidence with your remembrance of past success. Trust yourself. Take definite steps to accomplish your goals. Enjoy the pleasure of completing each step. Adjust to the changes each success brings and go on to the next step. You do belong in the world and you do deserve to use your resources as fully as possible. By succeeding you will show others that it can be done. You will have more to give to people you care about, and you will have taken care of the person you are primarily responsible for—yourself.

SUGGESTED READING:

Brande, Dorothea. *Wake Up and Live!* New York: Cornerstone Library, 1974.

Canavan-Gumpert, Donnah, Katherine Garner, and Peter Gumpert. *The Success-Fearing Personality.* Lexington, Mass.: Lexington Books, 1978.

See also: ANXIETY, COMPETITIVENESS, DEPRESSION, FEAR OF FAILURE, GUILT, MASOCHISM, MID-LIFE CRISIS, PASSIVITY, PROCRASTINATION, SIBLING RIVALRY, STRESS, UNDERACHIEVEMENT

GAMBLING

Heywood Broun once said, "The urge to gamble is so universal and its practice so pleasurable that I assume it must be evil." Evil or not, to some extent we all gamble. Some of us drive just a bit too fast, betting against accidents or the highway patrol. Others fiddle with the numbers on their income-tax return and bet against an audit. Millions of us play church or charity bingo, buy raffle tickets for endless causes, go to Las Vegas, and sometimes join a private poker party—legal or not. For some of us the stock and commodities markets provide a subtle sort of gambling opportunity under cover of respectable financial investment. (It's no coincidence that the stock market news is generally reported near the sports section.) Many of us enjoy the challenge of playing with limits, and if the cost doesn't get too high—in either monetary or psychological ways—gambling can satisfy a craving for the excitement of risk in a relatively safe way. But it has been estimated that there are eight million compulsive gamblers in the United States.

Many theories have been advanced to explain the appeal of gambling. Nothing about the subject is uncontested, however; psychologists do not even agree on whether gamblers wish to win or to lose. One well-known psychiatrist who has studied gambling, Edmund Bergler, defines a true gambler as a neurotic with an unconscious wish to lose who (therefore) always loses in the long run. (Bergler excludes from this definition the occasional social gambler: the person who plays from time to time for diversion. The neurotic gambler is unconsciously driven to gamble, motivated by guilt feelings. Thus, gambling is merely a mechanism for masochistically appeasing a troubled conscience. It reflects the gambler's deeply rooted passive tendencies, his or her need to be the object of forces beyond human control.

As a neurosis, gambling is variously explained as: masochistic punishment for guilt, perhaps for guilt arising from sexual or aggressive thoughts dating back to childhood; an aggressive act against "the system" (representing father), in which one outwits it (him) by science or cleverness; a way of getting love from an unpredictable, withholding source (harking back to mother and food); penance for not suffering while someone else is (satisfying present guilt); a way of testing intelligence or a way of relying on Lady Luck to reveal whether or not Mom does love her child.

Gambling casinos seem to recognize that part of some gamblers that seeks love and nurturance, by providing attention (in the form of "friendly" service), glamorous-seeming surroundings, free drinks, inexpensive food, and reasonable hotel rates to their clients. They cater to another trait that many nongamblers share with gamblers, a kind of anxious hope that some one thing can transform their lives: a big win, a super vacation, the perfect tan, new clothes, a different job, improved cosmetics, the right food or liquor, more hair, or less paunch.

Professor Igor Kusyszyn and other researchers have come to reject explanations for gambling's appeal that, like Bergler's, insist on its fulfilling a masochistic need to punish oneself for past or even present guilt. Kusyszyn and his colleagues find the clue to gambling's appeal in the human need "to play the game," to have an action experience, to search for stimulus intensity, for some proof of one's existence and worth.

Gamblers harbor few illusions about the likelihood of winning. Even so, most of the 99 percent who never come out ahead continue to play. Kusyszyn believes that gambling reveals itself most fully when thought of as play, a play so all-engrossing that it shuts out everything else. It's not that gamblers play for money so much as that they play with it for the fun of betting on the possibility—not the probability—of winning.

At one time, gambling can satisfy two basic human needs: to prove that we exist and that we are significant and of worth. Unlike Bergler's passive victim of chance, Kusyszyn's gambler tries to influence his or her environment. This gambler may blow on the dice, root for a horse, talk to a roulette ball—all in the cause of effecting a win over the odds.

For some people the need to find life's meaning in this manner may be so compelling as to seem worth any personal or financial cost. Even

for the less extreme gambler, gambling can be rich in psychological rewards and stimulation. In fact, some gamblers who lose still maintain
their sense of self-worth and their zest for playing. Winning against
heavy odds or against a crooked opponent surely confirms one's existence, but gamblers can also point proudly to large past losses as a
sign of being significant individuals, serious players. Playing the game
is what counts.

• Take a close, detailed look at *all* your gambling activities. Does
gambling seem safer than the routine, common challenges and risks of
life? Why? What might gambling substitute for in your life—making
risky changes, developing closer relationships, working hard?
• Honestly add up the amount of time and money you spend
gambling. Is it increasing? Do you have control over it? Are you
gambling progressively more and more? Are you betting more than you
can afford to lose?
• If you simply find gambling enjoyable and aren't losing more than
you can afford to lose, no problem. Be aware, however, of who really
profits from your gambling "investment." Are you getting a fair return
in recreation and pleasure, or are you being ripped off? Are you really
having fun, or are you being used? Do you care?
• Remember that the occasional win—even if large—does not change
the overall nature or underlying problems of our lives. Million-dollar-
lottery winners have found that for the most part they continue to live
according to their previous lifestyles, values, and principles. Those who
were hardworking and thrifty before their win continued to pursue their
career and family goals; those who had had money or personality problems still had the same difficulties after they became millionaires.
• Recognize that you must take responsibility for keeping your
gambling in its recreational place. You are responsible for participating
in gambling activities, and you are responsible for keeping these games
in perspective. Don't blame friends for pressuring you into gambling.
Stay away from friends who gamble and tempt you to join them.
• Make sure you are continually developing other means to validate
your existence and worth. Take up substitute forms of risk: Try
nonmonetary gambling, participate in competitive sports, or become a
fan of some involving spectator sport. Develop a competitive hobby,
perhaps one that requires some financial commitment, such as building
and flying model airplanes or rockets, raising animals, or growing
flowers for competitive showing.
• Face the fact that if you are a compulsive gambler, willpower alone
won't be enough to stop your gambling. You need support from a group
like Gamblers Anonymous (P.O. Box 17173, Los Angeles, California

90017) and a dedicated program of personal growth so that your *need* to gamble won't overcome your willpower.

• Resign yourself to the conclusion that a compulsive gambler must totally give up gambling for money, in all forms, no matter how trivial. A little gambling, like one drink for the alcoholic, just starts the whole self-deception process going again.

• See the connection between stress symptoms (like nervousness, irritability, frustration, and disrupted personal relations) and your struggle with gambling. Even during periods of abstinence, if your life is not being enriched in other ways, these symptoms will eventually drive you back to gambling. Abstinence without personal growth is not enough.

• Answer these twenty questions listed by Gamblers Anonymous. Compulsive gamblers will answer yes to at least seven.

  1. Do you lose time from work due to gambling?
  2. Is gambling making your home life unhappy?
  3. Is gambling affecting your reputation?
  4. Have you ever felt remorse after gambling?
  5. Do you ever gamble to get money with which to pay debts or to otherwise solve financial difficulties?
  6. Does gambling cause a decrease in your ambition or efficiency?
  7. After losing, do you feel you must return as soon as possible and win back your losses?
  8. After a win, do you have a strong urge to return and win more?
  9. Do you often gamble until your last dollar is gone?
  10. Do you ever borrow to finance your gambling?
  11. Have you ever sold any real or personal property to finance gambling?
  12. Are you reluctant to use "gambling money" for normal expenditures?
  13. Does gambling make you careless of the welfare of your family?
  14. Do you ever gamble longer than you had planned?
  15. Do you ever gamble to escape worry or trouble?
  16. Have you ever committed, or considered committing, an illegal act to finance gambling?
  17. Does gambling cause you to have difficulty in sleeping?
  18. Do arguments, disappointments, or frustrations create within you an urge to gamble?
  19. Do you have an urge to celebrate any good fortune by a few hours of gambling?
  20. Have you ever considered suicide because of the difficulties resulting from your gambling?

• Don't be afraid to look outside yourself for help in ending your gambling. It takes maturity and wisdom to acknowledge a problem that you can't solve alone. If substituting other games, risks, or competitions doesn't satisfy your needs the way gambling does but gambling has become destructive and negative in your life, seek out a support group and work with others who share and understand your problem. It's a good bet that members of Gamblers Anonymous can help you find new ways to prove that you are alive and that you are a worthy, significant individual.

SUGGESTED READING:

Bergler, Dr. Edmund. *The Psychology of Gambling.* New York: International Universities Press, 1953.

Jacoby, Oswald. *Oswald Jacoby on Gambling.* New York: Hart, 1963.

Kusyszyn, Igor. *Studies in the Psychology of Gambling.* New York: Simon & Schuster, 1972.

MacDougall, M., and J. C. Furnas. *Gamblers Don't Gamble.* Las Vegas: Gamblers' Book Club, 1970.

Newman, O. *Gambling: Hazard and Reward.* London: Athlone, 1972.

See also: COMPULSIONS, GREED, MASOCHISM, MONEY WORRIES

GETTING FIRED

Losing a job is one of the difficulties of life that nearly all of us experience at some time. Anyone can get fired—even the president of the country or the head of a big corporation. Usually, the higher up we are in a company or the longer we have worked hard on a job, the tougher it feels to get fired. But no matter who we are, getting fired can make us seem small and vulnerable, useless and insignificant.

The reasons for losing a job are sometimes obvious and fair. Sometimes the reasons aren't clear, or seem very unfair, such as being pre-empted by a machine, getting blamed for something not your fault, or for personal reasons that should have nothing to do with your job.

Finding a satisfying career in life is a tough but satisfying challenge to meet. Replacing a job when you have lost yours is also a big challenge and can be even more satisfying. Being unemployed is a time for reassessment of yourself and your goals, perhaps an opportunity not only to start making more money but to achieve in more satisfying ways.

If you are struggling with the loss of a job, here are some constructive suggestions.

• Follow an active program of seeking work. Let friends and acquaintances know you're looking. Visit or write letters to prospective employers. List yourself with several employment agencies.

• Don't be afraid of failing at an interview or on a new job. Prepare yourself as well as you can and go ahead. Feel confident. Do your best. If it doesn't work out, don't put yourself down. Analyze what went wrong, try to correct it, and try again. Give yourself credit for trying.

• Reward yourself when you have done something that was difficult for you, like getting through a tough interview or persisting when you're discouraged. Buy yourself a book or record, a colorful T-shirt, a special lunch—something that will remind you of your achievement.

• If having all day free is undermining your initiative, create a new "job" for yourself that consists of a carefully planned day. Get up at a regular time and follow the schedule you have laid out for finding work, job training, volunteer work, meals, recreation, and/or self-improvement.

• Don't give in to discouragement and become passive or self-pitying. Don't overeat, sleep all day, overdrink, or complain excessively. Recognize that these are self-defeating behaviors.

• Keep your morale high by doing things that make your mind and body feel good. Learn techniques of relaxing, such as meditation, deep breathing, or yoga. Read the classics, or biographies of people who interest and inspire you.

• Don't be too proud to accept financial help, such as unemployment benefits, welfare, or food stamps. They are intended to help people through this difficult period. Your past and future taxes help pay for these resources.

• Don't allow your dependence on outside financial support to undermine your self-image or render you chronically dependent.

• Sort out the reasons you believe you lost your job. Search yourself carefully and honestly, because you need these answers to guide you at this crossroads point.

• Ask yourself whether you were doing your job properly and relating adequately to your supervisor and co-workers. If not, was it just a bad match between you and the situation, or was getting fired a signal that you need to examine your basic work attitudes, patterns of relating, and repertoire of skills?

• If you were working hard but not accomplishing what was expected, ask yourself whether you now see what you could have done differently. Are you willing to perform differently on your next job?

Do you need more training, or personal and career counseling? Help yourself in those ways if you need to.

• If you believe you were fired because "the system" is unfair, don't let that depress or discourage you so much that you stop trying. Carefully weigh the odds of your being able to change the system. Determine to succeed by sheer persistence, by learning to use the system to your advantage, or by seeking work in another field where the rules fit your values.

• If you feel strongly that the system is wrong and should be changed, consider involving yourself in trade-union, political, or social activities designed to do that.

• If you believe you were fired because of illegal discrimination, call the local Equal Employment Opportunity Commission (in the phone book under "U.S. Government") and talk to a Commission officer.

• Reassess your career or job goals. Take stock of your interests and skills. Ask yourself what you want to offer to society that it needs and will pay for. Ask yourself what steps are required for you to achieve that. Are you willing to get training, to serve an apprenticeship, to persist despite discouragements? How can you present yourself so convincingly to an employer that you will get the job?

• Examine your feelings about being a success in your work. Does the idea of high achievement make you uneasy? (See FEAR OF SUCCESS.)

• While you are not working, continue to be a creative, giving person by putting extra effort into personal relationships and helping others. Enjoy the comfort and warmth of your family and friendships. Help your children with homework, or play basketball with them. Help your spouse with some project you've been putting off. Play tennis with your spouse or friends. Do volunteer work.

• If you can afford to, refresh and nurture yourself by taking a vacation now. Take your camper and go fishing. Visit friends who live in Hawaii. See the Grand Canyon. Take a self-improvement course. Keep physically active by jogging, swimming, bowling, painting the house, or coaching Little League. Spend time teaching your kids how to do the same good things for themselves. Remain confident about finding work.

• Reassess the way you spend your money. Have you been working to finance a way of life that is not totally satisfying? Decide what expenses and possessions are really meaningful. Consider cutting back on things you don't really need. Buy a smaller, more economical car. Move to a smaller or less expensive home. Don't try to live up to others' standards and expectations.

• If you're having trouble deciding what kind of work you want or how to find it, ask yourself specific questions about what you need to decide, and then let your creative, unconscious mind work on the answers while you sleep at night or think about other things.

• Don't be embarrassed or discouraged if you decide you've been working at the wrong job, if you want to move on to a new kind of work, or if you're not sure what you want to do. Many people find their real direction and embark on a successful second career later in life.

• Don't panic and accept a job you really don't want, just because it's available. Don't let other people pressure you into taking a job because they think you should.

• If getting fired has depressed you greatly even though you are not in immediate financial difficulty, ask yourself whether your self-esteem has been too dependent on your profession or the fact that you had a job. Try to appreciate yourself as independent, unique, and valuable, aside from your work. Focus on ways in which you have succeeded in life—your marriage, relationships, helping others, sports—rather than on this temporary setback.

SUGGESTED READING:

Harding, William E. *Between Jobs*. 1976. Executive Enterprises, P.O. Box 6532, San Diego, California 92106.

See also: FEAR OF FAILURE, JOB DISSATISFACTION, MID-LIFE CRISIS, MONEY WORRIES, RETIREMENT, STRESS

GREED

"Greed" may sound like an old-fashioned, moralistic label for a problem. It was included as one of the original Seven Deadly Sins. Sometimes this problem is also called "avarice," or "miserliness." A more modern term is "materialism." It is related to envy and selfishness.

We are materialistic creatures by nature. Our physical needs are powerful and persistent. To survive we require money and the things it buys. We need food, shelter, clothing, transportation, etc. We easily get caught up in the belief that "more is better." If we have suffered from having been poor, hungry, or physically vulnerable, we may want to make extra sure that we have more than enough to protect us from ever suffering again. Acquisition of wealth may become an obsession, as if the bigger our supply of money and objects, the stronger and happier we will be. Hence the saying "Money isn't everything, but it's way ahead of whatever is in second place."

Our culture gives us many mixed messages about material success. We are taught that "money is the root of all evil" and that "money can't buy happiness." But we are also taught, in more subtle ways, that it is somehow shameful to be poor, and that visible success is a sign that we are among the favored few. Keeping up with the Joneses is a national pastime, even if Mr. Jones is a workaholic on the verge of a heart attack at age forty-three.

Are you a victim of your own greed? Here are some questions to answer and steps to take.

• Do you really enjoy the money and the possessions you already have? Do you make rewarding use of them? Or do you neglect to enjoy what you have because you are so busy trying to acquire more? If so, you may be hooked on getting rather than living.

• Take a careful look at what you have. Remember when you didn't have it, how much you wanted it, how hard you worked to get it, and how convinced you were that you'd be happy when you got it. Are you savoring it to the fullest? Or are you taking it for granted while you push on for more? If so, more won't help.

• Do you own your possessions or do they own you? Weigh the actual pleasure and meaning you get out of them against the amount of time, anxiety, and effort you spend trying to acquire them, hold on to them, maintain them, and pay for them. Some rich people become in effect the overworked servants of all the toys, gadgets, houses, and social roles they've purchased. Do you know how to make money work for you, or do you slip into working for it? Would more money really make your life better, or would you use the extra money to complicate your life in ways that would be more hassle than joy?

• Sort out your own true feelings and wishes regarding wealth from those attitudes brainwashed into you by your family, associates, or the mass media. Do you know what *you* want, rather than what you've been told to want?

• Drop the fantasy that rich people have it easy. Scott Fitzgerald said, "The rich are different from you and me." Hemingway replied, "Yes, they have more money." More often than not, having more money just means that you struggle with the usual assortment of human goals—trust, love, communication, purpose—in fancier settings. The pain of loneliness or self-rejection can be just as great amid luxury as simplicity. In fact, money can often serve as a dangerous distraction or shield to keep us from facing problems that we eventually must work through.

• Study rich people and learn how some use their money creatively, carefully, and pleasurably, while others use it self-destructively. Analyze yourself in comparison to those people. What are the areas of living where you'd trust yourself with more money, and what are the areas where you'd get into trouble?

• Be aware that greed focuses on acquiring and holding on, rather than creating and enjoying. Thus, greed may actually block your financial progress if it focuses you narrowly and selfishly on getting, instead of on giving something of value to society that people will pay you handsomely for.

• If you find yourself obsessed with greedy thoughts and schemes, look deeply at your relationships and career to see if you have neglected to build rewarding interpersonal exchanges that would naturally advance your well-being. Greed is often the consequence of failing to create a "rich" life composed of many assets in addition to money. Your efforts might better be aimed at establishing good "credit" with people by contributing effectively to common goals.

• Look at whether you are trying to cancel or disprove something by acting greedily. Is your self-esteem still suffering because you were poor as a kid? If so, try accepting yourself as a person separate from your life story, and *then* decide freely, not compulsively, what you want to do about money.

• Dedicate yourself to building up *all* your assets, including the ones money can't buy, such as health, capacity to love, appreciation of life. Learn to be grateful for small blessings. That way, if you do get rich you'll know how to enjoy it, and if you don't you'll be too busy living to notice.

SUGGESTED READING:

Goldberg, Herb, and Robert T. Lewis. *Money Madness: The Psychology of Saving, Spending, Loving, and Hating Money.* New York: William Morrow, 1978.

Wiseman, Thomas. *The Money Motive.* New York: Random House, 1974.

See also: COMPETITIVENESS, ENVY, GAMBLING, JEALOUSY, MONEY WORRIES, NARCISSISM

GRIEF

Grief is the natural, universal response to loss. In intense grief, you may become short of breath, your throat may tighten, and waves of uncontrollable crying may sweep over you. You may become listless and depressed, or nervous, irritable, and restless. You may become exhausted from sadness and crying. Grieving people often sleep poorly or not at all. When they do sleep, they may have nightmares. Some cannot eat or make love, while others overeat or feel desperately sexual.

The initial reaction to losing a loved one may be shock and disbelief, followed by a feeling of confusion, outraged anger, or guilt. It is hard to believe that grief is a healing process, but you must experience it in order to become whole again.

The most profound grief is usually felt at the loss of a spouse, child, or lover, and it is especially intense if the death was sudden and unexpected. You have had no time to say good-bye. You are caught in the midst of your life together—in mid-flight. There were so many things you wanted to do for that person, so much love to give, things you had always meant to say, restitution you wanted to make for past hurts. Even if a death has been gradual and expected, you may be filled with remorse and guilt for the things you have done or left undone. You may feel angry at your loved one for leaving you, and perhaps be ashamed of your feelings.

Some people torture themselves with the idea that they or someone else could have prevented the death. "If only I hadn't asked her to . . . then she wouldn't have been there when . . . ." "Perhaps the doctor could have prevented the death, if he were skillful enough, or if he had cared enough. Maybe it was the hospital's fault."

Such intense feelings are exhausting. You may begin to feel utterly hopeless and helpless. You feel you will never be the same again, that nothing will ever be the same. Coming to terms with the loss of people through death offers one of life's greatest challenges. The challenge is to survive, to grow, to feel finally strengthened and renewed, and to rebuild a full and satisfying life. You can help yourself do this through your mourning, your grief work.

• Face the fact of the loss. Denying it will prolong your grief. Even tell yourself out loud that the person has died. If you were not present at the death, see the body, if possible. This will help you confront the reality and begin your grief work.

• Release any self-torturing doubts you have about whether the death could have been prevented. What's done is done.

• Let yourself feel *all* of your feelings. The more fully you allow them to come out, the sooner they will begin to fade and gradually disappear. Then you can begin your rebuilding.

• If someone very close to you is dying, share your grief with him or her now, during life. Express any regrets for things you have done or not done; express your delight in the life you have had together. Try to resolve all of the unfinished business of your relationship. Above all, express the love you feel.

• Share your feelings with other people after the death. Accept their comfort and their help in making arrangements for the funeral or for seeing that you are taken care of.

• Take comfort in whatever religious or philosophical beliefs you have. Try to understand death as part of the process of life. Read one of the many encouraging books about creatively facing death.

• Participate in the rituals that have meaning for you. Go to the funeral and the burial; visit the grave and take flowers. Go to the memorial service or the wake, where you can share expressions of mourning. Talk about the dead person; eat and drink to his or her memory. Let yourself laugh about the wonderful and funny things you remember. Laughter may bring on tears—both are healing.

• Take time to sift through memories and objects, to build back into yourself that which you have lost. Help put the dead person's things in order. Help other survivors with their needs.

• Do not become bound to the past. Do something constructive with the dead person's belongings—give them to family members who care, to charity, or to someone else who needs them. Save only a few special things for yourself.

• Have a conversation in your mind with the dead person. Say all of the things you did not have a chance to say in life. Make apologies. Express appreciation and love. Forgive the person for leaving you, and ask forgiveness for yourself. Say good-bye.

• If there is some symbolic or practical action you can take to make amends for the past, do it.

• If there are children in the family, include them in the mourning and the talking. This will let them know they are not alone with their grief. It will also help them to understand death as part of the natural life cycle, and it will help them recover.

• Let go of the lost person by rededicating yourself to the living, including yourself. Understand that even though you are letting go, you will have him or her inside you always, as part of you. Live so as to honor the dead person's memory and to express the important values you shared.

• Fully accept the challenge to rebuild your life. When you have done your grieving well, you will have gained strength, wisdom, compassion, and an appreciation of life. Make specific plans to move forward in life. Celebrate and be thankful for the aliveness you find in and around yourself, and exercise your capacity to enhance it.

SUGGESTED READING:

Freese, Dr. Arthur. *Grief: Living Through It and Growing with It.* New York: Harper & Row, 1978.

Kübler-Ross, Elisabeth. *On Death and Dying.* New York: Macmillan, 1970.

Moody, Raymond. *Life After Life.* New York: Bantam Books, 1975.

See also: DEPRESSION, FEAR OF DEATH, LOSS OF LOVE

GUILT

It's one thing to feel guilt after actually doing something wrong or hurtful to another person. It's quite another to carry around a burden of excessive and unjustified guilt. The first sort of guilt is a signal from our conscience that we've violated our own sense of morality. This signal helps us regulate our social behavior and learn how to get along with others.

The second sort of guilt is a blight. It can paralyze us with fear, worry, anxiety, humiliation, and eventually a deep, possibly suicidal, self-loathing. The emotional fallout of needless guilt can range from chronic fatigue to such self-punishing behaviors as alcoholism, drug abuse, sexual dysfunction, accident-proneness, and psychosomatic illness.

A critical, unforgiving conscience turns against the self, nagging away at all sorts of thoughts, feelings, and acts. Frequently this crippling guilt is grounded in the past. We sometimes carry along harsh judgments from the past into the present, even though we have changed. The weight of this self-blame can be enormous: The guilt-ridden victim feels bad, worthless, unlovable, unfit for human companionship. Guilt can thus drive a wedge between an individual and the rest of the world. Perhaps even more painful and damaging, guilt can also separate us from ourselves: We can end up truly alone, without even ourselves for support and interior friendship.

This remorse and loss of self-esteem is like paying endless installments on a stiff fine for a past crime. Yet the guilt-ridden individual may never have done anything really wrong. Children are easily shamed into feeling unworthy and bad; some never grow out of this. Even if you can look back to some genuine past wrongdoing, beating yourself up with guilt feelings will only get in the way of your making changes and improvements that could enrich your life and that of others.

It's often very difficult to let go of guilt, whether or not it's justifiable. Some of us look for forgiveness by suffering—we think that if we endure enough guilty misery we will earn release. Some people find it easier to dwell on the past than to deal with the present—they concentrate on their old sins and avoid taking creative risks and assuming responsibility now. Compulsively paying off a debt of guilt to parents, spouse, or children can be a way of acting moralistically but actually neglecting to use one's freedom and power to do real good in the world.

Feeling excessively or inappropriately guilty is a psychological habit you can break. If you recognize guilt as a destructive force in your life, take this opportunity to look carefully at it so that you can understand it and get rid of it. By putting your guilt feelings into perspective you can begin working on becoming a more creative, self-assured, loving person.

• Distinguish between justifiable and excessive guilt. Have you really done something bad? Have you failed to do something you were legitimately obligated to do? How bad is your act or omission? How much real hurt has resulted? Have you exaggerated the seriousness of the situation?

• Try to make amends for genuine wrongs and then get on with living. If you've really caused some harm, what can you do to make things better? (Don't create a problem where there is none: Don't attempt to "make good" on something if the others involved do not feel that you've injured them, or if you would just make things worse.)

• Examine the standards by which you judge yourself. Are they standards you accept, or have they been drummed into you by others—parents, teachers, friends, clergy, bosses? Are they reasonable and necessary for the way you want to live? Would other standards seem more valid and meaningful to you?

• Accept your imperfections. Perfection may be a noble and sincere spiritual goal, but it is not part of the condition of human life. Perfection is an unattainable ideal, not a requirement for worthwhile, joyful living. People often have to act without full knowledge of the consequences. For example, even if they try their best, parents can never know enough to deal correctly with all the problems of child-rearing. Don't burden yourself with unrealistic demands. Don't expect yourself to be free of anger in oppressive situations. Don't punish yourself for lack of sexual purity in thought or deed.

• Accept that breaking old socially approved patterns and asserting your individuality may stir up some guilt in you, especially if others are affected. For example, a woman who has valued herself only in terms of her homemaking skills may have to deal with some guilt as she starts a career out of the house. A man who changes his job to find more fulfillment may feel guilty if he earns less and his family has to economize.

• Resist the guilt maneuvers of parents, spouses, friends, or employers. Watch out for the ways other people have a stake in keeping you guilty. It is not possible to win universal approval. No matter how hard you may try to mold yourself to external demands, you're not going to please everyone. The others in your life, however important to you, are all individuals responsible for their feelings. If you concentrate on living well and decently in the present according to standards that count for you, you will be able to deal creatively with other people's criticism or disappointment.

• Review your past. What have you actually done that makes you feel guilty? What can you learn from it? Face that you cannot change the past, but can learn from it and use its lessons to create a satisfying present.

• After identifying your guilts, look to the present. Do the guilt feelings you've dragged along out of the past keep you from doing things now? What things? What do you avoid now by living in a guilty past?

• Try confession. It is one of the most proven, traditional ways of absolving guilt. Use a religious form of confession, or a secular form such as talking to a friend or counselor. For example, perhaps you have some justifiable anger toward your parents that needs to be expressed to clear up a block in your relationship with them, but the guilty child in you makes you feel bad for that anger and prevents you from using it effectively. Don't overdo confession, though, as a means of wallowing in self-pity and guilt. Even strict religious systems allow for grace and forgiveness. One priest likes to point out that his church is a hospital for sinners, not a museum for saints. Excessive guilt in any form is destructive, so get it out of your system. Don't, however, get rid of it by dumping a hurtful confession on someone who is unprepared to hear it.

• Don't repress your guilt with alcohol, drugs, frantic activity, overeating, or other self-destructive escapist behavior. If you really believe you've done wrong, face it and do something about it. Apologize. Make amends. If you're bothered because you don't think you're living an honest, upright life, maybe you do need to change your behavior— maybe you have good reason to feel guilty. Mental and emotional health can be improved by choosing what you regard as worthwhile moral standards and living up to them.

• Talk to people who can help you review your decisions and feelings without imposing their own standards or jumping in too quickly with approval or disapproval, forgiveness or blame.

• Remind yourself regularly that past a certain point you are doing no one a favor by feeling guilty. There is no value to constant excessive guilt. It is far better to try to be cheerful and constructive. Forget your own past "bad deeds" and those of others.

• Watch out for guilt's close cousin, shame. Guilt can result from violating your conscience; shame results from not measuring up to an external standard. A shamed person feels small, unworthy, and embarrassed. He or she feels defective and fears being found out and exposed as inadequate and ridiculous.

• Identify the "judges" who try to guilt-trip you or shame you. Do they live in your own harsh conscience? Are they other people who hide destructive criticism behind a cloak of virtue? Do they speak for a repressive family or social environment? Recognize the way others use guilt and shame to diminish your self-respect and to control you. Resist this attempt to deny your worth and dignity. Recognize the way you may be using guilt or shame internally to control yourself. What are you afraid you might do if you weren't ashamed of yourself?

• Do not exploit shame and guilt as ways to control others, especially children. Sometimes shame is a handy way to "civilize" a child, to force conformity to important family and cultural rules. There are, however, ways to educate without encouraging shame and guilt. Do not make children feel that they are inferior or unworthy creatures. Give them the opportunity to try things, to take on new responsibilities, to make mistakes.

• Turn experiences of guilt into opportunities to clarify what your values really are, to practice the art of self-forgiveness, and to dedicate yourself more fully to living what you define as a good life in the present.

SUGGESTED READING:

Bry, Adelaide. *How to Get Angry Without Feeling Guilty*. New York: New American Library, 1977.

Smith, Manuel J. *When I Say No, I Feel Guilty*. New York: Bantam Books, 1975.

See also: ANXIETY, DEPRESSION, LONELINESS, MASOCHISM, PERFECTIONISM, SELF-HATE, SUICIDE

HALLUCINATIONS

Suppose while you are reading this book the printed page suddenly fades away and in its place appears the face of Johnny Carson telling you to relax and enjoy yourself. That could be a pleasant enough experience, depending on how you feel about Johnny Carson. What could make it unpleasant is the worry that your mind has gotten out of control. What will it do next? (What if the channel changed and you were confronted with J. Edgar Hoover back from the grave, telling you that you are a Commie pervert and he's coming to get you?) If you go back to the store where you bought the book and complain, you may find the clerk looking at you strangely.

Hallucinations can be entertaining and informative if you are prepared to accept and learn from them. But they can be terrifying if they intrude themselves on you and make you doubt your sanity.

Hallucinations can be visual or auditory, and sometimes people even smell things that no one else smells. Most people have had the experience, for example, of having a song's lyrics and melody unexpectedly go through their minds.

Hallucinations can be caused by deceiving external stimuli, drugs, physical illness, fatigue, or emotions and needs. The thirsty man crawling across the desert who sees a mirage of an oasis is having a hallucination caused by his desperate need for water, and possibly also by sunlight reflecting off the sand in a particular way. Many reports of flying saucers turn out to be the result of observers' misinterpreting unusual lighting effects in the sky. The kinds of hallucinations that are psychological danger signs are the ones traceable to a powerful disturbance within the person.

• If you have had a hallucination or worry that you may have had one, don't panic or jump to gloomy conclusions. Hallucinations should be taken seriously, but in a planned, constructive way.

• Talk to a trusted, supportive friend, relative, physician, clergyman, or counselor about your experience. Get some feedback on how unusual your experience was, and weigh it carefully.

• Ask yourself what else unusual is going on in your life that might be connected with the hallucination. Are you using drugs for recreational or medical purposes? Are you sick? Are you eating poorly? Have you changed your diet drastically? Are you getting enough rest? Are you under stress? Have you lost an important relationship? Have you done something or contemplated doing something about which you are in conflict? Are you lonely?

• If you fear that your hallucination may cause you to harm yourself or others, seek professional help. You may feel better if you are in a protected environment such as a hospital for a while.

• If other people are worried that you may harm yourself or others, listen to them carefully. Play it safe—if you feel you can trust them to have your best interests at heart, consider following their advice.

• Consult a physician to make sure your hallucination is not due to a physical condition. Choose a physician who will respect your feelings and needs, rather than one who will slap a label on you and push you into some treatment that may not suit you.

• Study the content of the hallucination carefully. Free-associate to it. Use it as a dream to tell you what may be going on in your unconscious. See if there is a message in it for you.

• Explore the possibility that you have gotten out of touch with some deep parts of yourself and you need to spend more time tuning in to what is happening outside your rational thinking. You may have become too controlled and practical, blocking out emotions that are now breaking through your defenses in the form of pictures and sounds. Or you may have neglected to maintain your security and support systems, so that your ties to the conventional world are too loose.

• Do simple, basic things that reaffirm your sense of who you are and that reconnect you to the parts of the world that you know and value. Call a close friend, reread a book you like, wear some favorite clothes.

• Draw and write down your hallucination in as much detail as possible. Describe and portray it methodically. If it frightens you, create a sequel that makes it come out the way you'd like it to.

• If you sift out what seems like a valuable message, see if you can plan constructive, realistic action based on it. Joan of Arc took her visions seriously against much opposition and changed the history of France.

• Remember, the definitions of what is normal and abnormal, real and unreal, visionary and crazy, vary from group to group and from time to time. Hallucinations can be reacted to and used in many different ways. Choose ways that suit you and that work out comfortably and safely in the environment where you must function.

Much of this advice also applies if you find yourself dealing with someone who appears to be having hallucinations.

• Be kind and respectful. Take the hallucination seriously as a powerful form of communication, even if you don't understand it. Consider whether the hallucination has some particular significance for your relationship to the person.

• Help the person check out possible medical problems.

• Encourage the person to follow the other advice presented here. Don't impose your own opinions, values, and judgments. Help the person make responsible, self-directed use of the experience to learn more about himself or herself.

SUGGESTED READING:

Fadiman, James, and Donald Kewman, eds. *Exploring Madness.* Monterey, Calif.: Book/Cole, 1973.

Shorr, Joseph E. *Go See the Movie in Your Head.* New York: Popular Library, 1977.

Wilber, K. *The Spectrum of Consciousness*. Wheaton, Ill.: Quest, 1977.

See also: DELUSIONS, NIGHTMARES

HOMOSEXUALITY

Research has shown that being homosexual doesn't necessarily mean a person is psychologically maladjusted or has a mental disorder. In fact, the 1978 Kinsey Report, *Homosexualities,* based on lengthy interviews with 1,500 persons, found that some homosexuals are happier than heterosexuals. However, the 40 percent of male gays who were classified as "asexuals" and "dysfunctionals" were tormented by their homosexuality and plagued with severe psychological, social, and sexual problems.

"The homosexual men," said the report, "tended to feel less self-accepting and more lonely, depressed and tense than did the heterosexual men. They also tended to worry more and to display more paranoia and psychosomatic symptoms." Twenty percent of the gay men had attempted suicide versus four percent of the straight men.

The American Psychiatric Association, which formerly classified homosexuality as a mental disorder, now uses the less negative term "sexual orientation disturbance"—and it is applicable only to gay people who feel depressed or upset about their sexual preference. Since the focus of our encyclopedia is on psychological *problems,* we will not be talking about the many gay people who feel comfortable about themselves. Our treatment of the subject focuses on the problems only in order to present the most effective current strategies for coping with the psychological difficulties of being a homosexual in America today.

For a while it was fashionable to expound at length on the "causes" of homosexuality, and there is now a vast literature on the subject, but is it relevant? One sentence will suffice: The male homosexual in his earliest years of life appears not to have completely "individuated" from his mother and not to have fully "identified" with the male role model set by his father. 'Nuff said.

The gay man's basic psychological problem results from the excruciating stress placed on him by the "homophobic," or antihomosexual, society in which he lives. Surveys show that over 72 percent of Americans believe that homosexual relations are "always wrong." From Dad's commands to "be a man," to schoolyard taunts, to the mass media bombardment with macho values, homophobia is all-pervasive. The growing gay male can't help but internalize the homophobic values of the culture. He feels a secret, unsharable differentness.

He succumbs to self-doubt, self-inquisition, self-hatred, shame, loneliness, anxiety, depression. "No one in the world understands or cares."

At first he is reluctant to admit his gayness even to himself. He denies it. He tries to change. He goes into psychotherapy and it doesn't work. He is burdened with guilt and despair. If he is living with his parents, he is forced to pretend interest in girls. If he is living with his wife, he is constantly worried about exposure. The experience of "coming out" is then traumatic. Whom should he tell? He fears rejection, ostracism. He fears that his career will be jeopardized. Will he never be able to have a family and children? Will he end up alone and loveless? Will the world forever relate to him as "a homosexual" rather than as an authentic individual person in his own right?

Because of all these pressures, it is not surprising that 80 percent of U.S. gay males hide their homosexuality in the "closet." Having made this decision, a homosexual must live a double life with a public identity and a private identity, living a lie, "passing" as straight, enduring the strain of deception and fear of exposure. He has to stage-manage his every move, word, and gesture. Since he can't allow himself to be seen in a gay bar or in the company of other homosexuals, his sexual contacts are restricted to anonymous encounters in "one-night stands" or steam baths—relationships devoid of commitment or caring. Where is his self-esteem now?

Perhaps all of this sounds like the bad old days before the joys of gay liberation, but no, the new Kinsey Report says that the 40 percent of male gays classified as "asexuals" and "dysfunctionals" had the following problems: Regret about being homosexual. Difficulties in finding a suitable partner and maintaining affection for the partner. Disagreements with partner about what kind of sexual activity should take place. Concern about not being sexually adequate. Difficulties in reaching orgasm. Impotence and premature ejaculation. Psychosomatic symptoms. Feelings of loneliness, worry, paranoia, depression, tension.

Compulsive "cruising" for quickie sex is nothing less than addictive sex—the frantic pursuit of the next orgasm or the perfect fantasy partner. The average Kinsey male homosexual reported sex acts with hundreds of men, and 40 percent of them had had more than 500 different sex partners. Besides being debilitating, time-consuming, and destructive, cruising is highly competitive and rejection is commonplace. How do you handle your hurt feelings when someone turns you down? Self-hatred. Depression. Cruising is bleakly depersonalized. Unlike heterosexual sex, there is little talk between homosexuals once they get in the act. How do you handle your disappointment after sex when you have not received the simple affection you need? Depression. Self-hatred.

Few males in our culture—gay *or* straight—have learned how to relate warmly and closely with other males. Gay men suffer from awkwardness about intimacy even though they seek it. Who makes the first move? Who follows? Who "leads" while dancing? How can the partner who subordinates himself feel like "a real man"? Can a man who submits to anal intercourse avoid feeling powerless and helpless? Straight *or* gay, American males exalt aggressiveness and virility and devalue warmth, tenderness, and sharing. Homosexuals, paradoxically, carry this macho mentality one step further—by oversexualizing it.

Now for the good news. The new Kinsey study reported that one half of the male gays were in stable relationships, either "closed-couples"— those living in the equivalent of good heterosexual marriages characterized by self-acceptance, contentment, and a high degree of sexual fidelity—or "open-couples"—those living as partners but with a fair amount of outside sexual activity.

There were many more "open-couples" than "closed-couples," however. "This suggests that a monogamous quasi-marriage between homosexual men is probably difficult to achieve," said the report, "and that most such relationships involve the pursuit of sexual contacts with persons other than one's partner." The chief difficulty, according to one sex authority, is that of developing a warm intimate relationship with a partner whom we unconsciously devalue as a person for engaging in sex acts with us which we define as degraded.

As with many of the problems covered in this book, including those that don't involve sex at all, we find at the core of the problem the person's lack of self-esteem. When we don't know who we are, or don't like who we think we are, we try all sorts of things to create a positive identity. But the very things we try, such as various forms of sexual relationships, can make us more confused or self-critical because our actions are desperate attempts to cancel inner self-hate. It is a big enough job for a heterosexual man to develop a positive self-concept. A gay man has the added burden of handling family ostracism, social rejection, public ridicule, police harassment, and job discrimination. His anxiety, depression, guilt, and self-hate can make him even more vulnerable at times when he needs lots of confidence and assertiveness to protect himself from being victimized or exploited.

If you are a gay male facing some of the problems described above, here are ways to begin coping with them:

• Affirm to yourself as positively as you can that homosexuality is simply one particular way of sharing pleasure with men. It is not a sin or a sickness in and of itself. Like any human activity, it can be misused. But remind yourself that the physical, sexual acts involved do not automatically "mean" anything bad about you. What counts is the amount of caring that you put into these and into all other actions.

• Spare yourself a psychological self-inquisition. Don't obsessively question yourself: How did I get this way? Is it a disease? Am I sick? Should I ask a therapist to cure me? Tortuous self-examination wastes energy that can be better spent on making the most of the opportunities you have for self-development and self-expression in whatever forms satisfy you.

• Go easy on your parents. For better or for worse, they raised you in the only way they knew how. Don't avoid your present responsibility for managing your gay lifestyle by blaming them for what they may have done in the past to make you gay. They will have plenty to do to cope with your being gay now. Help them adapt to that, and don't burden them with defending their past behavior.

• Don't fixate on the goal of converting yourself to heterosexuality. Most such attempts are based on self-rejection, and that is no basis on which you can achieve anything. Strained efforts to make yourself do the "right" thing will fail, and you will intensify your belief that you are one of nature's misfits. Let yourself be, learn all you can about yourself and life from what happens, and choose ways of life that feel naturally good to you. In the long run, that is the way you will be the most loving person, straight or gay.

• When you stop thinking of homosexuality as a sickness, you can stop looking for a "cure." Free yourself of the one-down predicament of having to pursue a remedy for a disease. Instead, exert your efforts to build up your personal assets and to create relationships where they are valued.

• Set up a "buddy system" of mutually caring friends who respect each other and who look out for each other's welfare. Being a lone wolf is too hard. Choose comrades who demonstrate loyalty and supportiveness, and who are not excessively competitive and selfish. Don't let sexual acquisitiveness jeopardize your trust in each other. Tell your buddies what you want from them, what you are offering, and why you think it will be to your mutual advantage.

• Involve yourself with a local gay group which will provide psychological support and enhance your self-image. You will learn from other homosexuals who function as role models how to handle parents, how to deal with job discrimination, how to handle your homosexual identity. (Recommended: The Advocate Experience, a weekend "learning and self-discovery" encounter held in various U.S. cities. Write: The Advocate Experience, 681 Market Street, Suite 302, San Francisco, California 94105.)

• If you have problems performing sexually, consult the entry on SEXUAL DSYFUNCTION in this book and explore the various sex-therapy techniques available. You don't have to suffer from sexual inadequacy—there are steps you can take.

• Ask your gay friends to introduce you to other gays. This is the easiest, safest, and most self-respecting way to meet potential lovers.

• Keep yourself open to a wide range of sexual possibilities, including heterosexuality, until you are sure of what you prefer. Resist pressure from yourself and others to define you prematurely as a particular type of sexual person. Remain open to changes, too. New types of partners and new activities may appeal to you as you move through various developmental stages.

• Get rid of any gay "stigma complex" you may have by thinking of yourself—and thus causing others to think of you—as a person first of all. Shrug off the sexual labels that get passed around so easily. Concentrate on your humanness, not on your category.

• Accept that there will always be homophobes and that *they* have a problem of intolerance. Steer clear of them; let them work on their problem without using you as a victim. Don't take their judgments seriously or internalize them.

• If someone calls you a faggot, simply respond with a friendly smile. Don't be defensive or try to back away or explain yourself. Shrug it off as if to say, "The charge may well be true, but so what?"

• Don't retreat in panic or submit guiltily to antihomosexual treatment at school, on the job, or in a residential area. But keep alert to places where gay people are accepted or welcomed. Change job, school, or residence if you can do better. You don't have to put up with discrimination. Some church groups have welcomed gay members.

• Give careful thought to the possibility that "coming out" might relieve you of the stress of secrecy and open up new opportunities for you.

• If you do decide to come out, don't disclose your gay identity in one grand pronouncement. Often the best strategy is simply to be gay in a relaxed, self-affirming way and let people draw their own conclusions. If a friend or relative seems confused or troubled about you, however, you might be able to smooth out your relationship with a personal talk.

• Make use of gay rap groups, gay consciousness-raising groups, and gay therapy groups to help you develop your identity and lifestyle after you come out.

• Consider rooming with another homosexual. This might help relieve some of the stress of loneliness and expensive rent. Choose someone toward whom you do not feel possessive or competitive. Be clear with each other what your expectations are in terms of sexual loyalty and social availability. Living alone, with your parents, or with someone straight can put you under stress and make it harder for you to develop as a person and as a sexual being. Provide yourself with a secure and supportive home base.

• Consistently define yourself as a regular dues-paying member of society. Refuse to see yourself or to let others see you as belonging to a special category of freaks. You pay taxes, do your job, and help keep civilization going as best you can.

• Don't shun all heterosexuals just because you are gay. They are people too, and there is much you can share with them. The struggles of straight and gay people are much the same beneath the superficial differences. Learn to give and take in a wide variety of ways with many people.

• Choose some men who are good role models of the kind of gay man you want to be. Keep your own individuality, but learn from men you admire. There are authors like Merle Miller, athletes like Dave Kopay, politicians, businessmen, musicians, and mechanics who are gay and leading effective lives.

• Develop a clear, identifiable, positive image of yourself that you present to the world. You don't have to become pretentious and phony. Make a statement as to who you are that people will recognize and respect. Dress and talk with character. Learn to entertain well if you enjoy it. Polish up any amateur or professional performing skills you have. Don't hide your light under a basket just because you are gay. You have the same needs as anyone—to be acknowledged as an attractive and valuable member of the human race.

• Remember that you are not just a homosexual. You are also a person who feels and does lots of things besides sex. Don't get overly focused on your sexual orientation just because sometimes it is a problem. Cultivate passionate interests in other aspects of life. Give yourself fully to causes and ventures. Develop skills and caring, responsible relationships. This will give you a solid foundation from which to deal with whatever turmoils occur in your sex life. Helpful organizations: (to locate a nearby gay organization) The National Gay Task Force, Room 506, 80 Fifth Avenue, New York, New York 10011 (telephone 212-741-1010). Information on Parents of Gays chapters in various cities and towns may be obtained by contacting Parents of Gays, % Metropolitan Duane Methodist Church, 201 W. 13th St., New York, New York 10011.

SUGGESTED READING:

Bell, Alan P., and Martin S. Weinberg. *Homosexualities: A Study of Diversity Among Men and Women*. New York: Simon & Schuster, 1978.

Clark, Don, Ph.D. *Loving Someone Gay*. Millbrae, Calif.: Celestial Arts, 1977.

Silverstein, Dr. Charles, and Edmund White. *The Joy of Gay Sex: An Intimate Guide for Gay Men to the Pleasures of a Gay Lifestyle.* New York: Crown, 1977.

Tripp, C. A. *The Homosexual Matrix*. New York: Signet, New American Library, 1976.

See also: ANXIETY, DEPRESSION, GUILT, LESBIANISM, LONELINESS, LOVE ADDICTION, PROMISCUITY, SELF-HATE, SEXUAL PERVERSIONS, SUICIDE

HYPERTENSION

Hypertension is a treacherous problem in that it usually has no symptoms. The symptoms often thought to be associated with high blood pressure, such as anxiety, dizziness, and rapid pulse, are more often symptoms of stress instead. Thus, you usually don't know you have hypertension until someone (probably your doctor) or something (perhaps the blood pressure machine at the supermarket) shows you that you do. If you have a blood pressure with the first reading greater than 145 or the last number greater than 90, you are considered hypertensive.

Hypertension is now of epidemic proportions in the United States. The latest estimates are that one out of every three adults is hypertensive, with an even higher proportion among blacks. Out of the 60 million hypertensive Americans, only 23 percent are adequately controlling their blood pressure; 48 percent are aware that they have hypertension but are not adequately controlling it; and 29 percent are not even aware that they have the problem. The dangers of hypertension are definite and extreme—the higher your blood pressure is and the longer it goes uncontrolled, the greater your chances of serious organ damage, heart attack, stroke, and/or death. For example, a thirty-five-year-old male with a blood pressure of 145/95 is expected to live *nine years less* because of his elevated blood pressure level; with a blood pressure level of 150/100, he is expected to lose *sixteen years* of life!

It is important to keep tabs on your blood pressure by checking it a minimum of once a year if you have no history of hypertension, once every three months if you have a hypertensive history. Your local American Heart Association chapter can tell you where to go for a free or inexpensive reading, or you can purchase the equipment and learn to take your blood pressure at home. If you learn to take your own, do it once a week.

There are two types of hypertension: essential (sometimes called "primary") and secondary. If you discover that your blood pressure is high, you should see a physician to help you determine which type you have. Secondary hypertension is diagnosed when the hypertension has some clear cause whose correction allows the blood pressure to return to normal.

Unfortunately, more than 99 percent of hypertensive individuals have essential hypertension, the exact cause of which is unclear. Contributing factors seem to include heredity, a lack of proper exercise, excess weight, and excess salt intake. Psychological stress also seems to be a major factor in essential hypertension.

What can you do to lengthen your life by lowering your blood pressure and/or reducing the amount of medications you need to take to control high blood pressure? A lot!

• Realize that you have a great deal to do with what goes on in your body. You are probably contributing to your hypertension. If you want to overcome high blood pressure and preserve your body's health, examine what you are doing to "feed it," and commit yourself to change. You can achieve reassuring results by putting time and energy into healing yourself.

• Adjust your diet to lose excess weight. If you are ever going to do it, do it now. Find a way that works for you, that you can tolerate. Yes, it's difficult, but there are good programs to help, such as Overeaters Anonymous. If you slowly but surely make the necessary basic changes in your food habits, you can probably lengthen your life.

• Reduce the amount of salt you use. Do it by willpower for two weeks, and suddenly you'll start recognizing the subtler tastes of foods. Then you won't need salt for the taste anymore.

• Work more exercise into your lifestyle, the kind that strengthens your heart and improves your circulation. This includes running, rapid walking, swimming, and bicycling. Begin slowly and build up. Choose activities that you like and that fit with your age and physical condition. (Consult your physician.) Exercise at least three or four times each week. Build up your wind slowly. Try exercising with other people—it's fun to share being healthy!

• Release stress! Learn to let it go whenever it starts to build up. Several facts are important here. First, stress does not result only from negative events—any change involves stress, even if it is a positive change (marriage, for example, or a job promotion). Second, the goal is not to avoid stress—stress is both a natural part of life (since change is a part of life) and an unavoidable part of living in this culture today. The idea is to *deal well* with stresses—to release them appropriately, rather than expressing them through your blood pressure.

• Make yourself aware of the several types of negative stress.

• First, there are little stresses you can't do anything about, like having to wait forty-five minutes for an appointment. Catch yourself as you begin to get upset, as your stomach starts to get tense and your head starts to react. Say to yourself, "Hold on a minute—there's nothing I can do about this wait. It's a part of life. It won't help anything to get upset, and it will harm my body. And my body is my friend. I really need it to do things for me, so I'll choose to take good care of it and protect it."

Consciously begin to allow whichever muscles have become tense to relax, to loosen. Allow the tension to release, to melt and flow away. Loosen your jaw, shake your arms, and breathe slowly and deeply into your stomach.

If you must unexpectedly wait for something, decide early if you will wait or not, and then either leave or make use of the waiting time. Engage in some other activity or consider it a gift of time just for you, to relax and daydream, since there's nothing else you can do anyway. Keep reminding yourself to make positive use of the time. Concentrate on allowing whatever tension you find accumulating in your body to melt away, fade away.

• Second, some little stresses keep repeating themselves, like a co-worker's annoying behavior or a friend's continual lateness. Become aware of your repeating stresses. As soon as you recognize one, take action. Consider these possibilities: *Try to change the situation.* For example, talk to the other person(s) involved. Identify for him or her what it is he or she does and how it makes you feel. Negotiate how the two of you can deal with the situation better to minimize discomfort on both ends. *Accept the fact that the situation will not change.* Then, whenever it recurs, remind yourself that it is nothing new. Acknowledge that you have chosen to allow it to recur for reasons that you feel are more important than forcing a change. *If you must, leave the situation,* because the stress it causes you is greater than the reasons for staying. Be conscious about choosing one of these approaches.

• Third, you may experience fairly continual stress and tension. This often means you are avoiding change. It is likely that you are involved in something you should change (for your own well-being) but are resisting changing because change will require some upheavals in your external circumstances and/or your internal world. Face that there is no such thing as successfully avoiding: Right now the conflict is being expressed in your blood pressure. You must begin to face whatever is wearing at you and at least consider taking some action to change it, even if it implies major changes and is frightening for a number of reasons. You don't even necessarily have to make a change —but you must at least face your upset and allow yourself to feel the different emotions associated with it. Talking about it with others helps; explore the situation with friends or a therapist, even for a short period of time. Meanwhile, the general relaxation technique described below can help somewhat.

• At the end of each day, take twenty-five minutes to do the following writing: For each significant event of the day, describe what happened, write down your emotional reactions to the event (as many as you are aware of, even if some seem to contradict each other), and write down possible actions you might take to deal with this situation or event. Do this also for any situations, past or future, that are on your mind. If you seem to run out of things to write about before the twenty-five minutes are up, just sit and relax; often more will come to mind. When you are writing about your emotional reactions, allow yourself to feel the emotions, thus allowing the writing to be a stress-releaser.

Do this for three to four weeks consistently. Then review your writing; you may be surprised to find it quite revealing. Identify the types of stress you deal with most often, and use the suggestions just discussed to deal with them. You might want to continue (or occasionally return to) this writing to deal with stress in your life.

• Learn a meditation or general relaxation technique. If you are looking for just one relaxation technique to start with, see the one that follows. Once it is working for you, you may be pleased to notice that you are becoming eager to make some of the other changes, even those which had been difficult for you to carry through in the past.

Use this technique once each day. This minimum frequency is critical to develop the effects. Choose a relatively regular time to do it so that it becomes part of your daily routine. Try before dinner, if this is workable for you. Make a written record of your sessions. Close yourself off to minimize distractions and insure that you won't be interrupted: This is *your* time.

Lie down on a bed or the floor and get comfortable; loosen any tight clothing; take off jewelry. Each time before you begin, take a few moments to remind yourself what this is about and how important it is to you. You are trying to do something for your body, for your health. Realize that this day's practice, each and every day's practice, is important. Know that this session will take you twenty-five minutes whether you are restless or relaxed, so you might as well relax and really get into it. If your mind begins to wander at any time, bring it gently back; allow yourself to be fully involved in this relaxation experience.

Begin your relaxation session by closing your eyes, and taking a few slow, deep breaths. For the first two weeks of practice, you will be tensing and relaxing each major muscle group in your body, moving progressively from head to foot. Start by tensing your forehead—tense tightly, but do not strain. Feel the tension, then let out half the tension and hold—feel it—and then let all the tension out, allowing the muscles to relax completely. Repeat this, then move on to the next body area, always continuing to breathe slowly and deeply. Take approximately twenty-five minutes to move through your body.

With consistent practice, by the end of your sessions you will be achieving a very pleasant state of deep muscle relaxation. You will also have learned how to recognize tension, so that you will start becoming aware of unnecessary muscle tension and begin to allow the muscles to relax. Avoid falling asleep during your sessions by keeping the room cool or working on the floor. Losing awareness for brief periods of time, however, is fine; it is likely that you are entering a very relaxed state of consciousness.

After two weeks, change the exercise to leave out the deliberate tensing. Move your awareness progressively down your body, allowing what tension you may find in each muscle group to melt away, flow away. Move through your scalp, forehead, face, front and back of your neck, shoulders, chest, back, waist, upper arms, lower arms, wrists, hands, fingers, groin, buttocks, thighs, knees, calves, ankles, feet, and toes. Continue to breathe slowly and deeply as you allow all the tension in your body to melt away. When you have finished with your toes, take a few moments to survey your body with your awareness, and wherever there may still be tension, allow it to melt away, flow away.

When you end your sessions, do not jolt yourself out of the very pleasant state of relaxation that you have achieved, but carry this feeling with you into your next activity.

You can use parts of this second technique at any time during the day that you notice you are tense. Allow twelve weeks of daily practice before you evaluate the effect on blood pressure; the blood pressure effect will happen on its own and takes this amount of time to develop fully. Then work with your physician to determine what level of medication you need at this point to maintain a normal blood pressure. Although the full blood pressure effect takes twelve weeks, you can expect to experience some nice side effects much sooner. These can include a greater sense of relaxation, a new perspective on various aspects of your life, and a greater sense of general well-being.

• Now begin to integrate this technique into your regular lifestyle in whatever way works best for you and maintains the positive effects you have derived from it.

• Learn to use imagery for self-healing. Recent biofeedback research has demonstrated that people can learn to use their minds to affect physical processes that were previously thought to be beyond conscious control. Imagery seems to be the language our bodies understand. You can use imagery to ask your body to do what you need it to do to achieve a lower blood pressure. Developing this mind/body connection takes time and practice. You must be willing to work to develop it. It is like a never-used muscle: It takes time to develop control over it and make it strong. The rewards, however, are great; the potential for self-healing may be unlimited.

To use imagery you must first learn about hypertension, what is actually going on incorrectly in your body with your blood flow and pressure. Look at pictures. Learn what needs to happen to allow lower blood pressure. After working with the first relaxation exercise described earlier for two weeks, progress to the second exercise described, and condense it into a ten-minute period. At the end of each ten-minute exercise, image in your mind as best you can exactly what is going on in your body in its elevated blood pressure state. See it happening, feel it, hear it—sense the situation as fully and as vividly as possible. Dramatize it in your mind in any way that feels right to you. Practice—your ability to image vividly will increase over time.

Now image the situation being healed—see, feel, sense exactly the changes that need to take place for your blood pressure to become normal. Then image your blood flowing perfectly, freely, with no excess pressure. Pour your energy into imaging both the healing process and this final, totally healthy state. Image it fully.

Now move to imaging yourself bathed in a healing white light. Pull some of this healing energy into your body with every slow, deep breath—into every cell in your body, nourishing, soothing, healing, and revitalizing every cell. Then, with your every exhalation, send this white healing energy down your spine, out your feet, and into the ground. Spend approximately fifteen minutes on these images. Then slowly bring yourself back to the external world, feeling refreshed, energized, and well.

You may be surprised and pleased to find that with the use of these techniques your life can become not only longer but also deeper and lighter! Use them and *enjoy.*

SUGGESTED READING AND LISTENING:

Fineberg, E. Janna. *Relaxation and Hypertension Cassette Tapes.* Blood Pressure Self-Management Program, c/o Psychology Clinic Office, 2191 Franz Hall, UCLA, Los Angeles, California 90024.

Galton, Lawrence. *The Silent Disease: Hypertension.* New York: Crown, 1973.

Margie, Joyce D., and James C. Hunt. *Living with High Blood Pressure: The Hypertension Diet Cookbook.* Bloomfield, N.J.: HLS, 1978.

See also: ANXIETY, OVEREATING, PSYCHOSOMATIC ILLNESS, STRESS

HYPOCHONDRIA

A person with hypochondria is overly concerned with his or her health, believing it is worse than the doctor says, and persisting in this belief in spite of all evidence to the contrary. "I've had this indigestion and this pain in my stomach for years. I know it's an ulcer, but the doctors can't seem to find it." The pain or other symptom usually doesn't respond to treatment: "I've tried all kinds of medicines, but nothing really helps." Sometimes hypochondria is a fear of something fatal: "The doctors tell me there's nothing wrong with my colon. But I know these pains mean I have cancer. It's in the family—my grandmother died of it. Why won't the doctors believe me?"

Perhaps each of us has a touch of hypochondria from time to time, fearing that a lump or ache may turn out to be the beginning of a dreaded disease. We are certainly deluged with enough information about diseases to make us fearful of them. But a true hypochondriac becomes obsessed with what each symptom "really" means, talking about them constantly and going from doctor to doctor, never finding a cure. Each symptom may be from any number of causes, such as tension, indigestion, poor circulation, or whatever, but the hypochondriac "knows" it is something far more serious and becomes anxious, depressed, and exhausted with worry.

Hypochondria seems like a difficult way of life, yet a hypochondriac does receive the rewards of attention and caring from doctors, family, and friends, can control others by means of imagined or exaggerated illness, and also can escape from many kinds of life risks, such as meeting new people or being a vigorous, independent person.

If you recognize yourself as being obsessed about a worrisome illness that your doctors cannot diagnose and cannot cure, and if you do not enjoy such stress, you can do something about it. Determine to start building a lifestyle that provides you with nurturing attention, personal achievement, and other satisfactions in your everyday life that will make it unnecessary for you to continue to hide yourself in sickness.

• If you have a physical symptom that is painful, chronic, or frightening, go to a doctor. If you doubt the doctor's diagnosis, get a second or even third medical opinion.

• If the doctors can find nothing major wrong but your conviction that you are ill persists, consider the possibility that you are mentally exaggerating, or imagining, the seriousness of your symptom.

• Learn the difference between hypochondria and psychosomatic illness. A psychosomatic illness is a real disorder brought about at least partially by emotional stress. The cause of a psychosomatic illness may be hard to diagnose, but the symptoms of the illness are very real and troubling. Hypochondria is when we use our anxious imaginations to create or exaggerate symptoms and when we hang on to the idea that we are sick because we are getting something out of it. Don't let someone accuse you of hypochondria if you have pain or physical malfunctioning, even if it is hard to diagnose. But face the fact that you may be hypochondriacal if you find yourself searching eagerly for problems that hardly exist.

• Ask yourself whether your belief that you are ill has caused you to limit your relationships and lifestyle. If so, recognize this as a possible indication of hypochondria, and think about the possibility of making yourself well by opening up your life.

• Seek out nurturing relationships—people who give you a feeling of trust and confidence, who are interested and caring about you as a person. Try to enjoy them in a positive, joyful way, rather than overburdening them with your problems. Recognize that your doctor may also represent a mature, supportive parent figure to whom you truly enjoy relating, so appreciate that experience too. But don't cling to your doctor as your only friend.

• Practice giving and receiving physical contact with your spouse, family, or close friends. Enjoy massages, hugs, and affectionate gestures. Get some physical therapy. Choose medical practitioners whose professional touching makes you feel confident and cared for. Don't be embarrassed to acknowledge to yourself your very human need for physical attention.

• Ask yourself whether you have ever fully expressed your feelings of sadness, self-pity, anger, or resentment about the past, particularly your childhood. Most people have these feelings, and expressing them may make you feel better physically. If this seems difficult, find a professional therapist to help you relieve yourself of past hurts that may be making you fear you are sicker than you are.

• Try to imagine what you would be like if you were suddenly completely well. If you draw a blank, this may be because you now think of yourself mostly in terms of your illness and you need to build up a sense of yourself as an energetic, functioning person. Fantasize about getting rid of your illness and finding out who you really are.

• Consider the possibility that your symptoms stem at least partially from life stresses. (See STRESS and PSYCHOSOMATIC ILLNESS and start working on the suggestions offered.)

• Don't get hooked on medication, especially when it no longer seems to be helping. Try to follow a sensible diet and exercise program—whatever your doctor will allow, not what you think your sickness limits you to.

• Don't blame your illness for life difficulties or inadequacies that you feel. Accept and forgive yourself for being imperfect, as we all are. If you feel inadequate in a specific area, think about how you can remedy that, such as through classes, exercise, or reading. Stop thinking you have to have an illness as an excuse or disguise for normal human feelings of shyness, self-doubt, or anxiety.

• Don't use your illness to blame, punish, or control others. If you hear yourself thinking "Look what you've done to me" or "I can't have fun, so others shouldn't either," recognize that these negative thoughts keep you from growing free of your obsession with sickness. Try to relate in more positive, health-producing ways.

• If you think you eat, drink, or smoke too much, don't punish yourself by suffering guilt-produced fears of illness. Find out the facts about the consequences of what you do, and deal realistically with that knowledge.

• If you hear a story about someone's disease that doctors didn't diagnose until too late, don't use that to prove your beliefs about your illness. Admit to yourself that such cases are quite rare.

• Try extending yourself to other people in life-affirming ways through such activities as volunteer work. Help in a day-care center, read to the blind, teach arts and crafts in a parks program. Pass along your own life knowledge for the benefit of others. Appreciate yourself as a caring person who is more healthy than unhealthy.

• Don't fall prey to quacks, but do look into alternative healing philosophies or therapies, especially the holistic approach that treats both mind and body. Try to follow a philosophy that makes you feel like a good person inside and promotes your independence. Be aware that investing money in a healer's enterprise is never part of a legitimate healing process.

• Spend time planning what you would like to do when you start feeling better. Find out what's going on in the world that you want to participate in. Think back to your earlier unfulfilled dreams and ambitions. Let yourself turn on and determine to pursue some goal. Start now, in whatever way you can, despite your concern about illness. Let yourself become absorbed in living instead of in your symptoms. Take genuine pleasure in whatever you accomplish, and keep going.

• Don't pass your fear of illness on to your children by making a big deal out of their symptoms. Take them to the doctor only when necessary. Treat them lovingly when they're ill, but don't pamper. Teach them to expect good health and to trust that their bodies can heal most minor ailments. Teach them respect for their bodies through nutrition and exercise. Don't talk unduly about your own health problems.

• Learn that expecting good health tends to promote it, just as expecting ill health can contribute to illness.

• If you are the spouse or close friend of a person troubled with hypochondria, don't fall into the trap of restricting your life because he or she must restrict his or hers. When you do choose to limit yourself for his or her sake, take pleasure in the rewards you get for being a caring and loving person, and then get on with the rest of your living.

• If you feel you want to, try to give your friend or spouse nurturance such as touching and sympathetic listening, and acting as a loving parent would. This may lessen his or her need to consult doctors. Give this nurturance especially for positive, health-producing behaviors rather than for illness. Do what you can to encourage the person to pursue outside interests and activities.

• Keep in mind that hypochondriacs usually cannot believe that part of their illness is imaginary, and they resist professional therapy. Consider trying to persuade the person to try it anyway.

SUGGESTED READING:

Taylor, Dr. Robert B. *Doctor Taylor's Self-Help Medical Guide.* New York: Signet, New American Library, 1977.

Ulene, Dr. Art. *Feeling Fine.* Los Angeles: Tarcher/St. Martin's Press, 1977.

See also: DEPENDENCY, FEAR OF SICKNESS, MASOCHISM, OBSESSION, PAIN, PASSIVITY

HYSTERECTOMY

It is very difficult for a woman to give up her uterus—for any reason —without feeling some anxiety about her femaleness. Even women who have chosen never to bear children can find the finality of a hysterectomy scary and unsettling. The womb is that organ so especially woman's that it has acquired great symbolic significance. Even if she chooses never to use it, the potential for creating life is a part of nearly every woman's sense of wholeness and self.

Many women associate the capacity to bear children, the regular monthly cycle of fertility, with sexual attractiveness and sexual appetite. They fear losing their sex appeal and their desire along with their uterus. Many women worry that the aftermath of the surgery will be disfiguration—a scar that will make them less wanted by their husbands or lovers.

Hysterectomy, like any other major surgery, requires a time of recuperation and dependence on others for help. Women who are used to caring for themselves or for others—family, friends, a career—may find it hard to accept the physical needs and limits imposed by surgery. They may find it difficult to relax and let others help by preparing food, cleaning house, or taking care of business responsibilities. Dependency can be uncomfortable and upsetting.

Major surgery always carries risks. It is almost impossible to face it without worrying about the safety of the procedure, the effects of the anesthetic, the likelihood of postoperative complications. The need for such surgery, which always forces us to consider the possibility of death, may occur at a time when we are not prepared to confront our mortality. (See FEAR OF DEATH.)

It is not foolish or immature to have these feelings. Currently, hysterectomies are performed more often than any other major surgery in the United States. Some medical authorities estimate that over one-third of these operations are unnecessary. Hysterectomies produce a startling 50 percent complication rate. Many of the complications are quite serious: excessive blood loss, unexpected clots, negative reactions to anesthesia, infection, pneumonia, urinary problems that sometimes require additional corrective surgery. Some women do not survive a hysterectomy.

• A hysterectomy should not be agreed to for any reason but compelling medical necessity. Do not remove a healthy organ just because you've had all the children you want. The mere chance that cancer could develop doesn't justify removing your uterus; by the same logic you could remove every part of your body that could possibly develop a cancer.

• Hysterectomy is not a cure for lower back pain. It is not an appropriate treatment for fibroid tumors (benign overgrowths of uterine muscle), either. Fibroids often atrophy during menopause. In the absence of bleeding or other discomfort, they can be left to themselves. They are most unlikely to develop into malignancies.

Hysterectomy is indicated for treatment of uterine cancer, procidentia (protrusion of part of the uterus through the vagina), and excessive bleeding that does not respond to other methods (such as hormone therapy or a D-and-C).

How do you know if you need a hysterectomy? How do you deal with the feelings and changes it will bring?

• Choose a gynecologist you can trust. Seek out someone who has time for you as a person, who respects your feelings, concerns, and fears. Don't stay with a physician who refuses to answer your questions or who discourages you from asking about your diagnosis and treatment. Don't stay with a physician who demands that you turn over your one and only body, no questions asked. Don't stay with a physician who makes you feel childish or foolish because you are curious or afraid. (See FEAR OF SICKNESS.)

• If the gynecologist you have been seeing for your regular pelvic exam and Pap test (*Never neglect these!*) diagnoses a condition requiring a hysterectomy, get a second opinion from a surgeon who knows he or she will *not* be the one to perform the operation should you decide to have it. A competent, reliable physician will never be disturbed by your wish to get an outside opinion. Ask your health plan, your family physician, or the county medical association for a referral to an appropriate specialist. Check his or her credentials in a reference such as the *Directory of Medical Specialists* at the public library.

• Inform yourself thoroughly. Insist that your surgeon, the anesthetist, and all the other medical personnel you encounter explain what they will do and why. Have your surgeon explain your physical condition and the operation in detail, including the preoperative and postoperative procedures. Make sure you know what to expect, so you won't be frightened by standard procedures. Don't be put off by a bossy technician or surgeon—it's your body.

• Before making your decision, discuss alternatives. Find out what other treatments might be considered first. Think about how the surgery will affect all the aspects of your life. Discuss it with your husband or lover. If possible, give yourself time to get used to the idea and to prepare yourself emotionally.

• If only the uterus is removed, and not the ovaries, the surgery will not bring on menopause. You will heal, your scar will fade, you'll be as sexy and desirable as ever—maybe more so without the concern of unexpected pregnancy. If your ovaries are removed, however, the sudden sharp drop in estrogen production will cause menopausal symptoms to begin. You will need to confront—perhaps much earlier than expected—the significant changes of menopause. (See MENOPAUSE.) Remember, though: Menopause is not a disease. It does not end your sex life, ruin your attractiveness, or brand you as worn out.

• Expect to be emotionally upset by the surgery. Expect to have feelings of loss, anxiety about dying, fears about the future. Accept your feelings. Don't blame yourself for normal depression. (See DEPRESSION.)

• Expect to go through a period of mourning for your lost fertility—even if you thought you would never want children or if you think you have had all the children you ever wanted. (See GRIEF.) As time passes, you may find that even if you can no longer give birth you would still like to share all that you are with a child. If so, investigate adoption opportunities in your community. Find a child who needs you (and whom you need) and begin to do that sharing. We all have a lot more to give than just our genes.

• Move into action again as you regain your physical strength. Return to your work optimistically—you did survive; you're alive and have more to contribute to your world. Think about new things you want to undertake, skills you want to renew or acquire, a career change you've put off. We all need meaningful work, in our homes and out in our communities—in civic, church, recreational, or business activities —in order to feel productive and significant. Go back to your commitments and/or develop new ones. With or without a uterus, you are a complete and necessary person.

• Pay attention to your own needs. Keep up or develop refreshing side interests, crafts or hobbies, or sports. Deepen your friendships— there's nothing like the scare of mortality to make you recognize your affection and need for other people. Take care of your appearance. Watch your weight and your general health. Restore your feelings of attractiveness.

• Renew your sexual activity with confidence. Your feminine nature does not depend on your reproductive organs after all. You may in fact experience a heightened sex drive and an increased willingness to share and experiment with your partner. You will discover that your sexual responsiveness has not been reduced (and this is true for menopause, too). A positive attitude toward yourself will be rewarded with a return to the positive sexual experiences that preceded your surgery.

SUGGESTED READING:

Boston Women's Health Book Collective. *Our Bodies, Ourselves,* 2nd rev. ed. New York: Simon & Schuster, 1976.

Jameson, DeeDee, and Roberta Schwalb. *Every Woman's Guide to Hysterectomy: Taking Charge of Your Own Body.* Englewood Cliffs, N.J.: Spectrum, Prentice-Hall, 1978.

See also: FEAR OF SICKNESS, MENOPAUSE, STERILIZATION, VASECTOMY

IMPOTENCE

This problem consists of the inability to get or keep an erection in sexual activity. Some men just don't get an erection even though they are sexually excited. Other men get an erection, but lose it before they can engage in intercourse, usually just before they are about to insert their penis into the vagina. (If you lose your erection before intercourse because you ejaculate or come, then you have a different problem—see PREMATURE EJACULATION.)

Some men have this problem all the time, while others have it just with a particular partner or in a particular situation. If you have trouble getting or keeping an erection just with a particular partner, begin by asking yourself honestly: "How do I feel about her as a person? As a sexual partner? Am I angry or resentful toward her? Do I really want to make love to her? Does she frighten me in any way? Do I feel anxiously pressured to measure up to her expectations?"

Similarly, if your difficulty with erections is limited to a particular situation—after oral sex, in hotels, during your partner's menstrual period—ask yourself what is different about that situation and how this affects you emotionally and sexually. Your body is designed so that it will not function sexually when you are anxious, so the solution to your problem may lie in discovering what makes you anxious and dealing with it. For example, if your fear of your partner's bleeding during menstruation makes it hard to get an erection when having sex at that time, you may need to explore the source of your fear and dispel it.

Sometimes men think they have a problem with erection because it doesn't happen easily or quickly or often enough. If this is the case with you, you need to examine your expectations. Do you expect to have an erection without having your penis touched? Many men, especially as they get older, need direct, strong stimulation of the penis to get an erection. You may simply need to explain this to your partner. Also, there is a natural limit to how many erections a man can have one right after another. Are you expecting too much of yourself? Are you willing to be realistic about your sexual functioning?

If you conclude that you do have a problem with erections, you may need to examine your own attitudes about this. A lot of myths and prejudices surround impotence. The word itself means "powerless," and a lot of abuse is heaped on men who have this sexual problem. Often men who have difficulty getting or keeping erections feel that they are therefore less masculine. It is simply not true that having erectile difficulties has anything to do with a man's masculinity or sexual prowess.

Erectile difficulties simply occur when distracting thoughts or worries interfere with the body's natural response to sexual excitement. Unfortunately, men often place so much importance on getting an erection as soon as they are aroused that their worry about getting an erection may keep them from getting one. If after a short period of sexual excitement a man notices that he has no erection and begins to wonder "What's wrong with me—am I impotent?", he usually becomes too uptight to get more sexually excited and get an erection. As someone once said, "The harder you try, the softer it gets."

Another myth about erection problems is that a man naturally becomes "impotent" as he gets older because his body deteriorates. This is not true! Most men are *physically* able to have erections well into their senior years. However, because they don't expect to have erections or are worried about them, older men *do* more often have trouble getting erections.

There are a few physical states which interfere with getting an erection. Common ones are being on alcohol or taking sleeping pills. Blood pressure medications, prostate gland troubles, and diabetes also sometimes interfere with erection. If you think these are contributing to your difficulty, see a doctor. Most of the time, though, the cause of erection problems is the pressure a man feels to have an erection and "perform" sexually, and the way to deal with these problems is to take the pressure off yourself.

• Do the exercises recommended in the section on SEXUAL DYSFUNCTION, but *do not* expect to get an erection! That's not the point. In fact, you will learn a lot by *not* having an erection. Pay attention to how much feeling and pleasure you can experience without an erection. Tune out worries about having erections, and you'll discover that they're not very important. If you *do* get an erection during an exercise, stop the exercise, wait for the erection to go away, and then continue. Some men, when they get an erection, want to "strike while the iron is hot" and go on to an orgasm, whether alone or with a partner. Don't do this—it just puts more pressure on you.

• Throughout the exercises, let yourself lose any erection you have, at least at first. Do this both on your own and with your partner. This will help you focus less on your penis. It will also teach you that erections can come and go while you go on having pleasure, and that losing an erection once doesn't mean you'll never have one again. Practice becoming comfortable losing your erections.

• After you feel comfortable having and losing erections, try the following if you have a partner (or imagine it, if you don't). When you get an erection during an exercise, insert your penis slowly into your partner, *if* she is ready. Then, *do not* thrust or move; just lie quietly with your penis inside her vagina. After a while, you'll start to lose your erection. When this happens, your partner should *slowly* move or thrust a few times. If you get your erection back, continue for about a minute, stop, and repeat. If not, go back to caressing each other, and repeat if you get an erection again. Again, *do not* go on to have intercourse yet. Slowly, over a few sessions of this activity, the woman should increase her activity in a nondemanding way. After a while you will find, almost without noticing it, that you are having intercourse without worrying about your erections. Don't rush it, though; remember to go at a comfortable, nonpressured pace and, most of all, to enjoy your journey.

By working this way on what at first seemed like the worrisome problem of impotence you will discover that you have created the opportunity to open yourself up to your total sensuality more fully, to make closer emotional and sexual contact with your partner, and to gain confidence in yourself based on knowing that you now have a way to conquer a problem that formerly made you feel helpless and inferior.

SUGGESTED READING:

Masters, William H., and Virginia E. Johnson. *Human Sexual Inadequacy.* Boston: Little, Brown, 1970.

Zilbergeld, Bernie, and John Ullman. *Male Sexuality: A Guide to Sexual Fulfillment.* New York: Little, Brown & Company, 1978.

See also: DELAYED EJACULATION, MASTURBATION, PREMATURE EJACULATION, SEXUAL DSYFUNCTION

INCEST

People involved in incest or troubled by incestuous feelings have a hard time getting help because of the strong taboo against incest. Guilt, fear of punishment, and reluctance to blast a family apart cause participants in incest to delay or avoid facing its consequences.

Sexual abuse by parents—probably the most damaging variety of incest—is inflicted on infants and children of all ages. Girls are more frequently victims than boys. But there are many cases of father-son incest, and those are very destructive too. Incest means any genital contact, not just intercourse. Although most of the cases of incest that come to the attention of the civil authorities occur in poor or broken families, recent investigations suggest that most incest actually occurs in intact families. Such cases generally escape the attention and intervention of social agencies.

The experience of incest can be a crippling one for a child and can devastate a family. Sometimes a child overcomes fear and guilt enough to go to the police or other authorities for help only to have her story denied by her parents and disbelieved by the authorities, leaving her more alone and vulnerable than before. Or the authorities may descend with horrified and righteous severity, imprison the father, and place the child in a foster home. Few families can recover from such a trauma, and the child is often left feeling guilty for having broken up the family.

The emotional harm of incest comes from the child's awareness that society condemns it and from experiencing the relationship as exploitative. The child faces condemnation and suffers from a sense of having been "bad," of having been sexually used. Guilt, isolation, and loss of self-esteem compound the social stigma and pain of betraying a parent. Victims of incest find their social and sexual development blocked. They can't move on to behavior appropriate for their age. They may seek out self-punishing humiliation by becoming recklessly promiscuous.

• Face up to the fact that incestuous behavior is not always easy to identify. There are many fine gradations between showing loving concern for a child's developing sexuality and sexually exploiting a child who is not in a position to resist. Make sure you know what you are doing, and don't play with fire. If you have sexual feelings toward your child, don't panic—such feelings are normal up to a point. It's how you handle them that counts.

• If you have been the victim of an incestuous relationship, don't make yourself feel any worse than necessary by inflicting punitively harsh judgments on yourself. Devastating judgments by moralistic representatives of society are one of the worst consequences of incest. Don't waste your energy blaming yourself or feeling bad for the sake of society. Learn what you can from your experience about how sex, emotions, and the misuse of power cause problems and put the experience behind you.

• Don't automatically assume that incest always has terrible permanent consequences. In some instances incestuous behavior can occur without long-range or devastating results. A few people report having had a nondamaging incestuous relationship with a sibling, or even a parent. The deeper problems resulting from such incest may not always be apparent, however. Researchers suggest that the key to some children's escaping serious emotional damage is found in their having developed solid self-esteem earlier in their lives. Given the nature of our all-too-human difficulties in coping with power, dependency, sexuality, and guilt, however, harmless cases of incest are rare.

• Look at the probability that incest involves the exploitative misuse of power over a needy, frightened, and dependent person. In incest, especially involving a young child, genuine reciprocity and freedom are rarely involved. Confront the way sex is used to control, oppress, and dominate a weaker person. Children just don't know the moves: They are generally less experienced than adults, and more dependent. In a power struggle, particularly with a parent, they are rarely able to take care of themselves. Is that really how you want to treat another person and obtain pleasure for yourself?

• Low self-esteem is usually the source of incest, and eventually its result. If you are drawn to incestuous sexual behavior, you face a learning challenge: Try to understand that incest is less a sexual problem than a problem of diminished self-worth—for both parties. Are you using sex to get self-worth artificially, by forcing someone else to submit to you?

• Look at the way an incestuous relationship means striking a desperate bargain. The child submits: "I'll do this and then you'll love me." The adult commands: "Do this so I'll feel loved and powerful." For the child, the relationship is paralyzing: The child has the power to destroy an adult by revealing the forbidden act, but is kept from exercising that power by guilt and fear. Don't involve yourself or another person in such a desperate bargain. It won't work.

• "Psychological incest" can be as crippling as the physical sort. Children need parents to support their growing independence genuinely, to let go over the years, and finally to accept their eventual "desertion" of the family when they start out on their own. Parents who come between their children and their experiences of the world—ever-widening intellectual, emotional, even sexual options—can also block and distort social and sexual development. (See TEENAGE SEX.)

• If you are sexually using your child, get outside help. Don't minimize the problem, make excuses, or blame it on the child's seductiveness.

• Be aware that the law now requires any professional (physician, social worker, psychologist, minister, etc.) to report to the authorities any cases of incest that they learn about, even in an otherwise confidential counseling situation.

• Call a child-abuse hot line or the protective-services agency of your local department of social services. Great progress has been made recently in developing humane, caring programs to help families in which incest has occurred. Perhaps the best model program is that headed by Dr. Henry Giarretto, the Santa Clara County Child Sexual Abuse Treatment Program, 840 Guadalupe Parkway, San Jose, California 95110. In such programs expert counseling and support are provided for the entire family. Also, other people who have experienced an incest problem are available in confidential groups.

• If you have reason to suspect that a child is being sexually abused by a parent or relative, you can report the problem confidentially to a child-abuse hot line or to your local protective-services agency. Go to the police if necessary, but be aware that they may be trained to respond only in condemning and punitive ways. Try to contact a police officer or department with special training in child abuse. Increasing numbers of police departments now have special Abused Child units. They know how to intervene in ways most likely to help the family. Many incest offenders are put on probation with the requirement that they seek psychotherapy.

The Center for the Improvement of Child Caring is an excellent source of guidance and referral: 3727 West 6th Street, Suite 507, Los Angeles, California 90020.

SUGGESTED READING:

Armstrong, Louise. *A Speak-Out on Incest.* New York: Hawthorn Books, 1972.

Forward, Susan, and Craig Buck. *Betrayal of Innocence: Incest and Its Devastation.* Los Angeles: J. P. Tarcher, 1978. (Susan Forward can be contacted for further information at the Sexual Abuse Treatment Program, Valley Psychiatric Center, 15243 Vanowen Street, Van Nuys, California 91405.)

Kraemer, William. *The Forbidden Love: The Normal and Abnormal Love of Children.* London: Sheldon Press, 1976.

Meiselman, Karin C. *Incest.* San Francisco: Jossey-Bass, 1978.

See also: CHILD ABUSE, MASOCHISM, RAPE, SADISM, SEXUAL PERVERSIONS

JEALOUSY

We get jealous when we fear that a rival is taking away from us someone we count on for love, affection, sexual affirmation, or even just friendship. Jealousy is an acute sense of loss, defeat, or rejection in which we focus on the real or imagined superior enemy who is the cause of our pain. Jealousy has its roots in our childhood experiences, in that time when we learned to define ourselves and measure our worth based on the amount of love we received from our parents and other significant people. We got the idea that the only proof of being lovable is in getting direct loving attention. As a result, we think our own worth and lovability are something we can get only from others, and are in constant danger of losing.

Jealousy, like envy and greed, is destructive and self-negating. It is an emotional combination of anger, dependency, hurt, and self-devaluation. When we feel jealousy we focus on what we're not and compare ourselves fearfully to what our rival is. We're convinced that we can't be happy if someone we depend on for love also loves someone else.

• If you find yourself in a fit of jealousy, restrain yourself from reacting as if you are less of a person just because a spouse or lover or friend shares time, caring, or perhaps even sex with someone else. Such reactions are destructive to your efforts to develop an inner-directed sense of wholeness and individuality. Stop yourself from causing further damage to your relationship by expressing jealousy in violent, blaming, threatening, or clinging behavior. Being upset because someone shares himself or herself elsewhere for sure won't force that affection to be returned to you.

• Prevent jealousy by developing independence. The less you need to lean on someone to validate your basic worth, the stronger and freer you will be to give the kind of love that will bring you love in return. Focus your efforts on developing more confidence and attractiveness, rather than focusing on what you don't have compared to someone else. Your own wholeness and ability to live and grow regardless of what is happening in your relationships enhance your attractiveness and defuse the tension of competition and anger.

• Keep in mind that love is not limited to some specific quantity. Someone who really loves you can also love another without loving you less.

• Don't be programmed into someone else's definition of faithful love and grounds for jealousy. If you don't mind that your wife goes to see art movies—which you hate—with a male friend, don't feel obliged to feel jealous because other people think you should. If you do feel jealous, don't throw a tantrum if all you really want to do is talk it over constructively.

• Don't harbor the illusion that your jealousy shows how much you care. Expressing jealousy doesn't prove you love someone—it just proves you're jealous and uncertain of your own worth. Jealousy warns you that an important relationship and your self-esteem seem threatened and that you want to do something about that threat. Jealousy can be useful as a signal to pay attention to a relationship you value and to how you're feeling about yourself.

• When you're feeling jealous you have an opportunity to look at how you might be trapped in a poor self-definition. Jealous behavior often takes the form of trying to extort attention from someone else. It reflects your opinion that you aren't really worthy of attention and reveals your fear that you won't get cared for unless you force it. You have work to do on your negative self-concept.

• Study your "rival." You can learn much about what you want to be and how you want to develop. What wonderful traits make your rival so attractive? Are his or her traits really beyond you? Are you really in competition for the same things from your spouse, friend, lover? Do you really have a rival? If you do, and if your partner does choose him or her, are you therefore less of a valuable or lovable person?

• Be aware of the tendency to idealize a seeming rival. Make sure you're not setting up a superperson with which to torture yourself. You have your own set of strengths and weaknesses. You appeal to some people and not to others. So, too, does your rival. If the rival resembles you in some positive ways, remember that you have not been outclassed by someone totally different. If the rival differs from you in other ways, acknowledge that your partner clearly has some needs that you don't fill.

• Decide to develop new qualities to fill more of your partner's needs. Keep working on enhancing the qualities you already have. Even if you were willing to give up your own selfhood and individuality to fill all of someone else's needs or desires, you could never succeed. Your best bet is to be your best self.

• Even if you feel that your jealousy is an uncontrollable reaction, take control of what you do about it. You always have several options. You can terminate the relationship. You can concentrate on your own growth. You can ask your partner to change. You can work together to understand and improve your valuable relationship.

• Don't overreact and magnify minor jealous twinges. If you feel temporarily jealous because you've been left out of something—a party, a lunch, an excursion to the zoo—accept this as only a temporary irritant. Serious jealousy is grounded in the fear of loss: of face, of reputation, of control of yourself, your partner, the relationship.

• Don't let your insecurity and low self-esteem cause you to become withdrawn and aloof. This can cause your partner to pull away, creating the very distance and loss you fear.

• Get clear about the difference between possessive dependency and real love. Dependency tries to control and own. Love gives and receives flexibly and freely in whatever ways feel good to both people. Much of what is called "love" doesn't deserve the name. If such a relationship is destroyed by jealousy, it is actually no great loss. If you are plagued by jealousy, this is your challenge and opportunity to confront and clear up the immature, selfish qualities in your "loving."

• Honestly, and perhaps painfully, face the question of whether the person who is acting in such a way to make you jealous is worth your suffering. Is that person really so wonderful, and are you really so worthless without him or her? Take stock of yourself, of your lover, and of what you want in life. Is holding on to this problem lover the best way to fulfill yourself?

• When you feel jealous, take the opportunity to work on your relationship. Jealousy can be used as a learning device to identify and understand your needs and those of your partner. Talk about past experiences with jealousy. This may give you clues to the nature of your immediate worries. Talk about your expectations in this relationship. Many times serious and important expectations are left unspoken, leading to deep anger and disruption when one partner violates them. Ask for what you want honestly and fully. Don't make your partner guess. Define the limits of the relationship. What kind of sharing can you tolerate? Of time, affection, interests, sex? What can you not tolerate? Be realistic—don't expect your partner (or yourself) to give up fantasies about others or to stop feeling affection for others.

• Use some preventive precautions. Talk over situations that make you jealous, before they happen. Discuss with your partner situations from movies, plays, books, television, or your fantasies. Share your feelings about the flirting and seductiveness you notice at parties. Try to work out your expectations and define the underlying assumptions of your relationship before you feel it is threatened. Learn to recognize situations that make you jealous. Acknowledge them and share them with your partner. You may be able to work out the necessary mutual reassurances before there's a problem.

• If talking about jealousy-provoking situations that are occurring in your relationship is disruptive rather than helpful, and if you and your partner are committed to continuing the relationship, consider getting professional counseling. A neutral third person can help you work on de-escalating the jealousy and understanding its sources in ways not apparent to you when you are caught up in it.

• Don't deny your jealous feelings. Sometimes they are reasonable and based in fact. There are practical inconveniences and real hurts when a close friend, spouse, or lover becomes involved with someone else. Outside involvements do carry certain risks for close relationships. Sort out the real problems from those caused by your dependency and low self-esteem.

• If you feel good about yourself, you are less likely to react with jealousy when someone important to you shows an interest in someone else. Depression and self-dissatisfaction make you susceptible to jealousy. If you are secure in your relationship and secure in your self-confidence—if you recognize what makes you valuable and lovable—you will remain attractive and desirable. Growth and independence reduce your need for jealousy and enhance your progress toward being a loving, giving, self-directed person.

SUGGESTED READING:

Clanton, Gordon, and Lynn Smith. *Jealousy*. Englewood Cliffs, N.J.: Prentice-Hall, 1977.

O'Neill, Nena and George. *Open Marriage: A New Life Style for Couples*. New York: M. Evans, 1972.

Smith, James R. and Lynn, eds. *Beyond Monogamy: Recent Studies of Sexual Alternatives in Marriage.* Baltimore, Md.: Johns Hopkins Univ. Press, 1974.

See also: DEPENDENCY, ENVY, EXTRAMARITAL SEX, LONE-LINESS, LOSS OF LOVE, LOVE ADDICTION, MARITAL QUAR-RELING, SIBLING RIVALRY

JOB DISSATISFACTION

Being satisfied with our job or career is extremely important to each of us, because we spend most of every weekday at it. Feeling challenged and creative at work can give us a vital sense of well-being. Feeling bored, disappointed, angry, or frustrated all day has a suffocating effect on our lives.

What makes us satisfied when we work? Money? Yes, we need to feel adequately compensated financially for our time and effort. But we need more than that: We need to feel that we are accomplishing something worthwhile, that we are expressing ourselves and growing through using our talents or skills, that we are appreciated as individuals, and that we are at least partially in control of what we do and how we do it.

If you are presently dissatisfied with your job or career, you can fulfill more of your potential to become a vital, creative being if you accept the challenge of finding more stimulating, rewarding work or creating satisfactions in the work you now do.

• If you feel bored, resentful, or lazy at your job, don't let that convince you that you don't like to work. You need to get back in touch with your natural human drive to be creative and to make a valued contribution.

• Examine everything about your job to see whether you are over-looking some challenge or opportunity. Look for ways to make yourself feel good on the job regardless of the official assignment you have. Take on an additional responsibility, if necessary, and try to move your job ahead in that direction, so that you do more of the interesting work and less of the boring. In effect, try to re-create the job to suit you, while still giving the boss what he or she wants.

• Ask whether you are expecting the boss or the company to make life interesting for you. Face the fact that unless it is a very enlightened company, you will have to be responsible for your own job satisfaction. Feeling frustrated and resentful about "the system" is a dead end. Collecting injustices and documenting your complaints may give you a sense of moral superiority and righteous indignation. It may also tire you out, get you fired, or keep you from finding ways to fulfill yourself.

• If you are dissatisfied with your pay or advancement, ask yourself whether your money expectations are realistic for the job and your level of skill and experience. Ask whether you have really earned the raise or promotion you want. And have you done a good job of letting your boss know what you are worth?

• If your mind is primarily focused on demanding more pay and benefits, ask yourself if you have withdrawn emotionally from your work and are counting on money alone to keep you happy. That is a dangerous trap to fall into, and a hard one to get out of. Before it's too late, try to salvage some deeper satisfactions from some aspect of your work, or plan to find a job where you can.

• If you are really being underpaid, discriminated against, or are in danger on the job, use a grievance procedure to remedy the situation, organize a movement to change it, or look for a different job. Don't sink into passive resentment and hopeless resignation, no matter how impossible the situation looks. It is essential that you keep your active, creative energy flowing somehow, either on the job, on ways to change it, or on ways to get out of it.

• If you're stuck with a boring, dangerous, or underpaid job, think about how you happened to get into this situation, so that you can plan better next time. Do you focus on how bad the job is to avoid having to take more responsibility for your career? While you consider the secret payoffs you may get from having a lousy job, protect yourself from exploitation or danger as best you can, and get clear about the satisfactions and rewards you want the next time you have the chance to choose a job.

• Set your own standards, goals, and pace for your work, or make a game or contest out of it. If you load boxes all day, do it more neatly or more efficiently, or as a kind of ballet. Experienced workers often develop a graceful flow to their movements that is beautiful to watch. A worker in an aluminum mill, whose job it was to remove the rough ends of metal cut off aluminum sheets as they came through the rollers, perfected the art of doing it with the greatest speed and accuracy and the least effort. This skill also saved him from back strain, made his work safer, gave him aesthetic pleasure, and made him feel proud when he taught new workers how to do it.

• If your work game or technique gets the job done faster and your boss or the company benefits from it, don't let that spoil your fun. If getting your work done faster gives you free time, use it to rest, read, play, learn new skills, talk to friends, or plan ways to advance yourself.

• Look for ways to restructure your job, either with or without management permission. For instance, trade off tasks or responsibilities with other workers. If you're bending company rules, don't get caught. Make sure that your private techniques get the job done well enough to keep you out of trouble, and be sure they give you real satisfaction.

• Try to persuade your company to institute a job-enrichment program, such as flexible workweeks and schedules, or rotating jobs so that everyone periodically learns or experiences something new. Introduce the idea of shared work, in which teams work together on projects, rather than each person doing only one task. The Volvo factory in Sweden does this, and increasing numbers of American companies are trying it.

• On days when your job makes you feel bored, angry, frustrated, or restless, work your stress off afterward with physical exercise or sports. Plan a regular program if you need it.

• Recognize that unhappiness in your work can make you ill. If you are frequently sick, look at whether that is a symptom of serious job dissatisfaction. It may also have the payoff of helping you avoid your job or the necessity of finding a different one.

• Ask yourself whether some of your dissatisfaction is because you don't have good rapport with co-workers. If so, try to reach out and make friendly contact. (See SHYNESS.) Pleasant relationships with others should be a major fringe benefit of working.

• If you absolutely can't be creative or expressive in your work and can't change jobs, express the stifled side of yourself by decorating your office, studying on coffee breaks, doing isometric exercises at your desk, or enjoying relating to co-workers.

• If you don't get recognition or praise from management for what you do well, give yourself a pat on the back anyway for your good work. If you achieve something special, reward yourself with a symbolic gift or treat that will remind you of your success.

• Instead of focusing just on what your job is not giving you, ask yourself what you want to do with your life, especially what you want to do for other people. Clarify your personal goals, both short-term and long-range. See if there are ways you can help other people with their goals, and maybe they will help you with yours.

• If your job used to satisfy you but no longer does, don't think there is something wrong with you. Maybe your needs have changed or the work no longer is a challenge. Think about in what direction you now want to grow, and evaluate your work plans in those terms. Nowadays people change jobs and even careers more often than ever before. Don't get stuck in a job you have outgrown.

• If you are looking for a new job or a different job within the same company (or if you are looking for your first job), make sure you really know what the job involves and whether you can meet your needs in it. Don't just drift into it and then complain helplessly that it disappoints you.

• If you need additional training in order to improve your job situation, don't waste time regretting that you didn't start earlier. Begin now. Take classes on the job, at night school, or by correspondence. Also, keep your eyes open for informal opportunities to learn something new. One man learned Spanish from his fellow factory workers, and eventually landed a job as a bilingual teacher.

• If you expect to continue in your present line of work, keep yourself challenged by learning absolutely all aspects of the business. Know every job in the place. Understand what's involved in each step of manufacturing, management, sales, research, or whatever. This will not only help you do an outstanding job, both now and later, but will provide a real source of satisfaction.

SUGGESTED READING:

Bolles, Richard Nelson. *What Color Is Your Parachute?* Berkeley: Ten Speed Press, 1978.

Dauw, Dean. *Up Your Career*. Prospect Heights, Ill.: Waveland Press, 1977.

Haldane, Bernard. *Career Satisfaction and Success: A Guide to Job Freedom*. New York: AMACOM Executive Books, 1978.

Terkel, Studs. *Working*. New York: Avon Books, 1975.

See also: BOREDOM, DEPRESSION, MID-LIFE CRISIS, PASSIVITY, STRESS

KLEPTOMANIA

A kleptomaniac feels compelled to steal. The thievery, however, has nothing to do with material need. In fact, some famous and wealthy individuals have been kleptomaniacs—including several movie stars. A poor person may steal for survival; a criminal steals as a business. A kleptomaniac steals to satisfy an inner, emotional need.

Very often the items stolen by a kleptomaniac are not worth a lot of money and are not needed by the thief for any practical purpose. Instead, the items have a kind of symbolic worth. One woman stole sunglasses (more than she could ever use) because they symbolized for her the glamorous life and pretty face she lacked. Stolen objects become trophies of stealth and craftiness. They represent getting away with something, outwitting the merchants and the police.

In some cases part of the payoff for kleptomania is found in the excitement of experiencing and conquering risk, danger, and suspense. The risk of getting caught, even for those who genuinely do not want to get caught, gives the act of theft a dramatic, intense, gamelike quality —similar to gambling.

Like the gambler, the kleptomaniac is sometimes asking fate to tell whether he or she is going to be favored or punished as a person. The question goes something like this: "Does God/Fate/Lady Luck/ Mother love me enough to grant me this bonus?" An explanation for some kleptomania lies in life's earliest experiences. Some people find it quite difficult to overcome the sense of worthlessness instilled by parents who didn't seem loving or indulgent enough. Such people grow up with painful unresolved hurts, anger, and jealousy.

Some people find it easy to justify stealing as a way of repaying themselves for the hurts and denials of life. After all, the reasoning goes, stores are clearly wealthy and impersonal—just "places," from which you can take without hurting anyone. Their prices are too high, their profit margins excessive, and they have already made enough money from your previous purchases. Anything you take can easily be rationalized as a deserved benefit.

The stolen goods, however, are only a material substitute for something else deeply wanted and needed. Like other compulsions and obsessions, kleptomania puts one thing in place of another. Fearing openness, a compulsive individual may check and recheck the doors to his or her house. Needing to fill a void where love could go, a kleptomanic accumulates his or her stolen bonuses.

The substitute cannot be adequate to the need. It cannot bring love, offer support and attention, release anger, relieve fear, or soothe anxiety. Additionally, getting caught stealing something you hoped would bolster your sense of worth and importance can only make you feel belittled, trapped, and shamed. If you are troubled by a compulsive need to steal, use the following methods to help you understand your problem and to work out ways to overcome it. Do yourself the favor of discovering what you really need and learning how to get it legally.

• What are you getting from your stealing? What does it cost you? Are you actually taking and then enjoying things that you need for your life? Are you scoring in terms of fun, excitement, or satisfaction? Do you get pleasure from stealing and using nice things? Do you steal for revenge—against parents or spouse or the world at large? Are you paying out sums of guilt, shame, fear of arrest, loss of self-esteem?
• Look at what you steal for clues to your real inner need. Do the various items have some common characteristic? Can you see any sym-

bolic importance to them? What are you thinking at the moment you make your decision to take a particular item?

• What do you do with the things you steal? Do you give them to others as a way of buying affection or winning status? Do you keep them for yourself, perhaps to fill a void where you would really like to put caring, friendship, intimacy, or love?

• Look at what you have stolen. Think back to when you were stealing it and try to remember your feelings at that time. Now you have the item you wanted then. How do you feel about it now? Do you still feel triumphant and satisfied that you took it and got away with it, or do you feel some guilt or a kind of nagging discontent with yourself and your stolen goods?

• Fantasize in detail about your stealing until you exhaust the possible outcomes. First, imagine yourself succeeding at ever more daring and materially rewarding thefts. See yourself outwitting complicated security systems. Think about how you will use and enjoy your loot. Move up from the dime store to Tiffany's. How do you feel? Where do you imagine your kleptomania can take you? Do you see your life improving or changing in important ways? How? Is anything still missing? What?

Second, fantasize about yourself as an unsuccessful thief. How will it feel to be caught stealing? How will you cope with being arrested and charged with a crime? What other unpleasant consequences will you have to face?

• Ask yourself if you do want to get caught. Are you hoping to get help or attention by getting caught? Do you hope to embarrass or punish someone else by being found out? Who? Why? Take responsibility for getting help for yourself. If you feel you need nonjudgmental outside support, begin psychotherapy. Learn to get attention in positive ways instead of self-destructive ways. No one else can be as hurt by your acts as you yourself.

• Stop deluding yourself about what you really need and what you're getting by stealing. Consider the following possibilities:

Covert anger. If you feel angry and deprived, you may see stealing as a means of compensation. Recognize this method as dangerous and inadequate. You're not getting anything of emotional significance, and you're risking becoming much worse off—if caught, you'll feel angry, deprived, and bad.

Victimization. If you feel cheated—by your boss, your parents, the government—you may use stealing to get revenge. Learn to express your discontent and anger in direct ways that encourage real change and reconciliation.

Showing off. Do you need an audience? Do you tell others about your stealing? Does this sort of activity fit in with the expectations of your crowd? Are you competing with others for respect and attention as master thieves? Does stealing serve to create an impression of importance, to yourself and others? Are you disguising a need to build a stronger sense of self-esteem?

• Recognize the basic self-esteem problem that causes kleptomania. Stealing is not just a fun game. The consequences of losing can be devastating to your sense of self-worth. Try to replace stealing with positive actions that will improve your self-concept. Discover the sense of pride and satisfaction that comes with performing a service and earning a reward, either money or good feelings. Don't continue to deprive yourself of this kind of satisfaction. Contrast it with the cumulative negative effect on your self-concept that accompanies continued stealing.

• Don't expect to get off easily if caught. This is an unrealistic fantasy. Stores are increasingly willing to prosecute shoplifters. Businesspeople and the courts recognize this as a very costly crime, and there is little hesitation to punish. Instead of risking criminal prosecution, work at taking the other, truly rewarding risks in life: the risks of change, growth, and intimacy, or of learning to express anger, overcome fears, and relieve anxiety.

SUGGESTED READING:

Cammer, Leonard. *Freedom from Compulsion.* New York: Pocket Books, 1977.

See also: ANGER, ANXIETY, COMPULSIONS, GAMBLING, GREED, LYING, MASOCHISM, TEENAGE REBELLION

LESBIANISM

Lesbians are women who choose other women primarily or exclusively for their sexual and emotional relationships. In our society, lesbian women have to contend with widespread oppressive and guilt-producing attitudes and prejudices. They are often caught up in serious and painful conflicts between these external negative views and their own internal needs, desires, and values.

Lesbian women encounter numerous popular myths about lesbian relationships that challenge their efforts to create a strong sense of self-worth and individuality. Here are some facts to counter these inaccurate views:

Homosexual women (and men) do not suffer from mental illness or psychological problems any more frequently than people in general. Lesbians have the same range of emotional strengths and hangups, abilities and deficiencies, physical attractiveness and unattractiveness as the rest of the female population.

Lesbians prefer women as erotic partners. They have not become lesbians because they can't "get a man"; they are lesbians because they are primarily attracted to other women. It's a question of preferring women rather than of hating or failing with men.

Generally, lesbian lovemaking is not an imitation of male-female intercourse. The dyke-femme stereotype is rarely accurate. Instead, many lesbian relationships are characterized by an equality and expressiveness that are very difficult to achieve between men and women in our male-dominated society.

Lesbians are no more likely to be promiscuous than are heterosexuals. The number of partners a heterosexual has sex with depends on his or her age, background, social environment, and values; the same is true of a lesbian.

All people, in the process of developing their own personalities, have to sift and evaluate the rules and opinions of the world at large. We all compare these outside demands to our internal beliefs and needs. We all try to sort out our own set of values and standards from among those held by the important people and institutions in our lives: our parents, family, school friends, co-workers, religion, political groups, and so on. This difficult job is even harder for people who, like lesbians, find that their internal wants and needs are viewed negatively by much of society.

If what you are is unacceptable to the important people and institutions in your life, it is very difficult not to judge yourself as unacceptable and unworthy. Accepting yourself as a lesbian can occur only by discovering and choosing to live by your own values.

Recent psychological research shows that homosexuals who complete the hard task of discovering, accepting, and committing themselves to their own values live rich and fulfilling lives. They have a highly developed sense of individuality and self-esteem, and they are resilient and self-sufficient in the pursuit of their carefully chosen life goals. Thus, compared to those heterosexuals who have been able to avoid difficult struggles for self-knowledge and self-acceptance, many homosexuals are practiced in the art of seeing through social masks.

Lesbianism, then, does not have to be a problem. It is one if being a lesbian—or thinking you might be a lesbian—puts you in conflict with yourself and/or with the important people in your life. It is a problem if you think of it as evil, and therefore of yourself as a bad or perverted person.

Try to sort out your feelings about lesbianism with the help of the following methods.

• Work hard at identifying your own values and needs. What do you feel and want—sexually, socially, emotionally? Who are the people who count in your life? What sort of lifestyle do you want to create? What religious and ethical values have genuine meaning for you? How might the atmosphere of the town or city where you live affect your choice of sexual relationships? What is workable for you, given these factors?

• Recognize that the wish for compassionate, tender, gentle loving is very basic and powerful. If you think you're turned on to women because such love is not possible with men, ask yourself what has made you believe this. Does this belief come from your actual experience? Does it express a prejudice against men that has not been checked out in actual encounters? Men are changing, and not all are stuck in unappealing macho roles.

• What are you looking for in a sexual relationship? Look at the people to whom you have been attracted. List all their appealing qualities, not just the sex-related ones. Loosen up on the question of gender preference, so that you can identify the *kind* of person—male or female—you find appealing.

• Are you convinced you are a lesbian and are you comfortable with that conviction? So be it. Don't hassle yourself—save your energy for fending off outside attacks on your self-esteem. Work on creating a life that suits you and fulfills you. Work on all the aspects of your life: your education, your artistic and creative skills, your friendships, your relationship and contributions to society at large, your spiritual development. By developing yourself fully as a person you will become a more attractive lover, and you will be less bothered by criticism of your lifestyle.

If you are attracted to lesbianism, and perhaps have intense lesbian fantasies, but are resisting actual involvement with another woman, follow these suggestions:

• Ask yourself if you think lesbianism is "terrible." If you do, maybe you shouldn't push yourself to act on your fantasies. If you don't think you can handle lesbian sex, if you are not sure your fantasies reflect a genuine desire for a real lesbian relationship, you don't have to live out your curiosity and erotic imagination. Instead, enjoy your fantasies as part of your sex life. Enrich them, perhaps by photographing or drawing female bodies. Get to know lesbian women if the opportunity arises—learn from them and share with them. Give yourself permission to have sexual feelings toward women without concluding that these feelings mean anything decisive about the kind of person you are or the kind of life you should lead.

• If you feel guilty about your sexual or affectional needs, try to discover the source of this guilt. Does it come from your religious training? Recognize that there are many responsible, religious, creative, loving lesbians both within and outside of traditional religious institutions. There are some supportive and understanding clergy and congregations who do not exclude homosexuals from their churches or synagogues. You may be able to find acceptance and help within your religion; homosexuality does not automatically put you in conflict with faith.

• Are you trapped in an unaccepting environment, such as a small town or an isolated suburban area? Try to counter the external negativism of your environment by learning about the sexual preference you think you share. Read books by and about lesbian women. Look for opportunities to meet and talk with gay women, perhaps at an urban women's center. A lesbian's life is no more likely than a heterosexual's to center around her bedroom. Lesbian women study, work, play, strive, succeed, and fail just like their heterosexual sisters. Open your horizons so that you can see that there is more to lesbianism than sin and guilt.

• Consider the possibility that the guilt you feel is about being sexual in any way at all, not specifically homosexually. There are many pressures in our culture that discourage women from being comfortable and assertive with their sexuality. These pressures apply to heterosexually oriented women as well as lesbians. Are you basically afraid of knowing what you want and going after it?

• Give yourself credit for the fact that you are confronting a fundamental human problem that you would face regardless of the gender of your lovers: It is scary to let yourself be vulnerable, to care about another person, and to let someone else be significant in your life. Many people, afraid of intensity and hurt, use teachings about guilt and sin as excuses to hide behind, not because they are actually that moral. Vulnerability is a risk in any love or sexual relationship. Allowing vulnerability is a wonderful growth opportunity. It has its dangers— you might get hurt or rejected—but it is a necessary step toward experiencing genuine sharing and closeness.

If you think you are a lesbian and you have actually had some lesbian experience, but you are burdened by guilt and uncertainty, try these suggestions:

• Look at whether you are trying to resolve all your complicated feelings and questions about your sexual preference too quickly. Perhaps you need more time to explore your lesbian sexuality comfortably.

• Give yourself a chance to evolve into the person you want to be. Don't cut yourself off from your nonlesbian women friends or from male friends. While you are learning about lesbian lifestyles and sexuality—by direct experience and indirectly through lesbian literature, films, or activist groups—keep in mind that you don't necessarily have to make an either/or, straight/gay lifetime decision. Give yourself all the time and flexibility you need.

• Remember that if you are feeling uncertain, it may be that your sexual needs don't divide neatly into hetero- or homosexual patterns. Don't let society in general or your particular social group pressure you into a more definitive choice than you are ready for. Everyone has a range of needs and feelings. We are all complex mixtures of male and female characteristics, woven together in obvious and in subtle ways. Ideal sexual gratification may require a range of partners—men and women, or different types of men and women. Focus on the characteristics you want in a lover and see where you can get them; if you're uncertain about your sexual orientation, try not to make gender a primary consideration. A really good sexual partner embodies a wide and flexible range of social and sexual qualities. He or she will also evoke and value your own individual range of qualities. Give yourself a chance to discover the right mix for yourself and your lover. Also remember that your preferences may change as you grow.

If you have no doubt that you are a lesbian, if you have come to reasonably good terms with your sexuality, but would like to be even more comfortable with yourself, try these suggestions:

• Look inside for leftover guilt and negative stereotyping. Are there times when you still judge yourself negatively, or label yourself in narrow ways? It takes a long and dedicated effort to discover and accept your own needs and values. Be on the lookout for those times when you still judge yourself in terms of external opinions. Remind yourself that you really want to be at peace with yourself and to measure up to internal standards that you have developed for yourself.

• Don't substitute one rigid stereotype for another. If you're trying to model yourself after some image of lesbian perfection—having discarded an inappropriate heterosexual model—you risk exchanging one tyranny for another. You are your own unique person, who happens to be a lesbian. There is no model you have to copy. There are no "shoulds" to tell you how you "have to be" now that you know your sexual and affectional preference. Let yourself be.

No matter how certain or uncertain you are about being straight or gay, you will find it enlightening as a woman to learn more about your gay sisters. Men who are puzzled or upset about gay women can also benefit from expanding their awareness of the wide range of human feeling and sexual expression.

SUGGESTED READING:

Abbott, Sidney, and Barbara Love. *Sappho Was a Right-On Woman.* New York: A Scarborough Book, Stein and Day, 1977.

Martin, Del, and Phyllis Lyon. *Lesbian/Woman.* San Francisco: Glide Publications, 1972.

See also: ANXIETY, GUILT, HOMOSEXUALITY, LOVE ADDICTION, SEXUAL PERVERSIONS

LIVING TOGETHER

The problems and pleasures of living together without the legal bonds of marriage are being explored by more and more couples. Some do so in order to keep their relationship free of stereotyped husband-wife roles. Others feel it is meaningless to legalize a mutual commitment to love each other. For many couples living together is a trial marriage, an opportunity to explore and evaluate their relationship. Many other couples live together without any long-term or exclusive obligation. Most people who live together do expect to be married someday, though not necessarily to their current partners. Most agree that it is best to marry if they are planning to have children.

An increasingly relaxed moral atmosphere, due partially to the women's liberation movement and modern birth control methods, has made it possible for couples of all ages to cohabit without too much social stigma, particularly on campuses and in larger cities. Even many senior citizens now live together instead of marrying, to keep from losing Social Security or other benefits linked to legal status.

Social scientists disagree on the advantages and disadvantages of unmarried couples' living together. Morally, of course, "living in sin" is still viewed as just that by many people. For a variety of reasons— moral, social, financial, sexual, emotional—living together presents some problems that can either undermine and destroy a relationship or provide great opportunities for the growth of both partners if the problems are dealt with constructively.

If you and someone you care for have chosen to live together, you have a special need and opportunity to keep your relationship ever renewed and fulfilling. This requires respect, caring, willingness to give, and flexibility about closeness and distance. Each of you needs not only physical but also psychological space. This means making allowances for different lifestyles, beliefs, moods, and energy levels. As in a marriage, you must continue to develop your individual identity and sense of worth. You also face the challenge of a unique financial and legal situation.

Here are ways in which you can reap the benefits and avoid many of the pitfalls of living together.

• Make sure that you are both clear about the degree of your commitment to each other. Is this a transition toward marriage, an exploratory expression of affection without obligation, a deep love commitment, an arrangement of affection and economics? Remember that all relationships change and grow continuously. Keep aware that both of you will experience change in some of your feelings and goals, and that the relationship will need to develop in response to these changes.

• Make the most of whatever increased security and stability you feel as a result of living together. Let yourself be open, trusting, and creative in the relationship.

• Recognize that living together is not a magic solution to problems of low self-worth or emotional dependence. Accept the responsibility of fulfilling yourself as a loving but individual person, with your own interests and identity.

• Be very specific about your ground rules concerning other relationships. Agree on whether you will have separate friends and activities or outside sexual relationships, and, if so, under what conditions.

• Agree on whether you want to have children and on what you are going to do about contraception and in the event of an unplanned pregnancy. Facing these issues openly ahead of time is less stressful than reacting impulsively when they are forced on you.

• Work out a mutually agreeable plan for your housing expenses. How will the rent or mortgage be paid? What about taxes, maintenance, chores? Decide which expenses you will share and which you will keep separate. What about checking accounts and credit cards? Try to avoid having one of you vulnerably dependent on the other for finances or decisions. Recognize that overdependence may weaken the relationship.

• Discuss together the viewpoint that one of the innovative but potentially problematic aspects of living together unmarried is that both the man and woman cannot as easily slide into traditional marriage roles. Look at how this frees both of you from being stuck individually with responsibilities that should be shared. For example, are you both willing to decide together what to do about birth control and housekeeping instead of making these the woman's problems? And will you both grapple with earning sufficient income, instead of relegating this burden to the man?

• Consider making a written contract between the two of you concerning your personal expectations, rights and responsibilities, and financial obligations. Treat this as a creative process of clarifying who you are and what each of you brings to the relationship, emotionally and practically. If you want help in doing this, talk to a knowledgeable counselor or read Paul Ashley's book *Oh Promise Me, But Put It In Writing: Living-Together Agreements Without, Before, During and After Marriage* (New York: McGraw-Hill, 1978). Another source is *The Living Together Contract Kit,* published by Nolo Press (P.O. Box 544, Occidental, California 95465).

• Recognize that living together can present legal and financial problems if you later split up. If either of you has substantial personal assets or income, consult an attorney about the implications of the recent Lee Marvin case, in which the issue was whether the defendant should be required to divide property as if he had been married. If you want to consult the attorney who handled this and other similar cases, he is Marvin M. Mitchelson, 1801 Century Park East, Los Angeles, California 90067.

• Find out about other important legal implications of your living arrangement. Is living together legal in your state? In all states many of your rights are different from those of married people. Read *Living Together, Married or Single: Your Legal Rights,* by Nora Lavori (New York: Perennial Library, Harper & Row, 1976).

• Recognize that you may be using living together as a way to avoid making a deeper emotional commitment. If so, ask yourself whether you really want to hold back in this way, and examine the reasons for your reluctance. Look for growth opportunities, those special moments when you can become more open and vulnerable to a loving commitment.

• If emotional or sexual problems arise in your relationship that you cannot mutually resolve, consider consulting a professional counselor, just as if you were legally married. Recognize also that breaking up can be as emotionally difficult as a divorce.

SUGGESTED READING:

Alternative Lifestyles (journal). SAGE Publications, P.O. Box 5024, Beverly Hills, California 90210.

O'Neill, Nena and George. *Open Marriage: A New Life Style for Couples.* New York: Avon Books, 1973.

Rogers, Carl. *Becoming Partners: Marriage and Its Alternatives.* New York: Dell Publishing Co., 1973.

See also: COMMUNICATION BLOCKS, DEPENDENCY, MARITAL QUARRELING, PREMARITAL SEX

LONELINESS

When is loneliness truly a problem? When is it more than just missing someone you care about, just wishing to share your time and yourself with someone else? What is it that turns being alone into a depressive, sad, self-devaluing experience? When does it produce a sense of meaninglessness so strong that the lonely person doesn't even have himself or herself for company? Loneliness can become a serious problem if not dealt with—it can deprive a person of the will to go on; it can kill.

The consequences of loneliness can also be serious problems in themselves: depression, boredom, restlessness, psychosomatic illnesses. These are, however, rather generalized symptoms of unease, and you need to ask yourself if they really spring from aloneness or from other aspects of your life that need changing.

As miserable as loneliness can be, we sometimes impose it on ourselves. We may cultivate it, indulge in it for secret payoffs. Perhaps we seek to avoid social risk-taking, or the responsibility and hard work of making a relationship flourish. Perhaps we're comfortable with self-pity. We may be tempted to make the subtle shift from recognizing an unpleasant situation to blaming circumstances or other people for it. There is a certain security in complaining that "they" did it to us. This sort of indulgent, passive protest may even give us enough leverage to manipulate others into allowing us to rely on them.

Sometimes loneliness can cover a secret arrogance. It permits us to cloak our distance from others in claims of superior sensitivity. Loneliness can be worn as an outward sign of an artistic, suffering, creative nature. We dream of turning out the ultimate Gothic novel. We sing the blues. Aloneness *can* lead to creativity, which is one of the best reasons not to shun it or fear it, but real loneliness usually undermines our creative powers. The act of creating doesn't just happen because one chooses to be lonely or reclusive. It happens when one works to reach inward to oneself and outward to others, when one makes a commitment to communication.

Loneliness can be a test and an opportunity rather than a complaint or an affliction. In one sense, we are all alone, individual, separate. This realization can cause genuine pain, just as other experiences of aloneness can do: when we lose a loved one to change, or death, or just to a business trip, when we ourselves are isolated by travel, or obligation, or illness. Recognizing loneliness as a basic, inescapable part of our lives can be energizing rather than depressing, however. It can help us resolve to deepen, extend, and sustain our relationships with other people. It helps us think of our fellows as each being a lovable, lonely person—like ourselves.

If we try to avoid this recognition, we shut ourselves off from an important avenue of growth and sharing. We run from loneliness, but in fact we're running from ourselves, from a confrontation with our human nature. Fear of loneliness can inhibit us from deepening human bonds, enriching our appreciation of life and the world in which we live, understanding our inner needs and aspirations. Even when we feel least alone, even in the middle of an intense love relationship, an awareness of the separateness, changeableness, impermanence of our lives can bring us some comprehension of our true loneliness. This awareness can only increase our ability to love, to share, and to be compassionate.

Feelings of loneliness sometimes spring from a kind of fear of dying. Being cut off from what we think we need, we fear extinction. We can be too dependent on external validation of our worth, and then interpret aloneness as proof of worthlessness. We can come to feel that our value rests in someone else's estimation. If that person isn't always around to remind us of this value, we have no way of sustaining it. Our definition of self comes from an outside support. We're afraid we will vanish without that support.

What loneliness does to us can be brought under our control. We can learn to deal with feeling alienated from others and, perhaps more important, from ourselves. We can experience loneliness and learn that it doesn't really threaten our existence or worth. We can discover renewal and creativity in solitude. We do not have to accept loneliness as helpless victims, or with boredom, self-blame, or depression. Loneliness can teach us self-reliance. It can force us to take responsibility for our own lives. It can enrich us.

• We all need to be alone sometimes. Even in the most intense relationships we need a haven of solitude and self-nurturance.

• Welcome time alone as an opportunity to build a relationship with yourself. If you feel miserable because you are alone, ask if you yourself might not be the missing companion. Examine your degree of dependence on others. If it's extreme, try to find the weak spots in your internal self-estimation, and work on creating a personal, independent sense of worth.

• If your aloneness is externally imposed, by someone else's absence, illness, or death, do not take this as proof of your worthlessness. Your value does not depend on someone else's opinion of you. Even if someone does choose to stop seeing you—even if a spouse, lover, or friend ends your relationship against your wishes—you are not worth less because of this.

• Learn to enjoy being alone. At some time, everyone experiences some degree of loneliness. It is not to be dreaded. It has a place in a productive, happy life.

• Learn to meditate in some way. Take the opportunity to think about yourself and your life without distractions. You may find that keeping a journal or diary helps you concentrate on your feelings and insights.

• If you are lonely and yet there are many people in your life, ask yourself what is missing. What connection do you yearn for that you lack? Do you need to develop new relationships or to deepen existing ones?

• Many people are lonely not because they lack friends but because they lack intimacy. One practical approach is self-examination by a lonely person of how much he or she shares of himself or herself. Self-disclosure usually is reciprocated by self-disclosure by others. Learning how to be open with other people is even more risky than learning how to contact people. Groups where self-disclosure is valued and encouraged can be helpful.

• Lonely people are usually also depressed and blame themselves for the problem. Besides feeling inadequate, they begin to feel angry and desperate. These feelings can make them unattractive to others. Recognizing and dealing with these feelings as part of loneliness may help clear the way to creativity or reaching out to others.

• Examine how your present state of loneliness came about. To what degree are you responsible for it? Have you chosen to live in a way that encourages loneliness? If you find loneliness unacceptable, yet you have chosen it, recognize that you are free to make a new choice.

• You can foster your inner life, encourage yourself to pursue interests, appreciate the people and life around you, nourish your sense of humor. Keep in touch with the world surrounding you, with external events, and with your interior life and your goals. Exercise your creative powers: Use art as a way of communicating with yourself and with others. Paint, dance, sing, make music, take up a craft hobby, read for the good advice others may have about living and flourishing. Try to be patient, to take each day as it comes. Involve yourself with others and their needs—but not to the detriment of your own. Rediscover the joy of sharing with and helping another person.

• Loneliness can be a positive choice, too. It may reflect a desire for independence from a social network you no longer wish to maintain. You may simply want to break free of uncomfortable entanglements you inherited, stumbled into, or have clung to for too long.

• Some of us seek out, even purchase, aloneness. It is something to be valued. Meditation techniques of all kinds are franchised by purveyors of creative aloneness and enlightenment. Religious retreats invite us to get away from our surrounding relationships in order to reestablish contact with the timeless values of our faith. Sometimes we choose—as Anne Morrow Lindbergh describes in *Gift from the Sea* (New York: Random

House, Vintage, 1978)—to suffer loneliness in order to do needed work on the self.

• Loneliness cannot be escaped by using drugs, drinking, overeating, or oversleeping. These escapes are unproductive and dangerous, and merely prolong and aggravate the condition you need to change. Fantasies and daydreams may be of some comfort and value in constructive planning, but they too can degenerate into mere escapes.

• Practice what musician Mason Williams calls "true asking." Use lonely periods to search for what you really want from yourself and from others, to separate your true needs from the ones you or others think you *should* have or express.

• Sometimes loneliness simply comes from being parched for human company, for warmth and contact with other people. Learn to share with others without becoming overly dependent on them. You can learn to foster friendship and loving through conscious practice. You can reduce your loneliness by reaching out. Some people are lonely because they are low in social risk-taking. It is difficult, especially when you are feeling bad about yourself, to make initial contacts. The only way to break this barrier is to be assertive and take risks. People who have problems with shyness do well to join activities and clubs that give common ground for contact. If you want extra help and reinforcement, seek out a support group at a club, church or synagogue, or community center. Some community-service agencies, like the Los Angeles Free Clinic, have even started surrogate-family programs to help reestablish ties of closeness for people who feel lonely and isolated and who miss the experience of family.

SUGGESTED READING:

Moustakas, Clark E. *Loneliness and Love.* Englewood Cliffs, N.J.: Prentice-Hall, 1972.

Potthoff, Harvey H. *Understanding Loneliness.* New York: Harper & Row, 1976.

See *also:* DEPRESSION, DEPENDENCY, LOSS OF LOVE, LOVE ADDICTION, SHYNESS

LOSS OF LOVE

It's not easy to let go. Even if you have no choice. Even if *you* decide to end things. Even if you know things have worked out for the best.

Sometimes a lover dies. Sometimes a lover walks out. Sometimes you send a lover away. It's not easy to live with any of these changes.

If you lose a loved person to death, to divorce, or to a split-up, you are likely to experience some combination of the following unpleasant emotional reactions: depression, loneliness, restlessness, fatigue, guilt, anger, helplessness, fear, emptiness.

For a while after a painful loss of love you may be deeply pessimistic and afraid of new relationships. Won't reaching out again seem disloyal? Won't a new love be hurtful? Won't you always see the lost lover in the face of any new one? Won't you always carry the burden of diminished hope and deadened enthusiasm?

Even after you lose someone you love—parent, child, friend, relative, spouse, lover—you still feel a psychological bond to the lost person. Even when the loss is to death, you can't seem to make an end to the relationship. Any separation leaves you with unfinished business to work on. There are always many unresolved disagreements and hurts, many words of affection and caring left unspoken. It's painful to realize that there's no further chance to correct mistakes. It hurts to know that there's no way to make things right. Tied to the past, you may find it almost impossible to start living again in the present.

If you know a time of loss is approaching, there are some things you can do to make it less difficult.

• Make sure you say good-bye. This is important if you're leaving one job for another, moving to a new neighborhood, or helping someone you love face imminent death. Saying good-bye helps everyone involved feel that the unfinished business has been dealt with. It gives you all a chance to acknowledge the separation, to prepare for it, to accept it.

• If you're leaving friends behind, get together for a farewell gathering. Say good-bye, because even with the best of intentions to write or call, the new distance between you will change your relationships. Return borrowed items. Unlike gifts, which are pleasant reminders of past relationships, borrowed things keep you tied in a guilty, anxious way to the people you have left behind.

• If you have decided to end a relationship that the other person wishes to continue, think about how your parting meeting might go. Rehearse in your mind the arguments, anger, manipulation, or clinging you might have to face. Ask yourself how you will counter it; be prepared to respond to whatever you imagine you might encounter.

• Meet privately with the person you want to leave. Try to acknowledge and identify the problems between you, even if you can't resolve them. (This is true of just moving away, too: It's easier to get on with your new life if you haven't left disagreements—small or large—unacknowledged in the part of life you're leaving behind.) Give yourself—and the one you're leaving—a chance to recognize openly that the relationship is really over.

If you lose a love, if you're the one left behind, you can get yourself through the hard times and restore your sense of worth and your enthusiasm for life.

• Expect to feel miserable for a while. The emotions that come with loss are important to the healing process. Your loss is real. Recognize it. Accept the pain as natural and normal. Take it as a sign that you are reacting in an understandable, human way and that you will survive the loss. You are strong enough to survive.

• Human beings in pain after a loss are normally depressed for a while. They often give over some time to tears and mourning. Confront your feelings; you'll get through them sooner if you admit them than if you try to hide them or hide from them.

• Do your mourning for a dead or simply vanished love, but keep in mind that you are not the only person to suffer such a loss. Remember that loss is a commonly experienced part of life.

• Reaffirm your sense of worth. You are—alone, without anyone to tell you this—a lovable, worthwhile, valuable person. Your value doesn't depend on having a spouse or lover or friend to prove it. Even in a new environment, without all the supports you are used to from family, friends, work, or lover, you are still valuable for your own unique self. Take stock of who you are—what you like about yourself, what you enjoy doing, what you want to do in the future. Learning to be comfortable with yourself alone will make it all the more comfortable to be with others.

• Don't be scared by the bad days. Time is an ally. You will heal at your own pace. Your pain will end. Don't let someone else determine your rate of healing: Trust your emotions and let them guide you. Don't feel put down by someone who expresses surprise that "you're not over it yet"—only you know the personal, individual way in which you are putting your feelings back in order. By the same token, don't let anyone tell you that you haven't "mourned enough." There is no rule governing our feelings and needs. Being mournful for six months doesn't prove your love is greater than that of someone who mourns for three months.

• Treat yourself kindly. Let your spirit recuperate. Give yourself over to the healing process. Rest as much as you feel you need to; get help for those chores and responsibilities that seem burdensome. Try to avoid decision-making. This isn't the time for new emotional commitments, major moves, or large purchases.

• Involve yourself in productive work. This will help give your life a sense of purpose and order. Schedule your work wisely, however, to avoid pressure or stress.

• You may find that keeping a journal will help you recognize and sort out your feelings. It will also help you see the changes that come with time and will convince you that you are capable of healing. Some form of meditation might also help you regain your sense of calm and orderliness. It might help you accept and welcome your emotional changes.

• Let other people help you. Lean on friends or family if you need to. Get professional help if you feel you want it. Plan ahead to get through the hardest times, such as anniversaries, birthdays, weekends, or holidays. Let the people in your "support network" know that you would appreciate company—or would like to be company—at these times.

• Involve yourself with living things. Rediscover the joys of natural places, the satisfactions of caring for beautiful plants or growing animals. Go to the beach or the woods, to a zoo or garden, to the mountains, to the park. Let the world show you its wonder, liveliness, and growth. Let music back into your life. You may find yourself singing along.

• Suicidal thoughts are natural symptoms of the pain you are feeling. Thinking about suicide doesn't necessarily mean you really want to die. You don't have to act on these feelings. If they hang on, however, and you begin to feel drawn to suicide, *get help immediately*. Don't be ashamed to call a hot line or to go for professional psychological help. Many, many people need support during difficult times. Care for yourself; suicide is only an end, not a solution.

• You may feel intense anger. You may be angry at the one who died for abandoning you. You may be angry at the lover who deserted you. You may be angry at yourself for "letting this all happen." Express your anger, but not against yourself or others in a destructive way. Drive to a secluded place and scream in your car. Hit a tennis ball furiously against the backboard. Attack your pillow. Kick a snowbank. Throw rocks into a field. If you play an instrument, play it loudly and angrily. Speak your anger, to yourself and to trusted friends.

• Keep away from the dangerous addictions. Alcohol will depress you further. Drugs, including marijuana, will only interrupt the natural healing process. Pay attention to your health. Eat well, but be aware of the temptation to comfort yourself with food excessively.

• As you gradually become aware of your own survival, you'll gain strength and calm even more rapidly. Soon you will be able to forgive the one you lost for whatever unfinished business needs forgiving. And you'll forgive yourself for your feelings of guilt, or anger, or resentment.

• With time and healing, you'll be able to take stock of your loss in an encouraging and positive way. You'll be able to sort out what you gained—in love, sharing, commitment, growth—from the lost relationship.

• Give yourself credit for having given love. Be proud of your reviving interest in life and living, in renewing intimacy and sharing. Now you can invite new people into your life. You are ready to pursue new interests and/or deepen the old ones.

• Do things for others. Enjoy the satisfactions of caring. Provide yourself with a mix of activities done alone and in a group.

• Don't be shocked when you have sad days—memories will flood back in, but now you know time brings restored health and perspective.

SUGGESTED READING:

Colgrove, Bloomfield, and McWilliams. *How to Survive the Loss of a Love.* New York: Simon & Schuster, 1976.

Wanderer, Dr. Zev, and Tracy Cabot. *Letting Go: A Twelve-Week Personal Action Program.* New York: G. P. Putnam's, 1978.

See also: DEPENDENCY, DEPRESSION, GRIEF, LONELINESS, LOVE ADDICTION

LOVE ADDICTION

Love addiction, like other forms of dependency, negates ourself. It shows we don't feel worthwhile inside or in our relations with others. Love addicts suffer an emptiness of spirit and look to others to fill it. They are fixated on the idea that there is someone *out there* whom they absolutely must possess to survive as human beings.

Love addiction is based on craving and needing "love" and approval as absolute requirements for survival, in contrast to wanting to share love out of a feeling of strength and fullness. Love addicts look to their lovers to guarantee the quality of their lives. They are preoccupied with the fear of losing love, and burn themselves up in the effort to avoid that loss.

Perhaps this insecurity and need for reassurance goes back to infancy, when parental love did guarantee physical survival. It is easy to understand a small child's feeling that "if Mommy and Daddy don't love me and take care of me I'll die." Indeed, studies of infants in institutions show that, even if fed and protected from disease, infants who are not cuddled and loved regularly often die.

This doesn't have to be true of adults, however. Having survived into adulthood, you can work at erasing the inner negative tape that tells you "You're nobody till somebody loves you." You can learn to silence this voice without having to turn to something outside yourself: drugs, alcohol, cigarettes, food, a dependent relationship.

We're used to thinking of drugs, alcohol, smoking, overeating, even overworking as being addictive. Clutching at a love to solve your life can be equally addictive—a search for the perfect high that brings peace, fulfillment, and satisfaction—but from the outside, and at a high cost.

This kind of addiction is especially tempting and dangerous because it's legal, socially respectable, romanticized, widely shared, culturally encouraged. Lots of nice people share it. A whole "love industry" caters to it with songs, soap operas, music, valentines, mushy advice to the lovelorn.

In a culture that teaches us to rely on external associations—marriage and family, schools, clubs, business contacts—for our self-definition and sense of accomplishment and worth, it is difficult not to become a love addict. It is hard to shake the belief that the person we know ourselves to be through our relationships is all there is.

You are more than your relationships. For sure you are more than those relationships you desperately seek and cling to out of a sense of inferiority and deficiency. It was bad relationships that taught you to think so poorly of yourself in the first place, and that set you up to be an addict who goes around looking for a "fix" from a lover now. More bad relationships aren't going to cure you. Any relationship you need with an addictive intensity is merely repeating an old pattern and making you worse.

Look into your own life for the signs of love addiction and then choose some of the following suggestions for kicking the habit.

• Answer these questions: Do you think you'll die if you are not someone else's love object? Do you feel vulnerable and unprotected? Why? If you are someone's love object, do you hold on tightly and clutch your lover for safety and security? What do you fear? Don't you know that too tight a grip can strangle love?

• Are you someone's pawn? Do you define everything in terms of your lover's preferences and wishes? Do your feelings of well-being or depression depend on your lover's behavior? Do you need to see or talk to your lover in order to feel comfortable? Can you be alone with yourself without worrying about your relationship—can you give your attention to yourself without bringing in thoughts of your absent lover? Are you a puppet who merely reacts to someone else's action?

• Addictive behavior is not involuntary. You can learn to control it—but only if you first admit that you are an addict.

• Be aware of the ways you are encouraged to be dependent. Do your parents urge you to "settle down"? Do your friends hassle you about being a loner? Are you made to feel uncomfortable in social situations when you don't have a date? Are you looking for a mate because you yourself want one, or do you feel you have to have one to survive in this society?

• Apply this test to what you call "love": As one of your ways of expressing your love for the other person, can you let him or her have all the freedom and distance he or she may sometimes want? Love means caring about the well-being and fulfillment of your lover. If your lover needs some separateness, are you loving enough to grant that, instead of clamoring about your needs? An addict can't do this.

• Begin to practice small steps to smoke out and reduce your addictive behavior. Stop yourself before you make "just one more good-night call" to your lover. Ask yourself if your relationship would really suffer if your lover or spouse took an occasional business or pleasure trip separately. Consider the possibility of developing more interests for yourself—would that detract from your relationship or give you more to share? What threat is there in growing, in learning, in liking or even loving others besides your special lover, in having a career, or in going skiing alone?

• Begin to love yourself. Do things for yourself. Work at becoming the person you want to be, at developing the characteristics and abilities that you value. Don't depend on others to prove your worth. Learn to live fully as an independent person. Then you'll be ready to share yourself in a healthy, nondependent relationship.

• Accept yourself. Study yourself. Define your strengths and weaknesses. Set goals for change and growth. Make a list of your strengths, goals, and accomplishments. Your persistent and courageous work on your internal being will give you an understanding of other people's struggles. You'll be more accepting and compassionate, more able to work on your relationships with others. You will have the inner resources to deal with the change that is central to life. You won't be afraid of losing external support, because you'll be strong enough to stand on your own. You won't be afraid to share, because you'll know there's enough of you to survive giving.

• Learn the difference between addictive love and genuine love. Addictive love costs too much. It depletes you. It steals your energy for living. It gives you intense, temporary highs that you pay for with dependence, fearfulness, and sometimes self-disgust. Genuine love enriches and strengthens givers and receivers. It is shared, supportive without being controlling. It can accept separation, differences, and independence.

• Turn the disappointment and self-disgust you feel in an addictive relationship into a tool for cure. When you see how it is you and not your lover who keeps you in a relationship that makes you feel miserable, you will generate the determination to change.

• Take the following steps toward genuinely loving relationships: Stop thinking of love as a scarce commodity that must be collected from others. Develop your sense of worth and integrity. Appreciate other people as full, equal beings. Don't look to control others or to be controlled by them. Gain the strength to be supportive of others by learning to support yourself. Be willing to give serious attention to the nature of your relationships with others. Loving involvements take confidence, concentration, and patience. As your love progresses, take stock of its strong points and of the aspects that need work. Talk to your lover about these. Try to reach joint conclusions about ways to improve the relationship. Give yourself and your lover time and space to find ideas, talents, interests, other people to share with each other. Take all the joy you can from this giving and sharing. Be confident that if necessary you can survive the loss of love.

• The work you do to kick the habit of love addiction, painful as it may be, will help you develop into a stronger and more truly loving person—one who loves himself or herself and who can use that love as a source from which to love others nonpossessively.

SUGGESTED READING:

Fromm, Erich. *The Art of Loving.* New York: Harper & Row paperback, 1974.

Peele, Stanton. *Love and Addiction.* New York: New American Library, 1975.

See also: DEPENDENCY, DEPRESSION, JEALOUSY, LONELINESS, LOSS OF LOVE

LYING

When W. C. Fields said, "Never trust an honest man," he may have meant that lying is so universal that we should not believe someone who claims he or she never lies. Opportunities to lie occur often. There are many kinds of lies—from fibs to perjury—and we tend to evaluate each according to its circumstance. A lie may serve to avert harm or protect an important confidence, or it may be an intentional, self-serving deceit.

Lies which are told allegedly to protect others and not for personal gain are often called "white lies." Most of us use them at times. We may say "I'm sorry, but I can't go" in place of the needlessly abrasive "I don't want to go." Nobody is maliciously deceived by the false excuse, and nobody's feelings are hurt. We sign letters "Sincerely yours," greet strangers with "Very pleased to meet you," and are repeatedly encouraged to "have a good day" without much attention to whether these phrases express true feelings.

There are many kinds of well-intentioned lies. We might not hesitate to lie about our best friend's whereabouts to protect him or her from an enemy. Yet well-intentioned lies often pose the greatest moral dilemmas. Should a couple lie to an adopted child about his parentage? Should a physician tell a patient she is dying? Should a husband cover up an affair in his past? In these cases, the relationship between the individuals involved must be examined. If one person expects and relies on the honesty of the other, an irreparable rift may result from lying. People who learn they have been deceived in a matter important to them are likely to be resentful, disappointed, and suspicious. They may feel wronged and become wary of all future overtures from whoever lied to them.

The usual aim of lying is to make another person believe something that is untrue. However, the unconscious aim of habitual or pathological liars is to reassure themselves of their own power. Such lying may express a struggle to maintain personal self-esteem. A compulsive liar may even lie about irrelevant details or say things which are obviously false because he or she needs to feel in control. In effect, habitual liars are saying, "You must see things the way I describe them to you." Their lies are attempts to force the world into their own mold—one they feel able to cope with. Children often experience this sense of powerlessness. They sometimes invent imaginary playmates or concoct tall tales of adventure to make themselves feel more loved or important.

Lying is a problem when you use it to manipulate people who trust you, to cop out from facing reality, or to fool yourself and others as to who you really are. Recognizing why you lie offers an opportunity to learn more about yourself. Why do you think you have to make yourself seem other than what you are? Overcoming a tendency to lie will present you with the challenge of becoming more competent as a person and the opportunity to develop reality-based self-esteem. Try these steps.

• Notice when you lie. What do you lie about? Your age, sexual conquests, income? Are you seeking to disguise an inadequacy? Do you pay false compliments to win approval? Do you exaggerate your accomplishments to boost others' confidence in you? What needs or self-image problems are involved? Are you also lying to yourself? Recognize the areas in which you may need to develop more solid self-esteem. Keep a record of the lies you tell, the circumstances in which you tell them, and the advantages you seek by lying. Then write down what qualities or skills you would have to develop in order not to feel the need to lie.

• If you lie to avoid punishment, examine the long-range price you may end up paying for the short-term gain. Are you actually compounding your problems?

• How does the knowledge that you have lied affect you? Do you think less of others when they believe your lies? Do you think less of yourself because you need to lie?

• Do you often try to excuse a lie afterward by claiming it was just a joke or an exaggeration, that you did not intend to mislead? Justifying your lies shows that you are worried and that you need to examine your own feelings about lying.

• Do you blame or overestimate the forces pushing you to lie? Do you excuse deceit when it arises because "the system" is unfair? Do you lie to avoid the challenge of risking action? A couple may decide to falsify their address to qualify for less expensive automobile insurance because they—and all their friends—think the system of varying premium rates by residence area is an unfair practice. Instead of lying, however, they could have challenged the system, protested, and lobbied for a change in policy, as has been done successfully in some places.

• One man persisted in lying to his girlfriend about his age because he was afraid she would reject him if she knew he was younger than she. Actually, she became increasingly annoyed because she suspected he was lying. His age didn't bother her—his lying did. They both felt better when he told her the truth, and he saw that his lie had been unnecessary and disturbing.

• If you lie to protect yourself because your political beliefs or sexual preferences are unacceptable in your community, ask yourself if you can be comfortable living a lie. Recognize the risk that you may distort something of value in yourself by denying a central part of your identity.

• Even lies which seem justifiable involve risks. Be aware that many more lies may be needed to cover up or embellish the first one. These may soon need additional mending. How much energy are you willing to invest? The great thing about telling the truth is that it is easier to remember what you said to whom.

• Recognize that a lie that seems harmless or even beneficial to you may not seem so to the person deceived. A child who is lied to may feel deeply betrayed, and may conclude that all grown-ups bend the truth when it suits them. In any situation in which a lie is a possible choice, first examine a truthful alternative. Instead of telling a child that medicine will taste good, you can simply state it will help him or her get well. Instead of pretending to a friend that you have to work and thus can't play bridge, you can tactfully tell the truth, which might be that you need some time for yourself and aren't up to socializing.

• Look carefully at the consequences of the lies you tell. Be aware that you may lose the trust of others. How do your friends view lying? Double-check your environment before you get too comfortable with your lying. Don't kid yourself that lying is easier than telling the truth. Ask yourself if you expect others to be honest with you. How much do you value and depend on trust?

• Recognize that lies are frequently symptoms of life problems. Lying results from inner conflict, whereas truthfulness does not. Look for the motives and fears behind your lies.

• Is it really helpful to lie to protect someone's feelings? Certainly it is easier to reject a job applicant by saying the post has been filled, instead of that he is unqualified—but the applicant may then continue to pursue unrealistic career goals, and may even become resentful and blame others for his failure to get ahead. Look at the possible results of your "kindhearted" falsehoods, as well as your motivation. Are you afraid to deal with some of the more negative aspects of life? Do you lie to be a nice guy? Do you want others to lie to you to spare your feelings in the same kinds of situations?

Sometimes whole families practice mutual deceits to sustain illusions or suppress a painful memory. Parents may insist that discrimination—not poor grades—kept their daughter out of law school. Or a couple may suppress any mention of a child who died. Such attempts to avoid facing reality stifle growth. The student is not motivated to improve her skills. The couple are not allowing themselves to grieve.

• When you discover that someone has lied to you, face the challenge of becoming more realistic and alert, less indiscriminately trusting. Try not to let yourself be easily lied to. Insist that others take responsibility for doing what they say they will do. Don't accept repeated lying behavior. Object. Challenge it. Don't try to sustain a faltering relationship because you feel so insecure that you will overlook being lied to.

• Can you recognize when someone is lying? Facial movements offer clues. Rapid changes, particularly blinking or nervous jaw motions, reflect a liar's subconscious mind reacting to his or her false statements. The liar may try to mask this by other gestures, such as lighting a cigarette to distract the listener's attention.

• Train yourself to look for the negative potential of lies and to eliminate them from your speech. The need to resort to lies will diminish when you cease to see them as a useful alternative to the truth. If you can make it clear to others that you do not want them to lie to you and that they can expect you to tell them the truth, many needless and painful interpersonal complications will be avoided. And you may be surprised by how much freedom you gain by telling the truth. You will be able to be more open and spontaneous, because you won't have to worry about being caught in a lie. Take the risk. You'll probably find the consequences of truthfulness less difficult to manage than the consequences of lying.

SUGGESTED READING:

Bok, Sissela. *Lying: Moral Choice in Public Life.* New York: Pantheon Books, 1978.

See also: DELUSIONS, GUILT, PARANOIA, SELF-HATE

MARITAL QUARRELING

Some conflict is natural in any close relationship. Two people sharing time and space are certain to affect each other's freedom of choice and action in many ways every single day. How they choose to deal with their differences determines when routine friction escalates into a problem.

Fighting can be an exciting, liberating, and productive aspect of intimacy. A couple who never bicker may simply have very little emotionally at stake in their relationship. Other couples know how to argue in a problem-solving manner and avoid quarreling to punish, control, hurt, or belittle each other. The ability to argue constructively can be learned—just as supportive, caring behavior can be learned. In fact, some couples feel so strongly that open communication is essential to their marriage that they say it is "worth fighting for."

Conflict offers many positive opportunities for people to grow in marriage. In coming to terms with your differences, you can learn to empathize, to maintain flexible marital roles, to tolerate ambiguity, to be open-minded, and to communicate effectively. Conflict can teach you about the areas in which you still need to grow and develop as an individual *before* you can meaningfully share yourself with the person you love.

Marriage challenges both our capacity for intimacy and our need for separateness. How do you regard your marriage and your mate? Are you looking to your partner to "complete" your picture of yourself?

Perhaps to provide what you feel you lack? Did you think marriage would bring total happiness? Are you prepared for your marriage to change? Examining what you seek in your marriage and in your lover can help you to better understand your marital conflicts and begin to deal with them.

• Face your conflicts openly and clearly. This first step in solving a disagreement may seem quite simple and obvious, but it cannot be overemphasized. Discuss your areas of friction together when you are both in a calm, constructive mood. Remember, conflicts grow if they are ignored. Put aside the tendency to blame either your partner or yourself, and focus on getting a realistic picture of the conflicts you must work on.

• When you feel anger toward your mate, stop and look at where it's coming from. Realize that you created the anger from within yourself. You don't *have* to be angry. Is there an assumption lurking behind your anger—a demand that your spouse *ought* to behave a certain way? Look at these demands. They may be fundamental, such as that your partner should recognize your sexual signals, should come directly home from work, should devote Saturdays to family activities, and so on. How reasonable are your demands? Have you ever discussed them in a true spirit of negotiation and compromise? Try to separate your wishes from your demands, and change the "shoulds" into personal statements. If you change "He should want to make love tonight" or "He should go with me to the party" into "I wish he'd . . ." your partner may be better able to respond to you as a person rather than a dictator. Recognize how inappropriate and destructive it is to feel that your partner must do, feel, or think as you demand. Look for your spouse's hidden demands about you, too, and help him or her eliminate them.

• Train yourself to make "I" statements whenever you argue. Say how his or her behavior makes you feel, rather than putting a judgmental label on the behavior or person. You have a right to your feelings, but not to appoint yourself as Grand Inquisitor.

• Recognize that some areas of conflict are predictable at different marital stages, such as the birth of the first child, moving, job change, or an in-law's joining the household. Acknowledge these as "no-fault" situations and be careful not to blame your partner for creating tensions around them. Stress normally accompanies change—even if it is a pleasant and desired change.

• Begin to listen for recurrent themes behind your arguments. The three major conflict areas in marriage are sex, money management, and child-rearing. Problems in these areas can wound people in vulnerable parts of their identities. Look for the emotional touchiness beneath the friction. A bitter disagreement over how much allowance a child should receive may mask the wife's fear that her husband loves the child more than her. A husband's complaints about the cost of a new sofa may cover his fear of being an inadequate wage earner.

• Sort out your needs, wants, and expectations. Learn to tell them apart. Basic needs include needs for shelter, food, and sex. But we also need a sense of inner worth and outer attractiveness. How dependent are you on your spouse to provide for these needs? Is this a desperate dependency, a preference, or a self-righteous expectation? Are you both comfortable with each other's dependency needs? Are you looking too much to your spouse to bolster your self-esteem? Are you asking for more than you're giving?

• Learn to say what you want even when it seems unrealistic or selfish. First get it out in the open; later you can explore whether it is possible or fair. Try to transform negative wants ("I don't want our marriage to be so boring") into positive statements ("I want you to excite and surprise me, to initiate interesting activities"). Now you can begin to deal with the problem concretely. You may be surprised to learn how unaware your partner is of something you want. Don't expect your spouse to read your mind. If you're expecting guests in fifteen minutes and the house is a mess, instead of thinking that your partner ought to realize that you need help, ask for it.

• Learn to detect the clues your partner may be sending out. He or she may want your support but be unable to tell you. When your mate is cranky or moody, find out what's the matter. Don't guess or try to interpret his or her behavior on your own.

• List your expectations of your marriage and of your partner. Go over them together and determine which to try to satisfy and which, if any, to change. Discuss your mutual goals.

• Ask yourself if you are in touch with your expectations. Stop and examine the moments when you feel angry, hurt, disgusted, or upset with your partner. Often they will turn out to be times you expected something other than what you got. For example, a husband arrived home and was greeted by his wife's complaint that her new dishwasher had broken down and she had had to spend an hour doing dishes. He was expecting her to be happy with the new dishwasher, and she was expecting him to be sympathetic. He snapped, "What do you expect me to do about it?" She snapped back, "I told you to buy the more expensive one." Instead of combining resources to cheer each other up in the face of a disappointment, they stubbornly held on to expectations about how each other, the dishwasher, and life *should* be.

• Recognize that everyone is different, and do not expect your mate to change just to suit you. You can accept your individual differences without necessarily liking the way your spouse does things. Examine why you feel a particular way about a problem you are having. Are you influenced by the attitudes of your parents or a former spouse? Shake off what you've been taught to expect and value, and look for the good in what you have.

• Concentrate on your areas of mutual support and agreement, rather than on what divides you. Give each other plenty of credit for the adjustments you have made and for the pleasant times you have created together. Try to emphasize the positive.

• Ask yourself if "winning" an argument is important to your self-esteem. Do you keep score against your spouse? Do you regard compromise as "losing"? Do you store up grudges? Do you put down your partner in order to control him or her? Remember that your happiness will not come from winning but from solving conflicts.

• Once you recognize destructive, nonproductive arguments, you can seek to change the pattern. Stop fighting to win. Instead, learn what your most frequent and intense confrontations are really about. Remember that marriage is a cooperative venture, not a competitive one. A compromise which works, even though not ideal, is better than a brilliant but imposed solution which a resentful partner will try to sabotage.

• Practice new ways of arguing. There are certain sure-fire traps which you can learn to avoid by following a few simple rules:

1. Set aside a time and place to thrash out a problem without distractions. An argument may even benefit by being postponed until the air has cleared—so long as it's not too long a delay.

2. Don't argue in ways which alienate your partner. If you know he or she cannot stand it when you yell, practice keeping your voice down.

3. Learn to recognize and avoid misplaced emotions. If you come home angry at your boss, it's not a good time to discuss a hot emotional problem with your spouse.

4. Stick to the issue at hand. Steer clear of generalizations ("You never . . ." "I always . . .") and stereotyping ("There goes your Latin temper . . ."). Avoid emotional blackmail ("If you loved me, you'd . . ."), and refrain from sarcasm.

5. Be honest. Avoid withholding information. Say what you need and want. Don't test your spouse's memory or hope that your wish is his or her command.

6. Listen attentively. If you're not sure of your partner's message, restate it and ask for verification.

7. Try to keep your sense of humor.

8. Reconcile as soon as the conflict is solved. Apologize and put the problem behind you. Celebrate with some fun.

• If you have difficulty in communicating the strength of your wants, you may find it helpful to rate your feelings on a scale of 1 to 10 in order to bargain or arrive at a compromise. For instance, when you see that the idea of going out to dinner rates a very lowly 1 with your spouse, you might propose getting some take-out chicken and find it rates a 6 and is a workable compromise.

• Examine how your marital situation now differs from earlier, happier days. List all the things which have happened: career changes, sexual infidelities, the birth of children, and so on. Has one of you had more opportunity for emotional growth than the other? Are you uneasy with the changes in your relationship? Do you regard them as threats to your happiness?

It goes without saying that both partners must be willing to work at their problems if fighting fair is to succeed. Is there anything you can do to remedy your conflicts without the cooperation of your spouse? First, recognize that you do play a role in the conflict. Then confront your partner with the problem, even though you suspect that he or she may deny it. Be careful not to let your partner dump it all back on you with "You expect too much of me" or "You want more than I can give." Instead, use this opportunity to find out what you can expect and exactly how much he or she is willing to give. Then you can judge whether you can be comfortable in the relationship on those terms.

If the uncooperative partner has destructive or compulsive habits—such as drinking—recognize the advantages of professional counseling and peer self-help groups (such as Alcoholics Anonymous). Be sure you're not counting on your partner's remorse the next morning to prevent future occurrences of destructive fighting. He or she will need to deal with his or her own problem before being ready to solve mutual conflicts.

If your partner will not join you in a counseling or self-help program, there are still plenty of good reasons to go yourself. For one thing, the question "Why am *I* in this predicament?" bears looking into.

SUGGESTED READING:

Bach, George R., and Peter Wyden. *The Intimate Enemy: How to Fight Fair in Love & Marriage.* New York: William Morrow, 1969.

Lasswell, Marcia, and Norman Lobsenz. *No-Fault Marriage.* New York: Ballantine Books, 1977.

Wanderer, Zev, and Erika Fabian. *Making It Work.* New York: G. P. Putnam's, 1979.

See also: ANGER, COMMUNICATION BLOCKS, COMPETITIVENESS, DIVORCE, LOVE ADDICTION

MASOCHISM

There are two kinds of masochism—psychic masochism and sexual masochism—which may or may not coexist in the same person. What we are concerned with here is the psychic kind—when you enjoy your own suffering, revel in your own helplessness, arrange your life so that it is filled with failure, bad luck, or a continued round of mysterious mishaps.

We are usually blind to our own masochism, but we can easily spot it in others. We all know people who gravitate toward insufferable jobs, miserable relationships, or disappointing life circumstances—in short, "born losers." They loudly protest their cruel fate, yet seem secretly to enjoy it. There's a wicked smile playing about their lips as they tell us about their most recent catastrophe.

In fact, masochists go out of their way to inform us of how they have been misunderstood, offended, insulted, deprived, humiliated, underrated, defeated, wronged, exploited. Some professional comedians have made "looking pitiful" their *shtick*. They want the whole world to know. Psychoanalyst Theodor Reik, Sage of Masochism, has labeled this "The Demonstrative Factor." Masochists feel compelled to *demonstrate* to themselves and others how much they are suffering. This merging of pain and pleasure has been aptly termed "the joy of suffering."

Troubles happen to all of us. Normal people roll with the punches, remind themselves that "you win some and you lose some," and look for the silver lining in the cloud. If you are a masochist, you collect "injustices," complain that your glass is half empty, and end up believing that you have a claim against the world due to the hardships you have endured. To bolster your claim, you continually create and display new hurts.

If you are skillful at inviting others to mistreat you and then blaming them for it, your ploy is called "provocative suffering." You win by losing. You achieve a moral victory by making your "villain" feel guilty. If you are a really dedicated masochist, you will find and stick with a sadistic, exploitative, punitive, abusive mate—the long-suffering housewife married to an abusive alcoholic husband is a common example.

Your masochistic secret payoffs are always in danger of being "wrecked by success." If good luck should happen to strike you in spite of your best efforts, you will need to put on further displays of unworthiness and incompetence. At all costs you must protect yourself from envy or the accusation that you are happy and well off in this vale of tears.

Masochism "works" because it helps reduce guilt and anxiety about being punished. If you were punished erratically and inconsistently as a child, you may feel unable to bear the suspense of wondering when and how and for what you are going to be punished. You seek out punishment or inflict it on yourself, end the suspense, and get the worst over with. "Pay as you go" is the philosophy—suffer, sneak in a little pleasure, suffer some more. And by taking the punishment into your own hands you control the feared situation. As a child you were the victim. Now you are the playwright, director, hero, villain, and critic.

Another hidden reward is the chance to punish one's parents. "Cut off your nose to spite your face." Go out in the garden and eat worms. That will show them how mean they've been to you. "They'll be sorry." A miserable life stands as irrefutable testimony that your parents raised you wrong. To forget about them and live happily would let them off the hook.

Self-attack is a "safe" and "approved" outlet for anger. But if you are clever you can arrange it so that self-defeat becomes self-and-other-defeat. As Reik puts it, you can achieve "victory through defeat."

Because of the basic and ingrained self-deception involved, masochism is one of the hardest of all psychological problems to overcome. For starters, try these suggestions:

• Acknowledge your role in hurting yourself. Admit that you are a masochist if you see yourself in the above description. Take responsibility for causing this trouble for yourself. True, it may have started out as a childhood strategy, but that child was and is you. Only you can develop new and more effective strategies for coping with the world.

• Accept that it is natural to be somewhat divided inside, to have self-enhancing and self-defeating tendencies. Become more aware of these contradictory impulses, learn to detect the hidden martyr and saboteur in yourself.

• Recognize that masochism is essentially a power play that you designed for self-protection in a hostile world. Work on making a transition from your overemphasis on defense through individual, separate power toward self-affirmation through love and sharing.

• Learn a new skill: self-compassion. Practice it in small and large ways. Take pity on yourself and stop putting yourself through the tortures of the damned. You've taken enough punishment already. Take the energy you've put into self-attack and manipulation of others and put it to work in taking care of yourself.

• Since masochism is self-inflicted pain, counteract it by the opposite —self-administered pleasure. Put more fun into your life.

• Don't indulge in ostentatious suffering to forestall what you sense to be imminent attacks by others. Don't display weakness or take pleasure in weakness.

• Since you invented masochism originally as a defense against anxiety, find new ways to achieve anxiety-reduction. Try meditation, exercise, a trip to the country.

• Welcome good fortune. Accept lucky breaks, cherish praise. You deserve it after all you've been through.

• Forgive your father, your mother, God, your boss, and all the authority figures who have "driven" you to a life of pain and suffering.

• Be alert to the psychology of "reversals" which are characteristic of masochism: submission expresses unconscious rebellion, yielding equals obstinacy, servility stands for defiance, and self-humiliation stands for arrogance. Underneath it all, there's a raging child screaming to get out.

• Stop playing "poor little me" in your threadbare suit. Stop trying to make people feel sorry for you. Get a new outfit and go out on the town.

• If you suffer a reversal at the hands of fate, don't advertise it all over town. It's nothing to brag about. It won't earn you love.

• Let go of the whole drama you have created with you in the star role as all-enduring saint. It's a worn-out melodrama. Your audience is probably tired of your sanctimonious, "holier-than-thou" moral superiority. Your masochism is only going to earn you an early old age, not an Academy Award.

• Act *as if* it were impossible to fail. That is the talisman, the formula, the command of right-about-face which turns us from failure toward sucess. Dorothea Brande's "as if" strategy advises you to psych yourself into success. If one of your beliefs is "everything happens to me," find a new and better belief—because beliefs become self-fulfilling prophecies.

By facing masochistic tendencies and replacing them with self-affirming behavior, you will be gradually conquering one of the most troubling of all human problems. Active, responsible caring for yourself is more satisfying in the long run than the self-pity, the sympathy, and the concessions you can extort with masochism. Life is not easy, but it can be a lot easier and happier than we make it or allow it to be when we are masochistically proving that life in general or some people in particular are unfair. Drop the old argument; it's time to live.

SUGGESTED READING:

Menninger, Karl. *Man Against Himself*. New York: Harvest, 1938.

Reik, Theodor. *Masochism in Sex and Society*. New York: Pyramid, 1976.

Warner, Samuel J. *Self-Realization and Self-Defeat*. New York: Grove Press, 1966.

See also: ANXIETY, FEAR OF FAILURE, FEAR OF SUCCESS, GUILT, PSYCHOSOMATIC ILLNESS, SADISM, SELF-HATE, SEXUAL PERVERSIONS, SUICIDE, UNDERACHIEVEMENT

MASTECTOMY

Tens of thousands of American women every year face the prospect of mastectomy: the surgical removal of one or both breasts because of cancer. Mastectomy is presently the most common and perhaps most sure way of combating breast cancer, which is a leading cause of death in women.

The chances for cure of breast cancer depend on how far the cancer has spread and its location and size. For this reason, early detection is one of the most important factors in successful care. Yet the possibility of breast cancer is so terrifying that many women delay reporting the presence of a lump in their breast.

The causes of breast cancer (and all cancer) are not really known. It may be partially hereditary. It appears related to menstrual and childbirth history. Oral contraceptives, stress, obesity, virus, race, and country of residence are also possible related factors. Even mammograms (an X-ray procedure for detecting breast cancer) were once suspected of contributing to the disease.

For many years the most common type of surgery has been the Halsted radical mastectomy, which is the removal of the breast, axillary lymph nodes, and pectoral (chest) muscles. There is increasing controversy as to the necessity for removal of the chest muscles, and even the removal of the breast itself in some cases, rather than just the lump and some axillary lymph nodes for biopsy. The lymph nodes are the body's first line of defense against breast cancer, and only a surgical biopsy can determine the extent of the cancer's invasion. Even when cancer has spread to some of the nodes, some experts believe that the healthy nodes should be left in place to fight possible remnants of cancer cells following the surgery, or to fight against recurrence.

Breast surgery may be followed by chemotherapy, less frequently by radiation, depending on biopsy findings and the doctor's orientation. Opinions and treatment techniques change as more is learned.

The loss of any part of the body is very painful not only physically but emotionally. The shock and grief of mastectomy is greatly intensified if the patient has gone into the hospital for a breast biopsy and awakens to find a breast missing. The best eventual adjustment to mastectomy is usually made by the woman who has a solid image of herself as a valuable person, is in a satisfying emotional relationship, and has made an informed choice about her medical treatment.

If you are faced with the possibility of breast cancer, your immediate challenge is to inform yourself and make the best decision about your treatment. If you choose mastectomy as best and necessary, see it as an opportunity to discover or strengthen yourself as a valuable, attractive person, to rebuild your physical and emotional self after surgery, and to use this time of emotional pain to build a stronger love relationship with your partner.

• Consult your physician if during self-examination of your breasts you discover any of these warning signals of cancer: a lump anywhere in your breasts; changes in the skin of the breast, such as scaling or cracks; cracked nipples or secretion from the nipples; pain or swelling in the breast that is not related to the menstrual cycle; an asymmetry in appearance of a breast or a change in one breast but not the other.

• Do not be rushed into agreeing to an operation. Unless your doctor feels your life is in immediate danger, you might prefer to schedule your treatment in two steps: Have a biopsy first, then make your decision about surgery. Wait the few days for results of a permanent-section biopsy rather than depend on the immediate results of a quick-frozen section, which can be (though rarely is) in error.

• Investigate alternate biopsy procedures. Ask your doctor about fine-needle or wide-bore-needle techniques, which are done in some other countries but are not yet common here. Ask about having a surgical biopsy with a local anesthetic in your doctor's office or as a hospital outpatient. A simple biopsy does not usually require hospitalization. A small lump may be a cyst that can be diagnosed by your doctor in his or her office.

• If cancer is diagnosed, ask your doctor about doing a radioactive scan of your body to see if the cancer has spread to other organs. If it has, it may be best not to go through a mastectomy but to begin other treatment, such as chemotherapy, immediately.

• If a mastectomy is recommended, ask your doctor about each of these surgical options:

1. Having only the lump removed, with some tissue, as well as lymph nodes for biopsy. This operation does not usually change the appearance of the breast.

2. Having a partial mastectomy, in which the lump and a greater portion of tissue and skin are removed, along with some of the lymph

nodes. The breast is not removed but is changed in appearance.

3. Having a subcutaneous mastectomy, in which a portion of skin and sometimes the nipple are retained, as a base for reconstructive surgery of the breast. (Reconstruction can be done following other procedures as well.)

4. Having a simple, or total, mastectomy, in which the breast is removed but not the axillary nodes. A node biopsy may also be done.

5. Having a modified radical mastectomy, which removes the breast and lymph nodes, leaving the pectoral muscles.

6. Having a Halsted radical mastectomy, which does remove the pectoral muscles. (This is seldom done.)

7. Having an extended radical mastectomy, in which some additional nodes are removed, necessitating removal of some rib sections. (This is seldom done.)

• Ask your doctor about interstitial radiation therapy—the temporary implanting of radioactive isotopes in the breast—as an alternative to surgery. This is a relatively new procedure in this country. It involves discomfort and sometimes minor surgery, as well as radiation or drug treatment.

• Recognize that all surgery, radiation, and drugs have both benefits and risks, and there is much controversy about probable results.

• Remember that all positive and negative predictions about cancer are probabilities, not guarantees.

• Discuss your choices and their consequences with those you love and trust, such as your husband and family. Remember that the more thoroughly you explore, express, and accept your feelings now, and the more support you have from loved ones, the better off you will be in the future.

• Even though you discuss and consult with others, make your own decisions about what is best for your body. Take as much time as you need, or as your doctor will allow you, to choose thoughtfully.

• If there is any doubt about the diagnosis and recommendation, get a second or third medical opinion. Remember that surgeons think in terms of surgery.

• Before you decide anything, read *Why Me?* by Rose Kushner. This is more than the story of one woman's surgery. It is an informative, interestingly written, emotionally supportive report on the total picture of breast cancer that will help you make intelligent decisions about your various options and adjust to surgery if you do have it.

• If you decide that surgery is necessary, be sure you feel totally confident about your surgeon's experience and competence in the specific operation you have chosen.

• Find out what to expect while you are in the hospital, both before and after the operation. Ask what physical symptoms, such as pain or numbness, you should expect immediately after the operation. Remember that the intensity and duration of aftereffects vary from person to person.

• Find out what postoperative treatment your doctor recommends, such as X-ray therapy or chemotherapy. Ask about possible side effects of each as well as potential benefits. Ask what further treatment to expect if the cancer is estrogen-dependent—drug therapy or removal of the ovaries?

• By all means say yes to a visit from a Reach to Recovery volunteer following your operation. She is a recovered mastectomy patient who will help you with exercises, give advice and information and emotional support, and give you a "lounger," or temporary prosthesis (artificial breast). If a Reach for Recovery volunteer does not call, contact the American Cancer Society and ask for one. Her visit may be against hospital policy or your doctor's philosophy, but insist on seeing her.

• Expect to go through difficult emotions after the operation, possibly including grief or depression. Try to help your husband or lover experience his feelings of sorrow, disappointment, or anger about your suffering and loss. Be alert to his (or your own) denial of the facts. Don't allow feelings to be pushed under the surface. If necessary, get counseling both before and after surgery.

• Don't blame yourself for having cancer, and don't blame fate or the world. Guilt and blame are useless emotions that only slow down your recovery.

•Obey your doctor's instructions carefully regarding dos and don'ts following surgery. Since the surgical area is especially prone to infection, avoid cuts, burns, sunburn, and pulling and strain on your arm.

• Follow your doctor's instructions about frequent regular checkups after surgery, especially the first two years when recurrence of cancer is most likely. Follow a home program of regular breast self-examination (BSE) and report any menstrual irregularities or persistent hoarseness or coughs.

• Reach out to other women for emotional support—find out you're not alone. Join a rap group of other ex-patients. Talk to friends. Be aware, however, of the limits of support with women who haven't been through mastectomy or haven't worked through their feelings about it.

• If for a while after your surgery you don't feel ready to resume lovemaking, allow your husband to show his caring in other ways, and express your warmth and love for him. Perhaps he now finds you even more precious and valuable than before, because of the danger you have escaped.

• Examine the interactions in which you nurture and are nurtured by others, and deepen those kinds of relationships. Try to build your own self-nurturance. Be good to yourself—eat well, dress attractively, buy something you've wanted for a long time. Seek new avenues of self-expression and growth.

• Allow the seriousness and pain of your operation and your escape from illness to give you a new perspective on what is important in your life. Go in the direction most enriching to you. Recognize that an orientation toward openness, activity, and creativity helps your immune system resist negative forces of illness.

• Investigate alternative philosophies of wellness as a supplement to your medical treatment. See FEAR OF SICKNESS, and PSYCHOSOMATIC ILLNESS for information about visualization exercises, relaxation techniques, and other holistic approaches to health. Learn from this that your mind and body are not separate entities and that your positive emotions can help cure you, even of cancer.

• Think about wearing a prosthesis, which will make your figure look natural even in a bathing suit. They're expensive, so shop around, ask questions, and make sure you're getting the right size, shape, and weight for your figure. Silicone looks and feels most like a real breast, but it's not suitable for everybody. Check your medical insurance— some plans will pay for it, but some consider a prosthesis merely cosmetic! Get advice and instructions from Reach to Recovery, which is an American Cancer Society service. Contact any ACS office or write to 777 Third Avenue, New York 10017.

• Consider eventual reconstruction of your breast by silicone-pad implant. Even the nipple can be reconstructed, through grafts. Read about the benefits and risks in *I Am Whole Again,* by Jean Zalon with Jean Libman Block.

• If you continue to have severe emotional difficulties following surgery, ask yourself what your breasts represent. If they are for feeding infants, what does this loss mean to you? If they are for attracting and pleasuring men, does your self-worth depend on them? In what other ways can you now feel valuable and fulfilled?

• Get nearly any kind of information you need—for instance, locate a doctor or psychological support, or find out about current research and treatments—from Cancer Information Service (CIS). To locate one in your area, call toll-free 1-800-638-6694. Or write Office of Cancer Communications, National Cancer Institute, Bethesda, Maryland 20014, and ask for their information pamphlet.

• Consider joining Reach for Recovery—helping others helps your own psychological healing. Or join an organization for cancer patients and relatives called Make Today Count. To see if there is a group in your area, write P.O. Box 303, Burlington, Iowa 52601.

SUGGESTED READING:

Kelly, Orville, and W. Cotter Murray. *Make Today Count.* New York: Delacorte Press, 1975.

Kushner, Rose. *Why Me?* New York: Signet, New American Library, 1977.

Rollin, Betty. *First You Cry.* New York: Signet, New American Library, 1976.

Silverstein, Melvin and Karen. *Side Effects.* New York: Doubleday, 1978.

Zalon, Jean, with Jean Libman Block. *I Am Whole Again.* New York: Random House, 1978.

See also: CANCER, FEAR OF SICKNESS, PSYCHOSOMATIC ILL-NESS

MASTURBATION

Masturbation has had a lot of bad press, starting with Biblical condemnation. Generations were brought up to believe it was a sin. Children were warned of terrible consequences—everything from growing hair on their palms to insanity. It has been labeled dirty, shameful, and self-destructive.

In fact, masturbation is a problem only if you think it is a problem. If you believe it is wrong to masturbate and you go ahead and do it anyway, you will feel bad. If you feel guilty enough about masturbation (or anything else, for that matter), you could end up sick or socially withdrawn.

If you are concerned about masturbation, you need to take time to explore with yourself, or with a friend or counselor, what your values, attitudes, beliefs, and needs really are. And don't limit yourself to a focus on masturbation. It is not an isolated act disconnected from the rest of your life. It ties in to your feelings about your body as a whole, your genitals in particular, sensual pleasure, self-assertion, loneliness, frustration, society's taboos, and other related areas of life.

Why do people masturbate? Are there "good" and "bad" or "healthy" and "sick" reasons to masturbate? As usual, experts disagree, but there is a strong trend to be not only supportive and accepting of masturbation as a normal human sexual outlet, but even to recommend it for certain people in certain circumstances. For example, Lonnie Barbach's book, *For Yourself: The Fulfillment of Female Sexuality,* describes a highly effective sex-therapy program which includes teaching women to learn about their sexual responses through masturbation. Many people benefit from opportunities to explore by themselves how they respond to stimulation, without outside distractions and pressures.

Unfortunately, even people who are free of old-fashioned guilts about masturbation have now fallen victim to new-fashioned guilts, sometimes called "achievement anxiety" or "performance pressure." Thus, they feel masturbation is a failure as a sexual experience because it is not "the real thing." Such people are helped by viewing masturbation in a more relaxed manner, as simply a convenient option, a comfortable alternative, and an experience that contributes to the sum total of one's sexual aliveness and adaptability.

• Security, control, sensitive physical caring, and tuning in to unique personal preference and needs are all part of good sex. Developing these qualities in a sexual relationship takes time and skill and a motivated partner. Masturbation provides a way to get in touch with yourself. This is valuable in its own right, and serves as an essential basis for getting in touch with a partner and showing that partner how to get in touch with you. Freedom and openness are scary. Many people need to venture into the new territory of passion in the safety of privacy.

• Are there pitfalls and dangers to masturbation? What about the old fear that you will get addicted to it? Will masturbation replace intercourse? There is no evidence to suggest this will happen in the absence of other causes for avoiding intercourse. Actually, the physical loosening up achieved by masturbation, especially of the blood vessels in the pelvic area, tends to make a person more desirous and capable of satisfying intercourse.

• A person who relies exclusively on masturbation and avoids venturing into other ways of being sexual may have problems, but they are not caused by masturbating. At worst, excessive masturbation may be used to avoid experiencing other needs and feelings. Almost any human activity can be used this way as a narcotic to dull pain, anxiety, guilt, or responsibility. Even if used this way, masturbation is a lot better for your health than driving fast or drinking to relieve feelings of inadequacy or loneliness.

• Repression can cause the problem it is intended to stamp out. Strict prohibition of masturbation can drive some people into compulsive, defiant masturbation which serves more of a rebellious than a pleasuring purpose. A person who is more stimulated by the fantasy of social disruption surrounding his or her masturbation than by the physical delight is exploiting his or her own body for perverse purposes. Eventually this will deaden true sexual responsiveness. It is okay to take off on other "trips" from masturbation, but not if they take you out of touch with basic caring about yourself.

• Sometimes people fear that if they get turned on by their own bodies they will then be too turned on by other bodies of the same sex, and end up homosexual. The choice of a sex partner has much deeper determinants than that, however. To value and enjoy opposite-sex bodies, you must first value and enjoy your own and be convinced that a partner will feel as you do.

• A man will sometimes fear that if his mate feels free to masturbate she won't need or want him as much. This is true in one sense: She will be released from the emotional tryanny of believing that she absolutely must depend on him for sexual pleasure and her feeling of self-worth as a woman. But that releases her to be more sexual and loving toward him than if she is anxious and dependent.

• Learning how to masturbate enjoyably takes practice and knowledge. Take time to explore yourself thoroughly. If you are into masturbation, choose it wholeheartedly. Read sex manuals; look at photos and diagrams of genitals so you know what is what. As with other forms of growth and change, you need to make a determined commitment and carry it into practice.

• Privacy and fantasy are important if you want to explore your feelings about masturbation. If you have never before included masturbation in your sex life or if you've never let yourself accept it as a regular part of your sex life, give yourself some private time to find out if you are comfortable with it. (You may later want to include masturbation among the sexual practices you share with your partner.) Plan some time alone, time when you can lock the bedroom door (or any convenient door) and not be disturbed for an hour. Give yourself a chance to relax and get acquainted with your body. Use a mirror if you like. Provide yourself with nonirritating lotions, a variety of fabrics (even a vegetable or two) to create novel touch sensations, or a vibrator. (Avoid sharp or glass objects—anything that could cause injury to your body, inside or out.)

• Let your mind wander freely among images of sexual excitement. Imagine a situation that turns you on. Let your hands roam in tune with your fantasy. Men may find it satisfying to surround their penis with a soft fabric or to coat their hands with an oil-based nonirritating lubricant. Women may find that moving against the bed or a pillow while on their stomach or pressing their thighs close together while moving to their fantasy will be complementary pleasures to direct clitoral or vaginal stimulation. Don't neglect any part of you—if it turns you on to touch yourself someplace, do it. Pleasure yourself.

• Do not rely for a long time on a single method or pattern of masturbating. You can become fixated on the pattern and then find it difficult to reach orgasm in any other way. Be imaginative and allow yourself varied experiences.

• Expand and learn from your masturbation fantasies. Free of a real partner, you can trip out and discover what kinds of partners and acts turn you on.

• Remember, masturbation is not a problem unless you make it into one by your attitude or by your misuse of it to avoid dealing with other real problems. If that happens, you need to examine and revise your attitudes about masturbation, or replace it with a sexual outlet acceptable to you, and shift your focus to the other problems you've been avoiding. Learning to deal with your feelings about masturbation provides you with an opportunity for heightened awareness of yourself and what life has to offer, and a stimulus to more responsible, self-affirming action.

SUGGESTED READING:

Barbach, Lonnie. *For Yourself: The Fulfillment of Female Sexuality.* New York: Doubleday, 1975.

Zilbergeld, Bernie, and John Ullman. *Male Sexuality: A Guide to Sexual Fulfillment.* Boston: Little, Brown, 1978.

See also: GUILT, SEXUAL DYSFUNCTION

MENOPAUSE

The physical changes of menopause are generally predictable, unlike the psychological changes, which are often dependent on individual and cultural beliefs about how a menopausal woman "ought to feel." With the end of ovulation and menstruation there is also a virtual end of estrogen production by the ovaries. The results of this hormonal change include the thinning of vaginal tissue, a decrease in vaginal lubrication, some loss of hair and muscle tone, and hot flashes—brief experiences of feelings of warmth, flushing, and perspiration.

Most women—contrary to the stereotype—do not find the physical changes of menopause hard to handle. Only a relatively small number seek medical attention for menopause symptoms. Some cultural attitudes, however, can make menopause an extremely painful psychological experience.

Although some women do genuinely mourn the loss of their ability to conceive and bear children, many more women face menopause with fears of aging, loss of meaningful life roles, and feelings of uselessness because of cultural traditions that define the woman's role in life solely in terms of sexual attractiveness and fertility. We may think of some men as improving with age—becoming mellower, wiser, and, some say, sexier. Most women, however, are thought to decline with age— becoming unattractive, silly, useless.

Menopause happens at a time in a woman's life when many losses may occur. Children are frequently grown and gone, youth has passed, and with it, perhaps, her sense of physical attractiveness. Her husband may have died. These other losses amplify the sense of sorrow that can accompany the end of menstruation, which had been a monthly reminder of fertility and femininity.

Unless a woman has some purpose in life other than her sexual and reproductive roles, she can find the transition through menopause very difficult to endure. Change does not have to be a problem, however. Biology does not decree that a female human being must be depressed, useless, or purposeless after menopause. Women can plan for this significant life change and meet it with energy, enthusiasm, and joy.

• Think of menopause as a time for development and reorganization. If you are healthy and no longer need to devote your time to childbearing and child-rearing you have a wonderful opportunity to set new goals for yourself. Intelligence in healthy people does not decline radically with age; you are not significantly less able to learn now than earlier in life. What do you want to learn? How do you really want to live in your community? What do you already have to share? Unfortunately, there are serious barriers of custom and prejudice against middle-aged or older women—but keeping yourself out of the world will only strengthen them.

• For many women the freedom that comes with age and menopause is frightening. For the first time, perhaps, they can try things for themselves—not as so-and-so's daughter, or wife, or mother. Women who have kept all their self-esteem in the basket marked "wife and mother," however, feel lost without these roles. They feel useless, unwanted, valueless. The depression so commonly associated with menopause and aging in women arises from these circumstances, not from the hormonal changes.

• Combat depression by moving yourself ahead. Set a goal and go after it. Create interesting and meaningful work opportunities: Go back to school, volunteer your talents, get a job, develop a craft or artistic skill you didn't have time for earlier, polish your tennis game. You are no less a person because you are going through a change. Let go of the responsibilities, struggles, and joys of the past and move toward the options, obstacles, and pleasures of the developing present. Dr. Juanita H. Williams, in *Psychology of Women*, observes that "women whose self-esteem is intact, whose lives continue to be interesting and rewarding, and whose work, whatever its nature, helps them to feel that they are making a continuing contribution to the society, are the least likely to have negative reactions to the change of life."

• Menopause is related to aging, of course. And, like aging, it is sometimes confused with a disease. *It's not a disease.* It's ordinary, predictable change. You can do much to help yourself age well and healthily. Keep your weight down. Eat a well-balanced diet. Stop smoking. Involve yourself in stimulating work. Get regular, moderate exercise to maintain muscle tone and body functions. Don't wait until you're sixty-five—begin now to develop the physical fitness that will ward off premature old age.

• The adage "Use it or lose it" applies to your sexual activities as well as your general physical fitness. Just as staying physically active will help you age comfortably and with continuing vigor and ability, so too will continuing to express your sexuality help you retain your "sexual fitness." When menstruation ends you're not old, nor have you ceased being a sexual person. You're not through with sex, just with worries about pregnancy. If you continue to act attractive and interested in sex, you and your partner will continue to find you so.

• Our society is afflicted with youth mania. We seem to fear aging, which is natural, normal, and unavoidable. Do not seek the fountain of youth in estrogen-replacement therapy; not only does this therapy *not* keep a woman young forever, it has serious side effects and carries the potential for significant harm. Estrogen-replacement therapy is appropriate only for treatment of severe physical symptoms of menopause, and it requires extremely rigorous medical supervision. If your physical symptoms do not demand medical intervention, deal with change and aging out of your own resources: your mind, spirit, and willingness to face challenge and opportunity.

SUGGESTED READING:

Cherry, Sheldon H. *The Menopause Myth.* New York: Ballantine Books, 1976.

Clay, Vidal S. *Women: Menopause and Middle Age.* Pittsburgh: Know, Inc., 1977.

Williams, Dr. Juanita H. *Psychology of Women.* New York: W. W. Norton, 1977.

See also: AGING, DEPRESSION, MID-LIFE CRISIS, SEX IN LATER LIFE, SEXUAL DYSFUNCTION

MID-LIFE CRISIS

A mid-life crisis can hit us anytime between young adulthood and old age. That span of years can range from age twenty-five to seventy-five, depending on how we define young and old. And in that fifty-year period we have time for more than one mid-life crisis. What do you think of as the midpoint of your life? When is your life half over? Your answer may change from time to time.

One man was concerned that he would die before he reached fifty, because his father had died of a heart attack at forty-nine. For this man, age twenty-five was his midpoint, and he went through a major crisis then, when most of his friends were happily embarking on what they saw as the beginnings of their lives. As the result of counseling and a physical-fitness program, he revised his expectations and lifestyle, so that when he reached fifty he felt better than he had at twenty-five. Then he had another mid-life crisis over what to do with all the extra years ahead of him that he'd never planned on living long enough to worry about.

We too seldom have positive pictures of growing older. Middle age, we say to ourselves, means no longer being free, young, sexy, beautiful, strong, and full of dreams. We think in terms of loss and decline, rather than growth and development. We look back to our youth, idealizing it and forgetting its crises. Our vision isn't trained to focus on the unique opportunities open to us now and in the future. We live in a youth-oriented society that romanticizes young adulthood and devalues or nervously cosmetizes the aging process.

We have few maps or charts to guide us optimistically and creatively through mid-life. Too many people trudge and stumble through those years, coping stoically with responsibilities and following the "programming" built into them from childhood without regard for their unique needs and capacities.

If that is how you've been living, you may gradually or suddenly find that you just can't do it anymore, that you've lost your energy and sense of direction. To deal with a mid-life crisis you first must recognize that you are having one. Since you are reading this entry, you probably already have some concern about this problem. Asking yourself the following questions will help you clarify the nature and degree of your problem. Facing yourself and your life may stir up anxiety. Don't panic —your anxiety is a sign that you have important work to do that can pay off in valuable ways. On the other hand, just because there is a lot of talk about mid-life crises these days doesn't mean you have to be fashionable and have one. Here are some questions to help you take stock.

• Do you find yourself repeatedly bored, restless, discontent with your work, family life, or leisure activities? Marriages are especially vulnerable to mid-life crises. Divorce is often only a partial or substitute solution to the need for a radical revision of one's whole orientation toward life.

• Do you fail to get the kick out of things that you used to? Sometimes we hold on to jobs, hobbies, and relationships that we have outgrown.

• Do you feel old, jaded, negative, cynical about life's possibilities? Life probably hasn't changed, but maybe you have.

• Do you find yourself without dreams, plans, enthusiasm for what lies ahead? Maybe you have completed a major phase in your life and need new visions.

• Do you have a sense of waste, futility, of your life being over? It could be that the first half of your life *is* over, and that trying to keep it alive is a waste of effort.

• Are you excessively preoccupied with fears of death or illness? Such feelings may reflect a deep crisis within you about life slipping away.

• Do you get sick or tired more than you used to? Illness and fatigue can be signs that you are not engaged in life in ways that are enlivening for you.

• Are you plagued with insomnia, fears, or depression? These symptoms may express a struggle with mid-life issues such as revising your lifestyle to include more meaning, love, and joy.

• Have your children, relatives, and friends moved away geographically or emotionally, leaving you lonely? Other people have their own courses of life which may take them away from you as you grow older. Such losses can cause mid-life crises as you are forced to let go, endure aloneness, and reach out to new people.

• Do you feel a kind of emptiness, despair, and lack of real purpose even in the midst of what used to feel like enjoyable, worthwhile activities, and even when you try new involvements that are touted as turn-ons? You may be lacking an internal "compass," "gyroscope," or guiding star to steer by.

If you've answered yes to any of these questions, you probably are experiencing some form of mid-life crisis. Rather than being a specific problem that you can attack, solve, and move on from, a mid-life crisis presents a set of interlocking problems that require several strategies and sustained creative work. Knowing that there is such a thing as a mid-life crisis, that most people have at least one at some point in their lives, and that it is a major growth opportunity rather than just a "problem" can give you immediate relief and a way to begin working on it.

Try these methods to relieve the crisis and begin growthful changes:

• Start creating a map of your life. Take an 8½ x 11 sheet of paper and write "Birth" at the top and "Age 10" at the bottom. Make an additional separate sheet for each ten-year period of your life:

11–20, 21–30, on up to 100 in case you should live that long. Fill in the sheets with the events that have been important in your life so far, the events that you predict will be important in the future, and the goals you would like to achieve. Mark with a red line in the left margin that span of years you regard as your mid-life phase—it may be anywhere from one to ten years long. Put red X's beside the various turning points in your life, such as job changes, marriage, divorce, or death of a parent. This map of your life will help you gain perspective on your life course. Keep it up to date, including changes in your goals and your view of your future. The crises of middle age can be relieved and transformed into a healthy concern for creating a meaningful life.

• Make a list of the people in your life who are really important to you. Promise yourself that you will give high priority to doing whatever seems necessary to honor and strengthen your relationships with those people. This will protect you from the danger of letting time go by and contact with them fade until one day you wake up in a crisis fearing that it is too late. Don't wait until a dear friend dies to deal with the fact that you don't have unlimited time.

• Do the same for pet projects and postponed trips as you did for friends. Make a list of things you want to do before you die or get too old to enjoy them. Write them on your map. One man kept having a dream that he was in an airport frantically trying to find out where and when to catch the plane to France. Finally he realized that he really wanted to see France but had dismissed his wish as impractical and irrelevant to his current life. Only as he listened to what his dream was telling him and began to fantasize about a trip to France did he discover how much it meant to him. When he finally made actual plans for a trip he felt more energetic and optimistic than he had in years.

• Celebrate mid-life events and transitions in ways that help you feel their significance and share it with others. Make a ritual or a symbolic gesture of letting go of the past and welcoming the future. When one couple saw their last child leave for college they sold the weary station wagon that had served in so many car pools, bought a sports car, and drove across the state to see old friends who were also facing the "empty nest" syndrome. A fortieth- or fiftieth-birthday party can be a grand occasion for summing up the past and looking toward the future.

• Cultivate some friends who are five or ten years older than you. Observe how they cope with mid-life transition, and talk to them about their feelings and strategies. You can learn from their successes, and their mistakes.

• Remember that a crisis is usually not just an external event that is upsetting you, but an internal lack of faith in your ability to grow and learn. It is easy to lose faith when we have avoided facing a problem or challenge and it suddenly forces itself upon us. But when the initial stressful impact wears off we can usually mobilize our resources. Give yourself time to do that before you worry that a crisis is going to overwhelm you permanently.

• This may be a time to consider a job or even a career change. If you are going to do this, get all the facts, advice, and guidance you can, but don't delay until it is too late. On the other hand, many people resolve their crises by choosing what they have already chosen—that is, by deepening and reaffirming their commitment to the occupation they are already in. A surgeon who had gone into medicine in response to family pressure thought of leaving at age forty-five to become an architect, his lifelong suppressed ambition. But he discovered he had come to love surgery, and satisfied himself with designing an addition to his house. The movie *Lifeguard* is a touching portrayal of a no-longer-young lifeguard who turns down a chance to become a Porsche salesman and rededicates himself to the work he loves.

• Use your mid-life crisis to motivate you to pursue a better diet and exercise program. The fear of aging and death can be a powerful stimulus to get people to value their health and the years they have left. Take stock of just what condition you are in and what you are doing for your health and well-being. A crisis can sometimes be the result of your deeper self warning and protesting about mistreatment and neglect. Pay attention, value the "messages" you get in your crisis, and do something about them.

• Consider whether this is the time in your life when you are ready for and in need of more philosophy, religion, or some other source of meaning. Check out your heritage of religious practices, ethnic traditions, or folk wisdom. It may be of more use to you now than when you were busy growing up and separating from your parents. Or you may have truly outgrown it, and need to select and create a new heritage that better suits you and the times you live in. A hardworking lone-wolf dentist who had become bored took time to have long talks with his grandmother. Previously he had thought of her as narrow and old-fashioned, but he found himself being inspired by her devotion to the welfare of others, often expressed in quaint little acts of kindness. He saw that he needed more of this orientation in his life, and as he began to give more of himself he felt younger and past the crisis.

• Develop the fine art of letting go graciously. You are going to have to let go of some dreams, friends, hobbies, and vanities whether you like it or not. Your mid-life crisis is a sign that it is time to get on with a new phase of life, and to let go of an outgrown one. Do it with style. Letting go will make you lighter and freer to move into the future.

   • Remember that it is your own unique life and your crisis, no one else's. Do it your way. Create your own timetable. Allow yourself as many months or years as you need. Talk to other people, read books, but in the end remember that only you can evolve the course that is right for you. Enjoy the process of discovery that blossoms out of the darkness of crisis.

SUGGESTED READING:

   Gould, Roger. *Transformations.* New York: Simon & Schuster, 1978.
   LeShan, Eda. *The Wonderful Crisis of Middle Age.* New York: Warner Books, 1973.
   Levinson, Daniel. *The Seasons of a Man's Life.* New York: Alfred A. Knopf, 1978.
   Sheehy, Gail. *Passages: Predictable Crises of Adult Life.* New York: E. P. Dutton, 1974.

See also: AGING, ANXIETY, BOREDOM, DEPRESSION, FEAR OF DEATH, JOB DISSATISFACTION, LONELINESS

MONEY WORRIES

   Many people have self-defeating negative life-scripts about money. Some nurture the myth that the rich aren't happy anyway, so making money isn't worth the effort. There's the myth of the "honest poor" that says the process of getting money would only dehumanize you, so you're better off staying poor and pure. "Money is the root of all evil." There's the sabotaging myth that says the time when you could make it big has already passed, so there's no use trying now.

   For some people whose real motive in life is to be "right" about their position, they'd rather be right than be rich. They rationalize that it's better to be righteous and "rich in spirit." They may even demonstrate a perverse form of materialism, showing off their virtuous poverty by driving a battered VW.

   The positive thinkers assert that the real source of money is in your head. You have only to blast loose from your bankrupt mental constructs to become a self-generating source of greenbacks. As long as you think and say things such as "Money is hard to get," that is just the way it will be.

   Their message is that you can psych yourself rich. The trick is in counteracting your childhood poverty programming. The kid caught sucking on a penny ("Take that filthy money out of your mouth!") unconsciously keeps that dirty stuff away from him for the rest of his life.

But the positive thinkers tend to discount the fear of success, the masochistic will to fail. Their simplistic "mind over money" philosophy can make but the slightest dent in such thick character armor. To make big money you must take big risks, yet to take any kind of risk you have to be able to endure suspense. The "risk theory" holds that people generally would rather avoid suspense—and the tension that goes with it—than have money. "I'd rather be poor and content than rich and anxious." Which is why most people operate much below their potential earning capacity.

If you're two days old, how do you get "rich"? You scream, try to find mother. She's got what you need. After thrashing about for a while, you may learn that the most important thing is not to move, not to give her any trouble. Later in childhood you have to be vigilant and competitive toward anyone who might be in your way. If it's Daddy you want to eliminate, you project that Daddy wants to get rid of you. The consequent fear and guilt may neutralize you as a competitive striver for riches. But people who are free to go after money learn in infancy and childhood that it's okay to want, to scream, and to grab.

Psychologists believe that we each seem to know unconsciously exactly how much we are "worth." To the extent that we feel powerless, we dream of money as remedying that condition. To some people, money becomes a symbol of power; they strive to accumulate it so that they can bend other people to their will. These power grabbers, manipulators, and empire builders are quite often persons who felt rejected by one or both parents in childhood, and they have channeled all of their rage into getting the money and power to dominate and control others instead of being at their mercy.

For others, money becomes a symbol of security. Having money reduces their anxiety by making them feel less dependent on other people. Having money "papers over" their fear of rejection, fear of loss of love, fear of humiliation. Eventually, the fear of financial loss takes over their lives. They become self-deniers nurturing a "poverty complex" or they become compulsive bargain hunters or fanatic collectors.

To some people, money represents virility; they hate to part with it. To some love-starved creatures, money becomes equated with affection. Other guilty souls try to throw it away.

All of these "pseudo money motives"—using money to achieve a sense of worthiness, love, virility, power; for anxiety-avoidance, being right, showing up father—are going to blind you in the long run. They won't let you have money or enjoy it. They'll sabotage your efforts every time. Just as you're about to get the money you'll lose it through some kind of atonement gesture. Or you'll be so uptight about the money that you won't be able to use it.

One psychologically valid technique you can practice to raise your money consciousness is "visualization," which refers to the use of mental imagery to achieve goals. Anthony Norvell, whose Carnegie Hall lectures have drawn capacity crowds for decades, tells you to visualize a gigantic "magnetic whirlpool," where, on the outer periphery, you will see all the things you want swirling around—TV sets, refrigerators, $1,000 bills. "Now mentally begin to pull in to the center of the psychic whirlpool each of the things that you want to attract."

Such visualization exercises take us into the realm of modern brain research and right- and left-brain thinking. The left cerebral hemisphere is rational, analytical, and logical, whereas the right half of the brain is metaphoric, intuitive, and imagistic. It might seem that the path to riches would be rational and logical. Wrong. The capacity to generate "hunches" is right-brain stuff and fortunes cannot be created without that power of intuition. After all, the oldest way in the world to get rich is to tune in to what people want and to give it to them. That comes straight from the right hemisphere.

Don't let "money worries" get you down. Try some of these techniques:

• Dissolve the barriers between you and your money. Are you running money or is money running you? Take a look at your secret payoffs for psyching yourself poor. Maybe you're resigning from the rat race with a sense of moral superiority, and your secret payoff is piety.

• Uncover what it is that you really want subconsciously. Are you overloading your attempts to get money with too many other needs as well? Is making money a desperate way to prove your worth as a human being? Are you trying to show that you deserve love? Or that you are macho? If all of this is riding on your drive for wealth, you've got a lot more to lose than money. You could end up lonely, helpless, worthless, abandoned, unloved. Focus on the problem of making money without asking it to solve all your other problems.

• If you're trying to find a feeling of safety in money to offset a feeling of emotional insecurity, there is only one course of action: You must learn to take a chance on people and trust them with your feelings. Money won't ever buy that for you. Real security comes from creating good relationships with yourself and others.

• If you're plagued with negative thinking and you grew up with the idea that you're no good, that you can't do it, that nobody in your family did it, turn that around. Develop a positive self-image so you'll say, "I'm going to find ways to make it happen."

• Deprogram yourself of your poverty programming. Write down on 3 x 5 pieces of paper: "Money is the root of all evil." "Rich people lead miserable lives." "Poor is pure." Crumple up the papers into balls and pitch them into the nearest wastebasket.

• Activate your fantasies to increase your motivation and anticipatory pleasure. Imagine what you'll do with the money you get from a raise, how you will decorate your new office when you get that promotion, where you will live when you've "made it big."

• Impecunious people image what they fear, so instead image what you want. Write out a check to yourself for a million dollars and carry it in your billfold at all times. Cut out a magazine ad for a Rolls-Royce and paste it behind the door of your medicine cabinet.

• Learn to concentrate. The "millionaire mentality" displays self-confidence, enthusiasm, and a tremendous capacity for hard work. But one trait stands out above all—concentration. The successful tycoon worries, of course, but he is more single-minded. His business is all. Faced with a problem, he will tackle it with dogged determination.

• Don't *worry* about money, say the Zen Buddhists. Just go ahead and involve yourself in your "right livelihood," your particular passion, or whatever you are doing. Try to separate the problem of money from what you are doing for a living and money will come to you—if you are doing the "right" thing.

• "Be an individualist" is the advice of the late billionaire businessman J. Paul Getty in his book, *How to Be Rich*. Be a nonconformist, a dissenter, a rebel who is never satisfied with the status quo. Be an original, imaginative, resourceful, and entirely self-reliant entrepreneur. Take risks. Seek new horizons. Constantly seek new and better ways to do things.

• "Admit openly and inwardly that you like money. Say, 'I like money! I need money! I want money!'" Such is the advice of Reverend Ike, promulgator of the doctrine of Green Power. "Money is like a woman," he preaches. "You have to let her know you love her, you have to caress her, you have to say nice things about her all the time, or she'll leave you for sure."

• "Whatever you vividly imagine, ardently desire, sincerely believe, and enthusiastically act upon must inevitably come to pass," says Paul J. Meyer, founder of the Success Motivation Institute of Waco, Texas. In his course, How to Become Financially Independent, he counsels: Avoid irrelevant activities. Set priorities. Procrastination is suicide on the installment plan. Avoid the temptation to stop and start, stop and start. Do it once. When you want to become more like something, act "as if" it were so and you will become it.

• Face up to whether you are really willing to do something that people want enough to pay you money for it. Maybe you are stuck in a stubborn pride position or righteous argument about how the world *should* recognize your worth by giving you more money. That won't work. Like it or not, you have to make, do, give, or create something people need or think they need.

By clarifying how much money you feel you want and deserve, you will become more aware of the role in society you have assigned yourself or allowed yourself to be assigned. As you determine what you are and are not willing to do to get money, you will develop your value system. Overcoming self-defeating patterns in regard to money will help you deal with other forms of self-limitation and self-sabotage. True, "money isn't everything." But it is an unavoidable part of life that we must come to grips with. Solving money problems, or putting them in their proper perspective, frees us to get on with the rest of life.

SUGGESTED READING:

Goldberg, Herb, and Robert T. Lewis. *Money Madness: The Psychology of Saving, Spending, Loving, and Hating Money.* New York: William Morrow, 1978.

Wiseman, Thomas. *The Money Motive.* New York: Random House, 1974.

See also: COMPETITIVENESS, ENVY, FEAR OF FAILURE, FEAR OF SUCCESS, GAMBLING, GETTING FIRED, GREED, JOB DISSATISFACTION, MASOCHISM, SELF-HATE, TIME-WASTING, UNDERACHIEVEMENT

NARCISSISM

Is what we popularly call "narcissism" or "egocentrism" always a problem? Or is it sometimes appropriate to view self-love, self-actualization, self-affirmation, self-interest, self-realization, self-centeredness, even selfishness as healthy, protective, and developmental?

The nurturance of a valid sense of self, identity, and worth is an essential part of growing up. We must learn to accept and value ourselves as individual human beings, distinct from all others. We have to spend time on this process even at the risk of appearing selfish occasionally. Sometimes we're obliged to fight for our independence against people who protest that we are rejecting them, who criticize and disapprove of us, or who actually try to stop us.

If we are not to be parasites, we must bring to our relationships with other people our own inner resources and self-valuing. We can't healthily live off someone else's life. We can work toward mutual supportiveness only if we believe in ourselves and have the capacity to give

something of worth. That means we have to take time to develop ourselves, often in ways that temporarily take us away from other people
and into ourselves.

All of us have some amount of self-love that we seek to supplement
and confirm by winning aproval from others. This "normal narcissism"
underlies part of our pleasure in receiving praise and affection. As we
are growing up, such "positive strokes" help us develop independent
regard for our own worth. We become more able to ask the people in
our lives to give us space and support for our own growth and change.
Then, when we have achieved sufficient inner contentment, we are able
to lend our loving and caring to our friends and family in their own
struggles and searches.

The problem of unhealthy, pathological narcissism occurs when our
efforts at self-nurturance exceed wholesome limits. Some people are
stuck in defensive self-absorption. Their growth process is blocked and
their self-focus serves only to maintain their own comfort and distance.
They have no real contact with others.

Problem narcissists are truly selfish, inconsiderate, and withholding.
The payoff they get for being this way comes in the form of personal
protection, safety from the risks of involvement, distance from other
people's needs and demands, and indulgent fantasies of superiority un-
tested by real human encounter.

The pathological narcissist is unable to distinguish his or her inner
wishes from the rest of the world. The world exists only to fulfill his
or her needs. The narcissist manipulates, exploits, and controls others
in order to gain admiration and advantage, and then looks down on
them with contempt.

The traits that mark a narcissist's personality were formed in childhood. Such a person did not receive consistent parental love and guidance to help form a solid sense of self. Instead, there was usually a
confusing mixture of rejection, criticism, superficial approval, sporadic
indulgence, and lack of constructive feedback. The narcissist suffers from
a negative self-image, or the lack of much of an image at all. Narcissism
has more of self-hate in it than self-love.

Lacking true affection for himself or herself, the narcissist craves but
disbelieves the affection of others. No amount of gratification fulfills
the narcissist. He or she is incapable of love and genuine sharing. Other
people, even lovers, are sought only as admirers and not for their own
sake. Once a person responds to a narcissist, in fact, that person loses
the narcissist's respect. The narcissist "collects" the affection but thinks
less of the giver. "How could I love someone who loves me? They
must be hard up or stupid. Either I fooled them with my act, or they
just have no taste."

A true narcissist does not even realize that a problem exists until forced to see it because of some external crisis. Most of us, however, become aware from time to time that we may be behaving in a narcissistic way. Both the pathological and the "normal" narcissist need to consider the following.

• Examine your behavior toward other people. Do you act in a self-important manner that fails to show positive regard for others? Do you get others to pay attention to you and praise you a lot? Do you upstage other people or hog the show? Are you more concerned about how you appear to people than about tuning in to their concerns?

• Admit it to yourself if your self-examination reveals a narcissistic pattern. If it also reveals a sense of loneliness and separation, let yourself feel that pain. It may provide the motivation for change and improvement. Seize the opportunity presented by your new self-awareness. Experiment with listening carefully to others talking about their feelings and needs. Try to support and share with others. Even if it's at first mechanical, see if you can find a new kind of pleasure in returning caring to those who express concern for you.

• The solution to narcissism grows out of a commitment to something larger than your own ego. First, work at nurturing a real sense of self-acceptance. Value yourself as a unique life in process. Have patience with yourself; it takes time to gain confidence in your ability to change. Praise yourself for any effort you make toward self-acceptance. Self-approval is far more valuable than the outside approval you've been hoarding so far. Now, reach out to others. Give of yourself. Receive affection warmly. Try to return it instead of turning the giver away.

• Don't deny yourself occasional, necessary self-absorption. Sometimes you may have to concentrate intensely on your own problems or needs. Temporary self-nurturance can strengthen you and prepare you to return to your relationships refreshed. Wise self-care will keep you from getting stuck in endless self-absorption.

• Have faith in your ability to affect the world and its problems, no matter how humble your steps. Nurture yourself so that you can say, "I am a whole, real person. My acts have real meaning. I can, therefore, change my world for the better. I do make a difference." Every day you have an impact on at least the part of the world with which you have direct contact. Smile at a stranger and make your world bigger.

• Nurture yourself skillfully so that you can interact fully and joyfully with others, offering and accepting love. The goal of self-nurturance is to enable the self to interact satisfyingly with others, comfortable with its own needs and nature. It's not narcissistic to eat well, rest sufficiently, develop a rewarding work life, encourage your sense of self-worth and individuality, and choose your companions in life carefully to fit your emotional needs. It's not narcissistic to withdraw from involvement when your need for self-caring exceeds the importance of outside demands. Making it possible for you to act in the world is the opposite of narcissism—it is a commitment to living and sharing.

SUGGESTED READING:

Kernberg, Otto. *Borderline Conditions and Pathological Narcissism.* New York: Jacob Aronson, 1974.
Nelson, Marie Coleman, ed. *The Narcissistic Condition: A Fact of Our Lives and Times.* New York: Human Sciences Press, 1977.

See also: DEPENDENCY, ENVY, JEALOUSY, LONELINESS, PROMISCUITY, SELF-HATE

NIGHTMARES

A giant enraged bear chases you through a dark forest. You push ahead in terror, looking back repeatedly only to see that the bear is gaining on you steadily. Your movements are painfully slow. No matter how hard you try, you can't move faster. A huge paw reaches out to grab you as you cringe away in fright. Just as the bear's claws are about to sink in and tear you apart . . . you wake up. Heart pounds, body perspires, chest heaves. You're safe at home, in bed, but terrorized. You've had that nightmare again.

Nightmares shatter our sleep and our peace of mind. They leave us shaking and scared. Sometimes we can get back to sleep; sometimes we can't. Sometimes the nightmare's anxiety pursues us into the next day.

As you lie in bed trembling after a nightmare, you might find it hard to believe that such dreams provide us with ways to work on and master feared situations. But they do—if we don't push them out of our minds or medicate them into seeming oblivion. Dreams offer us a natural and free form of self-therapy. They represent a safe way for us to deal with frightening forces in our lives that we can't always recognize or confront in our daytime reality.

Bad dreams are a sort of safety valve. In the disguise of dream figures and situations we are able to express inner feelings that seem so fearful or wrong to our waking consciousness that we have locked them in our unconscious mind.

A common anxiety dream, for example, involves an examination, testing, or interview situation in which the dreamer must justify himself or herself. Most often this sort of dream reflects a concern about "measuring up" in some way—at work, at school, to our parents, children, spouse, lover, the world at large.

Most of the dream figures we encounter represent disguised aspects of ourselves. If we repeatedly face hostile dream images, we need to take them seriously and work with them in order to become more at peace with ourselves and the world. These hostile images stand for things we fear in ourselves. Deep inside we're sure that acting out our feared needs or desires will bring on disaster. Confronting our impulses and feelings—in waking fantasy or in a dream—can help free us to be more expressive and assertive in daily life. Dreams can help us get familiar with and "tame" our wild side. For example, we may learn from a dream that we have some unexpected sexual yearnings. By getting in touch with this aspect of our nature we can sort out our feelings and values prior to acting on our impulses. We may then gain confidence that we won't be struck dead by an avenging angel for behaving in new ways.

The dream state reflects our inner reality, including the positive processes of personality change and growth. Unfortunately, unless we focus on remembering our dreams, most of them slide back into our unconscious. We can go through life allowing our conscious and unconscious experiences to remain separated. Or we can choose to use our dreams as a source of "conversation" between these parts of us, to enrich and expand our lives.

• If you take your dreams—including nightmares—seriously and decide to work with them, be aware of the discipline you'll need to carry through on your decision. It's easy to let the busywork of daily life or other distractions get in the way of dream work.

• Learn to capture your dreams. The more scary the dream, the more likely you are to forget it. When you first wake up, devote a few minutes to retrieving the previous night's dreams. Don't give yourself over to the day's plans and demands immediately.

• Keep a dream notebook by your bed. Record your dreams regularly. Doing this for weeks or months will reveal repetitive themes and patterns. If a dream wakes you during the night, try to jot it down right away.

• Study your dream records for clues to problems you may be working on in your dream life. Try to identify your own dream vocabulary, cast of characters, and stock situations. What waking events or personalities do they remind you of?

• If you have a particular problem you want to work on, concentrate on it before going to sleep. Invite your dreams to help your waking life. You may find the next morning, or after a few mornings, that your creative dreaming has provided a solution.

• Discuss your dreams and dream work with others. Perhaps you can get a friend or family member to undertake systematic dream study too. As you increase your sense of the importance of your dream life by sharing it (and by sharing in the dream experiences of others), you may also find that you are increasing your sense of the overall importance of your whole life. You may come to value yourself and accept yourself as you are more easily as you learn to value and respect your inner life.

• Negative or frightening dream images sometimes reveal a struggle to overcome an inner conflict. Sometimes the frightening figure from which a dreamer can never escape—but which never really catches him or her—disguises some frightening part of the self. Monsters sometimes show us our own anger, desire, or fear.

• Fear can conceal a wish. Is there something you secretly want that you also fear? Suppose you have a terrifying dream that your spouse gets killed in a car crash. Do you have a wish concealed behind this fear—a wish to punish or even get rid of your spouse? If a dream frightens you, ask yourself, "Why did I create this particular dream?" What result might come out of the situation that would give you something you want but are afraid to admit?

• Night terrors are frightening sleep occurrences but are not full-blown nightmares. They usually happen soon after going to sleep, and to children more often than to adults. Night terrors may take the form of an image of falling, or being smothered or crushed or suffering some other horrible fate. The victim awakes terrified of some disaster— perhaps screaming, with a rapid heartbeat, in tears, or feeling trapped and paralyzed. Night terrors terrify, but they don't seem to do any other damage. When calm again, you can let yourself go back to sleep; the terror is unlikely to recur the same night, nor are you more likely to have another nightmare than at other times. Some psychologists believe the cause of night terrors is the person's fear of relaxing, letting go, trusting, or surrendering to passivity, sleep, and helplessness. If you have a night terror, ask yourself whether you are keeping your guard up too tensely and constantly. You may need to provide yourself with more peaceful, relaxing, unwinding experiences, especially in the evening before going to bed.

• Appreciate the richness of your inner life. Enjoy the detail. Watch for puns: In her book *The Dream Game,* dream researcher Ann Faraday reported a dream in which a young woman saw herself sitting next to herself. She was (obviously) "beside herself" about something going on in her life, and her dream self was taking this way to point that out to her.

• Consciously acknowledge your frightening dream situations or personalities. "Redream" your nightmare in a waking state: Retrace the sequence, meet again the frightening people, animals, or monsters, and have an imaginary conversation with them. Ask them what they want. Question them about their significance. You will be surprised at how many answers emerge from a part of your mind with which you were out of touch.

• If you become aware in your sleep of being in a dream, particularly a nightmare, try to direct your dream. Rather than try to wake up and escape into consciousness, stay with the dream. If it's a pleasant one, extend and enjoy it. Look for its positive message. If it's a frightening dream, remember that once you're aware of it as a dream you are no longer vulnerable. You can confront the most horrible monster, secure that it can do you no harm. Interrogate at will. Confront the fearful elements. Redirect the dream to have it come out to your advantage. Learn from it.

• Whenever possible, try to let yourself go with a dream image. Where does it lead you? What can it show you about your real needs and wants? In your dreams, try to identify and accept the parts of yourself that you fear. You may find that letting these parts make their demands, and then fulfilling some of them, brings you closer to being the person you really are, with all the hopes, anxieties, needs, doubts, and loves common to human beings. You may learn that you're just an ordinary, lovable mortal who wants some consideration from other ordinary mortals—not a raving monster whose needs are so terrible and demanding that they could destroy yourself or others.

SUGGESTED READING:

Cartwright, R. D. *Nightlife: Explorations in Dreaming.* Englewood Cliffs, N.J.: Prentice-Hall, 1977.

Faraday, Ann. *The Dream Game.* New York: Harper & Row, 1974.

Thoresen, Carl E., and Thomas J. Coates. *How to Sleep Better.* Englewood Cliffs, N.J.: Prentice-Hall, 1976.

See also: ANXIETY, SLEEP DISORDERS

OBSESSIONS

Obsessions are repetitive, nagging, haunting ideas that seem almost to have a life of their own. A person troubled by obsessive thoughts feels driven to concentrate on them, as if that will prevent something horrible from happening. Obsessive thoughts pop up without being summoned. They make unwelcome demands on us to think about or do some special thing—or else.

Efforts to avoid or stop obsessive thoughts can make them even more powerful and disruptive. They stubbornly insist on pushing aside all other thoughts. This is the exaggerated effect of their basic purpose: Obsessive thoughts are a way to keep our minds off something we don't want to face.

An obsession can disguise a problem for us. It can make it possible for us to deny a wish or impulse that we fear or believe unacceptable to ourselves or to the important others in our lives. Obsessive worries about having left the house unlocked, for example, can conceal a desire to leave it—and the self it represents—more open and receptive. In similar ways, obsessive thoughts can cover over sexual feelings, anger, deep insecurities, or dependency yearnings.

Obsessions serve to bind anxiety, to contain fears, and to focus worry and mental energy on something that may be scary but still keeps us distracted from the thing we really fear. It keeps us "safe" from something more deeply troubling inside us. It erects a dam out of an idea. The dam holds back the full force of our feelings.

The function of an obsession is to provide safety and order to a confused person. Obsessives fear the consequence of neglecting or doing some special thing: locking a door, turning off the gas, putting possessions in perfect order, keeping themselves or their home free of contamination from germs or dirt. An obsessive person may be plagued by a frequently recurring thought, perhaps telling him to yell obscenities or reminding her to concentrate on the children's safety lest they be hurt at school. These thoughts can take over a person's life, coming many times in an hour or even in a minute.

Obsessive ideas often lead to compulsive actions, rituals of protection that must be accomplished in order to maintain safety. These obsessions and their related compulsions can have a paranoid flavor: "The IRS is out to get me, so I'll keep every piece of paper I write on." "If I leave the door unlocked they'll get me, so I'll never leave unless I've checked and rechecked all the ways into and out of my house."

Sometimes people function for years with powerful and detailed obsessions and their accompanying compulsive actions. They are characteristically consumed by doubt: "Did I wash my hands after touching the doorknob?" If the obsessive cannot be sure that a ritual act or thought has occurred as it should have, he or she must repeat it.

A lifetime may be taken over by the uncontrollable need to fulfill the obsessive ritual. Obsessives seek total control. They want to anticipate every possibility. They make endless mental lists. They require order and perfection, and intensely dislike uncertainty. They are tied to their obsessions by the fear of what awful harm would result if they forgot.

In the long run, obsessions not only prevent people from seeing, feeling, doing, and risking in life, they eventually rob them of self-worth and feed the guilty conviction that "I'll be bad, or a nothing, unless I busily think about ———— all the time."

• Recognize an obsession for what it is: a defense against a wish, need, or impulse that you do not want to face. It is an unsatisfactory attempted solution to the problem of anxiety. If you are reluctant to dip deeper and face your anxiety, calculate the cost in your life of the protection from anxiety provided by your obsession. Is it worth it?

• Do you overvalue control? Can you distinguish between reasonable caution and an obsessive ritual? Are you trying to avoid choice, risk, error, and responsibility? Have you reached a point of diminished returns in your thinking about preventing harm—has some particular thought or behavior taken over your life?

• Try to follow your obsessive thought to its conclusion. Some therapists have found that about half of their obsessive patients gain some relief by doing this. Following their obsession into fantasy, seeing where it leads them, helps to reduce its power. Try to learn from your obsession. Try to find out what it hides from you—what you are hiding from yourself. Admit to yourself that you are using the obsession to get away from something within you.

• Expect to be disturbed and frightened by this sort of exploration. Reassure yourself that this is necessary and important to the process of learning to know yourself better. In the long run you will gain more by investing energy in dealing with your real feelings than by feeding an obsession.

• Experiment cautiously with cutting the cost of control. Try to take a small action that violates your obsession. Let yourself learn, for example, that you do reliably lock your front door. Go out. Lock up. Leave immediately. Walk at least around the block before coming back. You'll find the door locked and perhaps begin to realize that you don't need your elaborate checking and rechecking ritual. You'll also learn that nothing horrible happens when you don't behave obsessively.

• If you have developed compulsive behavior to accompany your obsession, see COMPULSIONS. Some of the behavior-therapy methods used to eliminate unwanted habits may help you reduce your compulsive patterns.

•Learn to turn your mind off and to relax. Don't use drugs or alcohol to accomplish this. Start by addicting yourself to some regular form of absorbing, soothing, physical exercise if possible. You may have trouble learning to meditate because your brain is so busy with your obsession. If necessary, seek out individualized meditation training. Progress from carefully structured meditation and breathing exercises to more personalized and relaxed ones. Learn how to notice your obsessive thoughts without taking them seriously, without feeling compelled to pursue them. Try this for about fifteen minutes twice a day. Develop a loving, friendly, accepting, nonjudgmental view of yourself. Listen to your mind, accept it, be quiet with it.

• Remind yourself that having a fear does not make it happen. Your feelings or fears will not create disaster.

• Confronting an obsession and overcoming it can lead to serious depression. After all, the obsession (and its compulsive actions) may have taken up much of your day. Seek the support and understanding of your family and friends as you try to break away from your obsession. Ask them to help you learn ways to fill your time with nonobsessive activities.

• If your life has become painfully restricted by your obsession and its rituals, consider seeking professional counseling or therapy. A trained couselor can help you through the sometimes scary and slow process of searching out the inner causes of an obsession and discovering your untapped inner coping strengths.

• Remember, an obsession is a way of hiding from yourself because you distrust and dislike a part of yourself. Getting rid of your obsession will require that you get to know and like yourself better. It may also force you to face some problems in your life situation and make some changes. Embarking on the process of looking beneath an obsession is an exciting and rewarding challenge that can enrich your life.

SUGGESTED READING:

Bain, J. A. *Thought Control in Everyday Life*. New York: Funk & Wagnalls, 1928.

Yogi, Maharishi Mahesh. *Transcendental Meditation*. New York: Penguin Books, 1967.

See also: ANXIETY, COMPULSIONS, DEPRESSION, PERFEC-TIONISM

ORGASMIC DYSFUNCTION

By far the most common sexual problem among women is difficulty experiencing orgasm. This difficulty can occur in many different situations. For example, some women have never experienced an orgasm under any circumstances; others have orgasms when masturbating or during oral sex but not in intercourse; still others experience orgasms in intercourse but not as often as they would like. Wherever you fit in, the recommendations in this section may be helpful to you.

Before moving on to the exercises it is important for you also to know where you fit in the range of women in general. Many people still believe that most women or "normal" women regularly have orgasms from the stimulation they get from the penis during intercourse. This is not true. Scientists estimate that only about four out of ten women have orgasms under these circumstances. About one half experience orgasms only when they masturbate or when they are stimulated by a partner's hand or mouth or by a vibrator. The remaining 10 percent have never had an orgasm.

Most women are surprised by these numbers, and say that knowing them makes them feel more "normal" and less alone. You may want to spend some time thinking about this. Have you been assuming that you were unusual or abnormal? How much of your troubled feeling about orgasm is due to thinking there was something wrong with you? Even though it's not unusual not to have orgasms during intercourse, you may still feel dissatisfied with how often you experience orgasm and may want to work on changing this.

One of the things that interferes with "coming" is trying too hard to come. Worrying about orgasm leads to "spectatoring," and keeps you from becoming more sexually excited, so one thing you need to do is relax and stop pushing yourself.

Another factor that often makes it difficult to experience orgasm is fear of letting go and losing control. Some of the pleasurable feelings related to orgasm can be so strong that they can be frightening and can make a woman want to shut down or tune out. Explore this with yourself: Are you afraid of having an orgasm? How do you imagine your partner will react? What do you think you would do—moan? scream? Some women are afraid they will lose bladder control. Is this a fear you have?

One useful way to dispel such fears is to practice having outrageously explosive orgasms. On your own, act out having an orgasm the way you imagine it could be at its wildest intensity. Feel free to exaggerate it: Scream, fall off the bed, or whatever you want. Many women say that after trying this a few times they don't feel as afraid of orgasm anymore, since the real experience is seldom as far out as their fantasies.

If your difficulty reaching orgasm is limited to a particular partner or situation, explore what this means to you. How do you feel about this partner (or this situation)? Do you feel sexy, angry, nervous, confused? What are your expectations from this partner (or in this situation)? You also may need to think about your partner's behavior. Does he come very quickly? Perhaps your problem is related to his difficulty with premature ejaculation. Does he do things that turn you on? If not, you may need to help him discover what you find exciting.

In fact, the most important cause of orgasmic difficulty is a lack of the right kind of touching or stimulation. This point is very important and needs explaining, because it is the key to learning to have orgasms. In order to experience orgasm, almost all women need to be touched and caressed *directly on or around the clitoris*. (If you don't know what a clitoris is or where it is, learn about this.) Even though people talk about having a "vaginal orgasm," Masters and Johnson proved that *all* orgasms result from stimulation of the clitoris. Most men and women don't know this, and as a result the woman's clitoris is often ignored in their lovemaking.

In intercourse itself, the clitoris is rubbed only indirectly by the action of the penis moving in and out of the vagina. When a woman masturbates, however, she usually touches or rubs her clitoris directly. This is why nine out of ten women come while masturbating, but only four out of ten come in intercourse. So stimulation of the clitoris is very important for orgasm, and masturbation is the easiest way to have an orgasm.

The program for increasing orgasm is based on these two ideas and relies heavily on masturbation and on clitoral stimulation. Like most things we learn to do, learning how to increase your excitement requires practice, so the exercises focus on giving you a chance to practice getting clitoral stimulation.

• Do the exercises outlined in SEXUAL DYSFUNCTION and focus on learning what makes you excited. Be especially sure to explore all the parts of your genitals. Remember that you may or may not become excited when doing this. As you try out different ways of touching yourself, concentrate especially on the area around your clitoris (this is important even if you already masturbate and reach orgasm in masturbation). Explore different strokes: up and down, circular, slow, fast, tapping, and so forth.

• Expect that after a while the clitoris itself may become tender, especially if there isn't enough lubrication. If this occurs, move to the side of your clitoris or to the top, where it first bulges. Again, you may or may not become excited at first—don't have any preconceptions. You should *not* have an orgasm in this exercise, even if you can. Just explore yourself.

• Keep up your exploration for several sessions of at least twenty minutes each. Discover new pleasures. As you do, begin to concentrate on the things that feel most exciting, especially around the clitoris. Begin to increase the intensity and speed of your stimulation. Also, increase your sessions to at least a half hour three to four times per week. Your ability to have orgasms depends on this practice.

• Pay attention to yourself. You may find as you make yourself excited that you become distracted. Do you start wondering if you're going to have an orgasm? Do you worry about your job or how to-morrow night's dinner will work out? See what you can do to reduce these distractions. Does having your eyes open or closed make a dif-ference? Try using fantasy—that often can keep the distractions away. In any case, try to find out what you need to do to focus all your attention on the pleasant feelings you have when you touch yourself.

• Keeping up the practice is very important. Don't get discouraged. Many women practice for months before anything happens, so don't expect to have an orgasm after a few sessions. Concentrate on increasing your pleasure. Most women find a vibrator extremely exciting; try it. If you feel ashamed to buy one in a store, get one by mail order (or get an electric toothbrush—the smooth handle vibrates quite a bit). A vibrator can be especially exciting when placed on or beside the clitoris. Try this and other spots. Continue your individual exercises for as long as you are doing the program. Even when you begin to do things with your partner, your individual program is most important.

• In working with a partner, be sure to let him know what you like. A good way to do this is to show him—put your hand over his and help him learn just what feels best to you. He won't know unless you communicate with him. This may be harder than it sounds. Many women who masturbate know that they like and need clitoral stimulation but have never told their partners. Explore this. What makes it hard for you to tell him what you like? Are you afraid to seem too demanding? Do you feel that men should just know? Are you afraid he'll be upset if you tell him what to do? Discuss these concerns with him.

• An exercise which is very useful, particularly for women who come when masturbating but not in intercourse, is to masturbate with the partner present. This is difficult and takes some getting used to. You may not want to see him or have him see you. Perhaps you feel easier with the lights out and you under the covers while he sits on the edge of the bed. Start with whatever feels comfortable and then move him closer. Some women find that eventually they can masturbate to orgasm while in their partner's arms. This exercise may help you get used to sharing your pleasure and excitement with him, and can bring you closer together.

• After you have shown him what you like him to do with his hands or mouth or the vibrator, and have practiced this so that it feels com-fortable to both of you, you may be ready to try having his penis in your vagina. Remember that you still should not aim to have an orgasm, but just to make yourself relaxed and pleasured. After he has stimulated you and you have stimulated him for a while, he should be on his back while you sit astride or over his hips. Making sure that you are wet enough for this, slowly insert his penis and then be still, as though you were just sitting on him. Notice that in this position, both of you can reach your clitoris; this is important. When this is comfortable, one of you should begin gently to caress your clitoral area. You can each take a turn, and then you should decide which you like better. Many women initially feel uncomfortable touching themselves when making love with a partner, but soon find that this can increase the sexual pleasure of both people.

Try varying the way of rubbing or caressing your clitoris. Also, you can begin slowly to thrust by moving up and down. At first limit yourself to a few thrusts at a time. Add more when you are really comfortable. Your clitoris should continue to be stimulated directly while you increase the number or intensity of thrusts to the point where you are simply having intercourse.

Do not burden yourself with expectations of having an orgasm— just pay attention to what feels good. Many couples who have tried it decide to continue to excite the woman's clitoris directly whenever they have intercourse. They find this most pleasant and exciting, and it also makes orgasm more likely. If you relax, concentrate on your feelings, and get lots of clitoral stimulation, you'll find that your sexual pleasure and satisfaction will rise dramatically. You will have learned how your body works, how to ask for what you want, and how to give of yourself more fully. Enjoy!

SUGGESTED READING:

Barbach, Lonnie. *For Yourself: The Fulfillment of Female Sexuality.* New York: Doubleday, 1975.

Boston Women's Health Book Collective. *Our Bodies, Ourselves: A Book by and for Women,* rev. 2nd ed. New York: Simon & Schuster, 1976.

Friday, Nancy. *My Secret Garden.* New York: Pocket Books, 1974.

See also: MASTURBATION, PREMATURE EJACULATION, SEXUAL DYSFUNCTION, SEXUAL INHIBITIONS

OVEREATING

Caring about our health and appearance sometimes turns out to be more complicated and difficult than we expect. Excessive weight can creep up on us and turn out to be extremely hard to get rid of. If you're overweight by more than just a few pounds, you've probably already given some thought to the drawbacks of obesity. Fat can interfere with your social life, work life, sex life, and health.

What's so hard about keeping thin? For one thing, food tastes good.

Eating is a great sensual pleasure, and, especially in social situations, it's easy to eat more than your body really needs. We are surrounded by invitations to eat, nibble, snack, taste, sip, munch, swallow, stuff, and gorge.

For most of us food is easily and almost constantly available. Convenience foods pamper our most exotic urges as well as our simplest. We have to eat, and the ease and variety of modern shopping makes it simple to shift from necessity to overindulgence.

Some people, for a combination of genetic, psychological, and cultural reasons, have more trouble eating appropriately and maintaining normal weight than others. There is some evidence that a tendency toward overweight may be inherited. Fat people also eat under more circumstances than thin people, and are more susceptible to food cues in the environment. Research indicates that once a person becomes fat, he or she develops a compulsion to eat because of the larger number of fat cells yearning to be fulfilled.

Being fat may not bother you. If it doesn't, and if your health stays good, you don't have a problem. Often, however, overweight people are unhappy with themselves, suffer from lethargy and lowered metabolism, have health problems, feel unattractive, and are victims of discrimination.

Overeating may have some psychological payoffs for you. You may find it reassuring and comforting to feed yourself, to indulge yourself when you're feeling down, just as Mom used to feed you when you were little. You may be using eating, being fat, and ineffectual dieting to avoid other aspects of life, such as love, sex, creativity, competition.

Sometimes fat expresses a fear of being vulnerable. It provides a sort of shield against really being in the world. Since many people avoid looking at an obese person, the fatter you are the less visible you may feel. For other people being overweight is a way of emphasizing their sense of importance. They are big, feel very visible, and are therefore reassured that the world must notice them.

Some overweight people stay fat out of anger, to get even with a demanding parent or spouse, for example. Remaining heavy is a way to frustrate and punish your partner if you believe he or she places too much emphasis on looks. For the single fat person excess weight may be a form of protection against being available sexually, having to make choices, and risking acceptance and rejection.

Becoming overweight can be a way of testing the love of your spouse or lover: If you really love me, says the fat person, you'll love me as I am. This test is a cry for help, an appeal for love. The message is a legitimate and important one, but the way of delivering it may not work. If you recognize your own weight problem as fitting into this pattern, don't ignore the message—you do want more clearly expressed love in your life—but find more effective, less harmful ways to express your need.

What can you learn by working on this problem? How can you turn it into an opportunity for self-development? Take some time and look at the issues of love, comforting, nurturing in your life. How can you get these things some other way than through food?

Look at your relationship with yourself. Are you trying to be the sole source of support, the provider of all your needs, the soother of all your troubles? Look at your close personal relationships, and at your relationship to the culture around you. Do you feel deprived? Does life seem harsh? Are you starving in psychological ways?

Before listing many of the things you can do to help yourself reduce, let's look at some general approaches to weight loss.

• You alone have the responsibility for achieving your desired physical condition. Others can help you, but only if you consciously and willingly choose to take on the basic responsibility for changing.

• Seek out new sources of nurturance to help you decrease your dependence on food as a comforter. Reopen and deepen contacts with people who may have more to offer you, be they parents, siblings, friends, or co-workers.

• You won't lose weight just by eating less; you will need to gratify yourself more in other ways. If you've lost touch, you might enjoy rediscovering music, art, nature, socializing, religion.

• Look inside yourself. Is there a hole in the bottom of your personality that lets all the good things you take in leak out? Does guilt or self-hate eat up your self-worth, leaving a never-filled, always-hungry feeling?

• When you feel hungry, pay attention to what's going on. Breathe deeply. Take in some air to fill you and make you stronger. Call a friend who will help you talk yourself out of unnecessary eating. Join a group like Weight Watchers or Overeaters Anonymous. People who've been where you are and understand your struggle can provide valuable encouragement and support.

• Avoid weight-loss programs that provide an external prop, like a too-specific diet or a doctor's special plan. You need to activate and channel your own desire to develop healthy eating habits, not turn yourself over to a program that will do something *to you*. You use the program, not the other way around.

• Research shows that most people who lose weight gain it back again. This is because they haven't yet really chosen to commit themselves permanently to the change in lifestyle necessary for sustained weight loss. If this frustrating pattern occurs in your life—after you've invested time, energy, and money in weight loss—don't give up in discouragement. Accept that you have gone through one of the common and necessary beginning stages, and learn from it that you still need to make a real choice.

• Don't turn against yourself if you backslide. This is a frequent, typical part of the obese person's experience. It signals you that there is still something you haven't dealt with. There is still an unsolved problem, a root cause for overeating that must be searched out and confronted. Rather than putting weight loss at the head of your list of problems, resolve to deal first with whatever else is bothering you, be it job, marriage, sexual fears, shyness, or whatever else you can identify. You may find that identifying and working on other problem areas of your life makes it easier for you to tackle long-term weight loss.

There are almost as many useful aids to weight loss as there are calories in blueberry cheesecake. First, however, get a medical exam to be sure that your weight problem is only the result of overeating.

• Be sure that you want to lose weight. Not everyone wants to look like Madison Avenue's idea of beauty. If you don't mind fat, be assertive about it. Many people do find fat men and women sexually attractive. There are partners available. You have a choice. You can reject the cultural model of late-twentieth-century America in favor of the plumper, rounder models of other times and cultures. You can be fat and happy. There is even a movement for you: Fat Liberation.

• Some people—especially those who love food—manage to maintain their desired weight by practicing controlled overindulgence. Most of the time they stay on a satisfying low-calorie diet, but on certain occasions of their own choosing they allow themselves to eat whatever they want.

• Develop a gourmet appreciation for the subtle flavors of natural foods attractively cooked and served. That will help reduce your dependence on fattening rich sauces, salt, and sugar for your only taste sensations.

• You may be addicted to sugar. This can be a disease as powerful as alcohol or drug addiction. Kicking the habit will take determination, willingness to go through a painful period, and lots of support from other people.

• Never use food as a reward, either for yourself or for your children. Don't encourage your tendency to overeat by making food a payoff; don't teach your children to use food in this way.

• Always eat in the same place, the kitchen or dining room. Don't snack all over the house—doing this makes you associate eating with every place you go and everything you do in your home environment. Don't eat in the car.

• Eat slowly. Chew thoroughly. Use smaller plates to help you see less as more. Enjoy what you do eat. Stretch out your smaller portion by taking a mid-meal break for a few minutes. If you are not eating alone, take time to talk to your eating partners—but not while chewing. Put down your utensils between each bite. Go slowly.

• Get used to leaving something unfinished on your plate. You don't have to eat everything put in front of you. You are in control of your eating habits; the food is not in control of you.

• Involve yourself in a gradually increasing program of exercise geared to your ability, physical condition, and interests. Vigorous exercise actually reduces appetite. Even better, the weight you burn up in exercise is in the form of fat. When you merely diet without exercise, you lose lean muscle tissue as well as fat.

• Talk back to your hunger—out loud. Take turns being yourself and your hunger, and discuss your hunger's need to make you overeat. This will help discourage that extra trip to the refrigerator and will also help you say no to anyone else who tempts you to cheat on your diet.

• Study nutrition. Work with a physician or nutritional counselor to develop a diet that suits your personal needs. First you need a diet that provides fewer calories than you burn; soon you will need one to help you maintain your lower weight.

• Beware of hazardous crash weight-loss methods, such as pre-digested liquid protein. Such a diet disturbs your whole system and can have severe side effects. You must change your fundamental eating patterns and learn to eat properly over the long run. Weight loss achieved rapidly and with a gimmick will be only temporary.

• Behavior therapy teaches us that overeating is a learned habit that can be unlearned. You can begin to modify your eating habits by paying close attention to them. Keep track of when, where, and why you eat, especially if you find yourself eating when you're not feeling true physical hunger. Note how susceptible you are to food cues around you: other people eating, advertisements for food, the mere availability of food, the time of day, the sight or smell of food.

• Establish a calorie allowance that will cause you to reduce. You must cut out 3,500 calories for every pound you want to lose. You may find that this is relatively easy if you can content yourself with a steady pound-a-week loss. Set realistic goals and *reward yourself* every week for meeting your calorie allowance.

• Reinforce your successes, no matter how small. Set aside some of your pre-diet food budget to buy yourself a gift every week you keep within your calorie allowance. Weight loss is a long-term process, so you must keep reminding yourself of how well you're doing.

• Take a very precise list to the market with you. Shop alone, so you won't be tempted to buy something extra to satisfy someone else's impulse. Don't take extra money. Don't dawdle—shop quickly, staying away from the aisles that stock the empty-calorie foods: desserts, chips, soda, and so forth. Never shop when you're hungry.

• Stay out of the kitchen as much as possible. Let other family members prepare their own treats. Better yet, try to get them to agree not to bring forbidden foods that you like into the house at all.

• Seek outside support and encouragement, from friends, spouse, family, your physician, your dates, your lover. Let your dinner-party hosts know in advance that you will not eat much—then don't.

• You may find that it helps to eat before you are very hungry. This may help you feel satisfied with less food. When you prepare your meals, don't prepare enough to have seconds.

• Write out motivating statements on index cards and read them over often: "Soon I'll be thinner and will look and feel terrific." "I and everyone who cares for me will be very proud of my accomplishment." "I am in control of my appetite. I will eat only as much as my diet allowance permits."

• Interrupt yourself on the way to prepare a forbidden extra. Take a walk. Exercise. Meditate. Try progressive relaxation. Do anything that interrupts the chain of events between urge and gratification—you'll probably find you don't really want to do something self-destructive after all.

• It took time to put on that excess weight. It will take time to get rid of it. Be aware of the pressures of stress, depression, and boredom. Try not to use food to relieve them. When tempted to overeat, find a distraction. Eating is not a recreational activity.

• The key to weight loss is your determination to accomplish it. First, admit you have a weight problem. Acknowledge the physical and psychological damage it causes you. Second, bolster your desire to change. Don't create obstacles for yourself. Don't kid yourself about your need to reduce. Third, recognize that you are making a long-term commitment that conflicts with a whole lifestyle and with many deep-seated habits. You will lose weight successfully when you develop and sustain new eating habits that are part of a new approach to life. Fourth, keep your long-term goal clearly in mind. Visualize how you will look when you will reach your desired weight. Reward yourself constantly for doing things that help you meet your goal.

SUGGESTED READING:

Fanburg, Walter H. *How to Be a Winner at the Weight-Loss Game.* New York: Simon & Schuster, 1975.

Mahoney, Michael J. and Katheryn. *Permanent Weight Control: A Total Solution to the Dieter's Dilemma.* New York: W. W. Norton, 1976.

See also: ANXIETY, COMPULSION, DEPENDENCY, DEPRESSION, GREED, SELF-HATE

PAIN

Pain can be an agonizing problem, but it can also be a valuable warning sign of physical danger or illness. Growing up, we learn a lot about how to interpret the messages our bodies send us in the form of pain. We learn to avoid injuring our bodies with burns, cuts, and bruises. We also learn how other people react to our expressions of pain. Much of this learning is useful, but sometimes we learn to over- or underreact to pain sensations, and to be too stoic or complaining for our own good.

No two people react to pain in the same way. We all experience pain according to our individual emotional, cultural, and physical make-up. There is no simple relationship between the source of a sensation of pain and the amount of pain an individual experiences.

Acute pain—from an illness, injury, or surgery, for example—is usually short-lived and usually can be relieved by medication, heat, cold, or just rest. Chronic pain is something else: It eats away at the quality and value of human life. For people who find themselves living in constant pain, sometimes it is so great that they can no longer function: They must stop working, they cannot get around and socialize, they have trouble caring for themselves.

Chronic-pain sufferers characteristically endure some or all of the following feelings and conditions: hopelessness, depression, uselessness, aimlessness, passivity, hostility, anxiety. They are often alienated from friends and family, who sometimes lose their ability to deal with chronic complaints. They are frequently exhausted monetarily as well as emotionally by the search for medical relief. Many times surgical procedures undertaken to relieve pain only serve to increase it. Chronic-pain sufferers may become addicted to drugs to help control their pain, and then find that the drugs don't even work after a while.

The stress of chronic pain can also cause problems with breathing, digestion, blood pressure, heart, and kidneys. Chronic pain sometimes develops after a specific illness or injury, continuing long after any identifiable physical cause can be found. During periods of illness or recovery from injury, patients sometimes learn to express suffering of a nonphysical sort in terms of physical pain. Researchers and practitioners of pain control, such as Dr. Richard A. Sternbach at the Scripps Clinic in La Jolla and Dr. David Bresler at UCLA, point out how important the ways we perceive and interpret pain are in determining our experience of its intensity and location.

The fact that the ways in which we suffer are to some extent learned doesn't mean we want to suffer or that our pain is "all in the head" and without physical cause. Nevertheless, some people are incapacitated by conditions that others are able to accept and live with, even though they have some amount of constant pain.

The ways we learn to experience and cope with pain are related to the ways we learn to function in the world in general. A child who experiences an extended illness, for example, may have his or her feelings of dependence and sickliness unconsciously reinforced by family and friends. Sometimes being in pain is the only way to get love and support from others. In other situations, pain can provide a way out of life problems. Thus, the "problem" of pain may in fact be a "solution" to some other problem. A person who hates his job but cannot let himself give it up can gracefully retire because of a painful physical condition. If a person doesn't find satisfaction or a sense of worth from his or her life, being a chronic invalid can seem like an acceptable alternative. Some people believe that they deserve to suffer. They accept pain as a purifying punishment for their real or imagined sins.

Sometimes we may involve ourselves in pain games: We don't feel well, so we manipulate others into doing our work or looking after us, or just leaving us alone. Some people find a meaning for their lives in challenging the medical world to diagnose and treat their pain. Other times, we make our own pain traps. We give up as soon as we feel any pain, putting ourselves to bed and waiting for it to go away. Inactivity leads to muscle degeneration, itself a source of continuing pain.

If our minds play a large role in determining how we experience physical pain, they can also help us overcome it. Medical pain control in the United States has had only limited success. Recently approaches emphasizing psychological awareness and behavior change have begun to provide alternatives to reliance on surgery and drugs. Pain clinics, such as the UCLA Pain Control Unit, are being established around the country. These clinics try to teach chronic-pain sufferers to look at their pain in new ways, to look for the messages it brings about their lives. "My body hurts" often means "My life hurts."

Evidence from many quarters, including recent studies on the effectiveness of placebos, shows us the body's own healing capacities. The UCLA clinic operates in the conviction that the power of our minds to affect our experience of pain appears to be vast, and techniques that teach and utilize this ability offer great promise. Together, body and mind can relieve suffering and cure illness. Becoming an active, informed, responsible patient often provides some immediate relief from the distress of feeling like a helpless victim condemned to a life of unalterable pain. Gaining insight into the meaning and use of one's pain and learning alternative behaviors can generate a renewed sense of self-worth and restore a sense of control and optimism about treatment.

Here are some ways to deal with pain.

• Learn some form of conditioned relaxation. (See ANXIETY.) Reducing the anxiety that comes with pain often relieves some of the hurting. If your condition allows it, movement therapy, especially dance, may also serve to relax you and help restore underexercised muscles. A program of regular meditation—transcendental or otherwise—may also help renew your sense of calm and control. Some pain clinics offer biofeedback training, which can help you learn about the relationship between your body and mind and can increase your ability to exercise control over involuntary functions. Investigate this option if it appeals to you.

• Investigate acupuncture and hypnosis. Both of these techniques are extremely successful for about 10 percent of the patients who use them; 60 percent find the techniques moderately to very successful; 30 percent find no relief at all. In both hypnosis and acupuncture the relief tends to be temporary, but having the experience of controlling your pain can lead you to further success.

• Live in the present. Just because your pain made going out to a party difficult last year, don't give up parties forever. If you feel up to doing something you haven't tried for a long time because of your pain, try it. Now is now; it's the only moment there is. Don't let the pain dominate and direct your life. What you can do, do. Develop your capacity for risk and adventure—take a chance that you can put yourself back into living.

• Involve your pain in a dialogue. Talk to it or write it letters. Tell it what you want it to know. Express how you feel about it and about what it does to your life. Be honest—what do you really want it to do? After expressing your feelings to your pain, take its part and write or tell yourself in your pain's words what the pain wants. Why does it hurt you? What can you do—in terms of diet, or relaxation, or kindness to yourself—that will make it hurt less?

• Dream about your pain. Before going to sleep, ask your internal dream power to send you a dream that helps you understand your pain and its purpose. Keep a dream diary and study your dreams for useful information learned from your pain.

• Examine your life experiences. What have they taught you about pain and how to cope with it? Have other family members had (or do they now have) similar pain problems? Does your family reward pain with attention or love that is otherwise withheld? How do others in your family deal with illness or injury? As a child, how were you treated for sickness or after an accident? Does someone in your family need you to be in pain so he or she can nurse and take care of you in order to feel worthwhile?

• Why do you want to overcome your pain? Do you really want to end the pain more than you want to continue receiving the benefits that pain can bring? Do others tell you that you should "learn to live with your pain"—as if that's all there is to your life? Do they give you attention if you can prove that you hurt? Do you think you deserve to suffer? Does chronic pain get you out of doing things you don't want to do— even very small things? Do you get a secret boost out of suffering more than someone else, as if there were status attached to hurting? Is being in pain the only way you can get to do pleasant things you want? Does pain excuse you from not being "perfect" as parent, worker, spouse, lover, artist, farmer . . . anything?

• Allow yourself to recognize the gains that can come with pain. Don't berate yourself for having to use pain to get what you need in life. The better you understand the message your pain expresses, the better you will be able to control it and to create the kind of life you really want. You can learn from your pain.

• Take nourishment from all of your environment. Eat things that improve your health and feelings of well-being. Breathe slowly and deeply. Drink pure water. Become more aware of the activity around you, and join in. Give love and look for ways to get some back. Practice accepting affection and caring freely, not as an exchange for suffering. Give yourself the luxury of indulging your needs. Nourish your desire for beauty and inspiration through nature, music, companionship, poetry, and stories.

• Ask the people in your life to reward you for feeling well. Ask them to show you love, attention, and affection when you are not in pain, and to leave you alone when you are. Retrain yourself and your family and friends to associate love and giving with feeling well.

• Learn to use guided imagery to mobilize your built-in healing forces. In a relaxed state, form an image of your pain as something living, such as an animal, with whom you can communicate. Talk to this inner creature, let it become an advisor. Ask it to explain your pain to you, to tell you what your pain wants and needs.

• The regional headquarters for the International Association for the Study of Pain can help you locate pain clinics in your area where you can learn more about acupuncture, biofeedback, hypnosis, guided imagery, electrical nerve stimulation, and other methods of pain control. Write to the Eastern U.S.A. Regional Chapter, 550 First Avenue, New York, New York 10016, or the Western U.S.A. Regional Chapter, Department of Anesthesiology, RN-10, University of Washington Medical School, Seattle, Washington 98195. Also, a Pain Clinic Directory is available for four dollars from the American Society of Anesthesiologists, 515 Busse Highway, Park Ridge, Illinois 60068.

• Pain is real, complex, and sometimes mysterious in origin. It is a valuable warning sign that something is wrong. If you have a pain, take it seriously. Consider all possible causes, from the most simple physical ones to hidden medical ones to the most elusive psychological sources. Give yourself every opportunity to overcome pain before it takes over your life.

• Be aware of the amount of stress in your life. Change of any kind—positive or negative—can create sufficient stress to make you unusually susceptible to illness or accident. Stay in touch with your feelings. Slow down when you need to; keep yourself well.

• Addict yourself to things that are good for you: exercise, meditation, music, a craft. Give yourself some time every day for your healthy addiction. Get your mind involved in what your body does. This will prepare you to let mind and body help each other overcome illness, injury, or pain when you experience them.

SUGGESTED READING:

Bresler, David, and R. Trubo. *Hurting.* New York: Simon & Schuster, 1978.

Pelletier, Kenneth R. *Mind as Healer, Mind as Slayer.* New York: Delacorte, 1976.

Shealy, Dr. C. Norman. *The Pain Game.* Millbrae, Calif.: Celestial Arts, 1976.

See also: ANXIETY, FEAR OF SICKNESS, HYPOCHONDRIA, PSYCHOSOMATIC ILLNESS, STRESS

PARANOIA

Do you ever imagine someone is following you? Or that the slow driver in front purposely won't let you pass so you'll be late for work again? Or that someone laughing is laughing at you? Irrational feelings that you have been singled out for harsh treatment are called "paranoia."

In its extreme form, paranoia is the delusion of persecution. It is characterized by hostility, self-righteousness, perceptual distortions, and sometimes delusions of grandeur. In its mild form it consists of feelings of distrust, suspiciousness, or oversensitivity.

It is natural to feel wary at times. Alertness to danger serves to protect us from harm. Suspiciousness is a virtue for the policeman, the lawyer, or the poker player. But extreme suspiciousness can be a destructive force which fosters needless anxiety and closes us off from other people.

Paranoia often results from projecting your unacceptable feelings onto another person. A woman who is sexually attracted to a married co-worker may repress her desire, then gradually come to attribute it to *him:* "See how he looks at me. He's trying to seduce me. I wish he'd leave me alone." Some men who accuse homosexuals of being a danger to society are denying and projecting their own homosexual impulses or antisocial motives.

Paranoid worries commonly involve fears of personal invasion, rape, sexual overtures, robbery, being fired, losing love of spouse. Often there is some partial basis in reality for paranoid anxiety. Certainly there are many physical dangers and hostile people to avoid in the world. It is not always easy to tell when a suspicion is excessive enough to be labeled paranoid. Years ago, having the belief that smoking was harmful and that the government and the cigarette companies were concealing the facts might have seemed paranoid. Today it does not. Similarly, the radicals' accusations against the Nixon Administration may have seemed paranoid until Watergate brought more to light than even they had suspected.

The attitudes of an entire group may be paranoid. Our history books are packed with events which are examples of full-scale paranoia, from the Salem witch-hunts to the McCarthy hearings. Why are human beings so susceptible to paranoid fears? Perhaps because anxiety is common to us all. Whenever you care deeply about something and feel in danger of losing it, you can fall prey to paranoia.

The problem of paranoia provides an opportunity—and a strong impetus—to learn what is really going on in your life. Suppose you've begun to fear a co-worker is after your job. You're uneasy when you're around him, and you worry constantly about pleasing your boss. When you slip up, you defensively blame others for your mistakes. Your emotional state has begun to hamper your work. You may actually be endangering your position now. It would be better to discuss your worries with a friend or your boss than to continue to feel paranoid and act in self-defeating ways. You may discover that your job actually is in jeopardy. Now you know where you stand. Or, luckily, you may find that your anxiety is totally unfounded. Now you can try to figure out what caused your misperception. For example, your job might have become particularly important to you because your new wife finds it impressive and you are worried about losing her.

Paranoid feelings grow when you are insecure, fearful, or simply overtired—at those times when you lack emotional nourishment. Feeling threatened by an "enemy" outside you may be a sign that there is an enemy threatening you from within. When you recognize the inner fear or self-attack, you can begin to free yourself from unwarranted anxiety. Identify and work on your inner enemies. There are lots of them, such as low self-esteem, severe conscience, loneliness, stress. Learn to differentiate between internal and external problems. This is not always easy, and takes continual practice.

• When you feel distrustful, examine your suspicions. Are you harboring some impulse you don't want to admit? If the danger you fear is specific, such as rape or burglary, fantasize about the threat. What terrible things might occur if your worst fears were realized? Face the worst. You may be able to decondition your fear by delving into it in a safe setting with someone you trust, such as a therapist. Or you may discover a secret wish. Fear of rape may disguise a wish for sex without any responsibility attached. Many women have rape fantasies. Label this fantasy for what it is—a fantasy and nothing more—to differentiate it from a realistic fear of rape. Maybe you can even enjoy a previously fear-laden fantasy when you no longer allow it to take on the appearance of reality.

• Ask yourself if your picture of a threatening situation could be distorted. Examine anything else which is bothering you, even though it may at first seem unrelated to your fear. Perhaps you are getting mixed messages from someone you love, so that you feel uncertain of his or her affection. Sort out the various real and imagined threats to your well-being, and concentrate your worrying and constructive action on the real ones.

• If you realize you are trying to "construct a case" to document and support your hurt or distrustful feelings, stop and examine your feelings. Are you caught up in an obsessive game of playing detective or prosecutor? Are you putting more energy into this cause than it deserves or than you can afford? Look for a secret payoff. Could your evidence-gathering activities be a substitute for having a direct constructive encounter with the individual? What do you have to gain by holding on to irrational suspicions and grudges? Does righteous suspiciousness make you feel safe or more important? Are you afraid to risk dealing with a world which contains hurt and disappointment?

• When you feel overly suspicious, check out your feelings with someone you trust. Pick a neutral person with no stake in proving you right or wrong. Try a therapist or a clergyman if you cannot share with a friend. Listen to the feedback you get, rather than trying to argue your case.

• People who live alone may be particularly afraid of intruders. There can be a definite reality to these fears. If you feel endangered at home, seek out practical solutions to the problem. Install an alarm system. Take all normal precautions and see if the fear persists. If it does, look for additional internal sources of your distress. Perhaps you feel cut off from others. You may want to make room for strangers in your life but be afraid to take the risk or uncertain how to go about it. You may feel guilty and create imagined attacks as a kind of atonement.

• Paranoia is often a signal that you need trusting and supportive relationships. Learn to choose your associates wisely. Spend more time with kindly, caring people. Avoid cynics and abrasive personalities. Watch out for people who inflame or prey upon your insecurities.

• Survey your environment so that you can take appropriate steps to balance the hostile influences in your daily life with friendly and protective ones. What can you do to offset the stress of congestion, noise, smog, crime, all the pressures of urban life? Find nurturing environments. Retreat to the park for lunch instead of the bustling cafeteria. Spend a weekend afternoon in the country. Nature, art, music, the company of loved ones—all these serve to combat aggravating pressures and keep them from building up inside.

• Many people find solace and a sense of protection in spiritual faith, which helps them tune in to the loving forces in the world. The great religions of the world offer perspective and guidance for dealing with the eternal battle between good and evil. Don't get sidetracked into elaborate intellectual discussions of religious dogma—focus instead on the feelings of love and trust inspired by religious leaders.

• Avoid depending on drugs, alcohol, or material luxuries to insulate you from the harshness in the world. They don't really deal with the problem, and they can use up necessary resources, leaving you even more vulnerable than before.

• Being tired, hungry, or overworked can stir up paranoid tendencies because you are not being nurtured from within. Do something positive to care for yourself. Plan a vacation if you can. If that's not possible, find things which alleviate daily stress—such as meditation, yoga, relaxing exercises—and integrate them into your schedule. Initiate kindly gestures. Pay attention to the people around you. They may be suffering from the same pressures. Your thoughtfulness will elicit friendly acts in return.

• If someone confides his or her paranoid views to you, hear the person out. Don't be tempted to humor or debate the person. Offer your own views, and suggest ways of checking suspicions against reality. But respect the fact that a paranoid person may need to maintain his or her belief system for deep reasons.

Troubling through it may be, paranoia offers a chance to grow in self-knowledge and to sharpen your reality testing. None of us operates effectively when distracted by distrust and suspicion. Paranoia can be contagious and destructive. Recognizing when paranoia has a hold on you—and overcoming it—will enable you to make wiser choices about people and situations. You can learn the importance of trust and mutual support and the rewards they can ultimately bring to us all.

SUGGESTED READING:

Friedrich, O. *Going Crazy: An Inquiry into Madness in Our Time.* New York: Avon Books, 1977.
Laing, R. D. *The Politics of Experience.* New York: Ballantine Books, 1967.

See also: AGORAPHOBIA, ANGER, ANXIETY, COMMUNICATION BLOCKS, DELUSIONS, GUILT, HALLUCINATIONS, JEALOUSY, LONELINESS, OBSESSIONS, SHYNESS

PASSIVITY

Passive people are often seen as lazy, nonassertive, or easily taken advantage of. A passive person might allow someone to crowd in front of him in line without objecting, sit through a class without participating, or drift along in a dull job for years. Passive people seem to be waiting to be told what to do. Yet they often won't budge even in response to helpful suggestions. Or they may docilely obey without any real involvement. They can be very exasperating.

People are passive for a variety of reasons, both healthy and unhealthy. For instance, the passive person often feels "If I don't do anything, then I can't make any mistakes." "If I don't speak up, I can't be embarrassed." Passive people often expect others to act for them, and avoid the responsibility of acting themselves. "I can't talk to strangers, let them speak first." "It's not my fault, they forced me to do it."

Passivity sometimes includes a magical wish or fantasy: "If I wait long enough, things will get better." One very powerful use of passivity —both conscious and unconscious—is to resist or manipulate others. "You can't make me do anything. I dare you." "You'll have to give in and do it my way." These are all negative kinds of passivity, which can cause us to miss out on much of life.

There is also a positive side to passivity. This kind allows us to become peaceful inside and experience ourselves deeply or just relax totally. It enables us to be receptive to other people—to be an empathic listener, to receive love, to allow others personal space without controlling them. This kind of passivity provides creative, self-renewing experiences that enrich our lives.

If you feel you are a passive person, don't think you are absolutely obligated to become aggressively assertive in everything you do. Your challenge is to discover the negative, constricting behaviors that hold you back from life, and experiment with other ways of being that will open you to living fully. At the same time, you can develop and enjoy the positive benefits of creative quietness and receptiveness that enrich you and your relationships.

• First, learn the difference between self-assertion and aggression. Assertion means being clear about your needs and feelings and taking steps to meet them. Aggression means trespassing on someone else's feelings and needs. Decide to be responsible for meeting your own needs.

•Practice saying what you feel and asking for what you want. Simply put, that's what assertiveness is.

• List ways in which you feel passive and situations that frighten you. Ask yourself what your feelings are at these times. Fear? Wishing somebody else would act or would change? Do you feel obstinate and powerful in refusing to act? These insights will guide you in making changes.

• If you discover that your passivity is obstinacy or an attempt to get others to change, look at the deadening effect this has on you and your relationships. Try to become more open and direct about what you want. Say "I don't want to do that" or "Please do it my way" or "What I would really like is . . ." When you can do this, you will feel yourself coming to life.

• Don't think you have to rage or hit someone in order to be assertive about your anger. Just say how you feel: "I'm really upset about this" or "That makes me mad." Say it to the appropriate person if possible, or to your rap group or a counselor. Don't let negative feelings build up and stifle you. Don't think you can hide in passivity forever.

• Practice expressing positive feelings too—your love, caring, and enthusiasm. Look for opportunities to be safely active and expressive, so you can get in some warm-up practice. Do assertive caring things for other people. This will help you store up good feelings for when you must be assertive in conflict situations.

• When you take a stand about what you want, persist. But if you realize you are treading on someone else's rights—for instance, when you get an honest, definite, firm no to a sexual advance—make an active choice to respect the other person's feelings. This boosts your own self-respect too.

• Give up the idea that it's absolutely essential for everyone to like you all the time. Trying to please everyone is more likely to make you seem bland and boring, and lose you friends. Being self-confident and saying what you feel make you much more attractive.

• Rehearse and relive difficult situations before or after they happen. Say what you wish you'd said to the impolite store clerk. Practice asking your mechanic to redo a faulty engine tune-up. Rehearsing makes new actions easier to carry out in real life.

• Practice making eye contact with other people. This basic form of active reaching out will help you feel and look self-confident.

• If someone makes a demand or request that seems arbitrary, ask why you should do it. Ask with a sincere interest in the reason, not angrily or sarcastically. Then evaluate whether it is something you want to do. If not, say no, and state why not.

• When you are asked to do something you don't want to do or don't know how to do, turn it down. Don't set yourself up for failure because you are afraid to say no. Don't fall into a pattern of passive resistance or procrastination. Say no up front and get it over with.

• Don't blindly accept others' criticism or doubts about something you're doing. And don't feel you always have to defend or justify yourself. Practice trusting your own feelings about what's right for you.

• If you feel ignorant or inadequate, find a counseling or mental health center that will test your mental, occupational, and physical skills. If you test high, believe it. If you find areas where you need improvement, get that education or know-how through reading or taking classes or through on-the-job training. Passivity often conceals a fear of failure. It is natural to fear failure. Admit you have such fears, and take gradual, manageable steps to overcome the deficiencies that could make you fail.

• If someone is hostile or aggressive in response to your assertiveness, face the opposition directly to learn more about it, without giving up your position. For example, if you have complained about poor service and received a hostile response, you might acknowledge the person's feelings by saying, "Yes, I can see it must be hard to listen to complaints about the service all day, when you're so shorthanded." Show respect for your opponent as a person, and then go on to ask firmly for what you want.

• If you fear you're becoming overassertive, ask a good friend, counselor, or other trusted person to give you some honest feedback. Try to get specific feedback about precisely when you were overassertive, so that you don't get discouraged and retreat into generalized passivity.

• If you're afraid to do things because you might make mistakes, look around you and notice how often other people make mistakes, change their minds, even appear foolish. Nobody's perfect. Learn to accept a little anxiety when you risk acting. If you fail, try to roll with the punch. When you succeed, let that give you the courage to keep moving ahead.

• Pick out someone—friend, movie star, public figure—whose self-confidence you admire. Try acting like that person—not in a phony way but some way you can be relatively comfortable in trying. Pretend for a while that you really are active and assertive, and see if it begins to feel more natural. Don't passively accept an old self-concept that you are passive by nature. Realize that passivity is a role too, just one you learned earlier in life.

• Take an assertiveness-training course, or read one of the very good books on the subject.

• If your passivity takes the form of an inactive life, ask yourself whether it's because you haven't yet found a meaningful life direction in which to be active. Reassess where you are and where you would like to be. Face the fact that "doing nothing" is actually a very active way of resisting living.

• Inactivity breeds inactivity, so practice taking action—anything that gets you unstuck and gets your breathing and circulation moving. Do yoga exercises. Take brisk walks. Make a date to play tennis every Saturday, and keep it. Find physical activities that relate to some of your life goals—even mental work like writing or playing chess requires that you be physically fit to perform them at your best.

• Cultivate and indulge the part of yourself that truly enjoys quiet and relaxation. When you feel like being passive, make the most of it. Listen to music, soak up the sunshine, sleep. Contemplate nature. Learn deep relaxation exercises and meditation. Feel the ebb and flow of the rhythm of life, and let this creative passivity rejuvenate and refuel you for joyous activity.

• Appreciate and cultivate the part of yourself that enjoys being quietly receptive to others. Really listen and empathize when people talk to you. Enjoy receiving love and warmth. Recognize that this is only one part of a full relationship, but a very important part.

SUGGESTED READING:

Alberti, Robert, and Michael Emons. *Stand Up, Speak Out, Talk Back!* New York: Pocket Books, 1975.

Smith, Manuel. *When I Say No, I Feel Guilty.* New York: Bantam Books, 1975.

See also: BOREDOM, DEPENDENCY, FEAR OF FAILURE, FEAR OF SUCCESS, LONELINESS, MASOCHISM, PROCRASTINATION, SHYNESS, UNDERACHIEVEMENT

PERFECTIONISM

Perfectionists are basically very insecure people with a constant need for reassurance. No matter how well a perfectionist does anything, he or she is left feeling at least a tinge of failure. An internal voice that will not be quiet always reminds the perfectionist, "You should have done better."

Attempting to be perfect is a way of denying and overcompensating for a negative self-concept. Some people carry around a deep negative self-image without being consciously aware of it or of its origins. Without knowing why, they are obsessed with thoughts of achieving perfection, which they translate into compulsive perfection-seeking behaviors.

Often adult perfectionism has its roots in unrealistic parental demands in childhood. Parents who are never satisfied with their children's accomplishments raise children who are never satisfied with themselves. These children grow into adults who are intensely self-critical and convinced that they are inadequate. Their gnawing insecurity reflects a painful anxiety about failure to meet the standards by which they were raised.

Like other compulsive behavior patterns, perfectionism can be a way to avoid a problem—in this case, the problem of fearing failure. Perfectionists desperately hope to avoid failure by going to extremes to avoid errors.

Perfectionists have grown up with conditional love and have therefore come to believe that only the perfect are worthy of love. Love was doled out to them only as a reward for perfect behavior, perfect achievement, perfect obedience. No wonder the perfectionist thinks, "I must be perfect or else I'm terribly imperfect. Imperfection deserves and receives condemnation and rejection." At the same time, the perfectionist seeks the guarantee hidden in this view: "If I am perfect, I cannot lose love—people will have to love me if I'm perfect."

In this way, perfectionists indulge in the illusion of perfectibility. Unable to accept themselves or others as naturally mistake-prone human beings, they constantly seek to get closer to their ideal of error-proof living. The fact that perfectionists are often highly skilled in some areas gets in the way of their recognizing the illusion they're pursuing. Unwilling to rest content with their genuine excellence in some areas, they push on to achieve perfection in more and more ways. Their striving becomes a kind of addiction that can never be satisfied.

A perfectionist's inability to accept human frailty and error can cause serious and disruptive emotional problems. For example, the stress and depression that accompany normal mid-life changes are increased for perfectionists, who tend to exaggerate both their past failures and the limits of their future. And many marriages have been ruined by the "toothpaste-cap syndrome," in which one partner picks at little flaws in the other, eroding the trust and love between them.

When perfectionists tire of pushing themselves and others past the point of endurance, they may then pull back and restrict their activities excessively to avoid the risks of trying anything that might fail. These restrictions may include a tendency to procrastinate. In the extreme, such a restriction may keep the perfectionist from starting anything at all (a kind of protective withdrawal ranging from underachievement to suicide). Another strategy involves beginning many things at once but seldom finishing any. After all, an unfinished task cannot yet be labeled a failure by the perfectionist's never-satisfied inner judge.

Overcoming the restricting and counterproductive patterns of perfectionism takes a strong effort at redefining and strengthening your self-image. Begin with the following approaches.

• Rediscover yourself as more than the sum of your actions and products. Perfectionism is a way of living that overidentifies you with what you do and produce. It distracts from your awareness of what you are: an ordinary human, with all the inevitable mortal flaws. We seek love and fear rejection. We are curious and creative, but often stumble and bungle. Those people in your life whose love is worth having will love and value you for yourself, not for the perfect "display image" you've been trying to project.

• Recognize perfection as an unattainable ideal, not a possible or even desirable way for human beings to live. We need to make mistakes in order to learn and to grow. Don't waste your time stewing over errors or even failures. Look for what they have to teach you and move on. Joseph Kennedy wanted to teach his children that it was all right to try and fail, so he reminded them that "once you've done your best, the hell with it."

• Strive for excellence, and when you do a good job let yourself enjoy it. The antidote to perfectionism is not to give up striving for improvement but to learn to accept yourself as a living, growing, imperfect— but improving and well-intentioned—individual.

• Repeat to yourself a new motto to replace the old one: "Anything worth doing is worth doing badly." If we really care about doing something, we ought to be willing to do it for its own sake, not to demonstrate how well we can do it. Tackling complex and difficult projects with real significance necessitates suffering through times of uncertainty, frustration, and failure. In art, music, science, teaching, sports, and other creative spheres of life, excellence is reached only in specific fleeting moments. Tasks accomplished with too much control lose the human quality of creative struggle that makes them exciting. Some artists say they never finish a painting—they abandon it.

• Stress your accomplishments in your mind. Stop listening to your overdemanding, never-satisfied inner judge. Do not keep score of your failures or mistakes. Do not exaggerate the difference between what you achieve and the goal you are striving toward.

• Look at the specific ways in which you are a perfectionist. Do you focus on looks, work, housekeeping? Under what circumstances are you likely to behave in a perfectionistic manner? Are you competing? Are you compensating for some real or imagined flaw in yourself?

• Imagine not doing something perfectly. What are the external consequences (not your internal responses)? If there are none—as is likely —look at the self-destructive nature of your perfectionism. Look carefully at your internalized unrealistic expectations. See that they are, in fact, *enemies,* not helpful friends. Begin to revise, lower, or drop these expectations.

• Don't get hooked on someone else's standards. If your parents are never content with what you do, recognize that they have a need to be discontented—not that you have never done anything worthwhile. Identify your own values. Strive to satisfy your own needs. If it's really more important to you to develop your photographic skill than to have the best-trimmed lawn on the block, don't be pressured by your neighbor's disapproval. A nightclub singer got fed up with the perfectionistic demands she and others placed on her, quit, and went to college, where she enjoyed learning new things in an atmosphere she found more supportive.

• Refrain from self-criticism and from harsh criticism of others. Work at accepting everyone's efforts graciously and positively. As an exercise, keep track of how often you criticize yourself and others (both internally and out loud). Use a golf-score counter to tick off each instance. Now, reward yourself for reducing this negative behavior. Give yourself points for the actual number of reductions in negative thoughts and for rejecting such thoughts when they do occur. Do something nice for yourself each time you earn five or ten points.

• Work at becoming less competitive. Stop comparing yourself to others as if you were always involved in an important rivalry. Praise yourself for your real achievements and positive qualities. Don't dump on yourself because someone else does something better than you do. There is no absolute "number one" in life. We're all working, learning, growing, and changing in our relationships to each other.

• Laugh. Make jokes. Look at the funny side to life's dramas. Very few things in life are so serious that there isn't some opportunity for humor. Recognize and accept the comic aspects of trying and failing. So much is really beyond our control that there is ample room for humor in the distance between what we want and what we get.

• Don't pass along your perfectionism to your kids. Praise and encourage them sincerely and appropriately. Let them know that you love them no matter how they perform. Give them opportunities to learn to make decisions and to take responsibility. Help them learn from mistakes without feeling ashamed or unacceptable. Show them that your love is not conditional on their being perfect. You may find that while you're concentrating on treating them generously and lovingly you're also learning to treat yourself with the same consideration.

SUGGESTED READING:

Dyer, Dr. Wayne. *Your Erroneous Zones*. New York: Funk & Wagnalls, 1976.

See also: ANXIETY, COMPETITIVENESS, COMPULSIONS, ENVY, GREED, GUILT, NARCISSISM, OBSESSIONS, SELF-HATE, STRESS

PREMARITAL SEX

Sex before marriage is an accepted practice for the majority of Americans. Yet it is an area of great conflict—and frequently deceit—because traditional moral and religious values against it remain strong. It particularly poses a problem for young people who must struggle to balance their emerging sexual desires with their moral code. A 1978 Gallup Poll revealed that 59 percent of American teenagers approve of premarital sex, and 41 percent of male teens do not think it's very important to marry virgins.

There are many reasons to enjoy premarital sex: to be loving, to learn about your own sexuality as well as your partner's, to see how relationships work. However, indulging in it can also become an excuse for promiscuity. It can disguise hostility or self-serving, manipulative behavior.

It is wise to examine your feelings, expectations, and fears about sexual intimacy and share them with your partner beforehand. Relationships which are not entered into honestly are likely to have messy consequences, such as pregnancy, abortion, emotional hurts, and betrayals. For premarital sex to be an emotionally enhancing experience, the desire to explore and share sexual pleasures must be balanced by informed, inner-directed standards.

• If premarital sex is an issue that now concerns you, assess your level of readiness and maturity for a sexual relationship. Can you handle it emotionally, socially, morally? What are you expecting it to be like? Review your fantasies to check whether they are likely to be fulfilled by reality. What are some fears and negative fantasies? Review the steps you can take to prevent an unhappy outcome. For example, be sure you have made an informed, conscious, and responsible decision to deal with the chance of pregnancy in a way that you can really live with. Also ask yourself how prepared you are to deal with disappointment or rejection in case the relationship ends that way after you have tried sex. Hopping into bed can be easy for some people, but getting out of bed and sustaining a good relationship requires skill. Don't hurry into sex to prove you are grown up. First make sure you are grown up enough to make it a good experience for yourself and your partner.

• If you decide to enter into a sexual relationship, be careful not to have unreasonably high expectations. Naturally you will have your hopes and fantasies. You may be exploring whether you and your partner are compatible before you get into a marriage together. Don't condemn your relationship or each other if your experiments with sex are not as fulfilling as you want. Sex often improves within the security of a solid relationship or marriage. It can, of course, also deteriorate if either partner feels too confined by the marital bonds.

• Realize that premarital sex is not a full or fair test of compatibility. It does not tell you much about what it would be like to live with your lover. Sexual rapport can be an important part of the foundation for marriage or living together, but there are many additional complexities.

• Keep a clear perspective about what you are doing. Continue to examine your feelings as your relationship progresses. Are you enhancing your sexual identity, self-worth, and capacity for caring? Do you feel compromised or trapped?

• Consider how you feel about the possibility of marrying or living with your lover. Have you pushed these possibilities into the distant future? Watch to see whether your relationship is in danger of remaining stuck at the premarital-sex stage because one of you is afraid to commit yourself to anything more. Decide whether that is okay for you, or whether you are settling for less than what you feel is your potential for committed closeness.

• Keep track of the expectations you and your lover have about the relationship. Are there any unverbalized expectations as to where the relationship is headed? Does one of you feel it is more casual than the other does? If your degree of involvement can be mutually agreed on as you go along, it will help prevent feelings of entrapment or abandonment later on.

• Ask yourself how much premarital sexual experience you need. When does sex become collecting adventures, or an ego trip? Are you progressing and learning, or just chalking up scores? Are you using—or being used by—a lover in a manner you may regret later?

• Look at whether your potential lover is also a good friend. Even if you don't want to continue as lovers after you experiment with sex, you may want to continue your friendship. Will this be possible? Do you want the sexual experience enough to complicate and possibly damage a valuable friendship? Don't feel pressured to progress into a sexual relationship just to demonstrate to the world that you are a normal, sexually functioning man or woman. Allow yourself to prefer a nonsexual friendship if that is what you really want.

• Face your responsibility for contraception. If you choose to enjoy premarital sex, don't clutter it up with anxiety about pregnancy. Think ahead. If you're a man, be aware that many teenage girls want to get pregnant, sometimes unconsciously. Be careful not to be misled or to assume that your partner will take precautions. If you're a woman, plan consciously what you want to do about pregnancy. Don't let it happen as a passive-aggressive act to get back at your boyfriend or your parents. Don't be careless. Your local Planned Parenthood group is an excellent, confidential source of help and information.

• Realize that a sexual double standard still exists. Many otherwise liberated men are unaccepting of free sexuality in women. Find out where you and your partner stand on this. Men with a madonna/prostitute complex make a distinction between sexual activities in marriage and out of marriage. They think a man has good sex with a "cheap" woman but marries a "pure" one. Some women have a similar attitude: They feel aggressive and uninhibited having "sex for sex" but are less free with their husbands. These attitudes unconsciously reflect the notion that sex is bad—not something you'd want to do with a nice potential marriage partner, or something he or she would enjoy. Check to see whether such ideas may be influencing you. If they are, you need to work on shedding your old standards and affirming sex as good.

• If your moral standards condemn premarital sex, don't attempt to ignore or override them. You may be pressured by your partner or overcome by desires you haven't felt before, but you must first come to terms with your own feelings and values. Don't blame your lover or passion for what you do. You are responsible for the choices you make. Honor your principles so that, whatever you do, you will feel good about it.

• If you have a dilemma about sex, talk with friends or a counselor. But watch out for their biases. Don't assume they will be neutral or approving. Many people's value systems or upbringing will not allow them to sanction premarital sex, though they may be very liberal about other issues. Look for someone who cares about you and your exploration of your feelings more than he or she cares about telling you how to live.

• If you or your loved one feels unequivocally that premarital relations are wrong, also discuss your feelings about marital sex. A rigid moral stance against premarital sex may disguise feelings that sex itself is bad. Such an attitude could be a source of great conflict if you marry. Regardless of what you *do* about sex, find out how you both *feel* about sex.

• Make all the preparations for sex that you can. Read the other entries in this book concerning sex. Don't expect the relationship to be the whole teacher. Do some homework.

• Make your own choice and be responsible for it. You may decide you don't want premarital sex, and this decision could be as threatening to your friends as it could be pleasing to your minister. Realize that people are very touchy about sexual matters and tend to be judgmental. Also, their verbalized attitudes may differ from their actual behavior. Only you can decide what's best for you. It's your body, your feelings, your value system—your choice.

SUGGESTED READING:

Child Study Association of America. *What to Tell Your Child About Sex.* New York: Pocket Books, 1974.

See also: DEPENDENCY, LIVING TOGETHER, LOVE ADDICTION, PROMISCUITY, SEXUAL DYSFUNCTION, TEENAGE SEX

PREMATURE EJACULATION

Coming too quickly is the most common sexual problem that men have, even though it's hard to say what "too quickly" is. Some men find a few minutes of intercourse too short, others think it's all right. At other times, it's the man's partner who thinks he comes too quickly and wants him to last longer. In any case, if, for whatever reason, you want to have more choice about when you ejaculate, there is something you can do about it.

Sometimes men who want to delay their ejaculation try thinking distracting thoughts during sex—thinking about baseball or the stock market are common ploys. There are also products which, when sprayed on, deaden feelings in the penis. (These have physical hazards.) Both of these methods just increase "spectatoring"—instead of focusing on feelings, they make a man stand outside himself and worry about how he will do this time. This only makes things worse.

Odd as it may seem, coming too quickly is not caused by feeling too much or being too excited; it's caused by not tuning in enough. When a man is about to come, his body gives him a signal, as if to say "If you keep it up, you'll come." If he continues whatever he's doing, he reaches the "point of no return." At that point, no matter what he does —even if he stops moving—ejaculation will occur automatically. So when a man tunes out his feelings, he tunes out this signal and therefore has trouble controlling when he ejaculates.

You can learn to control when you come by learning to tune in and recognize this signal and then stop for a moment when you feel it during intercourse. This requires two things: learning to put aside your worries and practicing recognizing the signal; pausing and then starting sexual activity again. This is called the "stop-start" method.

• Do the exercises recommended under SEXUAL DYSFUNCTION. Focus initially on bodily feelings that are *not* in your penis; tune in to the rest of your body. You will probably come during some of the exercises, particularly the ones where you're asked to stimulate your penis. Don't worry about this; it's expected and perfectly normal. Coming during an exercise is *not* a failure—how can you expect to learn about coming unless you do it?

• After you have become comfortable with giving your body pleasure, begin to focus a bit more on feelings in your penis and testes. Learn about your genitals in detail (use a sex book with pictures). Masturbate in a way you enjoy, and pay attention to the feelings you have just before coming. Most men experience the point of no return as a spasm or squeezing sensation at the base of the penis or inside the scrotum. Do this a few times until you think you know the feeling or signal. Then try masturbating slowly just until you feel the slightest hint of this feeling, then *stop* and caress another part of your body that feels good. When the signal in your penis has died down (you may lose your erection, too, but that is okay), return to masturbating. When you get the signal again, repeat the procedure.

• Don't expect to succeed at delaying ejaculation all the time; at first, especially, you will pass the point of no return and have an orgasm. Even after you have much practice, you will occasionally come when you don't want to. This is an expected part of learning this technique, so don't burden yourself with worries that you're not doing it right. If you come accidentally, try stopping sooner the next time you practice. You may initially need to stop after only a few seconds or a few strokes, but to learn this technique it's better to stop too soon than too late.

• Masturbate using the stop-start technique for a number of sessions. At first just try to stop once, then continue masturbating to orgasm. Later try two stops before orgasm, then three and four per session, moving on only when you have comfortably mastered the previous step. If you usually masturbate with just your hand, try introducing some lotion or cream to lubricate your penis. Don't worry if initially this makes it harder to stop in time.

• When you are comfortable with your own ability to stop before the point of no return when masturbating, you may want to practice with a partner. After you have each caressed each other over the whole body (as described in SEXUAL DYSFUNCTION), have your partner stimulate your penis slowly with her hand. Your job is to focus on your feelings and, by a prearranged signal, tell her when to stop. When you tell her to stop, she should hug you or caress you elsewhere until you feel ready to start again. Practice this a number of times until you can do three or four cycles.

• The next step is for you to practice stop-start with your penis in your partner's vagina. Initially try inserting your penis and just resting without moving. When this feels comfortable, your partner can try a few slow gentle movements while you just tune in to your feelings. As she increases her movement, you will feel the signal you now recognize and tell her to stop. Practice slowly until you can stop and start several times while in her vagina.

As you practice this, you will probably find that you are not only able to decide when to come and when to hold back, but also that you are feeling more than ever before. Enjoy yourself! You now will have learned how to make love with control and caring. You will be more aware of your own pleasure and more able to give pleasure to your partner. What started as a problem will have turned into a gateway opening onto a new level of giving and receiving.

SUGGESTED READING:

Kaplan, Helen Singer. *The Illustrated Manual of Sex Therapy*. New York: A & W Publishers, 1976.

Zilbergeld, Bernie, and John Ullman. *Male Sexuality: A Guide to Sexual Fulfillment*. Boston: Little, Brown & Company, 1978.

See also: MASTURBATION, SEXUAL DYSFUNCTION

PROCRASTINATION

To procrastinate means to put something off until the last minute—perhaps forever. Most people do this to some extent in some areas of their lives. If you procrastinate, you will be able to find a thousand dodges and excuses with which to kid yourself and others that you are really going to get a task done just as soon as you can.

You can procrastinate about anything: menial or unpleasant tasks; difficult, challenging (and therefore scary) tasks; action leading to or requiring a basic life change, such as leaving a job, seeking medical help, filing for divorce; facing up to a confrontation with people you depend on, such as asking your spouse or lover to work out a sexual problem, expressing anger to your employer, asking a friend to repay a loan.

It's easy to cover up procrastination. The very effort required to avoid action and repress the anxiety and guilt created by this avoidance will naturally make you tired—so you will have to rest before getting down to whatever "it" is. You can also keep busy with distracting, petty tasks: Make a list of what you have to do, rearrange your work space, reorganize your files.

Other cover-ups are a bit more subtle. You might hide your procrastination under a false front of Zen transcendence, spiritual peace (letting it be), or *mañana* indifference. You might take time out for an extended coffee break, a little snack, or a drink. You might even avoid the issue by dwelling on self-study or the development of psychological insight into why you procrastinate.

Procrastination has several juicy secret payoffs. Obviously, it lets you avoid doing what you don't like or want to do. Sometimes it is clear to you that you don't like something. Other times you may be puzzled at your own procrastination because you are struggling with an inner conflict—part of you wants to do it and an opposing part doesn't.

Putting things off as a way of life is a method you can use to avoid doing and risking in the real world of action. You can thereby protect yourself from the risk of failure and even from the suspense of trying. If you delay doing a job until the last minute and thus have little time for it, you can justify a poor performance by reassuring yourself that you did the best you could in a short time and that you could do better given enough time. You don't have to face that what you did is what you did.

People who fear success and all its consequences—having to meet higher expectations, accepting new responsibilities, gaining frightening freedoms, losing familiar old excuses, and confronting negative self-concepts—may procrastinate conscientiously and never have to face them. Others procrastinate themselves into failure just to spite demanding parents or spouses, just to enjoy the hidden delight of thwarting someone else's plan for their lives.

Procrastination costs you, except when you consciously choose to delay something and are willing to take the consequences. If not, habitual procrastination can lead to the sort of self-critical feelings that underlie much depression, guilt, and anxiety. Procrastinators often come to think of themselves as helpless, worthless, and out of control of their own lives.

Putting off things without worry or self-blame can give you an enjoyable flexibility and freedom. Procrastinating to deny reality or stay uninvolved with your own life cannot. Procrastination can become a way to escape living intensely in the present and accepting life's limits. It can be an escape into the fantasy that you can do it all eventually, that your life circumstances and inner capacities will be different tomorrow. This is a very human but very limiting form of self-deception. You do not have unlimited time.

The more you procrastinate, the more you stall, the worse it will get. If you have been procrastinating and you finally decide to do a task, you will probably be surprised at how much energy you have. Procrastination is hard work; taking action may prove to be less work.

• Don't work yourself up into a depression over past things left undone. Forgive yourself for your past "sins" of procrastination; give up the self-punishing guilt in favor of honest regret, and get on with the present. If you have not done something, you are not by definition a failure; you are just a person—with many, many positive, negative, and neutral characteristics—who has just not done something.

• If you really can't or don't want to do something, be honest with yourself and with the other people involved so that they can act without you. If you have to put something off for external reasons, request a specific time extension. If this inconveniences someone, offer to compensate him or her in some other way. But do be open about your need to delay, and *do finish*.

• Set priorities. What do you have to do? What tasks are most important? If your life is disorganized, create a realistic routine that will make it easier for you to keep track of your responsibilities.

• Assess your needs realistically and honestly. Identify what you are willing to do in the present to gain something you want in the future. Gauge your frustration tolerance—what future rewards are sufficient to keep you working instead of procrastinating?

• Set practical minimum goals for yourself. Break down large tasks into more manageable smaller ones. You'll learn from your success with these that you *can* control your behavior. Practice making rapid decisions on minor issues that have minor consequences: Wear the first appropriate outfit you think of to work or to a party; order the first appealing item on the lunch menu; decide whether you want pepper on your Caesar salad without taking a poll of the others at your table. Do small tasks that pop into your head immediately if you are not occupied; if you are busy, make a note and do the little task as soon as you're free. Learn to trust your ability to make decisions and complete jobs.

• Focus on short time intervals and decide what you're going to do in them. For example, right now make a clear decision as to what you are going to do in the next fifteen minutes. Do it. As a general rule, try making yourself give five minutes to a task you've been putting off. At the end of the required time you will probably find you can stay with it without forcing—you'll already feel the energizing effect of pleasing yourself by fulfilling your responsibility.

• Keep track of your behavior. What do you like to do? What do you dislike? When you complete a task you had been avoiding, reward yourself by doing something you enjoy, like reading, working on your hobby, having sex, going to the movies. When you don't complete something, impose a penalty (not a punishment). Require yourself to do something you dislike: clean up the garage, fill in requisition forms, get up extra early to make lunch for everyone before they leave for work or school. Another handy tool of behavior psychology is to leave motivating notes to yourself where you can't fail to see them often—on the bathroom mirror, the refrigerator, the center of your car's steering wheel, by your phone at work.

• Get in touch with whatever feelings you have about doing an uncompleted task. How bad would it actually feel to get it over with? (How much self-criticism is it worth to keep putting it off?) What's the risk involved in tackling this task? Practice accepting a certain amount of anxiety and suspense as you take risky actions. Think of yourself as a heroic person embarking on a voyage of discovery, even if it's just to get the tires rotated. Try to let go of your performance anxiety; doing is the important thing. Doing well is great, but doing poorly is a frequent and potentially valuable human experience. It doesn't devalue you.

• Demand better of yourself. Get lovingly angry at the part of yourself that procrastinates. Tell that part of you to treat you better, to stop sabotaging you. You do have control over most of what you do or don't do; there's almost always an identifiable choice point.

• Maybe it's time to take stock of your life in a very basic way. What are your values and goals? Are you stuck because the the basic design of your life just isn't right for you? If this is the case, don't struggle to override your procrastination—it may be a valuable warning sign that it's time for a basic reassessment. Don't force yourself to get on with the wrong thing.

• Recognize the element of self-deception in procrastination. Look inside for the roots of your procrastinating behavior. Look for evidence of such deeper concerns as low self-esteem; fear of failure; fear of success; hostility, denial, or spite (turned inward or outward or both); passive-aggressiveness; or anger and resentment. Take responsibility for dealing more directly with your feelings, in a way that does not sabotage your life.

• Ask for help. Tell friends, family, and co-workers what you are trying to do. Engage them as "friendly monitors" or pep-talking coaches to hold you to your word. Let them know that you really need encouragement, gentle prodding, and lots of praise.

• Don't put off pleasant things. The time for these is also short.

SUGGESTED READING:

Ellis, Albert, and William J. Knaus. *Overcoming Procrastination.* New York: Institute for Rational Living, 1977.

Ringenbach, P. T. *Procrastination Through the Ages, a Definitive History.* Palmer Lake, Colo.: Filter Press, 1971.

See also: ANXIETY, BOREDOM, FEAR OF FAILURE, FEAR OF SUCCESS, GUILT, PASSIVITY, PERFECTIONISM, SELF-HATE, TIME-WASTING, WRITER'S BLOCK

PROMISCUITY

Promiscuity means having sex with lots of different people without much real closeness or caring. It has a compulsive, driven, even defiant quality to it. It is quite different from freedom to choose to have meaningful sex with various partners unrestricted by antiquated rules. Freedom does not mean giving up your right and need to choose sexual partners carefully. It does not mean giving up your right—and the obligation to yourself—to say no to a sexual opportunity that does not seem suited to your needs and values.

Many people who behave in a promiscuous way, who initiate or accept random, casual, emotionally detached sexual relationships, do not realize that they are using sex as a "drug" to hide from problems, rather than for pleasure, sharing, or love. Not all casual sexual encounters fit this pattern, but if your sex life consists mostly of casual encounters and one-night stands, you may want to give more thought to what you are doing.

Sometimes promiscuous sexual adventures represent a form of love addiction: A person who is anxious and insecure about his or her own worth gets caught up in an addictive search for approval. Sex, like gambling, can become a game in which the compulsive player hopes Lady Luck will bestow the jackpot—the ultimate turn-on, the perfect partner who will make life ecstatic.

For others promiscuity is a way of expressing hidden anger. It can be a method of taking revenge against disapproving parents, a cold and un-supportive social environment, an aloof spouse, or even against a judgmental, self-critical part of oneself. Some people, feeling themselves deprived and disadvantaged by a harsh or insufficiently nurturing child-hood, grasp hungrily at lots of sex to make up the pleasure, love, and affirmation they have missed.

Narcissistic individuals are often comfortable with a promiscuous lifestyle, because it protects them against emotional demands and the risk of rejection by someone they let count. Never getting involved is a way of never having to be truly supportive of and vulnerable to another person. For those who find such sharing too scary or difficult, promis-cuity is a tempting alternative.

Promiscuity can also appeal to the competitive and the greedy. People who seek evidence of their worth by keeping score of their victories can record them by marking notches in their nightstands.

Sometimes, though, promiscuity is instead a reaction to stress. The anxieties and depression of a mid-life crisis, for example, can push a person into a frantic search for sexual adventure. Some people turn to sexual experimentation in hopes of rejuvenating their lost sense of alive-ness and attractiveness.

Perhaps some people are really at ease with promiscuous sex. For them it may be a comfortable, deliberately chosen way of finding sexual gratification without personal complications. Perhaps they know it pro-vides limited emotional fulfillment, but find it otherwise appropriate in terms of their values and needs. Such conflict-free promiscuity is prob-ably quite rare, however. So if you are sexually promiscuous, or feel drawn toward promiscuity, use the following questions and suggestions to help you understand your feelings and behavior and to develop your ability to create a fulfilling sex life.

• Be realistic about the dangers of promiscuity. In addition to the genuine physical risks of venereal disease and of taking home a violent —even murderous—partner, there are serious emotional hazards. Pro-miscuity can look like a way of seeking intimacy, but by its very shal-lowness it really prevents such closeness. Getting sexually involved with a lot of people, none of them for very long, is a hedge against any real investment in vulnerable, genuine intimacy. If you are promiscuous you risk missing what a part of your deeper self is trying to gain. You can wind up feeling empty, cheated, and fragmented.

• Identify your motives. What are you looking for in sex—pleasure, excitement, the challenge of conquest, revenge, love, the narcissistic power and freedom to use and discard people, proof that you are sexual, evidence of your worth as a person? What combination of rewards does casual sex seem to provide?

• Look carefully at the partners you choose or accept. After identifying your emotional needs and the goals you are seeking in promiscuous sex, ask yourself how satisfying sex with these partners actually is. Do they give you the love or pleasure you want? Do you end up less lonely, or more? Are you using them to avoid facing depression, anxiety, anger, or guilt? Or to avoid focusing on one love relationship where you might have to confront your barriers to giving and receiving love? Is promiscuous sex really a means to a goal, or is it an escape from difficult but more important life choices and problems? How much can you afford to give each of your partners? How much do they give to you?

• Pay attention to your sexual fantasies. Where do they take you? Is your present sex life a true expression of these fantasies? How do you want your sex life to develop? Is it going in the right direction for you? To gain a greater appreciation of the importance of fantasy in male and female sexuality, read *Secret Sex* by Thom Anicar (New York: Signet, New American Library, 1976) and *My Secret Garden* by Nancy Friday (New York: Pocket Books, 1974).

• Are you really comfortable with your promiscuous behavior? Are you paying a high price in terms of guilt or reduced self-esteem? Are you violating religious or moral rules you still value but have pretended to discard? Is the payoff worth what it costs you?

• Take responsibility for your own sex life. Don't get caught in someone else's game. Are you playing to a particular audience? Is there some individual or group you feel compelled to impress or to hurt? If so, you're not making a free choice. Don't try a promiscuous lifestyle if you find you cannot choose it wholeheartedly. Don't be promiscuous in response to social pressure or to defy a restrictive family. Neither of these ways is a positive, free choice to pursue your own best interests.

• Is your promiscuous behavior related to your drinking habits? If you are only (or especially) promiscuous when drunk, you probably have an alcohol-dependency problem, too. (See ALCOHOLISM.) Deal with the alcohol addiction first, then see if you still behave promiscuously. If you do, at least then you can focus on the problem by itself, free of the complication of alcohol dependency.

• Do you separate sex from feeling? Why do you make this separation? Are you afraid of the vulnerability that you'd feel if you combined them? Has a fear of emotional expression, dependency, and involvement caused you to overemphasize the desirability of a carefree sex life? Does variety substitute for meaning? Do you want to continue risking your ability to feel and care? The cold separation of sex from feeling can eventually numb and deaden both your emotional and your physical responses. You can get so good at not feeling that you won't even need the drugs or alcohol some people use to maintain their numbness. Do you want to risk this sort of emotional death? If you're willing to take such a risk, why?

• Celebrate and develop your own sexuality as something you have and use for pleasure and love, not something you *get* from a succession of partners. If you don't have this strong sense of your own sexual identity and validity, you won't get it from promiscuous sex. Something important is missing from your inner store of self-affirmation and sexual confidence. Why don't you have a strong sense of individual sexuality? Did you ever have it? If so, where has it gone? Who took it? Where did you give it away?

• Recognize the ties between promiscuous sex, shyness, loneliness, and masochism. Look for sources of anger and frustration in your life. These strong emotions may lead you to use sex without love as a way of punishing yourself—perhaps because you can't find a good external target for your anger and frustration. Is promiscuity a way of turning against yourself, possibly because you no longer see yourself as worthy of love? Are you trapped in loneliness and despair?

• Don't pay too much attention to judgmental labels. We all have a need to establish our personal standards, in sex as in other areas of life. There are various degrees and types of promiscuity, and some are less risky than others. If you are exploring and experimenting sexually, if you don't want obligations or involvement at this point in your life, and if you know what you're doing and why, your sex life is probably not a promiscuity problem. If you've led a repressed, sheltered, or dependent life, it can be useful to have a period of experimentation and testing your standards and wishes. You need to find out for yourself—not for your family, friends, or anyone else—how much sex is enough or too much, what kind is pleasurable, how many partners you want, how much closeness and commitment feels right, and so on.

• Watch out for the fact that there often is still a double standard even in so-called liberated groups. Men may want their women to be experienced as the result of having had several "meaningful" relationships, but may still judge them as "cheap" if they've had a lot of casual sex, even though the men don't judge themselves negatively for the same behavior. Whether you are a man or a woman, take a look at the ways in which a double standard may be affecting your attitudes and behavior, and affecting other people in your life.

• Beware of succumbing to the hype of the sexual revolution. Not surprisingly, in terms of human emotional needs, few people opt (in the long run) for promiscuity instead of some form of relatively stable sexual relationship. It's not unhip to want sex with feeling. You don't have to exploit others or let yourself be exploited to be sexually liberated. In fact, liberation has as much to do with the freedom to say no as to say yes—you're not free if you have sex with everyone who asks without your knowing if you really want to.

• Use fantasy to enjoy "safe promiscuity." If you want more varied experiences without being actively promiscuous, do it in your head. Indulge your fantasies; include them in your usual sexual behavior. Share them with your partner. If you include masturbation in your sexual repertoire, work the fantasies into your self-pleasuring.

• Remember, sexual experiences cannot substitute for all the other relationships you also need to develop in the domain of work, creativity, recreation, learning, sharing, and giving. Just having a "healthy sex life" will not guarantee that you will find meaning and fulfillment in the rest of your life. Don't mistake working at sex for working at creating a generally rich and satisfying life.

SUGGESTED READING:

Cammer, Leonard. *Freedom from Compulsion.* New York: Pocket Books, 1977.

Ellis, Albert, and E. Sagarin. *Nymphomania: A Study of the Oversexed Woman.* New York: Manor Books, 1974.

Kaplan, Helen S. *The New Sex Therapy.* New York: Quadrangle, 1974.

See also: ANXIETY, COMPULSIONS, DEPENDENCY, EXHIBITIONISM, EXTRAMARITAL SEX, LONELINESS, LOVE ADDICTION, MASOCHISM, MID-LIFE CRISIS, NARCISSISM, SELF-HATE, SEXUAL DYSFUNCTION

PSYCHOSOMATIC ILLNESS

Nearly all illness is at least partially due to psychological factors. This does not mean that the sickness is merely "in your head." It means that your emotions influence the way your body functions. The word "psychosomatic" means "mind/body." The awareness of the unity of body and mind (and spirit) is part of ancient wisdom, and it is being freshly applied today in the holistic healing movement. In this approach, good health is promoted by dealing with the whole person, not just the body or a sick part of it.

Even conventional physicians believe that certain symptoms and illnesses are influenced by emotions: eczema, backache, headache, rheumatoid arthritis, asthma, fainting, fatigue, hypertension, heart disorders, ulcers, colitis, constipation, insomnia, low blood sugar, diabetes, sexual dysfunction, tics and tremors, stuttering, even cancer. Our emotions can set us up to be vulnerable to a disease, and keep us too weak to fight it off.

The psychological cause of illness is emotional stress, which makes body muscles tighten and triggers the release of chemicals into the bloodstream. Tense muscles, constricted circulation, and out-of-balance blood chemistry reduce our resistance to the germs and viruses that exist in our bodies. We are usually able to protect ourselves against these enemies by means of our natural immunological system, but stress weakens that system and makes us more susceptible.

Fortunately, our bodies also have remarkable powers for self-healing. Experienced physicians know that they function best when they help the body heal itself. Indeed, since we are always automatically fighting off various diseases, it is often more important to understand why we don't naturally get well than why we got sick. In research studies, many people have recovered from illness when given only a placebo, such as a sugar pill. They recovered because they believed they were receiving medicine that would cure them. They often recovered much faster than people receiving real medicine who believed it was only a placebo. People recover best, even from serious illness or injury, when they not only want to get well but believe that they will.

There is such a thing as "good" stress, meaning that it is healthy and enlivening. Pleasurable sports, intense lovemaking, and rising to a challenge to our creativity are examples. Of course, excessive doses of good stress could become harmful, but it is usually "bad" stress that triggers illness. Acute or prolonged anger, disappointment, grief, loneliness, humiliation, frustration, and depression can all make us sick, especially if we do not recognize our feelings and find expressive outlets. For health, energy must flow freely through the body. When it is dammed up by external barriers or internal constriction, the blocked energy sickens us.

Illness, then, is often a signal that we need to get in touch with feelings, resolve stresses, find new outlets, and even make lifestyle changes. Sometimes we are slow and reluctant to heed these signals. When illness occurs, it is sometimes held on to—usually unconsciously—to get what are called "secondary gains." It may be our way to get love and attention from others ("Please take care of me"), to control others ("Don't argue, you know I'm not well"), or to avoid living fully ("I can't go out, I have a cold"). Self-defeating patterns of illness can be stopped once we determine to promote, accept, and enjoy good health and full living.

• Take active, inventive responsibility for maintaining your own good health. Understand that everything you do to increase your physical, emotional, and spiritual well-being will help strengthen your body's immunological system. This includes activities you might not ordinarily associate with physical health, such as making up with an estranged friend, repaying an old debt, cleaning out the garage, developing an interest in religion, or laughing at funny movies.

• Eat nutritiously, exercise regularly, and get adequate rest. Be aware of what you put into your body, such as food, drink, and drugs. Be aware of what you breathe into it, such as cigarette smoke and polluted air. Try to eliminate or at least limit those elements that are harmful.

• Learn physical relaxation techniques and mind-control methods, such as meditation, yoga, biofeedback, prayer, guided visualization, muscle relaxation, and deep breathing. Take classes in these methods and devote time at home to practicing them. The money, time, and effort you spend will be an excellent investment that will pay you generous dividends in reduced medical bills.

• Become alert to your own stress signals, so that you can do something promptly to relieve stress rather than becoming a victim of it. Do you first feel tension as a stiff neck, a headache, sore back muscles? When you feel this signal, stop what you're doing and begin using one of your relaxation techniques. Then look at what the stress signal was telling you about how you were going about your life.

• Look at your sources of stress to discover ways of making your life happier. A woman who ran a hectic computer-programming school was constantly bothered by indigestion that expanded her stomach painfully. Her doctor treated her for the gas, but the bloated stomach persisted. One day she looked around at her busy classroom and said to herself, "I've had a bellyful of this place!" She instantly recognized her physical symptom as a signal that she needed to make changes in her way of working.

• Learn to use your intuitive mind to discover causes of your own illness. Talk to your body and let it talk to you. Develop pictures in your mind of what is going on in your body. Give your imagination free rein—don't try to be precise and scientific. Ask what your symptom is saying to you. Have you had more than you can stomach of your job? Is something about your life a pain in the neck? Do you wish someone would get off your back? Are you burned up about something? Have you lost heart?

• Take action on a plan to change your "sickening" situation. Train for a new job. Find more cheerful friends. Move to the country. Take assertiveness training. Get marriage counseling. Take your overdue vacation. Learn all about tasty health foods. Risk building a close personal relationship.

• Take an inventory of the illness-producing forces that you carry around inside you, such as excess competition, chronic fear, unresolved guilt, or low self-worth. Keep track of when and how often these patterns get activated in you. Work with a counselor, friend, or imagined inner guide to stop them and replace them with new, life- and self-affirming inner processes.

• Don't let your symptoms fall into a vicious circle. Worrying about not sleeping or about sexual "failure" is a sure way to make those problems worse. Remember that your body is naturally designed to function well in sleep, sex, digestion, and lots of other things if you can get your head to stop interfering. Try to get in touch with any disturbing emotions that may be causing your problems.

• During stressful times, or following a stressful episode, help prevent psychosomatic reactions by working off your physical tensions— jog, play sports, punch a pillow, or cry.

• Invest time in building close, satisfying relationships. When you relate warmly with others, you give yourself some very powerful health-promoting medicine.

• Allow yourself pleasures and enjoyment of life. Eat, sing, dance, make love. Go to the movies, to the theater. Listen to music. Enjoy nature. Watch children play. Let yourself be open to happiness. Seek cheer rather than gloom. And remember that laughter truly is medicine for the body.

• If you become ill or injured, trust your native ability to help the doctor's medicine cure you. Follow the doctor's orders, be cheerful, and look forward to getting well.

• If you have a persistent or recurrent illness, ask yourself what benefits you might be getting from it, or be hoping to get. Do you want sympathy, rescue, an excuse to avoid life, revenge, something to talk about? Add up the score—does being sick really pay off? Can you get what you want at less cost? Get counseling for help in dealing with your emotional investment in being sick if this seems to be an issue for you.

• If you have a long-standing illness that does not respond to treatment, be aware that your doctor may eventually feel helpless to do anything more than medicate the symptom. Don't keep taking medication without working on the underlying causes of the problem. Drugs often treat symptoms only, giving the illusion of cure but actually allowing the underlying cause to get worse. You may also become over-medicated or even hooked on the drug.

• Don't underestimate the importance of having a doctor you respect and trust. Even though you retain responsibility for your part of the healing, your faith in your doctor's ability to cure you is extremely important. If you do not already have a doctor you like, ask friends and other professionals for recommendations.

• If you know someone who is chronically ill, explore the possibility that he or she is unconsciously getting something out of it, such as control or a shrinking back from life. If this is so, try to help that person to find ways to meet emotional needs more directly, or to acquire a more confident approach to life. Don't allow someone to blackmail you emotionally with his or her illness. It could drive you into an illness yourself.

SUGGESTED READING:

Frank, Jerome. *Persuasion and Healing.* New York: Schocken Books, 1974.

Lewis, Howard and Martha. *Psychosomatics: How Your Emotions Can Damage Your Health.* New York: Pinnacle Books, 1972.

Pelletier, Kenneth R. *Mind as Healer/Mind as Slayer.* New York: Dell, 1977.

See also: ANXIETY, CANCER, FEAR OF DEATH, FEAR OF SICKNESS, LONELINESS, PAIN, STRESS

RAPE

Janice Y. works evenings in a department store. One night Janice was late in finishing work, and most of her friends had already left by the time she walked alone to her car. She was accosted in the parking lot by a man who clamped his hand over her mouth, pulled her into the back of his van, and raped her. He left her, bleeding and shocked, on the parking-lot pavement.

Marilyn R. was raped by her brother-in-law one evening when they were alone at his house. She feels that she has been part of a terribly shameful act. She doesn't dare tell anyone about it.

The rape victim is filled with anger, humiliation, guilt, and sometimes confusion about her part in the traumatic event. Frequently, from the way law authorities (and perhaps her husband) treat her, she gets the idea that she must be at fault for what has happened. If she decides to prosecute, her treatment in court is sometimes more humiliating than the rape.

Most rapes are planned in advance. The rapist is often someone who has been watching her, perhaps has spoken to her on several occasions to test her accessibility and the likelihood of her compliance. Sometimes he is a friend of the family. Some husbands commit rapelike sex. Occasionally the rape is a casual by-product of a robbery.

The man who rapes is satisfying needs he is not even fully aware of: the need to be sexually powerful and anonymous, to use a woman and discard her, to be intimate without intimacy; most of all, to achieve release without feeling his own emotional need for loving contact. In the rape he remains isolated from his vulnerability. He is the conqueror, she is merely an object. If he then kills her, this is simply a more total solution. There can be no contact.

A rapist may release his victim and then fantasy that the woman has fallen in love with him and wants him to come back. He is now a powerful, sexual man who doesn't need to worry about rejection from the woman or guilt over his crime.

Although rape can happen to a man, women are the usual targets. As a woman, you can reduce your vulnerability, partly through specific precautions and partly by increasing your sense of independence and self-esteem. If despite everything you do suffer a rape, you need to know how to survive and rebuild your life, so that you can come out of the experience with increased inner strength and self-confidence.

• Recognize that you are vulnerable when you are friendly with a stranger. He may be testing you as a target. If you feel suspicious when he tries to strike up a conversation, say a firm no. If he says something objectionable or touches you, tell him to get away. Shout or scream. Learn to trust your sense of when a man is encroaching on you, physically or verbally, and take action. Don't be polite.

• In your daily life, understand that acting like a helpless female who needs masculine care and protection can attract a man's sexual power drive. Recognize that your weakness means the rapist would not have to deal with a potent, sexual woman, just a compliant, frightened, confused object.

• Don't be naive about the incredible power of sexual signals and sexual situations. Don't send any sexual messages or be in any potentially sexual situations without knowing exactly what you are doing—to whom you're sending the messages and what the result might be.

• Recognize that you are extra vulnerable when using alcohol or other drugs, that you are easy pickings when you are out of money or in trouble and have to depend on a strange man to help you out. Some men see you as "fair game" when you hitchhike or otherwise make yourself available to a man in an isolated place.

• Get a pamphlet on rape from a community organization. Read a book such as *Against Rape,* by Andrea Medea and Kathleen Thompson. (See *Suggested Reading.*) Follow its instructions about protecting your home and yourself. Learn to lock doors and windows at home. Keep shades drawn at night. Don't open your door to strangers. Keep car doors locked and windows up. In your car or on foot, avoid dark, lonely areas; seek populated, lighted areas. Don't become paranoid, but train yourself to think in terms of personal safety.

• Take a self-defense course, or learn from reading how to gouge eyes with your thumbs, strike an Adam's apple with the side of your hand, pull or bite testicles. Carry a short, pointed weapon—pencil, pen, hatpin—and aim for eyes, neck, or ears. Hit hard on the head or foot with a heavy weapon. Rehearse in advance. Strike rapidly and fiercely if threatened. Disable him totally on the first try, even if it means causing serious injury or death. If he has a weapon, do not try to resist. Otherwise, defend yourself rapidly when threatened, even if it means being physically aggressive in ways you prefer not to be.

• Remember that the time to take action against a rapist is at the very first sign of danger, before he gets you in his control. Scream, use your police whistle or a weapon, gouge, hit, or run if you can.

• If you are trapped and overpowered by a rapist, begin talking to him as one human being to another. If this makes him angry, stop. Otherwise, speak calmly and courteously. Be friendly. Find something about him or his appearance to compliment him on, something that will make him feel good about himself. Force yourself to become sincerely interested in him. Remember that it is sometimes possible to talk yourself out of being raped, or at least to avoid additional violence and perhaps murder.

• If you are the victim of a rape, get help immediately. Call a friend and have her (or him) take you to a hospital with a rape unit if possible, or to the police. Vent your feelings freely—cry, scream, do whatever you need to express your anguish. It will help you to get the feelings out, and remember that the authorities will be more likely to believe you if they have seen your real despair and hurt. Have a physical examination by a doctor. Do not go home first, or wash, or do anything to make yourself look better.

• If the hospital or police do not have a rape unit, immediately contact a rape crisis organization. If no one will help you find one, call a radio or TV station for a hot-line number. Find sympathetic, supportive, organized, female help.

• After a rape, realize that you are going to have many strong feelings such as anger and guilt, as well as a sense of grief. Get as mad as you can at the rapist. Use your anger to get your energy flowing and help you to take positive, rebuilding steps. Let your guilty feelings flow too, but don't blame yourself for the rape. If you were careless or foolish, limit your self-blame to that. Resolve to change whatever it was that allowed the rape to happen. Remember that the bad person is the rapist, not you. Join a women's group where you can talk through your feelings and feel supported.

• If you prosecute the rapist, prepare yourself to withstand additional anguish and humiliation in court. Learn what to expect, and determine to use the experience to become a stronger, more centered, and more confident person. Remember that if you can get a rapist convicted, you have made an important social contribution toward making the world safer for women.

• Your main task, whether you prosecute or not, is to repair any damage to your self-esteem and reclaim your own body, your sexuality, and your worth as a person. Allow yourself time for rebuilding. If you continue to feel guilty and worthless, ask yourself why you are accepting this self-blaming role. Get counseling help if you need it. Try to use whatever you have learned about yourself from this experience to reshape and reaffirm your life. Make changes in your lifestyle. Learn to value your own independence and strengths, as well as valuing more deeply the qualities of the people you love.

• If someone you love has been raped, give her comfort and help, not anger at her foolishness and not ravings of revenge at the rapist. Allow her to sort out her feelings and go through a period of emotional convalescence.

• If the fantasy of being raped turns you on, go ahead and explore it. Be aware of it as fantasy and don't let it lap over into dangerous situations or actual behavior. Realize that the more aware you are of the powerful, volatile mixture of sex, violence, and power in our society, the better you can steer clear of it.

• If you are a man with fantasies about raping, give yourself permission to explore those fantasies. Make clear in your mind the difference between thought and action. If you have some sadistic, hostile inclinations, learning about them in fantasy will give you more control over them. If you suppress them, they tend to gain control over you. If you feel that your impulses are quite strong, get professional help to learn how to defuse some of your disturbing feelings and live more comfortably in your world.

SUGGESTED READING:

Burgess, Ann W., and Lynda L. Holstrom. *Rape: Victims of Crisis.* Bowie, Md.: Robert J. Brady–Prentice Hall, 1974.

Farkas, Emil, and Margaret Leeds. *Fight Back: A Women's Guide to Self-Defense.* New York: Holt, Rinehart & Winston, 1978.

Medea, Andrea, and Kathleen Thompson. *Against Rape.* New York: Farrar, Straus and Giroux, 1974.

Storaska, Frederic. *How to Say No to a Rapist—And Survive.* New York: Warner Books, 1976.

See also: SADISM, SEXUAL PERVERSIONS, SPOUSE BEATING

RETIREMENT

Retirement is a time that many people look forward to eagerly. For them it means freedom from work and an enjoyment of the just deserts of a lifetime of effort. Some people look forward to retirement with dread, fearing it means they will be useless and old, and perhaps poor and friendless.

It's true that retirement is a problem for many people. We have all heard sad stories of cases such as that of the hardworking family doctor who retired after a lifetime of service to others and then died a few months later, on his first vacation trip. These stories take some of the glow off the "golden years."

Retirement is a major life change and a mixed blessing, in which we must adjust not only to benefits gained but to losses. We are cut off suddenly from work companions whom we may have known for many years. We lose the structure, stimulation, and activity of our work routine. We may even lose the familiar way we think about ourselves. We can no longer say, "I am a doctor." "I am a carpenter." If our work-role identity is very strong, this is a particularly severe loss. Coupled with the other losses, it can make retirement a really depressing and potentially even lethal event. But it need not be this way.

The people who enter most joyously into retirement are those who have developed a strong identity and self-worth separate from their work. They realize that work is not the only worthwhile way to participate in life. They have fascinating other interests to follow. They approach retirement with more eagerness than reluctance. Although even the most eager retirees may to some degree mourn the losses of the end of work, their emotional vitality propels them into constructive new activity, whether it is creative loafing, volunteer work, or traveling around the world.

The best time to start building for retirement is when you are young, by building a full life and developing many aspects of yourself. But whatever your age or work status, seize now whatever time and opportunities you can find to prepare financially, intellectually, and emotionally for the freedom and challenge of not working. Now is the time to start developing an identity and interests outside your work, to learn an appreciation of leisure, and to take responsibility for making your retirement a self-directed, creative adventure.

• Develop a positive mental atittude about growing older—accept age as something precious you have earned. See AGING to help you understand the potential richness of your later years. A vital, forward-looking mental attitude is the most important ingredient of a happy life, whether young or old.

• Be sure to make adequate financial plans for your retirement. Make a realistic assessment of your expected income from Social Security, pension, savings, and investments. If you will need a second career after compulsory retirement, plan ahead for it.

• Even if you are not yet retired, learn now how to enjoy leisure and treat yourself well. Take vacations when they are due you. Pursue non-work-related interests, such as sports or cultural activities. Enjoy relating to friends and family.

• When you retire you will still be the same person you are now, so don't expect problems to disappear magically. Emotional difficulties that you have now are likely to affect you even more in later life. Take steps to do something about them now. If you are troubled with boredom, anger, hypertension, or anxiety, for example, read the articles in this book that relate to your problem, and follow the recommendations there. If you need counseling, get it. The sooner you start, the sooner your problems will begin to ease.

• As attractive as it may sound to you now, just sitting around the house is not going to satisfy you for very long, and hobbies that you do now for relaxation may not fill the gap. If you have few real interests outside your work, start developing them. Take classes or join special-interest clubs till you find something that really interests you. Whether you decide to embark on a physical-fitness program or to write poetry, be sure your retirement activities have real meaning for you. For example, if you travel abroad, visit places where your relatives or ancestors came from and trace your roots. If you like certain kinds of food, art, or sports, visit places that specialize in them.

• Spend time doing things for others, too. Make clothes or build doll furniture for your grandchildren. Baby-sit for neighbors. Volunteer at a community day care or mental health center. Your experience, wisdom, and maturity make you valuable to others. Create a temporary second career out of personal service to others. Consider joining the Peace Corps or VISTA.

• If you are physically limited by health problems, don't let that keep you from being mentally and emotionally active. Your limitations just mean that you must be more creative about finding your sources of satisfaction. For example, learn wood carving, make recordings for the blind, or write letters for hospital patients.

• When you retire you will need friends to replace the co-workers you no longer see. Make friends now outside of work. (If you have trouble relating to others, see LONELINESS and SHYNESS.) Make a special effort to get to know your neighbors or the co-workers who live fairly near you. Make friends in an art class or photography club. Prepare your current golf, tennis, or bridge friends for the fact that you're going to want to play more often. One of the benefits of retirement is having time to relate to others.

• Expand your personal vistas by deepening your sensitivities to non-work aspects of life such as art, music, relationships, philosophy, travel. Take someone with you to museums, concerts, or the ball game. Take a psychology or current events course, or join a discussion group. Learn to meditate.

• You probably don't have to retire at all if you don't want to. A bartender retired on company pension from his first job, took another job until he had a small second pension, "retired" to the National Park Service for two years as a technician, then tended bar a while longer until he was really ready to travel and relax on his pensions and Social Security.

• You can prepare ahead of time for a second career, or you can begin studying after retirement. Just be realistic about the physical, financial, and time requirements of learning your new trade or profession. This may be your chance finally to do something you've always wanted to do. One man who spent many years as an unhappy but successful businessman (because it was "respectable") finally let himself retire and became a fishing guide. A race-car driver finally admitted that he got scared trying to prove his manhood and turned to his secret love, sculpting.

• If you have financial problems after retirement and cannot work, don't become an unpleasant person by complaining excessively. Seek out and cheerfully accept the social programs your community provides for senior citizens. Help fulfill yourself by becoming a creative contributor to those programs, through either enthusiastic participation or volunteer work.

• Understand that the emotional impact of retirement, particularly compulsory retirement, can adversely affect your health. If you develop physical symptoms, consider the possibliity that they are at least partly the result of psychological stress. (See PSYCHOSOMATIC ILLNESS for a better understanding of stress-related illness.) Then take steps to reduce the stresses related to your new life status. Use your doctor, counselor, or spiritual advisor as a resource.

• Before you decide to move to an isolated desert or country setting, or live in an all-adult community, make sure you are willing to give up contact with those others, such as young people, who can help keep your outlook on life fresh and revitalized.

• Retirement counseling has proved valuable to many people, either before or after retirement. To find out what counseling programs exist in your area, write to these groups: Preretirement Education, Andrus Gerontology Center, University of Southern California, University Park, Los Angeles, California 90007; Preretirement Planning & Counseling Program, Duke University, Durham, North Carolina 27706.

• For an excellent all-round source of information and activities— health, politics, travel, lifestyle—join the American Association of Retired Persons (AARP), 215 Long Beach Boulevard, Long Beach, California 90802.

SUGGESTED READING:

Bradford, Leland and Martha. *Retirement*. Chicago: Nelson-Hall, 1979.

Comfort, Alex. *A Good Age*. New York: Crown, 1976.

See also: AGING, BOREDOM, DEPRESSION, LONELINESS, MID-LIFE CRISIS

SADISM

Jules Feiffer, the cartoonist, wrote a play called *Little Murders* about the cruelties we inflict on each other as part of "normal" everyday life. We honk our horns, laugh when someone falls, and tell Polish jokes. Children tease their pets, spouses beat each other, and nations go to war. We want mastery, power, dominance, visible reassurance of our strength and righteousness. Hurting or subduing a victim is a temptingly vivid way to gratify this need.

Sadism is an attempt to assert our will and control—either verbally or physically—over another living being. It can be motivated by vengeance or by the wish to make someone else feel bad, weak, or inferior.

Sadists seek to prove that they are strong, powerful, and right in order to deny or overcome their feelings of weakness, vulnerability, and guilt or shame. Inside they feel impotent and scared. They fear being hurt or abandoned, and thus will risk relationships only where they are in control. Sadists usually have little difficulty in finding masochists to be willing partners in their games, but if they can't find willing partners, they will seek out ones who are too vulnerable or weak to resist.

We all need to express our power and will somehow. But our aggressive impulses—even our healthy ones—meet with restraints in our society. When children act assertively in ways that don't suit their parents, they are blocked or punished physically or morally by being told such feelings are wrong and by being made to feel guilty. Other adults such as teachers continue the shaping and suppression of our expressiveness. Barriers to freedom such as poverty and prejudice add to the explosive charge of stifled energy we carry around. As a result, we look for opportunities to "let off steam." We not only want to discharge pent-up energy—we want to fight back against the image we get of ourselves as helpless and bad. A sadistic act is a way of saying "Look, I am powerful, and no one can stop me with physical force or frustrating and guilt-inducing rules." We seek targets and situations where we can score safe victories.

Sadism and masochism both stem from the same inner sense of physical helplessness and low self-worth. People inhibited by moral restrictions ("anger is bad") will behave masochistically and get victimized, but score moral victories. Those who were blocked by physical punishment or inadequacy are more likely to try to become tough and seek sadistic revenge.

Sadists value power more than anything else in life, and sometimes more than life itself. They admire and submit to those who have power, and despise and exploit those who cannot or will not fight back.

The authoritarian structure of some business, government, military, and academic organizations provides a chain of command in which subtle and obvious forms of sadism can easily be practiced. Military training camps, as well as fraternities and sororities, have been known to sanction physically sadistic practices in the initiation of newcomers. Cruelty can be disguised and rationalized in impersonal organizations as "enforcing the rules" or "getting the job done." The Nazis and the Spanish Inquisition justified gross sadism as necessary to serve a noble purpose. When sadism grows to affect an entire culture, as Nazism did, it becomes rationalized by political, moral, or religious ideologies. Individual sadists can then feel they are agents of a higher authority. The terror, confusion, and weakness of the victims is viewed as evidence that the sadist is superior and morally right.

Sadism is an age-old problem. The Colosseum in Rome is a monument to human sadism. Today we have our daily ration of murder on TV, and football on weekends. Watching other people assault each other in fictional dramas or in sports may provide a safe outlet for our sadistic impulses. Some critics, however, claim that being spectators of violence makes us more prone to act violently. A court case attempted to prove that a TV program helped incite a recent murder.

War legitimizes sadistic impulses and directs them toward the enemy as an agreed-on evil target. Outside of wartime, most violent crimes still occur within families. (See SPOUSE BEATING and CHILD ABUSE.)

Here are suggestions for how to handle your sadistic impulses in nondestructive ways, and how to learn and grow from having a problem with sadism.

• When you realize you are acting sadistically, stop and look closely at the exact form and content of your hurtful words or deeds. What are you angry about? Whom are you really angry at? What are you really trying to say to yourself and the world? Will cruelty actually succeed?

• Explore your sadistic wishes in fantasy. Own up to those wishes— that way they won't catch you by surprise when you can't control them. Are you carrying around old grudges? Are you seeking revenge for past hurts? Satisfy yourself in fantasy, and then ask whether you want to get involved in the effort and risk of acting out your feelings.

• Remember that sadism is a distorted form of a natural human drive. It offers short-term satisfactions but no long-term gain. Weigh the penalties and the payoffs realistically. "Living well is the best revenge," and you can't live well if you are supporting a sadistic habit. Shift your aggressive energies over to obtaining lasting satisfaction.

• Recognize that if you are sadistic you become dependent on masochists. You will need victims to maintain your contrived sense of power. But there is always the danger that the masochist may be pushed too far and strike back. Your relationships will be precarious. You will have to work hard to keep your masochist in line, or to recruit replacements.

• If you're involved in sadistic behavior with a spouse, you can learn to fight constructively by introducing some rules. *The Intimate Enemy: How to Fight Fair in Love and Marriage* (New York: William Morrow & Co., 1969), by Dr. George Bach and Peter Wyden, illustrates ways of fighting without victimizing or scapegoating. Agree to fight only about real issues. Avoid rehashing past hurts. Hire a referee in the form of a marriage counselor, to help you keep your fights fair and constructive. Keep in mind that your goal is to be close and to enjoy life, not to win a war.

• Practice safe physical aggression. Buy a pair of foam rubber clubs and slug it out with those. Beat your bed with a tennis racket, punch your pillow, and scream in your closed car.

• Switch over to friendly contests. Find legitimate channels for your impulses in physical activities and sports such as tennis, boxing, hockey, football. Remember that aggression is a form of raw energy. Even non-competitive athletics are an effective outlet. Figure skating or skiing can be as fulfilling as aggressive team sports. You move assertively through space, cut ice or snow, seize recognition. Symbolic games like chess, poker and bridge offer additional opportunities to conquer and destroy . . . safely.

• Face the fact that you must find some way to express your energy and power. Channel these drives constructively. Choose work that permits you to attack something which actually needs to be destroyed, controlled, or refashioned. Surgeons, barbers, butchers, woodcutters, firefighters attack the physical world. Housecleaning can be an aggressive outlet.

• Attack the physical world through gardening, landscaping, or home improvement. Teen probation camps have found that putting delinquents to work on the land has resulted in improved behavior. They attacked trees, brush, and rocks to clear and improve the terrain. Seek constructive outlets such as these. Put your energy to work.

• Consider the violence you're doing to yourself when you abuse others. Being tough takes a lot of energy and traps you in a phony role. Examine how you feel about yourself after you've behaved sadistically. Is it worth the strain and the separateness from others? Are you actually more of a victim of your own programming that requires you to be strong and hard even when you don't feel like it or when it doesn't work?

• Be aware that accomplices and supporters who help or applaud you today may desert or turn against you tomorrow. Groups and gangs can be fickle and demanding. Have you assumed a sadistic role you may have trouble sustaining on your own? You may be replaced by someone who is more sadistic or more effective in accomplishing the goals of the group.

• Realize that you may be used by a group as a sadistic leader or agent and then get disowned later. The others can claim they are innocent and leave you stuck with the rap. Your temporary illusion of strength and adequacy is ultimately self-defeating.

• Don't forget that there is always a bigger, tougher, or cleverer sadist looking for someone like you to score points off. When you are on top you attract resentful envy. When you slip the wolves will be at your throat.

• To triumph over feelings of sadism, acknowledge and accept your vulnerability. You must make peace with your human limitations and fears. Try to get past thinking of life as a jungle or a game which has winners and losers. Practice creating relationships based upon mutual support and caring. A little love will do a lot to soothe the savage beast in you.

SUGGESTED READING:

Bach, Dr. George R., and Dr. Herb Goldberg. *Creative Aggression: The Art of Assertive Living*. New York: Avon Books, 1974.

Rubin, Theodore Isaac. *The Angry Book*. New York: Collier Books, 1969.

See also: ANGER, CHILD ABUSE, EXHIBITIONISM, MASOCHISM, RAPE, SPOUSE BEATING

SELF-HATE

In its various forms—low self-esteem being the mildest—self-hate is *the* human problem. Nearly everyone has taken in a critical, negative, judging voice from the outside and made it part of himself or herself. We all feed our "inferiority complex" or inadequacy feelings on the damning opinions of our inner critic, our harsh conscience, or the internalized judgments of critical parents.

Self-hate results from the neglect or abuse of the self, a devaluing of our unique individual being. It can lead to negative feelings such as boredom, anxiety, guilt, and depression. These self-hating feelings can then cause self-destructive behavior such as overeating, alcoholism, drug abuse, gambling, procrastination, self-derision, masochism, accident-proneness, and suicide.

Self-hate has to be learned. We learn it from people and events, especially during childhood. We accept negative attitudes about ourselves taught to us by others. Sometimes we go further and judge ourselves even more harshly than others have judged us. Children have a tendency to exaggerate outside criticism when they turn it on themselves. Once begun, this process unfolds as a continuous experience of self-blame and self-rejection.

Unpleasant as self-hate sounds, it does have secret payoffs that make it a difficult emotional habit to break. Hating yourself can be a way to keep control of the script of your life. It can keep you from ever being surprised by someone else's disapproval or rejection—because you always attack and reject yourself first.

Self-hate can also keep you from becoming independent and responsible for yourself, and thus rescue you from that scary part of human development. You can resign into self-hate and passively hope that others will do the work of praising and encouraging you. If they do, fine. If they don't, you can blame them along with yourself. You don't have to take active responsibility for affirming yourself and developing a solid positive identity.

Another payoff you get is the comfort of old familiar ways. If you're used to being self-deprecating and putting yourself down, you may not like the prospect of risking your familiar (though painful) life pattern for the chance of developing a positive self-image.

The risk, however, is more than worth it. Few prizes in life can compare to the discovery and creation of your own personal worth and value as a human being. Nothing else you will learn will be so liberating or so energizing. Nothing else will make it possible for you to give—or receive—so much love.

• Begin by looking back over your life. Where did you learn self-hate? Who taught it to you? What experiences can you recall that contributed to your poor self-image? What have you ever done that realistically merits hatred?

• Tally the self-attacking statements that you continually make in your head throughout the day. Bring your self-hate out into the open and look at it directly. Don't let it continue as a hidden, hostile conversation with yourself. Label the part of you that makes these self-hating statements an "enemy." Be on guard against this inner enemy, and fight it whenever it attacks.

• Do a self-hate inventory. Rather than accepting a blanket judgment of worthlessness, be specific. What don't you like about yourself? What can you do something about, rapidly or slowly? Are the traits you can't change really deserving of hatred? Hating yourself won't make you a better person or benefit your real friends. Why do you focus on these negatives rather than on the combination of all your qualities— positive, negative, and neutral?

• Look at whether someone benefits from your self-hate. Family dynamics often demand that someone be elected to be the scapegoat or whipping boy. Like a hot potato, this role is passed around until someone is stuck with it. Don't volunteer to be the fall guy. Try not to be a patsy in this game if you discover it is being played. Be alert to one of its variants: "You're just like your no-good Uncle George." You're not the "bad seed"—no one is. No one is destined to be bad, so don't let yourself be put down by some meaningless, superstitious belief in hereditary evil.

• Recognize that if you've been subjected to these sorts of self-hate-producing environments you may have come to behave in quite negative ways. Put-downs can become self-fulfilling prophecies. If you believe them, out of loneliness, desperation, and anger you may do bad things.

• Get to know yourself as you are, not as others define you. Take fifteen minutes a day to sit quietly and review how you have felt and lived that day. Don't judge yourself or compare yourself to others. Just try to discover yourself as an individual.

• Claim your rights. Take your needs seriously. Explore your freedom to choose what's right for you. Take care of yourself as if you were an important person. Give up the security of having others define you and your needs. Give yourself permission and encouragement to experience and enjoy what life offers. Do these things without guilt: Acting in your own best interest does not mean stepping on others or ignoring their rights. It does not rule out loving, sharing, or even honest self-sacrifice. It does rule out self-destruction, self-blame, and the denial of your personal worth.

• Try to let go of unpleasant, self-diminishing feelings and pay more attention to the good. Discover what makes you feel good about yourself, and do more of it. Discover what makes you feel bad about yourself. How can you avoid it? What can you change?

• Life is not either/or; you don't have to be either the best or the worst. There is more of a range than that to human experience. Don't distort your imperfections or mistakes out of proportion to their true seriousness. Appreciate your abilities and good qualities. Be realistic and kind in self-appraisal. Set expectations that are meaningful to you, and fulfill them for yourself. Give yourself the opportunity to succeed. Meet your ongoing responsibilities, even the tedious ones, so you won't tear yourself down over petty failings.

• Don't look to possessions to give you satisfaction with yourself or your life. You are not what you own. Material wealth is like a narcotic if you use it to gloss over self-hate. You will get addicted, and you won't solve your problem.

• Watch out for religion's contribution to self-hate. Most of the world's great religions do not really ask us to hate ourselves for our humanness, but distortion and exaggeration of various religious teachings sometimes do result in excessive emphasis on sin and evil. To balance this tendency, some faiths consider it sinful to dwell gloomily on your wrongdoings or to believe yourself unredeemable. Don't think that your religion or God wants you to be miserable and self-hating. Your faith surely makes provision for appropriate penance, restitution, and commitment to change. Religion is not meant to crush the human spirit, but to help it reach its highest potential.

• Identify your priorities. Find out what you need and want from life. Where do your fantasies take you? What would have to change for you to have the career, family life, sex life, recreational life you dream of? What's the first step you would have to take? Once you've identified what you really want, make your choices with these priorities in mind. As you begin to act on your own needs and wishes you will strengthen your sense of self-esteem and individual worth.

• Pay attention to your feelings—the real ones. Face your negative feelings; don't cover them up with false cheerfulness or phony optimism. Listen to yourself. Then learn to say no to your internal critic. Forgive yourself for your mistakes. After all, how important are most of them? It is part of the human condition to err, to suffer reverses, to fail sometimes. Such experiences are part of life, not evidence of your low personal worth or justification for treating yourself punitively.

• Let go of the past. Don't hang on to old grievances that make you feel bad about yourself and others. Are you able to forgive others? Now forgive yourself. How do you treat people whose feelings really matter to you? Try treating yourself with the same consideration and compassion.

• Learn that you can take a positive view of yourself and assert your needs and wishes without harming others. Feeling good about yourself will not make you irresponsible or selfish; it will most likely make you more able to be sensitive to the weaknesses and needs of others. Once cleared of sabotaging self-hate, your inner core will be a source of love and creativity for yourself and others.

SUGGESTED READING:

Newman, Mildred, and Bernard Berkowitz, with Jean Owen. *How to Be Your Own Best Friend.* New York: Ballantine Books, 1974.

Rubin, Theodore Isaac. *Compassion and Self-Hate: An Alternative to Despair.* New York: David McKay Co., 1975.

See also: ANXIETY, DEPRESSION, FEAR OF FAILURE, GUILT, LONELINESS, LOVE ADDICTION, MASOCHISM, PASSIVITY, PERFECTIONISM, SUICIDE, UNDERACHIEVEMENT

SEX IN LATER LIFE

The idea that people cannot function sexually or are not interested in sex after age sixty or seventy is pure myth. Extensive research and interviews with older people confirm that we are sexual beings all our lives. One of the secrets of having a satisfying sex life in later life is to keep sexually active, for in sex as with many other natural processes, what you don't use you may lose.

Sex does change in later life, but the changes can actually be for the better. For example, a man's erections may become less spontaneous and he may take longer to reach ejaculation, but this slowdown gives the couple more time to enjoy their lovemaking and give it creative attention. The woman may also get more satisfaction from prolonged intercourse than from faster, more youthful intercourse. This is especially true if her sexual appetite has increased after menopause, as often happens. A woman who has been unable to achieve orgasm when younger may even become orgasmic in later life, when pregnancy fears and child-raising responsibilities are gone and vaginal blood-vessel changes create more physical arousal.

Not all people retain sexual capabilities into advanced age, usually because they have other physical problems. Whether our sexuality is great or small, as we grow older we especially value our loving relationships. Love and affection with a longtime partner can become even more precious and satisfying as the years go by. When we can also express these feelings sexually, we achieve an especially deep measure of happiness.

Sexuality in later life is an affirmation of ourselves as physically vital, emotionally responsive human beings. It gives us a strong sense of ourselves. It gives us the pleasure of touching and being touched in caring ways. It is an expression of love, passion, and deep feelings of sharing. It is a continuation of our lifelong search for meaningful expression and growth.

Here are some suggestions for ways in which to retain your own fullest range of sexuality as you grow older.

• Don't accept the myth that sex isn't possible or appropriate for older people. Appreciate your experience and maturity as a sexual being, and recognize your right to continue this intense and vital part of life.

• Accept responsibility for your sexual functioning by keeping your body healthy. Eat nutritiously and follow a sensible plan of walking, jogging, bicycling, tennis, swimming, stretching and bending exercises, or whatever feels right for you. Relax through meditation or yoga. See AGING for many helpful suggestions.

• Find out what to expect from your body sexually as you become older, so that you do not have unrealistic fears or expectations. Talk to your doctor.

• Work on maintaining a loving closeness and mutual caring with your partner. Remember that the mind and heart are as important to sexual satisfaction as sex organs are.

• Do not think of slower erection and ejaculation as handicaps or sex problems. They are perfectly healthy, normal signs of your age. Accept a more leisurely pace in your lovemaking, and savor those long, loving moments.

• If you experience sexual difficulties, ask yourself whether they are problems you had earlier in your life as well and whether they reflect conflicts and stresses in other areas of your life. If so, don't blame your age. Try to resolve the problems as you would if you were younger. This includes seeking counseling if you need it. See SEXUAL DYS-FUNCTION—it will not only help you with problems, it will help you enjoy sex more even if you don't have problems.

• If you and your partner are having problems with sex, such as pain or bleeding, see your doctor. Such difficulties are often easily solved, or they may indicate a condition that needs medical attention. If lack of vaginal lubrication is a problem, try using a water-soluble preparation such as K-Y jelly. (Don't use petroleum jelly, as it isn't water-soluble and can increase the possibility of vaginal infection.) Consult your doctor about relieving dryness through estrogen therapy.

• Menopause often means a diminished estrogen supply, which can cause vaginal and other body changes. Your doctor may prescribe estrogen therapy, but remember that sexual activity sometimes keeps estrogen levels up too. Estrogen therapy is not recommended for every woman, because of possible side effects.

• Take pleasure in the fact that sexual activity tends to prevent prostate problems, too. Apparently sex is good medicine.

• Many drugs—alcohol, oral contraceptives, sedatives, tranquilizers, antidepressants, and others—can interfere with your sexual desire and performance. If your sexual appetite wanes, find out from your doctor whether this might be the side effect of something you are taking.

• Don't confuse reproductive capacity with sexual capacity. Meno-pause and operations such as vasectomy, hysterectomy, most prostate operations, and even removal of the testes do not physically interfere with sexual functioning, although the psychological impact can be great. If you have worries about this, consult your doctor for reassurance.

• If your sexual muscles are losing their tone, learn some techniques, such as Kegel exercises (described in Lonnie Barbach's book; see *Suggested Reading*), to strengthen muscle control and increase blood circulation in both male and female genitals. These simple tighten-and-release exercises improve sexual responsiveness as well.

• Don't feel that the man must ejaculate every time you have inter-course. If you skip ejaculation the man can become erect repeatedly, prolonging the pleasurable experience for both partners.

• If intercourse is impossible because of physical problems, learn about alternatives to intercourse, such as mutual stimulation by various other means. Many books deal with these subjects, including *The Joy of Sex,* by Alex Comfort, and *Love and Sex After Sixty,* by Robert Butler and Myrna Lewis.

• If you are becoming bored with sex, do something about your routine. Make love at different times of day, in places other than the bedroom. Go on a date with your spouse, or have a candlelit dinner at home. Read erotic material together. Go to a motel. Learn different sexual techniques from one of the books just mentioned. Take advantage of your increased leisure and freedom to be romantic, creative, and impulsive about your lovemaking.

• Don't let the absence of a sexual partner cause you to withdraw from sex and therefore forfeit sexual pleasure later. Even though you may have been taught that masturbation is health-destroying, it is not. It is probably much better than losing your sexual capacity through disuse. See MASTURBATION to help you overcome inhibitions you may have about keeping your sexuality alive this way.

SUGGESTED READING:

Barbach, Lonnie. *For Yourself: The Fulfillment of Female Sexuality.* Garden City, N.Y.: Doubleday, 1975.

Butler, Robert, and Myrna Lewis. *Love and Sex After Sixty: A Guide for Men and Women for Their Later Years.* New York: Harper & Row, Perennial Library, 1976.

Comfort, Alex. *A Good Age.* New York: Crown Publishers, 1976.

See also: AGING, MID-LIFE CRISIS, RETIREMENT, SEXUAL DYSFUNCTION

SEXUAL DYSFUNCTION

Problems with sex are among the most common sources of distress that people encounter. Nearly everyone has some sort of sexual difficulty at one time or another, though most don't admit it, much less do anything about it. While sometimes ignoring a sexual problem helps it go away, usually ignoring it only makes it worse. In any case, having a problem often is a signal that your sex life needs attention and presents an opportunity to examine and develop your sexuality. In addition, as you develop your sexuality you will find that you thereby also improve your relationships and personality in general. People who have had a sexual problem and have worked on it often say that their sex life became even better than it was before, and that they reaped other benefits in their lives as well. Giving and receiving sexual pleasure is a beautiful way to express love, so the more creative you become sexually, the more love you will be able to share.

Sexual problems come in a variety of forms for both men and women, so before moving on to what causes them and what to do about them, let's discuss the several kinds of sex problems. After that we will cover the general causes of sexual problems and how to begin to deal with them. As you read about various sexual problems, see which description fits the problem you have. It's not uncommon to have more than one problem, so don't worry if you recognize more than one description.

If you find you have trouble understanding the words used to describe the problems, you need some more education before proceeding. Buy some good sex books and read them thoroughly. Be sure you really learn and understand what you need to know in order to do the exercises we describe and to communicate with your partner.

(This section focuses on the problems men and women have in heterosexual sex. Much of it is relevant to homosexual relations, but it does not deal with problems that may be unique to those situations.)

Sexual Inhibition

This problem consists of general sexual disinterest and can occur in both men and women. Some people find that they don't feel at all physically turned on by sex and that their bodies don't respond pleasurably to sexual touching. Women with this problem may not get wet (lubricated) in their vagina, for example. Men may fail to get aroused or even to show interest in sex.

Impotence (Erectile Dysfunction)

A common problem for men is difficulty getting or keeping an erection. This may happen to a man only occasionally or just with certain partners, or it may be a constant problem. Some men get an erection but then lose it before they want to, which is another form of impotence.

Premature Ejaculation

This problem occurs when a man comes, or ejaculates, sooner than he or his partner wants him to. Sometimes a man may come before starting intercourse; other times, it may be just "too soon" during intercourse.

Delayed Ejaculation

Other men have a problem that is the opposite of premature ejaculation. They take too long to come, and may even start to find intercourse painful before they are able to come.

Orgasmic Dysfunction (Anorgasmia)

Many women don't experience orgasm at all or as often as they'd like. Some women have never had an orgasm, others have had one only through masturbation, and still others have one only with certain partners or only rarely with a partner. All of these are versions of anorgasmia, sometimes mistakenly called "frigidity."

Vaginismus

This problem occurs when the muscles of a woman's vagina close up so tightly that it becomes impossible or very painful for her to allow the man's penis to enter. This may happen even though the woman feels turned on.

Most people call any sexual problem a woman has "frigidity." This is a poor term, because it falsely implies that women who have sexual problems are cold or uncaring. This is not only untrue but very insulting and hurtful to many women who are actually warm, loving people but have some sexual difficulty. Using one word for all female sexual problems also implies that they are all the same; this too is untrue.

Most sexual problems for both men and women are caused by thoughts or fears which interfere with the body's automatic sexual responses. In other words, your body is beautifully programmed to respond sexually on "automatic pilot," but problems occur when the mind interferes with this response, usually by turning its attention to other concerns. (Physical causes of sexual problems are rare, but you should get a thorough medical checkup to be sure.)

Usually sex problems happen when a person feels anxious or troubled about some part of his or her sexuality and is busy worrying during intercourse. These worries are often made worse by things that we learn about sex from our parents and other sources, especially strict religious and moral training. Other times they may be connected with a particular partner or situation.

Do you recognize some of these common worries? "Is he or she enjoying this?" "Is that business deal going to fall through?" "What if my mother/father/child/roommate walks in?" "Is this going to hurt?" "This is dirty and evil." "I hope the birth control works." "Am I doing this right?"

Thinking about these sorts of things rather than feeling the sensations in your body is called "spectatoring," because you are watching or analyzing instead of feeling. A special type of spectatoring often occurs once a person has had even one experience with a sex problem. It goes like this: "Will I be able to hold off coming?" "Will I come this time?" "I hope I can lubricate/get it up this time." This causes the sexual trouble to get worse.

These worries keep the person's attention away from bodily feelings and interfere with the body's natural response, so the first step in changing things is to examine these worries. If you have a steady partner, discuss them with him or her. This may be scary, but people who have done it say it makes them feel closer to each other and better about sex together. If you don't have a partner, think about your worries yourself.

What do you tune in to or think about during sex? What are your worries about sex? What sensations or feelings do you like or dislike in sex? Do you tell your partner about these or wait nervously for him or her to catch on? Can you relax and be passive in sex without worrying about whether you're doing enough? Do you worry too much about whether your partner is pleased?

If you're honest with yourself or a partner about these questions and the others that come up in the discussion, you may find that much of your attention during sex is somewhere else. For most people this realization is not enough to remove the problem; they need to practice a new way of relating to sex.

The rest of this section outlines exercises designed to reeducate you about sexual feelings. The program contains exercises to be done individually and exercises to be done with a sexual partner. Working with your partner or lover on these exercises is extremely important. This is only natural, since both of you work together on your total relationship, including your sexual fulfillment. It is important that both people in a couple commit themselves to the program, including individual exercises.

Don't fall into the simplistic view that one of you has the problem and the other is going to help. Share the problem as something that happens between you, and share the work and pleasure of solving it together. Discuss the problem and your plan to remedy it openly with your partner—is he or she willing to take action to improve your sex life together? It is important that both partners participate willingly and lovingly in the program—doing things resentfully, halfheartedly, or impersonally can sabotage your best efforts.

The program will ask you to take some risks together, both emotionally and sexually. For example, you will be touching each other in ways you may not have tried before. However, it is important that neither of you force anything on the other. This is an important rule for working together.

Here are three other rules:

1. You must always take turns. Don't have one person always be the one who is active while the other is passive. It's as important for each of you to learn how to give sexually as it is to learn to take.

2. Communication between the two of you is crucial. Many people expect their lover to know automatically what feels good to them. This just doesn't happen. After each exercise the two of you should talk about what you felt and what you liked. Sharing your worries or fears can lighten them. Communicate!

3. Your attitudes in doing the exercises are very important. Be positive; avoid put-downs and criticism. Don't place any expectations on your partner (or yourself); don't have goals for him or her. Be patient and understanding. This will pay off in your relationship.

If you don't have a partner or lover, or if your partner is unwilling to participate, just do the individual exercises. You might also do the partner exercises in your imagination—how might you feel in each situation?

The program for dealing with sexual problems has three principles that are even more important than the specific exercises, so keep them in mind:

1. Proceed slowly and without pressure. Pressure, demands, or hurry keep you from concentrating on your sexual feelings. There is no "right" way or pace in these exercises—just do them in your way and at your pace. You'll probably come across things that are hard for you to do or think about, things that embarrass or scare you. Don't force or hurry yourself through them! That will work against you. Proceed first by exploring your fear: What exactly scares/embarrasses you? Why? Where did you learn to react this way? Then find the part of the exercise you feel *least* uncomfortable with and try it when you're feeling relaxed; a glass of wine or a warm bath often helps. When you become comfortable with an easy part (perhaps looking at a partner's body), move on *slowly* to another step (say, looking at his or her genital area). When you feel okay with that—and *not* before—move ahead another step (say, looking closely at your partner's genitals). Never move on to the next exercise or part of an exercise until you are comfortable with what you've just completed. Hurrying does not go with relaxing and enjoying.

2. Focus on feelings and sensations in your body. The major purpose of the exercises is to get you in touch with your natural sexuality. To do this you have to get away from distractions. Try to find a time when you are alone and aren't interrupted by your kids or the telephone. Try to clear away other important distractions; if you and your partner are fighting about something, try to clear it up before doing the exercise. Most of all, try not to let your mind wander. Pay attention to what you feel in your body and to your emotional reactions. Don't think, feel!

3. Explore openly. Be honest about your reactions: There are many kinds of touching you may not like. Acknowledge this to yourself. If you are working with a partner, open discussion after each exercise is crucial. Tell each other about your exprience, and *listen.*

The exercises are designed to get you in touch with your basic or natural sexuality. If you think back to your first awareness of your sexuality, you'll find that it took place long before you actually had intercourse. Similarly, the exercises don't start with intercourse, but with simpler sexual experiences. (It is important that you not have intercourse when an exercise doesn't call for it. This will keep you from worrying about intercourse, a worry that only adds to your problem.)

• Begin by spending some time looking at your body in the mirror. Also look at your genitals and become familiar with how they look and work. How do you react to looking at yourself? Do some parts turn you on or off?

• On a different occasion, try touching your body with a variety of objects from around the house and focus all your attention on the sensations in your body. How does a rough object like a sponge feel? A smooth one like an apple? Try hot and cold, hard and soft, and so forth. Really let yourself go on this one. Also focus on how things feel on different parts of your body. Do you like rough textures one place, soft ones in another, and none at all in a third part? After you've used a variety of objects on several occasions, use your hands. How is this different? Can you focus on being the giver and receiver at any one time?

• Many people tend to assume that most of their sexual or sensual feelings are in their genitals. Explore this by not emphasizing your genitals, trying other areas of your body. A few people respond sexually to this exploration; most don't. Be sure not to burden yourself with expectations of getting an erection or lubricating; just explore.

• Pay attention to what happens when you are distracted. Do the feelings change? What sorts of things make you tune out?

• In working with a partner, start by caressing each other's shoulders and heads *only,* taking turns. Do not talk. When you're being caressed, do you worry that the other person is getting tired? When you are giving caresses, do you worry that the other person is not enjoying them? Try focusing on the feelings in your fingertips as you caress your partner; get into giving sensually. This will take some practice.

• When you're ready to move on (remember, no rushing), explore each other's bodies, first just visually, then with touching. Stay away from the genital area for now; just explore the different sensations of giving and getting touching on different parts of the body. Try different pressures or speeds, and be sure to talk about it *afterward.*

• *On your own,* begin exploring the sensations in your genitals. Do not at this point give yourself an orgasm, even if you can and want to. However, if you have an orgasm during the exercise, that's okay too. Don't set any goal; just explore how different touches feel in different places. Try things you have never tried before. It is especially important for women to explore sensations around the clitoral area. (If you haven't already done so, get a book with photographs or drawings and identify the clitoris.) Where are you most sensitive? Least sensitive? How do you react to odors or fluids associated with your genitals? Does it make a difference whether your eyes are open or closed? Does music help or distract?

• After you have explored your genitals on several occasions, begin to concentrate on what feels especially good to you. Most men find that they have the most sensual feeling on the head of their penis. For most women the most powerful sensation is in the clitoris. Tune in on what increases your sexual excitement, but don't make an orgasm or any specific level of excitement your goal. Your only goal should be exploring and feeling. Some people find that fantasy helps them focus on their sexual feelings. Experiment to see if this is true for you. Published collections of sexual fantasies are helpful if you don't have a personal favorite fantasy. Look at the female fantasies recorded in *My Secret Garden,* by Nancy Friday, or the male fantasies in *Secret Sex,* by Thom Anicar. Try both, if you like—each has some fantasies that will turn you off and some that are likely to turn you on.

• If you are working with a partner, begin to explore each other's genital sensations only after you have *both* done the individual exercises. Take turns exploring different ways of touching each other's genitals, but *don't* stimulate each other to orgasm. At this point, avoid rhythmic or strong stimulation, focusing on trying different touches and being certain to avoid expectations of any sort.

• If either of you has a hopeful fantasy that *this* time, finally, he will have his erection or she will have her orgasm, share it and let it go. Focusing on this fantasy only pressures you and distracts you from feeling.

The specific instructions listed under each particular sexual problem in this book will tell you how to continue your exploration from here. Be sure to read them carefully before doing any exercise. If you are working with a partner, you should talk about the instructions beforehand to be sure you both agree about them.

Most people find that devoting the kind of time and effort this program requires is worth it. Not only can most sexual problems be helped, but most people find the sensual-exploration program enjoyable and interesting. Sex is like a vacation journey. When you are going somewhere on vacation, you can either fret impatiently about arriving or you can enjoy the journey. This program is an invitation: Relax, tune in, and enjoy the journey!

Both San Francisco and New York have sex-information hot lines that provide free help with sexual problems. Other cities are in the process of establishing similar services.

SUGGESTED READING:

Anicar, Thom. *Secret Sex.* New York: Signet, New American Library, 1976.

Boston Women's Health Book Collective. *Our Bodies, Ourselves: A*

Book by and for Women, rev. 2nd ed. New York: Simon & Schuster, 1976.

Comfort, Alex. *The Joy of Sex.* New York: Crown Publishers, 1972.

Friday, Nancy. *My Secret Garden.* New York: Pocket Books, 1971.

Golstein, M., E. J. Haeberle, and W. McBride. *The Sex Book: A Modern Pictorial Encyclopedia.* New York: Bantam Books, 1971.

Johnson, Eric W. *Love and Sex in Plain Language.* New York: Bantam Books, 1974.

Kaplan, Helen Singer. *The Illustrated Manual of Sex Therapy.* New York: A & W Publishers, 1976.

Zilbergeld, B., and John Ullman. *Male Sexuality: A Guide to Sexual Fulfillment.* Boston: Little, Brown & Company, 1978.

See also: DELAYED EJACULATION, IMPOTENCE, MASTURBATION, ORGASMIC DYSFUNCTION, PREMATURE EJACULATION, SEXUAL INHIBITIONS, SEXUAL PERVERSIONS, VAGINISMUS

SEXUAL INHIBITIONS

"Sexual inhibition" refers to a problem that some people have getting aroused or sexually excited. A man or woman suffering from this problem usually feels uninterested in sex. Also, even when he or she wants to have sex, his or her body doesn't respond sexually. A woman's vagina may not become lubricated, or she may not feel any pleasure in being caressed. A man may feel little sensation in his penis and feel generally disconnected and unresponsive.

Many people who are this way deal with it simply by avoiding sex. Usually they are not very interested in changing this pattern unless someone else, such as a spouse or a friend, urges or pressures them to do so. When this is the case, changing is very hard, since the person has trouble really making the commitment and taking the risks that are needed.

If this is the case with you, you may need to think about this issue for yourself, as well as discuss it with your partner. Do you want to change? Are you going through the exercises outlined below just to please your partner? Are you harboring secret resentment about the pressure to change? How would you feel if a program of change failed to work out? If it succeeded? Try to be sure of your (and your partner's) commitment before starting.

Most people with general sexual inhibition don't have any physical problem. (A medical checkup is a good way to find out for sure.) The cause of this problem is psychological—usually they learned to feel *very* fearful or guilty about their bodies and about sex especially. A puritanical or antisexual upbringing is often responsible for this attitude.

Explore this. How do you feel about your body? Can you look at yourself comfortably in the mirror? How do you feel about touching various parts of your body? What is your reaction to seeing sex scenes in movies? Are you disgusted or turned off? Where did you learn this response? What did your parents teach you about sex? What did you learn about it from religion? Have you had any frightening or painful experiences with sex? Sometimes such an experience causes a person to unconsciously shut off his or her sexual feelings.

• Talk about these issues with someone you feel comfortable with. Also, it is *very* important for you to read thoroughly some good books on sex. Parts of these books (for example, pictures and drawings) may make you uncomfortable. Don't force yourself, but slowly get used to them. Take your time.

• Follow the program outlined under SEXUAL DYSFUNCTION and continued under ORGASMIC DYSFUNCTION and IMPOTENCE. You will need to be especially slow and patient about the exercises, though. Your fear of sex is not going to disappear quickly or under pressure.

• Learning to talk about sex is an important start, and should be followed by beginning the exploration of your own body. Don't expect miracles—you probably won't notice any change in your reaction for a while. In fact, some of the exercises may be unpleasant or disgusting for you. Don't force yourself, but concentrate on your pleasant bodily sensations.

• Relax when you do the exercises. Try a hot bath, music, a nap, a relaxation exercise, or perhaps a glass of wine. Do whatever works for you. As you become more and more relaxed and more and more familiar with your body and its feelings, you will probably begin to find greater pleasure in it. As your sexual excitement increases, you'll discover a whole new world of comfortable pleasure.

SUGGESTED READING:

Comfort, Alex. *The Joy of Sex*. New York: Crown, 1972.

Johnson, Eric W. *Love and Sex in Plain Language*. New York: Bantam Books, 1974.

See also: IMPOTENCE, MASTURBATION, ORGASMIC DYSFUNCTION, SEXUAL DYSFUNCTION, VAGINISMUS

SEXUAL PERVERSIONS

Woody Allen was asked in one of his movies, "Do you think sex is dirty?" His answer: "It is if you're doing it right." His humor expresses our mixture of shame and delight in doing the forbidden. Few of us grow up without some hangups about sex being "dirty" or wrong. Most people outgrow these inhibiting beliefs with the help of some pleasant experiences which help them develop the attitude "If it feels good, do it."

But sometimes early prohibitions, rejections, and negative feelings about our bodies or impulses can leave us with blocks to easy, natural, and varied expressions of our sexuality. Freud believed we were born "polymorphous perverse," meaning we want it all, any way we can get it. ("If it moves, fondle it.") That degree of freedom would upset some families and communities, so restrictions get imposed.

These arbitrary rules about allowable sex may make life go smoother at times, but unfortunately they get carved in stone as righteous commandments, rather than convenient arrangements. People take them too seriously and feel bad about transgressions, or make other people feel bad. Instead of enjoying variety as the spice of life, self-appointed guardians of morality establish norms, denounce deviance, and pronounce that some acts are "perverted." Who can do what to whom, and who gets to decide, is a political power issue, and often turns sex into a battleground rather than a playground.

The dividing line between "normal" and "abnormal" is fuzzy and shifting. "Healthy sex" can be defined as "whatever feels good to two consenting adults." Inventive, imaginative, exploratory sexual activities add zest to life and relieve monotony. They can help us feel freer with our bodies and with a wide range of sensual as well as sexual sensations. They can provide varied and delightful ways to give pleasure and affirmation to another person.

So when does a sex act deserve to be called a "perversion," in the sense of being something "bad," hurtful, or unhealthy? When it damages your own or another person's body or self-respect. When it diverts energy into acts that do not allow the energy to flow smoothly and fully into comfortable stimulation, arousal, increased excitement, pleasurable tension, release, and relaxation. When full self-expression of feelings and energy is blocked. When after the act you experience frustration and unresolved tension.

By this definition, if a husband and wife have intercourse and both have orgasms but there is no feeling of personal closeness and caring between them, we could say that they have engaged in a perverted act. Looked at this way, perversion is not defined by what parts of the anatomy are used in what way by partners of which sex, but in terms of how limited is the physical, emotional, and even spiritual encounter between the two people.

Perversions often express dominance and hostility, although frequently in subtle or carefully ritualized behavior. The presence of hostility as a contaminant in a sexual encounter can divert it from being pleasurably loving. Carried to an extreme, energy that is diverted becomes what we call perverted. Instead of emphasizing giving, sex may be used to get something. Sex acts are used as symbolic ways to win points in a contest. Conquering, intruding, using, grabbing, engulfing are all actions that have more of a selfish than loving meaning. If an act is defined as perverted by society, and if you are angry at society or another person, then engaging in a perverted act can be a way to score a victory over repression and get revenge for past hurts.

Here are some ways to decide whether or not a sexual activity is perverted, in the sense of being a problem, and what to do about it.

• Ask yourself where you got your definitions of "perverted." What wisdom and value may be expressed in these definitions that are worth respecting? To what extent are these ideas about perversion narrow and naive, unnecessarily limiting, based on misinformation and prejudice?

• Consider whether someone else has a personal, selfish stake in foisting their definition of perversion onto you. For example, macho men with secret doubts about their masculinity are often intolerant of homosexuality. Puritanical women with rigidly controlled emotional hungers tend to be shocked by the idea of oral sex. Don't let someone else tell you what is perverted and what isn't. Learn from your own experience and from the reports of others about what seems to work. Decide on your sexual style for yourself.

• Keep flexible. What may be right for you this year with your present partner may not be right for you next year with a different partner. Keep in touch with your inner feelings and your partner's, and be open to change.

• Take an honest look at your basic motives in sex. Do you want to give pleasure, approval, caring, and love, or do you seek to dominate, degrade, conquer, humiliate, control, or punish your partner? Do your actions create closeness, trust, relaxation, and mutual caring, or guilt, shame, embarrassment, fear, and eventual distance? Experiment with emphasizing the caring, pleasurable aspect of whatever you do sexually, and see if you enjoy sex more.

• Look at whether you view sex as a beautiful, delightful way of playing, giving, celebrating, and loving, or as a contest, achievement, rebellion, or degrading submission.

• Does your partner enjoy and respond to your adventurousness? Are you adding to the range of ways you can enjoy each other, or pushing into areas that make one or both of you tense up?

• Talk over what you each like and dislike, and what you'd like to loosen up and try. Agree to experiment, and agree to stop whenever either one wants to. Discuss how it felt, and what you'd like to do next.

• Don't rely just on talking. Use nonverbal language to offer, request, stop, or encourage. Learn to read your partner's body and its many signals to you.

• Be gentle, gradual, and considerate, rather than abrupt and insistent. Introduce new sex acts in a spirit of play and invitation.

• Assess how the nonsexual part of your life is going, and whether you are seeking power, revenge, atonement, or punishment in sex to compensate for what you are missing elsewhere.

• Take stock of your health. Are you caring well for your body? Is what you do sexually helping you like your body better and feel better physically? Does your body hurt after sex in ways that suggest you may be damaging tissue? Do you develop any skin rashes or eruptions? See your doctor promptly if you have any symptoms, and consider carefully whether your sex life is giving you more pleasure or pain.

• Cherish sex in all its variations as a marvelous teacher from which you can learn many things about human nature. What we do—and don't do—sexually reflects our basic character and ways of relating to people. It reveals our way of dealing with power, pleasure, love, and the life force. Pay attention to what goes on for you sexually, and learn to regard it as a valuable window through which to see your whole way of being in the world.

• Refrain from passing hasty, closed-minded judgments on sexual wishes, fantasies, and acts. Instead of condemning them as perverted, ask yourself what they are saying. What are you or the other person really seeking through this act? Learn all you can from what you do or fantasize sexually, and choose what is right for you based on awareness, not on dictated rules.

• Remember that all sex contains at least some attempt to create closeness and acceptance. Even an act that seems impersonal, distant, and exploitative represents the best compromise the person could achieve between fears of rejection, anger for past hurts, and the need for physical love. Appreciate the effort to create closeness and caring, and look for ways to reduce the aspects that emphasize power or distance.

• Don't get stuck in a rigid, fixated sexual pattern that excludes spontaneity and responsiveness to the other person's feelings. When people are afraid of vulnerability, embarrassment, rejection, or guilt, they may set up precise rituals or rigid scenarios that must be followed to make sex safe. This approach creates emotional distance, because the partner is expected to follow a predetermined script and is not treated as a person. This amounts to forcing one's trip on someone else, and it usually backfires sooner or later.

• If you prefer a sexual outlet that excludes other people and focuses on objects (such as shoes or underwear) or animals, give thought to why you keep so distant from involvement with people. Don't be moralistic about it—that will just set up an inner conflict that will waste energy and obscure what you need to see. Study the exact nature of your activity to discover the satisfaction—and the protection—it involves. Regard this form of your sexuality as a developmental phase or a temporary compromise solution to the conflict between your needs and your fears. Don't try to stamp it out as "evil." That is more likely to drive it into an underground stubbornness. Look for safe, small, gradual steps that will move you from where you are now into slightly more contact with people and slightly more direct expression of your sexual feelings. Continue to allow yourself some indirect or remote ways of having sexual interests, but gradually shift these into sublimated forms, such as taking a life drawing class, developing an interest in women's fashions, watching children play, or whatever pleases you. Meanwhile, remember that your goal is to free up some time, energy, and courage for reaching out to people.

• Indulge your need for tenderness and gentle, sensuous caring. Many people need lots of comfortable stroking—physical and emotional—before they feel safe enough to proceed to sexual activity. People who focus their sexual feelings on objects, animals, or children, for example, often do so because in this way they are able to feel secure and safe from threat. Provide yourself with more warmth and kindness by recognizing your deep need for these qualities and giving them a higher priority in your selection of friends and activities. One very aggressive skier who practically made a fetish out of his ski clothes and equipment found that he felt more sexual toward women if he stopped skiing earlier in the afternoon and took time for a soak in the hot pool. He also learned to choose women he was comfortable with—gentle women who weren't driven to compete with him on skis. A farm boy who felt great guilt because of some sexual experimenting he did with his dog was able to talk about it with a counselor when he got to college. The counselor helped him see that this was merely an early and not very satisfying episode in his lifelong task of making pleasurable sensual and sexual contact with the world.

• Make full, wild, weird use of fantasy. Try everything—in your imagination. Learn what kooky stuff turns you on. Do it over and over.

See where it takes you—to satiation, or to some further variation.

• Remember that we are all imperfect, especially when it comes to difficult ventures like sex. We all hedge to some degree and avoid being fully present and open to our own sexual desires and to the total encounter with our partner. So-called perversions are places you may linger or get stuck on your journey from separateness to relationship.

SUGGESTED READING:

Ruitenbeek, Hendrik M., ed. *The Psychotherapy of Perversions.* New York: Citadel Press, 1967.

Stoller, Robert. *Perversion, The Erotic Form of Hatred.* New York: Pantheon Books, 1975.

See also: EXHIBITIONISM, GUILT, INCEST, LONELINESS, NARCISSISM, SADISM, SELF-HATE, SEXUAL DYSFUNCTION, SHYNESS, VOYEURISM

SHYNESS

In a way, a certain amount of shyness is natural, and nearly all people are shy in some ways. It's when shyness causes anxiety, loneliness, and withdrawal from living that it becomes a problem. If you are extremely shy, you know that any attention from others—sometimes even a compliment—can cause blushing, sweaty hands, a pounding heart, and a feeling of sheer panic. Your mind goes blank. Your voice may fade away entirely, or suddenly seem so loud that you're sure everyone must be laughing at you. Even the thought of such humiliating experiences causes turmoil inside you and makes you want to avoid social situations.

If you are a super-shy person, your basic fear is that you are somehow deficient as a person, and that when you are expressive and outgoing people will reject you. This becomes a self-fulfilling prophecy, for when you do express yourself, it is in an ineffectual or timid manner that is difficult for other people to respond to. Or when they respond, your expectation of failure makes you misinterpret them negatively. This confirms to you that they don't like you and that you are an unlikable person, and you withdraw even more.

The negative self-concept of a shy person usually begins very early in life. When we are small children we experience many failures in learning to walk, eat, use the toilet, dress ourselves. Little children (and adults too) need lots of encouragement and support to struggle through life's problems. This encouragement tells the child that his or her efforts are worthwhile. When other people are too busy or too critical to give love and attention, the child begins to have a feeling of inadequacy and self-doubt.

If you have been taught to be shy, you may now play it safe and seek the secret reward of getting other people to make the effort to come to you, so that you don't have to take that risk. But when you do that, you deny yourself the self-appreciation that comes through the hard work of extending yourself, of taking risks, accepting failures, enjoying successes. You can learn to expand, to become your own wellspring of self-confidence, to live your life more fully.

• Recognize that your shyness is an attitude you have learned which has nothing to do with your true worth as a person. Remind yourself that you perpetuate your problem every time you hold back from a conversation or turn down a party, every time you concentrate on deprecatory thoughts about yourself, every time you predict failure. Take on the challenge of testing the reality of these perceptions. Determine to make a plan to do this gradually, and to reverse your self-defeating pattern.

• Make a list of all the qualities and skills you have to offer, such as being a good listener, being helpful or caring, having information. Practice expressing these qualities with specific people who you *know* will respond favorably. Stack the deck for success. Enjoy the appreciation of those who value you.

• Choose a person whose respect or friendship is not really important to you and practice being more expressive and assertive with that person. If you're rejected, it's not too terrible. If you're warmly received, you've learned something good about yourself and the other person.

• Try the same experiment in a situation that you know is difficult, where you may fail. Wade in and do your best. If things don't work, check it off as just an experiment and learn what you can from it. If you succeed, consider it a bonus.

• Practice speaking to strangers: someone standing next to you in line, sitting next to you in a waiting room or a new class, or to a store clerk or librarian. Make a simple comment or ask for information. Practice saying hello to people you see often but do not know yet. Notice how often they seem pleased to be spoken to.

• If you are worried about an upcoming social situation, prepare for it. Make a list of your interests and experiences that you would like to share. Read about current events. Rehearse conversations. Make notes about what you want to say. Prepare to ask intelligent questions and pay attention to the answers.

• Practice concentrating on making other people feel at ease and overcoming their shyness. Show appreciation for what they have to offer. Practice making eye contact.

• Don't rationalize that being shy and aloof is attractive, or that others should make the effort to come to you. Admit your need for others and take responsibility for reaching out.

• Recognize that when you are focused on yourself and your fears, your mind isn't free to practice positive social skills—like learning people's names and thinking about things to say to them. Try to turn your self-conscious moments around by focusing on the other person.

• If friends or family place so much emphasis on image, appearance, and success that it makes you feel inferior, find new friends who value you as a person, not a performer.

• Don't accept put-downs from others, and never criticize yourself verbally. If people don't accept you, try to evaluate that objectively. But also consider that these people may not be nurturing for you and you would be better off elsewhere.

• Never put down a compliment. Have faith that most compliments are sincere, even if you find them hard to accept. Use them to help learn a new, positive self-image.

• If you feel inferior about your appearance, find out about clothing, styles, makeup, grooming, hairstyling. Talk to friends, salespeople, co-workers. Look in magazines. Integrate that information with your own characteristics, so that you will feel comfortable with your improvements.

• If you feel inferior about your job or education, or fear that you are not an interesting person, set some specific goals to remedy this. Take classes; pursue interests that really matter to you. Give yourself credit for each step of progress as you make it. Talk to other people about your efforts and achievements. Recognize that a person with real plans and interests is usually interesting to others.

• If your job or studies require solitude, balance this by making plans that put you among people at least part of the time.

• Don't depend on alcohol or drugs to relieve your shyness. Face the fact that any benefits are temporary and will keep you from making the real progress that you want.

• Become aware of how tense you feel in social situations. At these anxious times, remember to keep breathing. Tense people tend to hold their breath, which makes them more tense. Learn techniques of relaxation through meditation or physical exercises such as yoga, and practice them before social encounters.

• Join a group or class where others are trying to become more outgoing too—like a Toastmasters Club or Dale Carnegie course. Join a hobby or sports club where you can be a genuinely involved participant.

• If you are the parent or friend of a very shy person, make the effort to give him or her your honest positive responses, friendliness, and encouragement.

SUGGESTED READING:

Walters, Barbara. *How to Talk with Practically Anybody About Practically Anything.* New York: Dell, 1976.

Wassmen, Arthur C. *Making Contact.* New York: Dial Press, 1978.

Zimbardo, Philip. *Shyness: What It Is—What to Do About It.* Reading, Mass.: Addison-Wesley, 1977.

See also: COMMUNICATION BLOCKS, DEPENDENCY, EXHIBITIONISM, FEAR OF FAILURE, LONELINESS, PASSIVITY, SELF-HATE, STUTTERING

SIBLING RIVALRY

Every child with brothers and sisters has at least some feelings of competing for love, support, and attention from the parents, no matter how hard the parents try to give equally to each child. Although a certain amount of these feelings of rivalry, jealousy, and sometimes hostility is normal in children, they can become problems when they are carried over into adulthood.

Feelings of rivalry among grown brothers and sisters can affect more than just family relationships. Siblings compete not only with each other but with friends, strangers, and co-workers. Up to a point the competitive spirit helps people succeed, but consider the wasted energy of the person who has to be first through the intersection after the green light, or who absolutely must win every argument. More seriously, these siblings sometimes covet others' achievements, possessions, or family. This can lead to seriously hurt feelings, spouse stealing, open battles, and even murder.

If you as an adult suffer from sibling rivalry, you are responding to a childhood competitive situation that no longer exists, even if your parents are still living. If your parents are dead and you are still keeping score of the competition in your head, your behavior is even less realistic. If you picture yourself as always winning the rivalry, you may be doing so at the cost of your health or close relationships. If you picture yourself as the loser, you may be wallowing in the perverse pleasures of feeling inferior. This helps you avoid choosing your own unique life course and concentrating on succeeding in that. Your resignation can turn into self-pity: "My brother is better at sales/music/business/ life than I am. What's the use of trying?"

Defining yourself only in relation to your parents or siblings keeps you from discovering the real, unique, adult you. You need to develop a self-worth based on your own, inner, self-determined values and choices.

• Review all the past incidents of rivalry between you and your siblings. Recognize these as past history. Tell yourself that you are now starting your life from the present moment.

• List all of the qualities, experiences, achievements, and talents that you value in yourself. Ask whether you are developing them to the fullest. If not, why not? If your reason has anything to do with your parents or siblings, recognize this as only an excuse. Resolve to devote your energies to becoming a self-determining, self-fulfilled person.

• Make a self-development plan and start working on it: Take classes, get counseling, build new relationships, travel, work harder at your job. Enjoy learning and growing.

• Set long-range goals that matter only to you. Don't waste time comparing them with anyone else's goals, either favorably or unfavorably.

• Think about accomplishments and possessions that you envy in your siblings. Ask yourself whether you are wasting time wishing for something you really don't want, or that is unsuited to you as a person, or that you realistically can't have. If so, determine to keep spending your energies on your real goals.

• Accept the fact that not all things in life are "fair." Perhaps a sibling was given more love or advantages, or was born with superior intelligence or talent. Accept this as a fact and recognize that in no way does it diminish your capacity for building a happy, worthwhile life. And as you pursue your own life, you may discover you are better than you thought.

• Consider that your parents may now be perpetuating a rivalry in order to keep their children dependent. Examine whether they offer love, material possessions, or special privileges in a way that makes you feel you are competing for them. If so, quit competing. Find other sources of satisfaction among your own friends and in your own work.

• Consider that to become separate from your parents or siblings you may need to move away, leave the family business, or otherwise remove yourself physically while you develop your own uniqueness, standards, and lifestyle.

• Think about the birth order of you and your siblings and in what ways this may be affecting your feelings. Are you still trying to regain the center of attention you lost when your younger sibling was born? Are you still expecting others to care for you as the youngest, or give you special privileges? Determine to find a more appropriate way of relating to your peers.

• Understand that sibling rivalry may be affecting you at work. Have you unconsciously set the boss up as a parent whose approval you compete for, even at the expense of your co-workers? Recognize this as potentially damaging to your career, since you need support and cooperation of your peers to do your best work.

• Recognize that siblings can be a unique source of friendship, support, and joy to each other, and that it is a tragic waste to allow meaningless rivalries to rob you of this opportunity.

• As you gradually free yourself from jealous, competitive feelings, find ways to let your siblings know that you are no longer their enemy or rival. Maybe they can then relax their vigilance or hostility with you. Appreciate any positive responses they make to your gestures of truce or friendship.

• If your siblings continue to behave in antagonistic or rivalrous ways despite your new, relaxed attitude, accept that they may not be able to change. Put some self-protective distance between you, continue to focus on your own goals and satisfactions, and hope that change will come about eventually.

• If you and a sibling have an authentic, adult rivalry, such as in sports or business, confine that rivalry to its appropriate sphere. Don't let it contaminate your personal relationship. Enjoy the rewards of both healthy competition and sibling closeness.

• If memories of past events continue to haunt you, try to release some of the feelings. Talk about them with a spouse or close friend. Talk them into a tape recorder, and then throw the tape away. Pretend your sibling is sitting in a chair in front of you and tell him or her off, letting your feelings go. Pound furiously on a pillow or overstuffed piece of furniture, but don't do anything to damage yourself or your possessions. After your feelings are spent, seek out the companionship of people you care about and feel secure with.

• If your hostility toward your siblings is too intense to risk releasing, get counseling to help you deal with your feelings and put your life in perspective.

• Learn a meditation technique to help you maintain an internal sense of who you are.

• Help your children work through their own rivalrous feelings. Read child-raising books that deal with this problem, such as Dr. Haim G. Ginnott's *Between Parent and Child* (New York: Avon Books, 1965).

• If your spouse or a loved one suffers from sibling rivalry, encourage him or her to develop interests and set goals that will provide feelings of independence and self-worth.

SUGGESTED READING:

Toman, Walter. *Family Constellations*. New York: Springer, 1976.

See also: COMPETITIVENESS, ENVY, JEALOUSY, MASOCHISM

SINGLE PARENTING

There are many styles of single parenting. You may be a single parent by choice, having opted to have a child without being married, or you may be divorced or widowed. You may be a woman whose husband deserted her, or you may be a single man who has chosen to adopt a child. You may also be a single person, male or female, who has chosen to adopt a child from another race or with an emotional or physical handicap. The variety of lifestyles is very great; however, if you are single and have a child, you are by definition a single parent. In April 1978 the *Los Angeles Times* stated that a recent survey showed there are over 8.5 million single-parent households in the United States. So, regardless of how isolated or alienated you may feel, you are not alone.

Being a single parent may have its unique problems and difficulties, but it can also be very exciting. Traditionally men were considered the providers while women were the homemakers and nurturers. Single parents have to assume both roles, and in the process are discovering that women can be good providers while men can enjoy the nurturing role. Some men have even found that they like being fathers although they do not want to be husbands.

All parents create areas of conflict for their children. Single parents and their children may have some different problems, but they are not necessarily worse than those of married parents and their families. It is better to have a good relationship with one parent than a bad relationship with two, so never feel guilty about being a single parent. However, there are some issues and problems that all single parents face, regardless of whether they are single parents by choice or out of necessity.

One of the basic needs of all families is money. Single parents, particularly women, may have severe problems in this area, but there are several ways in which single mothers and fathers can help themselves. Consider some of the following suggestions.

• First of all, be honest with yourself and recognize that it is not the child's fault that there is not enough money. When you can take emotional responsibility for yourself and your child, you will find it easier to think about getting a job.

• Try to get a full- or part-time job which fits in with your child's schedule, and look for other single parents with whom you can share car-pooling and after-school responsibilities.

• Look for a job which will allow you to bring your child to work with you in an emergency. Many bosses and supervisors are more understanding than you might think. If you have a positive attitude toward your child and assume that other people will like him or her, other people are more likely to help you than if you see your child as a hindrance.

• Plan to go to school to finish your education, to be retrained, or to take a refresher course. A high-school diploma is essential, and you can usually get a better job and a better salary if you are trained in a specific field. If you are divorced or separated, your ex-spouse may be more willing to help you financially in the knowledge that the payments will decrease as soon as you are working.

• Contact the social service department in your community for information about day-care facilities. Investigate these places, keeping in mind that you must have confidence in the people who will care for your child while you are at work. Remember that as your child grows it is healthy for him or her to have regular and constant contact with other caring adults and other children. Also, if you are productive during your time away from your child, you will be happier and more relaxed when you are with your child.

• Investigate communal living. Some single parents find that communal arrangements offer more companionship and more freedom as well as lower living expenses. You might consider renting a house together with one or several other single parents, dividing the expenses and the responsibilities, or perhaps joining a commune. Remember to seek out people whose lifestyle is compatible with yours, so that you can fit easily into each other's routines and patterns.

Next to the need for money, the need for companionship is probably the one felt most acutely by single parents. Whether you are a single parent by choice or you are widowed or divorced, you probably want the companionship of another adult, and you may be concerned about how you can bring another adult into your life.

• Remember that if you are lonely and frustrated you will not be a good parent, so find time to do things you enjoy, away from your children and with other adults. Many single parents who work all day find it hard to go out in the evening because they feel guilty for having left their child all day. This guilt is nonproductive, and does not help your relationship with your child. Remind yourself that married parents who work also go out. Be attuned to yourself and to your child and you will know when you can take time for yourself and when you are needed at home. Don't live by rigid rules, and remember that when you deprive yourself you are not automatically helping your child.

• Be aware that single mothers tend to be more protective than married ones, so try to get insight into your own fears and anxieties in order to minimize their effect on your child. Children need to develop positive feelings about themselves; therefore, try to recognize that overprotectiveness can block this aspect of development.

Some single parents are unsure how to introduce their sexual partners to their children. The most important thing to remember is that children are always observing the behavior and the value systems of the adults in their lives.

• What you do is more important than what you say. Keep your sexual activities private. Consider that if your child sees you bouncing casually from one casual relationship to another, he or she may conclude that there can be no serious adult commitments. Your child may become reluctant to take any of your partners seriously or open up to them.

• Keep in mind that you, the parent, must be the constant and steady person in your child's life. Every time you change partners your child may suffer feelings of separation. Research has shown that children of single parents tend to worry more about separation than other children do. Although the presence of a person of the opposite sex who likes your child and with whom you have a stable and loving relationship will give your child a feeling of security, casual sexual partners will cause confusion and anxiety.

• Recognize that children who have lost a parent through divorce or death may have difficulty accepting another partner for their parent. Children often feel loyal to the absent parent or see dates as intruders or competitors for the love of the remaining parent.

• If you are divorced or separated, if possible encourage your ex-spouse to visit the child regularly and frequently. When parents separate and children no longer see one of the parents, they frequently feel abandoned by that person and blame themselves for the breakup of the marriage. These feelings of abandonment and guilt may lead to lowered self-esteem.

• Try to resolve your feelings about the opposite sex. Your child will pick up your attitudes, so you should make them conscious and talk about them. If you hated the boy's father, does that mean you hate all men? Be aware that your son may grow up feeling you hate him because he is a male and/or because he is like his father.

• Find satisfaction from other people besides your child, and don't expect him or her to fulfill all your emotional needs, because the child can't. When you are expressing warmth and affection toward your child, try not to be too intense, and avoid being seductive.

• If you are a woman, keep in mind that your child needs significant relationships with men. If you are a male single parent, your child will need closeness with mother substitutes. Don't be jealous of your child's relationship with other adults. Accept the fact that children also learn about themselves and their world through their contacts with people other than their parents.

• Make the effort, out of a sense of commitment to your child, to achieve a good working relationship with your ex-spouse. You may be able to develop a co-parenting arrangement in which you share responsibilities. Of course, co-parenting is easier if you had an amicable relationship when you were married, if you parted on relatively good terms, and, most important, if you are willing to share the responsibilities of raising your child. Those people who have made co-parenting work have found that both parents can have some of the satisfactions of raising children while experiencing some of the feelings of freedom and independence of being single.

• If you are contemplating remarriage, keep in mind that the work you do to become a better parent helps, not hinders, you in becoming ready to find a suitable partner and create a new relationship.

• Talk to your child about your feelings toward the person you plan to marry, but don't expect him or her to feel the same way you do. After all, it will take time for the child to adjust to the continuing presence of someone else in your lives. Try not to expect too much from either your child or your new spouse.

• Respect your child's reactions and be realistic about changes in discipline. If you are a woman, do not relinquish your responsibility as parent just because you have remarried. If you are a man, don't forget the mothering side of your nature just because you have a new woman to help you.

Discipline is often difficult for single parents, especially those who work all day. Consider that real discipline does not mean punishment— it means rules, order, structure, and rewards.

• Clarify for yourself what behavior you expect from your child and whether you are realistic in your expectations; then establish a few rules and be consistently firm. Always keep in mind that discipline must include warmth and encouragement, and that it does not have to be either harsh or excessively punitive.

• Remember that children feel more secure when they have definite limits set for them. They feel that their parents love them when they care enough to set and enforce reasonable rules for their safety and protection.

• Be aware of your own anxieties so that you do not restrict your child unreasonably, yet do not let feelings of guilt for being a single parent or for not being available as much as you would like to be cause you to give your child freedoms for which he or she is not ready.

• Open the lines of communication between yourself and your older children and/or teenagers. Clarify with them your and their needs, expectations, and responsibilities. Above all, avoid conflicts over trivia, and concentrate on the important issues that really affect their lives and their health. Maintain your credibility. Remember that if you are confident, respect yourself, and respect them, they will have the opportunity to learn from your example.

It is helpful to remember that there is nothing new about being a single parent. There are now more women than before who choose to have children without the benefit of marriage or husband, and society's growing acceptance of them is a fairly recent phenomenon, but there have always been women who raised their families alone. In previous times the men were away on crusades, at war, on long journeys, conquering the wilderness, or simply working far from home. Divorce was less common, but families were frequently left fatherless and even more frequently left motherless when a parent died from what are now curable diseases.

• If you are a single parent today, you have resources never available before. You can find child-care centers, and you can find support in groups of people who have a similar life situation. You can begin by calling the YWCA or a local chapter of Parents Without Partners. The women's center in your area will also provide you with ideas and suggestions, and if you are resourceful and energetic, you could start a group of your own.

SUGGESTED READING:

Jones, Eve. *Raising Your Child in a Fatherless Home*. New York: Macmillan, 1963.

Klein, Carole. *The Single Parent Experience*. New York: Avon Books, 1973.

See also: CHILDREN OF DIVORCE, STEPPARENTING, TEENAGE REBELLION

SLEEP DISORDERS

We may not need as much sleep as we sometimes think, but we most certainly require a regular, restorative, daily sleep allowance. If something interferes with our sleeping, we quickly notice poorer performance, especially at tasks needing sustained attention to detail. Prolonged sleep deprivation has more serious side effects. People denied sleep over extended periods demonstrate increasingly disoriented behavior. They become irritable and eventually incoherent. A string of sleepless days produces hallucinations and delusions; even further lack of sleep would probably bring on psychotic forms of behavior and eventual death.

For most of us, happily, occasional temporary insomnia is the worst of it. A significant minority, though, do suffer from any of a wide variety of sleep disorders, some more susceptible to personal correction than others.

If you think you may have a serious sleep problem, first rule out the medically related possibilities. Be aware of the signs of a physiological disorder, and find a physician who specializes in the treatment of sleep difficulties. This is an area of medical and psychological concern in which a great deal of research is currently being conducted, with new information coming to light frequently. It is important to seek out attention from someone familiar with this specialized, rapidly changing field in order to get proper diagnosis and treatment.

Medically related sleep problems include several neurological disorders. Among them, for example, are sleep apnea, restless-leg syndrome, and nocturnal myoclonus. Sleep apnea is the most risky of the group. A person with this illness may stop breathing for up to two minutes many times during the night without being aware of it. The sufferer characteristically experiences a peculiar, heavy, intermittent snoring. This snoring is a common symptom of the upper respiratory problem that causes breathing to stop. If breathing does not resume after eight to ten seconds it may not resume at all, resulting in a death that is usually attributed—reasonably but incorrectly—to stroke or cardiac arrest. If you find yourself complaining of frequent daytime sleepiness and find others complaining about your noisy, gaspy snoring, seek immediate medical attention in order to rule out sleep apnea or to treat it if you do indeed suffer from it.

People who experience restless-leg syndrome are distracted from sleep by a sort of "creepy-crawly" sensation in their legs. This sensation is so irritating to them that they feel compelled to get up and walk around to try to get rid of it. This makes falling asleep a battle between fatigue and discomfort, a battle the sufferer often loses.

Nocturnal myoclonus is a leg-jerk syndrome: The sufferer is repeatedly awakened by a sudden leg jerk that fragments sleep and deprives him or her of needed rest.

Other sleep disorders are more familiar to us. We know that disturbing our usual day/night body rhythm can make sleeping difficult. People who must work night shifts, for instance, need to adjust to an initially uncomfortable change in sleep patterns. Travelers through different time zones often complain of a similar disruption and need to readjust to an altered day/night schedule. Almost any of us may occasionally awaken too early, wake during the night and have difficulty getting back to sleep, or find it hard to fall asleep in the first place.

Perhaps the most common problem is this last one, insomnia. Dealing with it demands a multilevel approach in which you consider the possibility that a solution may be found through medical care, or through changes in your physical or emotional environment, or in some combination of all of these. Sleep specialists point out that temporary insomnia may arise from psychological stress, for example, but that long-term insomnia often develops out of the drugs and alcohol misused in an effort to restore normal sleeping.

Many physicians unfamiliar with current sleep research findings continue to prescribe drugs to patients complaining of insomnia, and many people treat themselves with over-the-counter sleeping pills and/or liquor. Hypnotic drugs may in fact be appropriate for only a minority of insomniacs. In general, these drugs only make the problem worse—and combining them with alcohol creates the well-known danger of oversedation.

People develop a tolerance for hypnotic drugs rapidly, and many are then drawn to increase the dosage to dangerous levels in order to maintain the effect. In some people a drug's pharmacological effect is the opposite of what is needed to resolve a specific sleep problem. Additionally, there are serious side effects to the medically supervised withdrawal necessary to treat drug-induced insomnia. At first the patient may experience nearly total insomnia. Subsequently sleep may be interrupted by horrifying nightmares. Getting free of the drugs, however, is just the first hard step in returning to normal sleeping.

Garden-variety, non-drug-related insomnia and middle-of-the-night sleeplessness often respond to techniques anyone can undertake safely and independently. Let's begin with the "don'ts."

• Don't watch television right up to bedtime. It can be too stimulating —the late news, an action movie, a piercing documentary can get you too agitated to relax easily. If there's anyplace else in the house to put it, in fact, you would do well to get the television out of the bedroom entirely.

• Don't use your bed for anything but sleeping (with the exception of sexual activity). Many insomniacs come to associate their beds with not sleeping. Therefore, avoid any nonsleep activities in bed—such as reading, eating, writing letters, or clearing up a few bills.

• Don't badger yourself about your sleep problem. Never go to bed unless you are already drowsy. If you don't get to sleep in a short time, or if you wake up and stay awake, get up and leave the bedroom. This will help you associate your bed with falling asleep quickly rather than with tossing about in insomniac distress.

• Don't take a daytime nap. Your body needs to readjust to a night-time sleep schedule.

Now, some positive suggestions:

• Even if you have to move to a different bed—something a spouse or lover might find surprising—make sure you use a bed that's comfortable for you. It doesn't matter whether it's medium, soft, firm, air, or water, just so long as it feels good to you and helps you get to sleep and stay asleep.

• Try to identify the sources of stress and tension in your life and develop ways to deal with them. Having some plan to reduce stress—and then acting on it—can greatly diminish those pressures that sometimes inhibit relaxation and rest. You may discover that you need to make some changes in the way you live to reduce tension and stress—facing up to problems with other people, or with your work, or within yourself, and then tackling them.

• Try to make your sleep room a refuge against the daily grind. Try not to bring work problems to bed. Try, also, to settle arguments with the people who share your home. It's hard to get to sleep when you and your spouse, stewing over some disagreement, are curled up, tense and angry, on opposite sides of the bed.

• Daily exercise, early in the day—not right before bedtime—can lead to a healthful physical tiredness.

• Relax awhile before bedtime. Take a bath, read a dull book (few things are more sleep-inducing), listen to soft music, drink some warm milk.

• Relax in bed. Perhaps you could use some form of relaxation technique, such as systematically tensing and then relaxing your muscles, starting with the face and working to the feet. You might wish to investigate such techniques as autogenic training and progressive relaxation.

• Once settled for sleep, think relaxing thoughts. Visualize peaceful scenes that you find reassuring, calming, and pleasurable.

• Focus on the comfortable feelings of your relaxed body rather than on going to sleep. Sleep is more likely to overtake you if you don't chase it.

• You may find sleep records useful. Inquire at a record store about records or tapes of restful sounds, such as falling rain, wind, the ocean, or simply white noise.

• Establish a sleep ritual. Devise a set of activities that you always perform just prior to bed. The precise order or content of the ritual doesn't matter. All that is important is the creation of a sleep-related sequence that signals to your mind and body that your day is at an end and that you are ready for sleep and rest.

• Make your sleep room a suitable environment for sleeping. Intermittent noise—barking dogs, the on/off of a heater, car doors banging —can be very disruptive of sleep. Try to muffle out this sort of distraction, even with earplugs if necessary. Unless you feel most comfortable with some light in your sleep room, darken the room as much as possible. Use blackout shades or try night blinders if you wish. Set the room temperature within a soothing range, somewhere between 66° and 72°F.

• Always set your alarm for the same time, no matter how late you go to bed. This will help your body adjust to a regular, predictable pattern of waking and sleeping.

• Even if you are dieting, don't go to bed hungry. Save part of your calorie allowance for bedtime if you need to. Avoid caffeine after noon; it might be just one more disruptive factor in your sleep problem. Drink something warm before bed—especially the old standby, milk. Hot milk becomes increasingly effective as a sleep inducer the more often you use it. This seems to be related to milk's high tryptophan content (tryptophan is a naturally occurring amino acid with sleep-inducing properties). Other natural sedatives or relaxers include camomile tea and the essential dietary minerals calcium and magnesium (found together in dolomite).

If the individualized sleep program you work out for yourself fails to resolve your insomnia, you may need to dig a little deeper for the cause and work a little harder on the cure. Reconsider the possibility of a hidden medical problem. Sleep disorders are often provoked by psychological strains, but persistent, chronic disorders can often be traced to neurological causes. A persistent sleep problem is less likely to be caused by psychological problems than is the temporary, manageable sleeplessness we all experience from time to time.

If you've ruled out illness and you still can't sleep regularly and satisfyingly, look again at your life. What's going on that's disruptive? What sorts of threats to your security—monetary, family, health, career, sexual—might you be struggling with? Nighttime can be a period of heightened vulnerability; a little sleep and rest, awakened to a dark and quiet room, we're vulnerable to a kind of sensory and intellectual deprivation that lets whatever torments may be hiding in our heads take over and menace us. As F. Scott Fitzgerald said in *The Crack-Up,* "In the real dark night of the soul it is always three o'clock in the morning."

For some people sleeplessness signals a time of spiritual or religious turmoil. Is this a time of major change or transition for you? Do you feel the need of a fundamental value reorientation or a deepening of your spiritual life? Are you working toward a transformation—of feeling, commitments, behavior patterns?

Others find sleep difficult because they are restless with a sense of a missing, unlived life that they desire. Is your sleeplessness caused by a need for more meaningful connections, closer ties to people, more self-expression in your work? Do you miss a loving, sexual relationship that you have failed to pursue or develop? The lack of engagement with life in a deep sense can produce much anxiety and sleeplessness.

In the susceptible hours of the night other fears can arise, akin to the fears that plague the lonely. If your inner self is weak and poorly developed, if your sense of self and value is insufficient, you may be afraid to sleep—afraid to be alone with yourself and your doubts in the vulnerability of sleep, afraid to let go of the external supports and reassurances that validate your waking life for you. You may fear that sleep is too like death, that you have so weak a hold on life that you may just vanish, that your own substance is too thin to withstand the loneliness of dark and quiet. Many people experience such night terrors, not least among them those who as children were taught that sleep and death are close cousins—that "Grandma went to sleep" and had to be buried in the cemetery.

You can work at discovering the feelings, needs, or fears that interrupt your sleep. If you can't get to sleep or stay asleep, leave the bedroom and try to meditate somewhere else. You might try a simplifying, mind-emptying, or mantra-centered meditation, or just sit quietly and drift with your wandering thoughts and feelings. You might call this creative worry: The late-night silence may make you freer and more receptive to concerns you neglect during the active hours of the day.

Try to let your fantasies go so you can discover what your mind is working on below the immediate conscious level. You might like to try a guided fantasy, such as this one:

You can't sleep—you're restless—decide to go on a trip—imagine yourself walking out of your home across a beautiful warm meadow—after a long walk you come to a range of sloping foothills—you begin the easy, safe ascent—the path leads through a stand of trees to a cave—you enter—a friendly person awaits you there to tell you something. Who is it? What does he or she look like? Imagine all the details of appearance and action—is this a wizard, an old wise man or woman? What is the message? Is it one of confrontation, reassurance, guidance, instruction? When the conversation seems over, ask if it's all right to return through your walk and go to sleep. Ask if there is anything you need to do before you may sleep.

At different times we all need this sort of soothing. We need to know that it's all right for us to give ourselves over to sleep. Like children, we need reassurance—if not from mother or the sandman, then from some part of ourselves. Sometimes it helps to objectify that part, to make it seem like some external friendly presence approves of our sleep, gives us permission to let go of the day and its obligations, and to rest ourselves.

SUGGESTED READING:

Dement, William C. *Some Must Watch While Some Must Sleep.* San Francisco: Freeman, 1974.

Goldberg, Philip, and Daniel Kaufman. *Natural Sleep (How to Get Your Share).* Emmaus, Pennsylvania: Rodale Press, 1978.

Rubinstein, Hilary. *Insomniacs of the World, Good Night.* New York: Random House, 1974.

Webb, Wilse B. *Sleep: An Active Process.* Glenview, Illinois: Scott, Foresman, 1973.

See also: ANXIETY, DEPRESSION, LONELINESS, NIGHTMARES, SLEEPWALKING, STRESS

SLEEPWALKING

If you sleepwalk, you're by no means alone. According to the American Medical Association, about 4 million Americans have consulted their medical doctors about this sleep disorder. Some estimates indicate that 1 to 6 percent of the population may engage in some nighttime wandering. More common in children than in adults, in boys than in girls, sleepwalking is a problem that is generally outgrown with no serious difficulty. In fact, it is probable that most children have some sleepwalking experience that both they and their parents fail to notice or consider too unimportant to report to pediatricians.

As is commonly known, sleepwalkers have been reputed to have accomplished some rather extraordinary and complex things: setting a table for a meal, crossing from rooftop to rooftop, driving, swimming. For the most part, sleepwalkers don't seek to harm themselves. They are, however, unaware of dangers, and they often do suffer injuries (scratch one myth). A sleepwalker who opens his front door and strolls across to the park may walk well enough, but he is not likely to notice the late-night driver rushing along his street.

People who sleepwalk sometimes contend with other sorts of sleep disorders, among them enuresis (bedwetting), night terrors, and nightmares. (See SLEEP DISORDERS and NIGHTMARES.)

Sleepwalking does not occur during dream sleep, so—again contrary to popular knowledge—sleepwalkers do not act out dreams by getting up and moving about. They function at a low level of awareness and with little judgmental ability. Sometimes sleepwalkers respond to questions or react to external stimuli, such as noises or lights or touch or being spoken to by an observer. Characteristically, sleepwalkers have no memory of their sleepwalking activities, neither the next morning nor if they are awakened immediately following an excursion. If awakened while sleepwalking, they are usually confused and disoriented, and have difficulty alerting themselves to the immediate situation.

Some research suggests that sleepwalking may be a disorder of arousal from non-dream sleep (also called slow-wave sleep). People who sleepwalk may have some physical condition that predisposes them to this arousal disorder. Sometimes, especially in children, sleepwalking seems related to a delayed maturing of some functions of the central nervous system. It is possible that psychological factors may trigger sleepwalking episodes in people with such central nervous system immaturity.

There may also be a hereditary aspect to this sleep disorder. Many sleepwalkers can trace a family history of the problem back through the generations. Occasionally several or all members of a family will have the problem in the same generation. An Italian doctor once reported an entire family—parents and four children—who all sleepwalked, once all at the same time.

Is the sleepwalker asleep or awake? This is still open to debate; in some ways the sleepwalker's state resembles both waking and sleeping. Some, but not all, sleep researchers think it possible that the sleepwalker is not really moving about while asleep, but when supposed to be asleep. It's as if he or she were awake, but not truly alert.

Sleepwalking is not necessarily a symptom of severe psychological problems. In children and adults it is often related to periods of stress or sorrow: repeated family fights, a death in the family, intense school or work pressures, moving away from a familiar environment. Like nightmares, sleepwalking episodes can have something to do with working out internal conflicts that are difficult to face directly in waking life.

If you or someone close to you experiences repeated sleepwalking episodes that last more than ten minutes, consult a physician who specializes in sleep disorders. Such a specialist may be able to define the cause for you and recommend effective treatment.

Similarly, consult a sleep specialist in order to learn about available and appropriate drug therapies. The study of sleep disorders is a complex, rapidly changing, experimental field. It is important, therefore, not to try to prescribe for yourself or to accept a prescription from an untrained nonspecialist.

Even the sleepwalker who is not bothered by his or her excursions and who has no particular anxiety about the condition needs to be protected. If the sleepwalking experience is not frightening or disruptive, protective measures alone may be enough in the way of "treatment."

• Lock doors and windows. If necessary, put a special night lock on outside doors. Do not leave the key for this lock anywhere the sleepwalker could get it.

• Put sleepwalkers in first-floor bedrooms—better to take a walk on the flower beds than on air.

• Remove dangerous objects, such as appliance cords that trail across the floor, freestanding heaters, scatter rugs. Don't leave the car keys out.

• Don't punish children who sleepwalk. Punishment could cause even more sleepwalking. It won't help to treat them as though they could control it. Just try to make their environment as safe as possible. Securely lock bedroom windows. Place a gate at the head of the stairway.

• Most of the time sleepwalkers can be guided back to bed without being awakened. If you must awaken a sleepwalker, do not grab or shake him or her; call the person's name until it sinks in. When you get a response, let the sleepwalker know that he or she is safe. Allow for some disorientation and explain gently what has happened, then help the person back to bed.

For the adult sleepwalker who is disturbed by his or her sleep disorder, protection alone may not be the answer. Some people suffer great anxiety because they sleepwalk. They may fear for themselves or others. Sometimes they are ashamed of sleepwalking and think that other people blame them for it, as if it were a failing they should have overcome.

Too often adult sleepwalkers who seek nonspecialist medical attention are told to ignore the problem, to expect it to go away untreated, or to take sedatives. These approaches won't work if the sleepwalking reflects a serious psychological disturbance.

Sometimes anxiety-producing sleepwalking is accompanied by disturbing nightmares or fantasies. The nighttime movements may reflect unreleased internal tension accumulated during the day. For example, some sleepwalkers are people who have difficulty expressing anger. Many of them notice a direct relationship between becoming angry or emotionally upset during the day and sleepwalking at night. Seeing this relationship, they may come to fear tension altogether, to fear the coming of night itself, and to struggle for total control over their feelings.

• If you notice such a relationship between your waking emotions and sleepwalking, try to identify and record for yourself situations that produce sleepwalking events. What emotions do you deny during the day that seem to disturb your sleep at night? What might you be trying to avoid saying or doing? What frightens you about expressing your feelings? What emotions do you feel you have to hide or deny?

• In as nonthreatening a situation as you can find, try to let yourself go with your feelings as soon as you are aware of them. Let a friend know that you're struggling with anger, for instance. Talk about it. Express your anger in safe ways. Give yourself a chance to learn that it's all right to have angry feelings. You can learn to express them without hurting other people; they don't have to cause a catastrophe.

• If you don't find sufficient relief on your own, use your observations and recognitions to start work with a professional counselor or therapist. Don't be afraid to ask for outside help when you feel over your head with confusing or scary emotions. Another person may help you make connections and see alternatives you would not be able to reach on your own—alternatives that may already be waiting in the self-study and recording you have done.

SUGGESTED READING:

Hartmann, Ernest L. *The Functions of Sleep.* New Haven: Yale University Press, 1973.

See also: ANXIETY, NIGHTMARES, SLEEP DISORDERS, STRESS

SMOKING

If you are reading this because you've already decided to kick the habit, there's no need to go into all the reasons to quit smoking. If you smoke and are still in conflict about whether to continue or quit, let's simply say that you'll live longer and be healthier if you stop smoking now. But, as with many habits we wish we didn't have, the habit of smoking persists because it serves a real need or purpose.

No matter how much you claim you want to stop smoking, you won't stop until you have dealt honestly and directly with the part of you that stubbornly wants to continue smoking. You may be one of those rare people who can do some blunt soul-searching, look clearly at how the costs outweigh the gains of smoking, and stop.

Try that approach—it might work for you. And if it doesn't, you will have learned something you must face up to in order to stop. You will have learned that you are more complex, inwardly divided, and tricky than you realized. Parts of you play games with other parts, and then still another part of you pretends that no such games are going on at all.

It can go like this: One part insists it wants to stop smoking, another part goes right on smoking, and a third part observes this contradiction and disowns it. Disowning behavior occurs when people assert that they could not possibly be capable of inconsistent and destructive behavior, and that some mysterious force or "devil" made them do it.

So if you think you want to stop smoking, the first step is to admit to yourself that you also want to continue smoking. Don't judge or condemn yourself, just admit it. Then the problem you must tackle is what to do with that wish to smoke. Here is a plan that is not easy, but that deals directly with the powerful pro-smoking forces within you.

• To start with, plan to quit cold turkey—just to stop smoking altogether. It's tempting to tell yourself that you can cut down a bit at a time until you get to zero, but it just doesn't work that way. People who try to cut down gradually usually find that they soon go back to smoking as much as ever. The smokers who are successful in quitting are those who do go cold turkey.

• Set a specific date for quitting; this will help keep you from putting it off forever. Announce to your friends and the people you work with that you are going to quit by that date. Get their support and make backing out embarrassing for yourself. Try making a bet with someone that you *will* quit—that may give you the extra push you need.

• The next part of the plan focuses on how to deal with your wish to smoke, so that the wish will be gone by the "stop date" you have set. Observe carefully what is going on for you emotionally each time you want to smoke. You must learn to see and hear the events within your head and between you and other people more clearly so that you will know exactly what triggers your wish to smoke. Don't kid yourself— it isn't that you "just want a cigarette." You want one because not enough is happening at that moment, or because something is happening that you don't like. Smoking solves a problem: It fills an emptiness in your life, or soothes an aggravation.

• Recognize something else that makes it especially hard to stop smoking: Not just your feelings and thoughts are involved, but your body has also come to depend on the kick from the nicotine. Even though the effect of this powerful drug is very unhealthy, your body has learned to like this effect of smoking, and in order to stop smoking you need to unlearn this liking. To unlearn such a strong liking, you need an even stronger negative experience.

• Psychologists at the University of Oregon have developed a method of teaching your body to dislike smoking by making it unpleasant. Nine out of ten people who use this method quit smoking in *one week!* If you have heart or lung problems, however, this technique may be harmful to you; if you're unsure, better check with your doctor.

Here's what to do: Sit facing a blank wall with a clock or watch that indicates seconds in front of you and a pack of your brand of cigarettes. Light a cigarette and smoke it *very* fast—take a deep puff every six seconds. You'll find that this is very unpleasant, but that's the point. Keep smoking the cigarette at this rate until you really start to feel ill, then stop and leave the room for some fresh air. Pay close attention to how unpleasant it is to breathe smoke and how good it feels to get fresh air into your lungs. When you feel ready, go back to your chair and light up another cigarette, again inhaling every six seconds and stopping when you feel that you can't take another puff. Do this as many times as you need (most people need to smoke four cigarettes) until you feel so turned off to smoking that you just can't think about lighting up another cigarette. Your body is learning to dislike cigarettes.

• In order for this dislike to last, you must repeat this procedure once a day for five days in a row. Also, it is *very important* that you don't smoke between sessions—this dilutes the effect of the treatment. When you get an urge to smoke, remind yourself how unpleasant it can be to draw smoke into your lungs. If you just can't resist a cigarette, then smoke it the fast way—one puff every six seconds. Remember, though, the method will be most effective if you don't smoke between treatments. That way, your body will learn that smoking is unpleasant, and you'll stop craving it.

• If you follow these instructions, at the end of five days you will have stopped smoking. Congratulations! Remember, though, that quitting is only half the battle—*staying* off is what counts. (Mark Twain used to say: "Quitting is easy—I've done it a hundred times.")

Smokers who have just quit often go back to smoking because of the discomfort they feel when they stop. Most say they feel more irritable and nervous than usual. If you do, pay attention to what's bothering you—you will discover problems or opportunities that your smoking has been hiding. For example, does a particular person or situation make you nervous? Why? What action must you take instead of the cop-out of smoking?

When you quit, you may also feel a bit more sleepy or less sleepy than usual, and you may be unusually hungry. You can help yourself stay off cigarettes by reminding yourself that these problems (withdrawal symptoms) will go away in a couple of weeks if you don't smoke. Don't worry about gaining a little weight during the withdrawal period. Find some substitute for smoking when you get an urge: Chew gum, whistle, practice slow, deep breathing.

• For the first few weeks avoid situations that make you want to smoke. For most people social drinking is a hard test, so stay away from it. Most of all, stay away from cigarettes; do not try even one "just to see if I can handle it." Learn to say no to people who offer you a cigarette—and to yourself!

Quitting smoking will make you feel better in lots of ways, physically and emotionally. However, if you find that new problems arise in the place of smoking, be prepared to deal with them in new ways. Look out for increases in anxiety, anger, or depression, for example.

If you want to know more about cigarette smoking and how to stop, get in touch with the local chapter of the American Cancer Society or the Heart and Lung Association. Both are listed in your phone book and both will give you information and help. Also, contact Smokenders, 210 Prospect St., Phillipsburg, N.J. 08865.

SUGGESTED READING:

Danysh, Joseph. *Stop Without Quitting.* International General Semantics, 1974.

Donaher, Brian G., and Edward Lichtenstein. *Become an Ex-Smoker.* Englewood Cliffs, N.J.: Prentice-Hall, 1973.

Pomerleau, Ovide and Cynthia S. *Break the Smoking Habit: A Behavioral Program for Giving up Cigarettes.* Champaign, Ill.: Research Press, 1977.

See also: ANXIETY, BOREDOM, COMPULSIONS, DEPRESSION, STRESS

SPOUSE BEATING

Recently the problem of wife beating has been increasingly publicized and legally prosecuted. Husband beating is also being revealed as surprisingly widespread. Previously, the battered spouse was assumed to be the wife. She was her husband's property, so he naturally had a right to punish her. This punishment ranges all the way from a sharp slap in the face to a severe beating. He may accidentally kill her. Or she may kill him in self-defense.

A battered wife is often too terrified of her husband to report the crime. She feels powerless and dependent, with nowhere to turn, especially if she has children to take care of. She sees no alternative picture of what life could be. Battered husbands report their plight even less often, because of shame and embarrassment. They often pretend to themselves that it's not really happening.

When a wife does contact the police, she often finds the law reluctant to interfere. A man's home is his castle, and his crime is difficult to prosecute. Police who intervene in domestic disputes sometimes become the victims of assault or even homicide themselves.

Who are spouse beaters? They are people from all walks of social, economic, and intellectual life. They have one thing in common: They are desperately dependent on their husband or wife to make them feel worthwhile. When they don't receive this validation inside the marriage, or when things go wrong in the outside world, they turn against the spouse as a scapegoat. They may project their own intolerable feelings —of weakness, inferiority, guilt—onto their spouse. The spouse "deserves" to be beaten.

Are you trapped in such a dangerous, degrading situation? You can stop being a victim by facing your problem and becoming a stronger, more self-valuing, self-sufficient person. Your immediate challenge is to survive, by defusing some of your domestic time bombs.

• Don't provoke your spouse to attack. Don't taunt, ridicule, mock, blame, accuse, or give cause for jealousy. Recognize that these put-downs are inflammatory, and that your spouse's way of feeling worthwhile again is to beat you up, to prove that you are the bad person.

• Be particularly careful when your spouse is tired, having a bad time at work or elsewhere, or drinking. Try not to get trapped alone at those times. Don't join in a drinking session with the false hope that it will smooth things over. More likely, it will set the stage for a fight.

• Learn to de-escalate conflict if it begins. Back down from an argument. Don't grovel, but don't risk your scalp defending your righteousness.

• Never crowd or confine your spouse physically by moving in too close, making threatening gestures, or yelling at close range. Some people react violently when they feel cornered.

• If trouble starts, try to stay out of range. Keep an escape route open—don't let your spouse get between you and the door. If you do get trapped, concentrate on escaping, not on fighting back.

• Never bring out a weapon. In many domestic murders the weapon was introduced by the victim. The sight of a weapon in your hand may trigger your spouse to even greater rage.

• When your husband or wife seems stressed, try offering genuine sympathy and concern. Try this even if he or she is blaming you for the problem. If your spouse can blow off steam verbally by complaining to a sympathetic listener, he or she eventually may not need to get so violent. Battering is often a crude way of saying "Hear me, take my pain seriously."

• Recognize that violence sometimes represents misdirected, frustrated sexuality. Discover whether you are inhibiting or preventing positive sexual action. If sex isn't possible for some reason, try some other vigorous, satisfying, physical activity together outdoors. Encourage your spouse to use his or her energy in sports, yard work, motorcycling, racing. Help your spouse get a sense of power and strength in some way other than beating you up.

• Find allies—friends, neighbors, clergy—who can give you emotional support. Alert them that you may need them to call the police or provide emergency shelter. Don't ask them to intervene, because they could become victims. Alert the police as well. If they seem cooperative, ask them for advice.

• Think about how you happened to choose for a spouse someone who turned out to be violent toward you. What cues and signals about this did you miss? Did you allow the problem to develop by not emphatically stating the first time he or she hit you that this was totally unacceptable? How could you choose better in a future relationship? If you are a woman, consider whether you think of women as second-class citizens. In subtle ways you may be inviting mistreatment and neglecting to develop your strengths.

• Consider leaving. If you cannot because of emotional or economic dependence, responsibilities, or fear, what are the practical steps necessary to get you free? Start work now on an escape plan. Taking even small steps will help you feel better. Recognize that protesting, complaining, wishing your spouse would change, or believing constant promises to change will accomplish little. Accept the responsibility for taking charge of your own life. If you do not want to leave a situation that you cannot change, think about why you are willing to accept a substandard and punishing existence.

• Recognize that you need to become more self-sufficient and self-valuing. Take classes or job training, find other outside interests, make friends. Try to develop an internal sense of your own worth and power. Keep up your emotional and physical health.

• Don't encourage your children to take sides against your spouse. Don't let them intervene, because they may get hurt. Encourage them to develop outside interests, make friends, and become independent, self-worthy persons.

• Line up hot-line and shelter resources for an emergency. Contact a local National Organization for Women or Family Service Association office. Get help or legal information from social agencies in your community. Join a group of people who have had experiences like yours and solved them. Recognize that relating to other men and women who are loving, peaceful, and noncoercive may be an important growth step.

• If you are the abusing spouse, learn to take a walk or physically work off your energy when you become angry. Get out of the house. Talk to yourself, a friend, a rap group, or a tape recorder about your problems. Try to develop interests and skills that make you proud of yourself. Get counseling. Learn what sets you off and what to do instead of using physical attack.

SUGGESTED READING:

Davidson, Terry. *Conjugal Crime: Understanding and Changing the Wifebeating Pattern.* New York: Hawthorn Books, 1978.

Martin, Del. *Battered Wives.* New York: A Kangaroo Book, Pocket Books, 1977.

See also: ANGER, CHILD ABUSE, LOVE ADDICTION, MARITAL QUARRELING, MASOCHISM, RAPE, SADISM

STAGE FRIGHT

Almost everyone who has had to appear before an audience at some time has suffered from stage fright. Experienced actors, successful businesspeople, and college presidents have had to deal with dizziness, sweaty palms, upset stomachs, and other familiar symptoms of stage fright. Some professionals never entirely lose the fear, but they have learned to control it and even to use it to their advantage.

The more common symptoms of stage fright are a rapid pulse, an upset stomach (butterflies), and sweaty palms. Sometimes the symptoms are more severe: Your voice seems uncontrollable—it either becomes inaudible or it sounds loud and shrill—and, worst of all, your mind goes blank—you can't remember anything. Actually, when you have stage fright you are experiencing an acute anxiety attack, which can be controlled with practice and determination.

Usually when you have to appear in front of a group of people you want to make a good impression, but you also are scared of revealing more of yourself than you really intend to. You may be plagued by fears that you are not sufficiently attractive, clever, informed, or convincing. As a child you may have been taught that it was wrong to "show off." Consequently, when as an adult you have to make a presentation in front of an audience, you may be caught in a paralyzing conflict between the wish to "let it all hang out" and your parents' prohibition against such behavior. Early shame experiences may also leave you with a fear that you will inadvertently do something to expose the awkward, embarrassed child beneath your fragile façade of maturity. You may even be tired of keeping up a front and unconsciously long to test out the response to your "true" self.

Regardless of the cause, stage fright can be controlled. Those people who master their fear gain not only the ability to appear before an audience but also a feeling of self-confidence which carries over into other areas of their lives. Stage fright is a very common affliction, so you can learn much from people who have analyzed it and conquered it. There are many things you can do to help yourself.

• First of all, recognize that you are not unique. Don't put yourself down for being afraid. Try to determine whether your fear is realistic and justified. Think about your audience in a positive way. The people who have come to hear you or see you are probably not your enemies. Hopefully they have come prepared to like you.

• Prepare thoroughly. You may be afraid that you will fail, so keep in mind that the best insurance against failure is preparation. Go over your material, be sure of your facts, and don't be afraid to express your feelings about your subject. When you are personally involved in your topic or your task, you think less about yourself and as a result are less self-conscious. By caring deeply about what you have to say or do onstage you won't have time to be self-critical. So in preparing your presentation, get clear with yourself the importance it has for you and the reasons you want to communicate effectively to your audience.

• Plan ahead. Know what you are going to wear, and be sure it is something that is comfortable and conveys the image of you that you want people to have. If possible, check out the auditorium, theater, lecture hall, or wherever it is you will appear. Become familiar with it so at least you'll feel physically at home there. Look at the empty seats and imagine people in them. Imagine those people being friendly and attentive. If you plan to use notes, print them large and clear. Time your presentation to be sure it is not too long or short for the occasion.

• Think about how you will present your material, and to whom you are addressing yourself. Practice your speech or your act either by yourself in front of a mirror or, preferably, before friends. The better prepared you are, the more quickly you will be able to overcome your fear and the symptoms which accompany it.

• Look on the experience as an adventure and an opportunity for learning and growth. Think about the pleasures of communicating with other people and reaching them with your ideas and your performance.

• Smile and look confident, even if you don't feel it. People will respond to your smile, and soon you will really feel the confidence you are trying to project. Although you can admit that you are suffering from stage fright (many famous people do admit it to their audience), don't put yourself down. People may sympathize with your nervousness, but remember that they came to hear you talk or see you perform, not to worry about you.

• If you have trouble controlling the feeling of panic just before you give a performance or make a speech, try relaxation exercises or yoga. Calm yourself by taking long deep breaths. Regular breathing has a soothing effect, and the extra oxygen will help your muscles to relax. One famous actress even used to take a nap just before show time.

• Use the anxiety you feel to add intensity to your talk or your performance. If you are so nervous that you must use your hands, try to make gestures which punctuate or accentuate the content of your talk.

• Look at the people in your audience and find someone who is listening and seems to be agreeing with or even enjoying what you are saying. Eye contact with another person will help to ease your tension. When you address yourself to a specific person rather than to a vague mass of people, you will be more direct and more persuasive and thus get a better response from your audience.

• Speak about things you know well. Don't bluff; the audience will realize that you don't know what you are talking about. When you are sure of your facts and convictions, even if you are momentarily confused, you can regain your composure. When you make a mistake, admit it but don't dwell on it. Remember, everyone makes mistakes. If you can graciously admit yours, you will probably have the sympathy of the people in the audience, because they can identify with your embarrassment. A supportive audience does a great deal to lessen the performer's panic. Even experienced actors often say how dependent they are on a good audience.

• Keep your attention on the topic you are presenting and not on yourself. If you are really involved in your subject, the interest of your audience will be focused on what you are saying, and your enthusiasm will communicate itself to your listeners.

• Be yourself and be natural. Do not try to be like some person you admire greatly. Remember, the audience came to hear *you*. You will be most effective if you are comfortable with yourself. Successful TV personality Barbara Walters reminds herself, "I am the way I am; I look the way I look; I am my age." Genuineness and sincerity are still greatly admired qualities.

• If you want to learn some of the techniques which have helped others gain confidence and become more comfortable in the role of speaker or performer, you might investigate courses in acting or in public speaking given at your local community college. The Dale Carnegie course has been taught since 1912 and is constantly updated to include modern techniques.

SUGGESTED READING:

Carnegie, Dale. *The Quick and Easy Way to Effective Speaking*. New York: Pocket Books, 1977.

Linver, Sandy. *Speak Easy: How to Talk Your Way to the Top*. New York: Summit Books, 1979.

Walters, Barbara. *How to Talk with Practically Anybody About Practically Anything*. New York: Dell Publishing Co., 1970.

See also: ANXIETY, EXHIBITIONISM, SHYNESS

STEPPARENTING

Very often today, when two people marry they bring to the marriage not only themselves but the children of one or both of them. This blending of families sometimes throws together a variety of expectations and lifestyles that are as hard to mix as oil and water. The children are used to their real parents. They have built-in expectations about relationships, duties and privileges, food, possessions, and personal space.

In addition, children separated from a parent through death or divorce are going through a very difficult period. This is greatly complicated by your appearance as a new parent whom they are supposed to love and obey. They may resist, for all sorts of reasons. They may feel a need to stay loyal to the real parent. They may resent you or fear that they cannot love both you and the other parent. They may be afraid to love you for fear of being left behind or hurt again. They may have been living for some time with just one parent and consider you an intruder. Almost inevitably there are emotional adjustments to make on both sides, for you as a stepparent cannot expect to love them instantly either.

Part of being a mature and loving parent is being able to keep on giving love and caring to children even at those times when they don't respond with all the love and appreciation the parent wants. Taking on this challenge as a stepparent gives you the opportunity to expand and deepen your capacity as a loving person, to be creative in finding ways to let your new child grow to love you. This doesn't mean masochistic submission to a bratty child, but it does mean giving to and supporting someone who needs you.

Here are suggestions for approaching your new life as a stepparent.

• If possible, get to know the children (or child) before you make a final decision to marry. Ask yourself whether you are willing to take on the significant obligation of stepchildren. Recognize that now is the time to discover what your feelings are about these particular children and start building a relationship.

• Discuss with your prospective spouse what your role will be with the children. Be sure you are not expected to be the ideal, perfect parent, or some other image that does not fit the real you. Try to understand what the children expect of you. Are you a potential friend, or a bad person who stole their parent, or a new playmate? Try to promote a realistic expectation of your life together by being open and natural.

• Become clear in your own feelings about what you are willing to give to these children and what you cannot give. If you pretend you like playing games with them or going on picnics when you really don't, they will recognize and resent your falseness. Try to discover activities that you will truly enjoy doing together.

• Agree in advance with your spouse about rules and guidelines for the children, modes of discipline, and who will administer it. Especially if you and your spouse disagree, discuss these matters alone initially, not with the children. If you appear uncertain, the children may feel insecure or try to manipulate you into doing things differently.

• If you already have children of your own, talk to them about their new siblings. Listen to their feelings, and reassure them that you will still love them. Discuss the changes that are coming and set out guidelines for their new lifestyle.

• As soon as you comfortably can, spend some time alone with each stepchild. Plan something that you can enjoy together without your spouse, to help establish you as a separate person.

• Be prepared to invest hard work in the relationship. Hang on to your sense of humor and your sense of self-worth. Don't try to change to fit somebody else's image of you, especially the children's images of the lost parent. When things do go wrong, recognize that it's part of the stepparenting process and that the relationship will eventually get better as you work on it.

• Recognize that if a stepchild has resistance or resentment toward you, it may not be your fault. Try to get the child to talk about his or her feelings about losing the real parent, feelings of mixed loyalties, anger, wishes that the real parents would get back together. Really tune in to what's being said. Reassure him or her that those feelings are okay, that they don't make you angry. Reassure the child that you're not trying to replace the real parent. If appropriate, explain that you like the real parent and hope you will become friends in time.

• Be honest with yourself about any negative feelings you have toward a stepchild. Try to analyze why and plan steps to eliminate the causes if you can, or let time work on the problem. Deal with any guilt you may have if you have left your own children and now are the stepparent of others. Talk with your spouse about your feelings. Get counseling if you need it.

• Above all, don't rush the relationship. Don't try to buy or force the children's love. Don't try to force yourself to have loving feelings. Try to be interested, caring, generous as a person, and give the relationship a chance to grow, on both sides.

• Remember that effective discipline must be based on caring and rapport, and don't come on too strong with corrections and reprimands at first. But also remember that you're the parent, and don't let things get out of hand. Be direct in explaining the rules.

• Hold family meetings at which everyone can talk about their feelings and make suggestions. This is especially important when two sets of stepchildren dislike each other. Be prepared to adjust personal space, duties, privileges, and general house rules from time to time. Never play favorites among the children.

• Accept that there may be times when the real parent reenters the children's lives. If the parent visits the children, be graceful about allowing them time and space for their relationship. Try not to feel rejected, but don't be a martyr and give up all of your rights. Expect that after the children spend time with the real parent they may return home with renewed sorrows or anxieties, critical comparisons between you and the real parent, or generally negative behavior. Try to take this in stride and keep working on the relationship.

• Remember that the most important ingredient for success in your family is a sound marriage. Enjoy devoting creative attention to the loving, growing relationship between you and your spouse.

SUGGESTED READING:

Dodson, Dr. Fitzhugh. *How to Parent*. New York: Signet, New American Library, 1970.

Gesell, Dr. Arnold. *Child Behavior*. New York: Dell, 1955.

Ginott, Haim G. *Between Parent and Child*. New York: Avon Books, 1965.

Gordon, Dr. Thomas. *Parent Effectiveness Training*. New York: Peter Wyden, 1970.

Rosenbaum, Drs. Jean and Veryl. *Stepparenting*. Corte Madera, Calif.: Chandler & Sharp, 1977.

See also: CHILDREN OF DIVORCE, DIVORCE, SINGLE PARENT-ING

STERILIZATION

More and more couples are choosing sterilization as their form of birth control. It is no longer uncommon, especially among couples who have had children, for a man to decide to have a vasectomy or a woman to decide to undergo a tubal ligation or some other sterilization procedure. In fact, sterilization is now the number one form of birth control for couples married ten years or more.

Women usually find that sterilization does not adversely affect menstruation (unless it has involved a hysterectomy, of course) or their sexual desires or responsiveness. If fear of pregnancy has brought considerable anxiety to sexual intercourse, sterilization can mean increased ease and enhanced sexuality. Lovemaking can become more spontaneous, relaxed, and enjoyable.

For the woman who chooses it, sterilization can have other advantages. It requires only a single decision and a single financial commitment, unlike the ongoing concerns and expenses involved in nonpermanent birth control methods. For many women, no other available form of birth control—the Pill, condoms, contraceptive foams and jellies, the diaphragm, IUDs, rhythm or other natural methods—provides sufficient safety or certainty. For some women, in addition to the threat of accidental pregnancy and the burden of an unwanted child, there is a significant health hazard in using some contraceptive methods, such as the Pill or an IUD, or in undergoing an abortion.

Sterilization can guarantee that a couple will not pass along a hereditary physical or mental defect (Tay-Sachs disease, for example). It can also guarantee the emotional and/or physical well-being of a woman who cannot safely bear more children, or any at all. Some women are too burdened with serious psychological problems to handle the responsibility of parenting. Others have physical conditions that make pregnancy and childbirth dangerous for them. Others have simply had all the children they wish to bear and raise.

In addition, there are some women for whom mothering is not a natural or appropriate choice. They may find the prospect unpleasant and undesirable. Others resist the loss of freedom. There are people who have no desire or ability to be parents and who responsibly wish to avoid the role. There are women who live with deep fears about becoming abusive parents like their own mothers. In an uncountable number of personal life situations, sterilization can be a positive, caring choice.

However, there are disadvantages to be considered. The surgical and anesthetic procedures involved in the various methods of female sterilization carry varying degrees of risk. No surgery is completely without hazard, and so no surgery should be undertaken casually, even outpatient surgery.

The other major disadvantage is that for all practical purposes there is no way to undo surgical sterilization. Restoration of fertility is still rare and expensive, although advances have been made in special microsurgery techniques. For almost all who choose it, sterilization is a one-time, no-going-back, absolutely permanent decision.

It is a decision that lets you trade the freedom to reproduce for the freedom not to. The freedom you gain—as is so often true—brings with it an important limitation. Before you decide to give up your reproductive ability forever, it is crucial that you prepare yourself to handle both the liberation and the loss. Even if you don't define yourself as a woman solely in terms of your ability to produce children, childbirth is an exclusively and intimately female creative experience. Before choosing sterilization, you may want to sort out your mixed feelings and list for yourself the many other ways in which you are creative and productive.

Use the following guidelines to help you define your feelings and needs.

• Inform yourself fully about available forms of nonpermanent birth control. You may find that there is a method that would be sufficiently safe, economical, and nondisruptive for you. If you can be comfortable without making an absolute decision—especially if you are not certain about wanting no (or no more) children—surgery would probably be an extreme and potentially regretted action.

• Inform yourself fully about the various surgical procedures that result in female sterilization. Ask a gynecologist you trust to explain in detail the techniques and risks involved in tubal ligations, laparoscopy, mini-laparotomy, hysterectomy, and the other, less common procedures. If you are involved in an apparently stable, permanent relationship with a man, consider the possibility of his having a vasectomy. (See VASECTOMY.) Which of you could better tolerate surgery, physically and emotionally? Which of you feels the greater need to end worries about conception?

• Allow yourself time to search your own feelings. Are you prepared to accept the freedom from conception? Will you view sterilization as a loss? How important is motherhood to you? Will you be giving up an important aspect of your self-concept? Is your image of your sexual role tied up with your ability to reproduce? How well do you handle endings? How do you now fill your creative needs? What will you do in the future that will fulfill your desire to be productive? If you decide to go ahead with surgical sterilization, be prepared for some depression afterward (some of it related to pain-killing medication) and for increased anxiety about the safety and survival of the children you already have.

• Learn to distinguish between your own feelings about having children and the social pressures that surround you. There are strong religious and social encouragements to be fertile; most economic and educational systems still steer women toward childbearing. Many people still have children to prove that they are grown-ups: The children are used as a visible sign of sexual maturity. If you decide against having children at all or choose to guarantee surgically that you will not have more kids, anticipate who will criticize and disapprove, and how you will handle this. Your own parents (especially if they want grandchildren), relatives, and friends may challenge your decision. Those who oppose sterilization may characterize you as selfish, unnatural, even emotionally disturbed. If you share any of these feelings, you will need to come to terms with them before you can comfortably face your own sterilization.

• Don't make your decision under pressure or stress, especially if you are still very young. Women commonly have mixed feelings about childbearing, and their feelings often change over time. Try to avoid deciding at the time of an abortion or when you have just delivered a child. Postpone your decision until you have resolved religious objections if you have them. Marital instability or a recent severe loss can also interfere with your ability to decide in your own best interests. If you are married or living with someone in a long-term relationship, talk it over thoroughly. Make an effort to determine if your husband or lover is pushing you to decide one way or another.

• Be wary of coercion from spouse, lover, or physician. Women who have chosen sterilization because they decided it was right for them report less subsequent regret than women who were sterilized out of medical necessity or to please someone else. If your self-image as a mother (and as a woman capable of producing more children) is central to your ability to share in a male-female relationship, you are likely to suffer considerable regret. Unless a severe medical problem leaves you no choice, don't be pushed into a decision you may not be ready to make.

• Take advantage of pre- and post-surgical counseling if it is available. Sympathetic and supportive counselors can help you reach a decision suitable to your life's needs and adjust to the consequences of that decision. A competent counselor can help you discover whether you really want permanent birth control. If you don't, he or she will help you choose a nonpermanent contraceptive method or combination of methods. If you do want sterilization, a counselor will help you identify and cope with the emotional effects of the surgery.

• Your local Planned Parenthood Association is a good source of further information and of referrals to counselors and physicians. But remember to make your own decision based on what feels right to you, regardless of the stands relatives, friends, and professionals take. They don't have to live with the consequences the way you do.

• Coming to terms with your feelings about fertility versus sterilization is an opportunity to clarify and deepen your knowledge of yourself. It is a stimulus to look at where you are in your life, where you want to go, and whether you want to go there with more children.

SUGGESTED READING:

The Boston Women's Health Book Collective. *Our Bodies, Ourselves,* 2nd rev. ed. New York: Simon & Schuster, 1976.

Wylie, Evan McLeod. *All About Voluntary Sterilization: The New Birth-Control Method for Men and Women.* Berkeley, Calif.: Medallion, 1977.

See also: ABORTION, DEPRESSION, FEAR OF SICKNESS, HYSTERECTOMY, MID-LIFE CRISIS, VASECTOMY

STRESS

Stress can catch us up in a nasty cycle of interconnected physical and emotional reactions. Physical conditions, such as illness or fatigue, can provoke emotional stress. Emotional stress, in turn, can cause a variety of physical symptoms (among them rapid pulse, increased blood pressure, and increased secretion of adrenal hormones) that have been linked to health problems ranging from heart attacks and ulcers to cancer and premature aging. If you find yourself frequently ill or especially susceptible to infection, you might want to look for the ways emotional stress may set you up for your particular physical symptoms.

Traditional stress reactions include such behavior as brooding, fuming, shouting, and the increased use of alcohol, tobacco, or drugs. These don't work, except in offering what seems like temporary relief, and they all have undesirable side effects. The last three add injury to already strained bodies, while the first three do damage to personal relationships. Friends and family may sympathize when we are under excessive stress; this doesn't mean they are willing to be yelled at or blamed.

Professor Hans Selye, the world's foremost authority on human stress, defines stress as the body's nonspecific response to any demand placed on it, pleasant or not. It is often associated with major life changes, good and bad, and with crises small and large, anything from burning the roast at a dinner party to missing a plane to finding out you do have that dreaded illness you've always feared.

Stress is not always negative. Selye suggests that eustress (good stress) occurs in a life situation toward which we feel positively. If, for example, you like your work, a high-pressure schedule may be just right for you. Most important, stress is individually determined. We stay in stressful situations for the rewards they offer, for approval, money, status, self-esteem. We need, therefore, to decide repeatedly throughout our lives if the rewards are keeping ahead of the costs or falling behind, and to try to modulate our life in accordance with our personal stress capacity in order to keep costs and rewards in balance. We can develop ways to cope with stressful situations. These can alter the physiological impact of stress to reduce the harm we do ourselves when we react to stress improperly. The hazard is not in stressful experiences, only in our reactions to them. The key to improvement is in recognizing and working with our individuality.

• Learn to recognize your own stress signals. Stress can creep up on you insidiously, sometimes as the result of prolonged anxiety. It has its signals, but they may not always be as clear as you would wish. Practice monitoring yourself for the signs of unhealthy pressure. Some common signs are irritability, sleeplessness, rapid weight loss or gain, increased smoking or drinking, little errors (physical or mental "dumb mistakes"), physical tension, nervous tics, and tightness of breath.

• Don't underestimate the importance of exercise and good nutrition. Daily attention to health care can significantly decrease the effect of stress on both body and mind.

• Keep watch—even during the best of times—for your own stress signals. If possible, withdraw a bit when they appear. Don't exceed your normal, individual stress endurance. *Protect yourself.*

• Try to locate the sources of dangerous stress in your life. Take a look at your personal relationships with family, employer or employees, friends, neighbors, lovers, and strangers. Take a look at your own personality. Do you make unreasonable demands on yourself? Do you insist on never failing, never being late, never making a mistake, never being in the wrong? You can minimize the stress of frustration by learning when to stop something, when to acknowledge that the aim is no longer worth fighting for, when to accept your own limitations.

• Train yourself not to carry grudges and not to dwell on past unpleasant incidents. Carrying a grudge can deplete your naturally limited energy to resist stress. For your own sake, end an unpleasant relationship, but don't wallow in feelings of enmity or revenge.

• Turn worry into plans and action. Stress can be thought of as a kind of readiness in the extreme, an activation without release. Taking on the task at hand, however complex or frightening it might seem— planning actions and doing the necessary work—will greatly reduce the strain. It will also get your work done—another of life's reliefs and satisfactions.

• Live in your own right way. Some of us need speed and intensity and would wither under the stress of a quiet job or an isloated, do-nothing sort of vacation. For those used to high levels of activity there is more stress in suddenly slowing down than in maintaining their usual frantic pace. In general, diversion from one activity to another is more relaxing than complete rest. Frustration follows swiftly on the removal of stimulation and challenge.

• Work at making the necessary adjustments to unchangeable situations. It makes sense to fight for your highest attainable goal; it does not make sense to put up resistance in vain. Don't waste your limited adaptation energy by resisting the inevitable. You do not have control of rush-hour traffic.

• Set your own goals. There is almost unbearable stress in trying to live out goals created for you by others, be they friends, parents, or the proverbial Joneses.

• Doing nothing is no substitute for doing what you feel you must. If confronted by a stressful situation you could change, take direct action to eliminate the source of the stress, even if it seems harder to do than accepting things as they are. It's often hard to come right out and deal with a problem, particularly when it involves someone intimidating. It's even harder to live with unrelieved stress.

• Learn to accept the possibility of failure without losing your sense of self-worth. Failing will not hurt your health; feeling like a failure will. Reinforce your sense of accomplishment, even in the face of failure, by recalling past achievements. No present failure can take these away from you.

• Learn and practice regularly one of the relaxation techniques. For example, sit in a quiet room for twenty minutes once or twice a day and simply concentrate on your breathing. Notice each breath as it comes in and goes out. It may help if you count one as you exhale, and then as you exhale again, count two, and so on until four. Then start counting all over again. This helps focus your attention and regularizes your breathing. Some people prefer to repeat a word like "one" to themselves as they exhale each time.

• Another useful technique is to lie on the floor and progressively tense and relax all the muscles in your body, starting with your feet and gradually working up to your jaw and eye muscles. Create a pleasant, relaxing scene in your imagination. Make it as vivid and detailed as possible. Visualize yourself in the scene, completely relaxed. Turn that scene on in your mind several times a day, especially when you feel tense. Think of it as a place you can always go on a moment's notice. Unfortunately, because of our years of adaptation to stressful modern life, relaxation is not a natural, passive skill for us. We have to practice it actively and regularly.

Professor Selye recommends a certain attitude toward living that he believes will help you reduce the occurrence of negatively stressful situations. He calls this attitude "altruistic egoism," something healthily between selfishness and self-sacrifice. It means looking out for yourself by being necessary to others and thereby earning their goodwill and support. If you strive always to be useful, to acquire ever-increasing competence in your chosen field, you have much to gain: the personal satisfaction of helping others, protection against purposelessness, the stabilizing support of constructive goals and caring fellow human beings. You have constant improvement—of skills, self, and relationships—as your permanent guideline; you avoid the terrible stress of purposeless drifting.

SUGGESTED READING:

Benson, Herbert. *The Relaxation Response.* New York: Avon, 1976.

McQuade, Walter, and Ann Aikman. *Stress, What It Is, What It Can Do to Your Health, How to Fight Back.* New York: Bantam, 1975.

Selye, Hans. *Stress Without Distress.* New York: Signet, New American Library, 1974.

Walker, C. *Learn to Relax: 13 Ways to Reduce Tension.* Englewood Cliffs, N.J.: Prentice-Hall, 1975.

See also: ANGER, ANXIETY, HYPERTENSION, SLEEP DISORDERS

STUTTERING

When Porky Pig stutters in a cartoon it sounds cute, but if you are a stutterer you know how frustrating and upsetting this problem can be.

Over 50 percent of stutterers begin to stutter before age five, and it is a troublesome handicap to grow up with. In many countries between 1 and 2 percent of the population stutters. In the United States this amounts to over two million people. Fortunately, well over 50 percent of stutterers get over it by themselves or with help. More could conquer their stuttering with proper professional assistance and self-help. Churchill and Moses did quite well, as have many other famous and ordinary stutterers.

Stuttering occurs when a person can't get words out smoothly, when speaking is blocked by a tongue-tied repetition of parts of words. In severe cases there is a sputtering expulsion of breath after a block in getting a syllable out. Sometimes a stutterer will also grimace, twist his or her body, or stamp the floor.

If you are male, a twin, and/or left-handed, the chances of your stuttering are increased, but no one knows why. Maybe learning to talk as an assertive independent person is scarier for boys, twins, and left-handed people. One theory has it that stuttering is caused by the fear that you will not be allowed to "speak your piece," especially to critical or repressive parents. Some support for this theory is found in the fact that stutterers usually are able to speak clearly to children and to people they view as socially inferior. Also, nearly every stutterer blocks when trying to say his or her own name, especially to someone in authority.

A specific traumatic experience may be the cause of some stuttering. One boy began to stutter after he was physically terrified by some older boys and unable to get his parents to believe his story. Severe punishment, or an overwhelming experience with surgery or general anesthetic, can have a similar effect on some children, but for stuttering to result there would probably have to be additional conflict specifically related to the act of speech.

Self-help is the method of choice for stutterers for two reasons. First, many stutterers do not have access to professional speech pathologists. Second, even with professional help, most of the work must be done by the stutterer anyway. Stuttering can be cured—many have done it. Knowing and believing this is a source of relief for many stutterers when they begin to tackle their problem.

Here are ways to deal with stuttering:

• Get a thorough medical checkup, including a neurological exam. Stuttering is rarely caused by a medical condition, but it's always a good idea to make sure. A physician associated with a speech clinic is the best person to consult.

• Don't get dependent on tranquilizers or other drugs as artificial ways to reduce the tension which may be a cause of stuttering. Drugs mask the problem; they don't solve it. Using them just lulls you into the delusion that you can cope, while the outer and inner stresses you are sweeping under the rug get worse. Stuttering is a valuable signal that something important is happening within you and in your relationship to the person you are addressing. Learn what is happening.

• Don't expect hypnosis, metronome timing of speech, or other gimmicks and distractions to cure your stuttering permanently. Such techniques often work temporarily, but avoid real confrontation with the problem and avoid sustained self-help.

• Remember that some children go through a temporary phase of stuttering when they first learn to speak and then naturally grow out of it. Don't make a big deal out of it. Certainly never laugh at or try to correct a stutterer.

• Don't jump to the conclusion that you are a stutterer unless you really are one. You may simply share with most people the common tendency to stumble over words when tense or embarrassed. Don't make this natural foible worse by labeling it a "problem" and by anxiously trying to stop it. Such focused striving to perfect your speech could make you more tense and aggravate your self-consciousness. Deal with the source of your tension and learn relaxation techniques. Then your speech is likely to smooth out naturally.

• If you are a stutterer, be an honest one. As Dr. Joseph Sheehan said, "You will remain a stutterer as long as you pretend not to be one." It is essential that you admit to yourself and other people that you stutter. Doing so is a decisive and effective first step in gaining relief from stuttering. A large part of the tension and fear that cause stuttering is caused by shame about stuttering and by attempts to conceal it. As stuttering expert Dr. Wendell Johnson put it, "Stuttering is what you do trying not to stutter again." Don't waste effort and tense yourself up more by trying to stop stuttering or by trying to hide the fact that you stutter. Go ahead and stutter.

• Don't dwell too much on the original cause of your stuttering. Even if you discover a past cause, your stuttering today has taken on an independent life of its own. Focus your efforts on curing your stuttering, not on theorizing about it.

• Stutter intentionally. Exaggerate it. Force yourself to stutter until you are tired of it. Do this by yourself, with a friend by prior agreement, or in some other safe setting.

• Practice stuttering easily, without struggling to prevent it. Also, stutter slowly. Don't try to hurry past it. Speak slowly in general, and in a firm decisive voice with natural inflection.

• Take advantage of the fact that stuttering often takes a vacation when you sing or when you speak in a foreign language, with an accent, or in a play. Give yourself some success experiences by enjoying speech in ways that are free of stuttering. You will gain confidence and social presence, and some of this will carry over to your ordinary speech.

• Talk a lot. Seek out conversations. Discuss your stuttering problem with people. Tell them your openness is part of your self-help program. Stop avoiding situations where you might stutter. Avoidance creates fear and tension, the causes of stuttering. Since you have decided to admit you are a stutterer, you now have no guilty secret to hide. Enjoy your new freedom.

• Make and maintain eye contact with people you talk to. Look them squarely in the eye most of the time. You don't have to hide your eyes in shame. Looking at people directly reminds them and you that you have decided to make contact whether or not you happen to stutter.

• Stutter while watching yourself in a mirror. Observe and analyze the blocks your muscles create. Experiment with those muscles, alternately exaggerating and relaxing the blocks.

• Also using a mirror, self-observation, and feedback from friends, notice and eliminate the physical mannerisms and habits that accompany your stuttering. Blinking your eyes, pawing the ground, pulling on your ear, or jingling your car keys doesn't really help. Bring these compulsive behaviors under conscious control by counting the number of times you do them, and by sometimes doing them deliberately.

• Record your speech on a tape recorder. Use the recorder when you practice talking alone, when you talk on the telephone, and even when you are talking face-to-face with people—whenever the recorder will not be an intrusion. Then carefully study the recording of your speech to determine exactly which sounds and words give you trouble.

• Learn to value leisure, patience, pauses, and silence in conversation. What's the rush? Stop pushing yourself and others. Take time. Anything worth saying is worth saying slowly. Anyone worth talking to will give you the time you need to say it your way.

• Beware of pressure from demanding and perfectionistic people. Some experts believe that parents of stutterers contribute to the problem by being too ambitious and strict with their children. Was that true for you? Don't allow the present to be a repetition of the past. Don't let critical bosses, impatient friends, or even curt strangers rattle you into stuttering. Grant yourself your natural right to pace your speech comfortably.

• Think of stuttering as an act of rebellion and defiance that you secretly enjoy. Instead of looking at it as a problem that was inflicted on you, the victim, by mysterious forces outside your control, claim it as a powerful tool you have for stalling and frustrating people. Look at people and think to yourself, "I'll speak as slowly and awkwardly as I want, and you are going to have to like it or lump it." Imagine yourself doing this with a famous and powerful person who eagerly or angrily awaits your words. Be smug, calm, and as slow as you please.

• You probably enjoy the way some comedians deliberately use pauses, "slow takes," or speechlessness for laughs. Learn from it too. One of Jack Benny's classic skits about his stinginess included the scene where a robber snarled at him, "Your money or your life." Jack's anguished pause brought down the house. You don't have to act as if it's "your words or your life." Lighten up.

• If self-help is not enough, consult a speech clinic or independent speech therapist. But don't get caught up in a heavy, grim "stuttering-is-a-sickness" atmosphere. Only work with a therapist you like and feel comfortable with. Don't let speech exercises become annoying tasks. Remember that you want talking to be fun and useful, not a chore designed to make you perfect. And remember, self-help is the essential ingredient in all stuttering-reduction programs.

By understanding what causes your stuttering you will learn more about yourself and how you feel about making your way in the world through speech. From your progress with this problem you will gain confidence that you can help yourself, with and without expert assistance, and you will have a greater appreciation of what goes into stimulating, mutually affirming conversation.

SUGGESTED READING:

Self-Therapy for the Stutterer: One Approach and To the Stutterer. (Both available from the Speech Foundation of America, 152 Lombardy Road, Memphis, Tennessee 38111.)
Other organizations to contact:

American Speech and Hearing Association
10801 Rockville Pike
Rockville, Maryland 20852

Council of Adult Stutterers
% Speech and Hearing Clinic
Catholic University of America
Washington, D.C. 20017

See also: ANXIETY, COMMUNICATION BLOCKS, COMPULSIONS, SHYNESS, STAGE FRIGHT, STRESS

SUICIDE

At one time or another, the majority of people alive have considered the possibility of suicide. Under sufficient stress almost anyone might choose this way out.

Suicide-prevention specialists point out three important shared characteristics of those who attempt suicide. First, the potential suicide finds himself or herself in the midst of a crisis. Life seems to hold no promise of escape from intolerable and unsolvable problems. Helplessness and hopelessness take over. Second, most poeple who plan and even carry out suicide efforts are ambivalent about their wish to die; most also wish to live. Suicide prevention succeeds when this wavering will to continue life can be nourished and strengthened. Third, suicide attempts represent desperate efforts at communication by people who have failed to get help in less extreme ways. Suicidal people feel overwhelmed by their problems, and despair of getting help from other people.

Any number of circumstances can bring on a suicidal crisis: stress, interpersonal difficulties, financial losses, social pressures, imprisonment, loss of a loved one, severe or terminal illness, a sense of futility or lack of self-esteem, guilt, which turns hostile and murderous impulses inward, a long stretch of dark and gloomy weather, threatening economic trends, the suicides of famous people, a desire to punish people who don't seem to care enough, a wish to win a moral battle.

A successful suicide is rarely a surprise to those who are left behind. If they think back they can usually recall some or all of the following clues. If you recognize these in the behavior of someone you know, or in yourself, take them seriously. They are real warnings of need, crisis, and danger.

• Not everyone who threatens suicide commits it, but most people who do end their lives have previously threatened to do so. An unsuccessful suicide attempt—which is too often dismissed as "just a way to get attention," *which it is*—is frequently followed by a successful attempt. Take anyone's threats or attempts seriously, including your own.

• Depression is the most common presuicidal emotional state. It is characterized by hopelessness and isolation. Watch out also for signs of unrelieved anxiety, tension, anger, and/or guilt, for insomnia and loss of interest in work, hobbies, sex, eating, and other usual activities. Be alert to sudden personality changes and wide mood swings, especially if the person seems to become increasingly withdrawn and isolated from his or her usual social environment.

• People contemplating suicide generally do not realize just how restricted their thinking has become. They lose sight of alternatives and opportunities for change and improvement, and concentrate on making an exit. Look for hints that a severely depressed person is preparing for death—making a will, perhaps, settling business or personal affairs, giving away treasured possessions, saving pills or acquiring a gun. The more detailed and complete a plan, the more likely a successful suicide. If someone talks to you about his or her plan (especially a violent one), and if he or she has clearly given it considerable thought and preparation, get help as soon as possible. If your own suicide fantasy seems to be taking on too clear an outline, get help for yourself. See DEPRESSION and LONELINESS, call a suicide-prevention center, and seek professional counseling.

• Self-destructive behavior, such as excessive drinking or reckless driving, may lead to gradual or subintentional (not consciously planned) or disguised suicide. Many suicides take the form of car accidents resulting from depression, anger, impulsiveness, and/or too much alcohol. Accident-proneness may disguise an unconscious wish to endanger one's life. An uncertainly suicidal person may simply leave it up to fate—but behave in so careless a fashion as to give "fate" the edge. If you are accident-prone, explore whether this expresses suicidal leanings.

The suicidal person needs to make contact with someone else who can provide support and interest and point the way to alternative forms of action. Above all, the suicidal person needs help in discovering that time brings change. He or she has forgotten that a crisis is time-limited, that his or her feelings and circumstances will not always be so painful or overwhelming. But, as someone once said, "Suicide is a permanent solution to a temporary problem." Here are some ways to help a person who feels suicidal:

• Put a suicidal person in touch with a helping professional. Suicide-prevention centers, crisis hot lines, mental health clinics, psychiatrists, psychologists, social workers, physicians, and clergy all provide suicide-prevention guidance. They make it easy for a suicidal friend, acquaintance, family member, or loved one to call on professional support without embarrassment. Praise any effort to reach out and cling to communication and life.

• Recognize suicidal talk ("My family would do better without me." "I'm no good to anyone." "I'll never get out of this bind.") and actions (carelessness, hoarding pills, making a suicide try) as expressing a desperate need for help. Such talk or actions are dramatic warnings sent out to the significant others in a suicidal person's life—screaming a message of hurt, confusion, and helplessness. Only a small minority of suicidal people really intend to die. Most are unsure. They may go so far as to leave the outcome of a dangerous act to fate, but all the while they're hoping for someone to show them another way out.

• Beware of too-rapid progress or seemingly total relief from suicidal feelings. People often relapse and commit suicide just when they seem to be recovered; at that phase they may become overly discouraged by normal setbacks. Sometimes a determined suicidal person may pretend improvement in order to get out of a hospital or free of surveillance so that he or she can complete a previously unsuccessful attempt.

• Don't moralize or use excessive force or coercion, which would further diminish the freedom or sense of self-worth of the potential suicide. Don't try to make a suicidal person feel guilty or ashamed. Some people stay alive in spite of suicidal tendencies because they treasure the sense of freedom and autonomy the possibility of suicide provides for them.

• Adolescents and college students make surprisingly frequent suicide attempts, and many succeed. Take signs of depression and withdrawal in young people very seriously. Few teenagers or college students take advantage of crisis centers or suicide-prevention facilities, so other people need to be alert to their need and direct them to help. Young people give warning of their suicidal intentions, so pay attention to their expressions of confusion and despair.

• Listen. Let the potential suicide talk about his or her feelings. Accept the suicidal person *as is*; don't offer advice or intrusive opinions. Try to learn just how bad the situation seems to the suicidal individual and just how well planned the suicide act has become. Don't be afraid to offer basic emotional support: "It sounds like you feel really terrible. Tell me more about how you feel. Have you ever felt like this before? What helped you get through that time? What can I do that will help you now? What can you do that will make it easier for yourself right now? Tell me specifically about the problem; maybe we can see a way out of it." Suggest therapy, a call to a suicide-prevention hot line, a call to the individual's current therapist, if there is one, and a medical checkup to look for possible physically or medicinally caused depression.

• Express your concern. If you think someone has taken an overdose of medication or some sort of poison, go ahead and try to get medical attention: "I'm concerned about you and I think you need to be checked over by a doctor." It is always better to offer help than to be sorry later on for having missed a warning.

• Try to be patient. Be aware of the feelings that suicide brings up for you, so that you can control them. Offer warmth and support to someone who feels worthless and unwanted. Show that you understand suicidal feelings and recognize that the suicidal person is not the first or only one to have considered death as an escape. Help find alternatives and strengthen hope.

• Know how far you are willing to go to prevent a suicide. Before the situation arises, give some thought to the possible need for suicide among the elderly or the terminally ill. Our life-affirming traditions and medical conventions teach us that life is to be maintained at all costs, under any circumstances. Many individuals, however, wish to make the choice for themselves: They plan what is called "balance-sheet suicide" in order to control their time and manner of death.

If you are reading this because you are feeling suicidal, don't wait for someone else to take over for you—help yourself.

• Feeling suicidal or thinking about killing yourself does not mean you *will* end your life or that you have to try to do it. Suicidal feelings are crisis-related; crises always pass. You will not feel this way for long. You can feel this way now and get over it—hopefully never to feel the same way again. Suicide is never an obligation, even if you plan it in detail and tell everyone you know about it; you can always choose to hope and to look for alternatives. You can always change your mind and choose life.

• Wait and see. Give yourself a chance to see if you are passing through a life crisis. (See MID-LIFE CRISIS.) Give time a chance to work its healing. Experience your feelings: despair, anger, loneliness, confusion. Experience your wish and fantasy of suicide . . . but don't do it. (You may find that knowing you always have the option to choose suicide *later* gives you the strength to endure a crisis *now*.)

• What is the real message you want to send to the others in your life? If you can't identify it clearly even to yourself, or find it too difficult to tell others directly, *tell them you feel like killing yourself*. Tell people. If you can't come right out and say you feel suicidal, hint around as best you can. This will increase the odds of someone hearing your call for help.

• Call a suicide-prevention center or hot line, a local mental health clinic or crisis center. Talk to your psychiatrist or psychologist if you are seeing one; if you aren't, *start* seeing one. Seek help from a social worker, your physician, or a member of the clergy.

• Face fully the consequences of your suicide, especially the lifelong burden on any surviving children. Don't delude yourself: Close survivors, especially spouses and children, may need years to work through their sense of loss or guilt or negation of life. Children of suicides are statistically at greater risk of suicide. Your self-inflicted death will "deaden" other people, cause them pain, challenge their faith in life.

• Even if you are alone in life, your suicide will have a depressing effect on others. Do you really want to do this to them? Don't have illusions that no one will care. We all need help from other people to keep up our faith that life is worth living. When one person gives up, it shakes us all.

• If you don't want people to feel guilty for your death, absolve them of responsibility for your decision. Make it clear that it's not your purpose to cast blame on them. If your suicide is intended to inflict blame and guilt, recognize the hostility of your act. Is suicide the best way to express this hostility or anger? Is righteous revenge worth killing yourself for?

• If you are contemplating or actively planning your suicide, take the full responsibility that is yours. Make sure you do the necessary life-affirming things first. Finish up the business of your life in any way you need to: Give thanks to those who deserve it, clean up any emotional messes or misunderstandings that you can, pay your financial debts if possible. In the process of tidying up you might find yourself reinvolved in life and willing to stay on.

• If you really claim your suicide is not a hostile act, don't dump a mess on others. Leave a will. Give as much of yourself as you can to others before you take yourself away. Give them something to remember and cherish.

• Suicidal feelings can sometimes be turned into creativity and positive change. The wish to die or to kill a disliked part of oneself has creative aspects to it if not acted on literally. An intolerable way of life may need to be ended so that a new way can be started. A self-hating part of oneself (a harsh conscience, excessive guilt, a negative self-concept) may need to be "killed" in order to free the rest of your being. We often carry "tapes" or aspects of judgmental parents inside us, and need to silence them. Sometimes atonement or penance serves a cleansing and freeing function that lets us get on with living in a less burdened way.

• Pay attention to your ambivalence. If part of you doesn't want to die, that's because at least part of you has hope of finding alternatives to death. Listen to that part. Nourish your hope and let others help you find alternatives.

• Think about the strong life-affirming traditions of our culture. Is it really your life to take? Is it possible you are planning to commit a truly selfish act? Do you belong only to yourself, or might you also belong to your family, community, society, or even to God? Others do need you. We all need each other. Try to identify proudly with other people who have endured pain and loss and who found new ways to affirm themselves and life.

SUGGESTED READING:

Alvarez, A. *The Savage God: A Study of Suicide.* New York: Random House, 1972.

Farberow, Norman L., and Edwin S. Shneidman. *The Cry for Help.* New York: McGraw-Hill, 1961.

Farberow, Norman L., Samuel L. Heiling, and Robert E. Litman. *Techniques in Crisis Intervention: A Training Manual.* Los Angeles: Suicide Prevention Center, 1968. Write: Suicide Prevention Center, 1041 South Menlo Ave., Los Angeles, Calif. 90006.

Menninger, Karl A. *Man Against Himself.* New York: Harcourt, 1938.

Shneidman, Edwin S., and H. Mandelkorn. *How to Prevent Suicide.* Public Affairs Pamphlet No. 406, twenty-five cents. Write Public Affairs Pamphlet, 381 Park Ave. South, New York, N.Y. 10016.

See also: ANGER, ANXIETY, DEPRESSION, GRIEF, LOSS OF LOVE, MASOCHISM, PAIN, SELF-HATE, STRESS

TEENAGE REBELLION

All adolescents eventually reach that stage of development in which they begin to assert themselves as individuals separate from their parents. The symptoms of this "rebellion" range from mild (staying out late, neglecting homework) to severe (pitched battles with parents, leaving home, getting jailed). Sometimes it drives the parents frantic.

The pressures on these young, developing adults are enormous, sometimes overwhelming. They must make adjustments to their changing bodies and confusing new sexual urges. They must win approval of their peers. Many suffer great anxiety about finding a life's work and fulfilling the heavy responsibilities of the adult world. They are struggling for values, identity, and a sense of self-worth in the midst of chaos. As their parent, you are both their friend on whom they are dependent and their enemy from whom they must separate themselves.

Not every teenager creates havoc during this period, but many do. If your teenager is in full rebellion against you and society, you may feel it's your fault. You almost certainly feel angry and desperate, perhaps hopeless. Don't give up. Your child needs your help and understanding through this turbulent time of life. You can help your child and also turn your difficulties into self-growth by becoming clear about your own standards and needs, communicating them, and taking a confident, independent stand on them with your teenager.

• Be the kind of person you want your teenager to be. To teach respect, be respectful. Show your real attitude about drugs by cutting out or limiting your own smoking, drinking, or pill-taking. Face the fact that your children learn from what you are and do, not what you moralize about.

• Recognize that a cooperative, loving atmosphere in your home is the best demonstration of the importance of love and caring. Your children need to know that these values are real and that they work. If your teenager temporarily refuses to be included, don't let that destroy the other good relationships.

• Avoid nagging or blowing up over small things. You can't possibly control everything that irritates you. Try to find ways around them. If your teen's room is too messy, keep the door closed. If your teen telephones incessantly, get an additional phone. Grit your teeth, and save your parental muscle for the important issues.

• In evaluating the importance of problems, keep in mind that your main concern is to help your child grow into a healthy, motivated, loving adult.

• If only a few issues are causing real problems, discuss them in those terms with your teenager. Say that the relationship is good but these few areas concern you. Ask him or her as a caring person to do it your way. Make it a request, not a self-righteous demand.

• If a difficulty is part of an overall uncooperative pattern, be direct about the fact that you have a difficult situation in the house and that trust and communications are low. Say that one specific problem (drugs, sloppiness, disregard for others in the house) is most intense, and be clear what the rock-bottom requirements are on this issue. Get your teenager to commit himself or herself to work with you on that issue as well as the larger situation.

• Make sure that your rules and the reasons for them are clear in your mind and that you communicate them clearly. Explain why they are important. Explain the consequences for infractions. If rules are broken, explain what the requirement was, how it was broken, and what the consequence is.

• Assess the positive ways in which you can achieve cooperation, such as through rapport or persuasion. Assess ways in which you can force cooperation, such as by controlling finances, TV, use of the car, or other privileges.

• If you have been lax about rules and now are trying to clamp down, don't go too heavy on punishments. Give warnings for early infractions as your child learns your new expectations.

• Don't explode excessively, but don't store things up and then over-kill. Say what's on your mind at the appropriate time, if possible.

• Try to talk with your teenager as adult to adult. If he or she won't do that and instead insists on a parent-child power struggle, make it clear that you will use your parental power if necessary.

• Don't get sucked into arguing on your child's level. Don't bait your child with put-downs or militant commands that invite rebellion.

• Don't impose your will arbitrarily, just to show who's boss.

• Never put down your teenager's feelings, no matter how silly or unreal they may seem to you. They are realities that your child is living with; he or she must discover how to cope with them. If you have good rapport, you can point out what you believe is the truth, but don't push.

• Give your teenager privacy, trust, and psychological space to do his or her own thing, within your basic rules.

• If you think you're being fair but your teenager opposes and argues with you sincerely, consider reexamining your position. Values and customs do change—remember how old-fashioned your parents' views sometimes seemed to you? But don't invite trouble by seeming wishy-washy or confused. Say you know what seems right to you but you are willing to listen to other points of view. Ultimately it's your house and you'll decide your way. Don't be inconsistent about your degree of power and your willingness to use it in a crunch.

• If your teenager is moody or bad-tempered, try discussing it, but it's probably best just to limit your interactions temporarily and wait for him or her to get over it. Get family counseling if the moodiness is really persistent and disruptive. Consider whether your child is sulking to blackmail you into submission, or to take a stand he or she isn't able to communicate in words.

• When your teenager disappoints you or rebels, look at the behavior to see whether it may have a positive aspect of being an attempt to try new skills or learn a new identity. If your daughter uses her mother's makeup and clothes, praise her for learning to be an attractive woman, but probably also discuss the issues of private property and appropriate appearance styles.

• Help your child learn adult responsibilities early, such as saving and handling money, buying clothes, and making decisions about social activities and household responsibilities. Do this in clear, manageable, graduated steps. If you neglect or indulge your child until adolescence and then abruptly require giant steps into adult responsibilities, expect problems and don't blame them all on the child.

• Keep problems from building up by having a weekly meeting of all members of the family, regardless of age. Air any problems, and brainstorm for possible solutions. Use your kids' creative capacities for problem solving. Don't try to manipulate the results. The best decisions are agreed on unanimously. Dictated decisions have less chance of working.

• Learn the art of contracting with your teenager—decide on privileges or compromises you are willing to give, in return for behavior or tasks important to you. The contract must be written down and very specific, with nonperformance penalties stated.

• If your child is in danger from activities such as driving too fast, sexual exploration, drugs, or defying authority, try to channel these activities into positive learning experiences. Share your own learning experiences with your child. Talk about others' experiences. Discuss books and movies about growing up, explore problems and solutions in fantasy. When possible, help your child test new behavior and its consequences. For example, try out the motorcycle in a safe area, driving a little faster than usual. Discuss how that feels, and what might happen if the pavement were wet. Help him or her get the most information for the least risk.

• If your teenager is in trouble but doesn't seem concerned or puts the blame on others such as the law or "the system," help your child realize that regardless of seeming unfairnesses in life, reality must be faced and dealt with. Don't preach conformity—teach reality.

• Try reducing your anxieties about your children by asking self-searching questions of yourself. If you doubt your children's ability to be independent, ask whether you are somehow dependent on them and fear their leaving. If their sexual experimentation frightens you, do you yourself have sexual anxieties or hangups? If they're in trouble with the law, ask yourself how good you are as a model of a genuinely law-abiding, happy citizen. If you discover a problem area, get counseling if necessary to deal with it, so that you can project a different kind of attitude to your children and become more comfortable yourself.

• Don't let anger, discouragement, or revenge make you shut out your teenager. Continue to care and to keep communication lines open. Your child may desperately need contact with you even if he or she won't admit it or doesn't realize it. If your child turns to someone else for advice, don't feel jealous—be glad your adolescent has someone to relate to.

• Don't give up hope, even on hard cases. Tell yourself that you're doing your best in a difficult situation, and take comfort in knowing that most teenagers, despite rebellion, end up being like their parents.

• If you are at your wits' end and need help, or just want to share feelings, join Families Anonymous, an organization for concerned relatives and friends of teenagers. Write P.O. Box 344, Torrance, California 90501, to find a group in your area or for information on starting your own group.

SUGGESTED READING:

Dreikur, Rudolf. *Coping with Children's Misbehavior.* New York: Hawthorn, 1972.

Ginott, Haim. *Between Parent and Child.* New York: Avon Books, 1973.

Gordon, Dr. Thomas. *Parent Effectiveness Training.* New York: Peter H. Wyden, 1970.

See also: ANGER, COMMUNICATION BLOCKS, STRESS, TEEN-AGE SEX

TEENAGE SEX

Most teens need far more constructive communication with their parents on sex than is common today. They need to learn more from Mom and Dad than how babies are made. They need to learn about sharing love, choosing sexual partners, understanding their sexual feelings, how to say no when they don't feel ready for sexual involvement, how to avoid unwanted pregnancy and venereal disease. Above all, they need guidance in making decisions—in choosing for their own good and in accordance with their own true feelings.

Unfortunately, too many teens feel that their parents are strangers or hypocrites who don't really know or care what their children want out of life. If neither parent nor child is comfortable discussing sex, they avoid conflict over sensitive, personal issues by talking in generalities and by not asking direct questions of each other.

As a result, most young people are at a loss to know what their parents would honestly like them to know about sex. Far too few of them learn about essential, sex-related matters from their parents. Instead, they gather information about masturbation, venereal disease, birth control, homosexuality, and other important topics from each other. They pool their ignorance.

Because for a variety of reasons parents often find it difficult to discuss sex with their children, too many teens come to believe that their parents never learned that sex is a natural or beautiful human experience. For the most part, teens find it hard to imagine their parents having a passionate sexual relationship with each other.

This absence of communication is a problem for parents, for sexually active teens, and for teens who are sexually inexperienced. Sexually active teens risk pregnancy, disease, and emotional harm. Recent studies show that teenage girls, who because of their age run increased medical risks in pregnancy and delivery and have limited ability to care for babies, are frequently not using any form of birth control. Sexually inexperienced teens are under great pressure from their peers. They may know that they're not ready for sex, yet worry about popularity and about their sexual adequacy so much that they become sexually involved against their better judgment.

From birth we are sexual beings. As we grow, we learn from our families and from the world around us—friends, playmates, school chums, books, movies, songs, television, the news media—how to express that sexuality. For a child, it may be the most difficult part of growing up. For parents, teaching a child to understand and manage sexuality may be the most difficult and complex of parenting tasks. Here are some guidelines.

• Encourage sex education and family-life programs in your children's schools. Fully informed teens tend to delay intercourse and to use contraceptives. This, of course, helps lower the rate of unwanted pregnancy, and may also help decrease VD.

• Be aware of the often biased influence of movies, television, books, magazines, and your teenagers' friends. Don't rely on the world at large or the local school to be your children's primary source of sexual information and values. Take that role for yourself.

• Discuss sex with your kids. Accept the fact that they are interested in it. It is unrealistic to pretend that even very young people are unaware of sex. Don't punish their interest. Teens whose parents can talk about sex comfortably with them are more likely to make healthy, inner-directed choices. For example, if they do become sexually active, they are more likely to use contraceptives than are teens whose parents react negatively and avoid such discussions.

• Examine your own feelings about teenage sex very carefully. Parents can give their kids confusing mixed messages; at the same time they can impose excessive restrictions and offer subtle encouragement to sexual experimentation. Some parents, for example, severely restrict their teenager's socializing and yet tell explicit sexual jokes that convey a permissive, anything-goes attitude toward sexual relationships. Look at the clarity of your message. Are you saying no and yet (unconsciously, perhaps) encouraging seductive behavior—early dating, excessive emphasis on appearance and popularity? Making a big deal about sex through either repression or encouragement makes it hard for a teen to experiment cautiously and gradually with his or her developing sexual feelings.

• Don't panic if you are suddenly confronted with your teenager's ability to discuss sex frankly. Just because your daughter can tell you in great detail "where it's at" in teen sex this year doesn't mean she's off to an orgy every time she goes out the door. Teens—even if they've accepted their own sexual feelings—still are uncertain how to deal with them and will welcome supportive, caring discussion.

• Think back to your own adolescence. Now as then, control based on fear doesn't work. In fact, too much control frequently leads to rebellious experimentation.

• Teach by example. If you want teenagers to save sex for marriage because your religion forbids nonmarital sex, be sure you're willing and able to honor your own marriage vows lovingly. Teens won't take your advice, even if they know it's good advice, if your own life doesn't reflect what you tell them.

• Recognize that the core issue in sex is that of self-esteem as the basis of decision-making. Help your children develop the independence not to be pressured into doing things they're not ready for. Help them learn to respect themselves and others as individuals who develop at different rates. Teach them to pay attention to their own feelings and not to do something just because someone else has done it.

• Help your teenagers find nonsexual sources of self-esteem at school, in easygoing socializing free of pressure for sexual involvement or early marriage, in sports, music, art, or work. Teens often want safe, social, presexual experiences to prove to themselves that they're attractive, without necessarily having to perform sexually.

• Recognize the power struggles that surround your young person. He or she has to develop a strong sense of self-worth and the independence to make decisions that reflect his or her individual needs. This must be accomplished in spite of the power of parents and peers to say "You are nothing unless you do as I say."

• Pay attention to your teens. If you think they're becoming sexually active, make sure they know how to take responsibility. Inform them about the availability of Planned Parenthood or other family-planning clinics. Reassure them of their right to privacy and to treatment by a private physician. Boys especially need to learn to share responsibility for sexual involvement and contraception. Don't deny your children this sort of information because you disapprove of their being sexually active. Express your values and wishes, but include your concern and understanding. You may not succeed in keeping them celibate, but the only way to remain an influence in their lives is to be approachable and supportive. Remember, many sexually active teenage girls do not use birth control because they're afraid their parents will find out. Would you prefer pregnancy or VD to responsible sexuality?

• Acknowledge your teen's sexual behavior. He or she will find it insulting to be ignored. Teens would rather not have to fend for themselves completely. Share with them what you've learned in your life about expressing sexual feelings, about showing love, about developing an intimate relationship, about giving and receiving pleasure. Recognize the importance of such sharing. Acknowledge your teenager's growing need to know more than anatomy.

• Try not to give the impression that you don't want to discuss sex. This creates a barrier that may become permanent between you and your young person. Teens resist confiding things they feel their parents don't understand. If you can talk about sex only in moral terms, if you can't accept your teenager's experiences and feelings, if you seem to worry excessively, your young person will probably not try to discuss his or her real feelings and experiences with you.

• Recognize that your teenager is as sensitive about his or her privacy as you are about yours, and very vulnerable to your attitudes and judgments. Your reaction to sexual confidences is a powerful element in forming your teen's perception of how you view him or her.

• Don't pry. Although some families use general discussion about "what teens are doing" to avoid exchanging personal information, sometimes it's useful to let a young person ask a sex-related question as if it doesn't have to do with his or her own experience. Don't force your teenager to admit that a question concerns them if they are not comfortable with asking directly. Respect privacy and allow indirect discussions so as to preserve your role as informant and advisor.

SUGGESTED READING:

Pierce, Ruth I. *Single and Pregnant*. Boston: Beacon Press, 1970.
Pomeroy, Wardell B. *Your Child and Sex: A Guide for Parents*. New York: Delacorte, 1974.

See also: COMMUNICATION BLOCKS, TEENAGE REBELLION

TIME-WASTING

You just never have enough time. You run madly around in all directions, and the faster you run, the less you get done. You're late to every appointment. Your work piles higher and higher. At the end of the day you're pooped, but there's still work to be done. All night long, in your restless sleep, you worry about how much work you have to do tomorrow. You dream of being buried in an avalanche of unwashed dishes or being pursued by an army of dissatisfied customers. You oversleep and wake up tired and behind schedule.

Do you really enjoy living like this?

Of course not.

Or do you?

There actually are benefits to being always out of time. It may be that you like being breathless and disorganized. It makes you look important. Other people take pity on you and want to take care of you. You may be inefficient with your time because you don't want to give up control of anything. You want the glory and martyrdom of doing it all yourself.

But if you are sincere about wanting the satisfaction of getting your essential work done and even having time left over to enjoy yourself, there are a multitude of ways to work toward this.

• Decide what's important to you in your work and your life. Write down your long-term goals. Write down some short-term goals that will help you get to your bigger ones. Don't forget to include some relaxation or personal enrichment in your goals.

• Make a detailed survey of how you actually spend your time, both on the job and at home. Keep a time log for a week. Take a hard look at your values and priorities. Face the fact that you can't do everything or be all things to all people. Decide which things you are doing that don't relate to your overall goals. Quit doing them.

• Decide which things you are doing that can be done well enough by someone else, and get someone else to do them. If you don't know how to delegate work or get cooperation from your family, you can learn. You may have to invest time in helping your subordinates or your children to organize their time, or in teaching them how to do the work. You may have to do some friendly bargaining with your spouse to get him or her to share certain responsibilities. Be prepared to be as cooperative with family members as they are with you.

• Make specific agreements or contracts with the people from whom you want more cooperation. Put these in writing, if necessary. For example, post a weekly calendar showing who will do what chores on what days. Have each person cross off the chore as it is done.

• Plan your day. All time management starts with planning. Make a list of essential tasks and make a schedule for doing them. Put two kinds of tasks at the top of your list: (1) urgent, high-priority tasks; and (2) tasks that will give you a big payoff for a short amount of effort. Follow your schedule.

• Do your most demanding work during the part of the day when you're fresh. Save less demanding work for the end of the day. Have a stack of essential but simple tasks with which you can fill in extra time, in case you suddenly have a waiting period during the day which would otherwise be wasted.

• Make double use of waiting time, driving time, or time when you're doing a routine task: Read, listen to music, dictate or tape letters or business reports, learn a language from tapes, make schedules, plan menus, do isometric exercises.

• Use waiting time for relaxing. Close your eyes for a few moments. Breathe deeply and let a sigh come out. Do this whenever you get a chance. You'll have a lot more energy during the day and feel less stressed.

• Organize your work area so that you know where everything belongs, and keep things in their place. When you receive a business letter, insurance policy, bill, or whatever, put it where it belongs. Re-arrange your work space to save unnecessary steps.

• Do things in multiples. Prepare several casserole dinners at once and freeze the extras. Invite three couples over instead of one. Buy in quantity. Use forms and form letters. Make telephone conference calls. Write one memo to cover material for several people.

• Get up a half hour early to gain some especially productive time. Stay a half hour late at the office, or wait till the kids are in bed, to gain some interruption-free time. Shift your schedule to avoid rush-hour traffic.

• Control interruptions. Don't take phone calls when you're in the midst of something important—return the calls later when you want to take some time out anyway. Schedule one limited time of day when you're available for appointments, consultation, or conversation. Sched-ule your out-of-office or out-of-house appointments all on one day.

• Invest money in time-saving devices and helpers: tape recorder, freezer, slow cooker, food processor, secretary, cleaning person, ac-countant, errand boy.

• Find a faster way to do a job, a shortcut to work, an easier way of getting the kids to yoga lessons. Explore alternative methods. Don't be the old dog who can't learn new tricks.

• Make time count when you're with your loved ones. Commit your-self to being with them, and really *be* there. Short amounts of high-quality time are worth more than extended periods when you are tired, distracted, and not all there.

• Bask in the satisfaction of getting things done. Enjoy being in control of your life instead of being a victim of time.

SUGGESTED READING:

Lakein, Alan. *How to Get Control of Your Time and Your Life.* New York: Signet, New American Library, 1974.

Efficient Time Management (cassette course). Audio-Forum, 901 N. Washington St., Suite 200, Alexandria, Virginia 22314.

See also: PASSIVITY, PROCRASTINATION, UNDERACHIEVE-MENT, WRITER'S BLOCK

UNDERACHIEVEMENT

Underachievement often refers to a problem we have in school or work, but it can plague us in many other areas of life as well. We suffer from underachievement whenever our performance falls below the level of which we are really capable. Then we feel disappointment and frustration. Or other people such as teachers or bosses may feel critical toward us and disappointed that we did less than expected.

Why do some people achieve less than they can? They may have deep-seated, unresolved psychological conflicts which show up in passive resistance and avoidance. Too often, school systems turn learning into a passive, force-feeding process. Information passes from the book or the teacher through the learner to the examination paper without being savored, digested, or absorbed by the student. Such an inactive process leaves the learner unnourished, emotionally empty, and disconnected from the experience of learning.

People also may become underachievers because their ethnic heritage or general living environment does not value achievement. Some families or neighborhoods just don't encourage young people to make the most of themselves. Teachers play favorites, and may neglect some students because of their color, sex, dress style, or even their names. One study showed that students with familiar names like John or Mary were graded higher than students with unusual names. Such hidden messages can lead students to define or label themselves as underachievers. Pegging ourselves at a certain level in school can cause us to lower our sights in other parts of our lives.

There is no quick way that we can change the social forces that cause underachievement. However, you can change yourself, and knowing how to do that is the best way to combat underachievement.

You have choices. Although you have been influenced by your background, family, school, etc., underachievement is not just something that "happens" to you. You make choices of action or inaction, struggle or surrender, hope or despair. Instead of just blaming outside forces for your behavior, you can take responsibility for changing that behavior.

• To learn, open yourself up to real contact with the teacher, the successful person, or the material you are trying to learn from. Make the new behavior part of yourself, not just an act you put on or a canned speech you memorize. Don't just observe and copy successful people. You will feel angry and betrayed when you can't achieve the same results. When you imitate others, you merely perform mechanical acts without appropriate feelings or full understanding. Personal involvement is crucial to learning and growth.

• Talk to people whose achievements you admire. Learn how they got where they are. Ask them to tell you about their hard times, their false starts and failures. Don't be overimpressed with the images of success you see. Learn about the struggles that went into that success.

• Accept that you will feel fear and embarrassment in the process of learning. Try to take small, safe steps with supportive allies around you to minimize these feelings. But change means some amount of loss and threat to old ways of being. If you cling to old, unrewarding behaviors and believe "that's the way I am," then trying something new is a threat to your security. We often fall back on worn-out habits of working or studying rather than risk opening up to new ways. Face the fact that achievement requires risk and effort. At the same time, learn to pace yourself, to take on new challenges you can handle, and to rest and recover between bouts.

• Achievers have a strong sense of personal power and acknowledge that their achievements (or lack of them) are direct consequences of their own actions. They take responsibility. Underachievers feel powerless, as though their goals are beyond their personal control. They attribute their failures to fate, circumstances, other people, or lack of inherited ability.

• One way to learn to be more responsible is to use responsible language. For example, say "I," not "you," "one," or "it," when you are talking about yourself. Say "I will," "I won't," or "I don't," rather than "I can't," which implies that you are helpless. Do not say "I'll try" when you really mean "No." That is just a way of getting some credit for something you really do not intend to do. Live in the present. Stop asking yourself *why* you do (or do not do) something—that question diverts you into seeking explanations and excuses. Instead, ask yourself *how* you can do something in a new way. Make statements whenever possible. Do not ask questions unless you really are looking for information. Take responsibility for letting people know what you think, how you feel, what you want or need, and what you really intend to do.

• Use feedback as information rather than reacting to it as personal criticism. What you *do* is not what you *are*. If you hear feedback as an attack or an accusation, you will defend yourself by arguing, explaining, and justifying—and you will miss the valuable information.

• Look carefully at the goals you set for yourself. Underachievers generally set either inappropriately high or extremely low goals. When you set goals too high, you are merely arranging a way to duck responsibility for a poor outcome. No one can do the impossible! If you succeed, it obviously is luck, a fluke, and you do not have to repeat the performance. If your goals are too low, success is meaningless. You have no sense of achievement because anyone could have had the same outcome. In both cases, you do not learn anything about improving your performance and you probably feel bad about yourself.

• Choose moderate goals. Pay attention to your limits and do not make promises that go beyond them. If you get over your head, admit it and get help.

• Take an honest look at how well you honor your commitments and fulfill your obligations. If you cop out often, you are inviting people to look down on you. They won't give you the help and opportunities that you need to succeed. Don't set yourself up for rejection. Clean up any messes you have made as best you can. Don't use past failures as an excuse to hide. Keep the commitments you make to increase your credibility with yourself and others. Show people you want them to count on you, and be sure you come through.

• Ask yourself whether the achievements you are trying to attain are really what *you* want, or something you have been told you should want. If your brother did well in business but you'd really rather be a musician, don't torture yourself trying to compete with him. You have to find your own path.

• If you are confused about your interests and abilities, call a local college and ask about vocational testing and career counseling services. Excellent tests have been developed to help you determine the direction in which you are most likely to be successful.

• When you have a task at hand, focus on what you are doing rather than on external distractions. If you drift off, bring yourself back to the task gently. Concentrate on doing the job, not on worrying about how good you look.

• Turn off the inner critic. Talk to yourself in kind, encouraging words. Do not "futurize" or worry over performance. This behavior leads to self-consciousness and away from involvement. Concentrate on how you will do your task rather than who is watching and what the person is thinking. Take responsibility. Things do not happen *to* you. You *do* things.

• Write out a list of ten things you would like to do that seem a bit risky. "A bit" means that ordinarily you would not do them, although they are not so frightening as to seem impossible. Rank them in increasing order of difficulty. Start with number one. Take one risk a day, and as you do so check it off your list. Give yourself a kind word and a pat on the back each time you risk. Tell a friend what you are doing and how you feel about doing it.

• If you have difficulty in saying no to others and find yourself feeling resentful about doing things you do not want to do, or not keeping promises you wish you had not made, make a point of saying no three times a week. When someone asks you for something, first consult your feelings. If you do not want to say yes, say no, and keep a record of each no. It's a victory!

• Ask for what you want. Do you have trouble telling people what you want? At least three times a week, make a statement, a request, or a demand that says clearly what you want. Keep a record of this assertive behavior. Let people know about your needs and desires. Learn the difference between assertiveness (taking care of yourself) and aggression (bullying others), and between cooperation (working with others) and submission (giving in to others).

• Keep a "time diary" to learn how you actually spend your time and how long different activities really take. One reason for being late or not finishing things on time is having a totally unrealistic notion of how long it takes to go somewhere or to do something. Your time diary will provide the data you need to plan your activities wisely.

• When you have a deadline, use a "backward" calendar. Start with the time or date you must finish and make a list of all the activities that must be completed from start to finish. Use your time diary to estimate the time for each activity. By working backward you then can figure out when you must begin.

• Take a few minutes each day to jot down something specific you appreciate about yourself: your looks, your behavior, your capacity for enjoyment, your achievements, etc. Give your kind inner voices some ammunition for their battle with your inner critic.

• Every time you feel excited, interested, or stimulated, jot down what you have been doing or seeking. After a month or two, you will have a good idea about the kinds of activities that turn you on. Use this information to plan work and leisure time to be more rewarding. You will achieve more if you attempt things that give you real satisfaction.

• Before you attempt to solve a problem, spend some time thinking about methods of solving it. Allow yourself to try out more than one method. Next, examine your assumptions. Do they really fit the situation as it is now? When you have found one solution, evaluate it. Then consider alternatives. There may be several workable solutions rather than one correct answer. Take a look at your problem-solving process and evaluate it along with the solutions.

• Finally, exult in your victories, including small ones. Congratulate yourself. Share your triumphs with others. Give yourself a present or some other reward when you accomplish something you have set out to do. If you treat yourself like the deserving person you really are, *you'll* begin to believe it.

SUGGESTED READING:

Canavan-Gumpert, Donnah, et al. *The Success-Fearing Personality.* Boston: Lexington Books, 1973.

Felton, Gary, and Barbara Biggs. *Up from Underachievement.* Springfield, Ill.: Charles C. Thomas, 1977.

See also: FEAR OF FAILURE, FEAR OF SUCCESS, PASSIVITY, PROCRASTINATION, SELF-HATE, TIME-WASTING

VAGINISMUS

Vaginismus is a condition in which the muscles of the vagina squeeze so tightly that it is difficult or impossible for a penis to enter. This is *not* a voluntary act; it happens even when the woman is excited and *wants* to have sex. Sometimes her partner may believe that the woman is doing it on purpose, which makes for much resentment and additional difficulty.

Often it is hard for a woman to know that she has tightened up. The first sign is usually her partner's difficulty inserting his penis. (Under no condition should a man try to force entry; this can be painful or cause injury.) This difficulty may reflect more than one problem, however; don't rush to diagnose yourself as a vaginismus sufferer.

Lack of lubrication may make penetration difficult. The absence of lubrication can have several causes and solutions. If you feel excited and turned on but don't lubricate enough for easy penetration, you may simply need additional lubrication. Try saliva (yours or your partner's) or a cream such as K-Y Jelly. Do not use Vaseline.

If absence of lubrication is the only problem, this simple solution will usually work. If, however, the absence of lubrication is due to lack of sexual arousal—that is, if you generally don't feel turned on or excited—then this needs attention. If this occurs only with one partner or in one situation, ask yourself honestly: "Am I attracted to this man? Do I feel sexy in this situation? If not, why am I engaging in sex?" If, however, you don't *usually* feel excited in sex, and want to change this, then follow the program outlined under SEXUAL INHIBITIONS.

If you are unsure whether the difficulty in penetration is due to tightening of muscles in the vagina, one way to check is to insert your own finger *gently* into your vagina and see if you can feel whether the vaginal canal is closed off or not. Check this in privacy just after intercourse is attempted and then again at a later time when you are relaxed. If the canal is closed the first time and opened the second, you almost certainly have this problem. If you're not sure, see a gynecologist; this is a good idea in any case.

Though many different things can cause the vaginal muscles to tighten up, usually this is caused by fear or anxiety. Explore your fears about sex: Were you taught at home or elsewhere that sex was bad or harmful? Do you imagine you could be physically hurt by entry of the penis? Have you ever actually been hurt during sex? Sometimes a woman's fear of sex and her tightness may be due to an actual hurtful or frightening experience. Women who are assaulted or raped, or even just pressured into sex, may later feel so frightened of sex that they tense up at the very thought of intercourse. If this is the case for you, take all the time you need to remember, reexperience in fantasy, and let go of the past so that you can be in the present. Talk to your spouse or lover about your fears and their sources. Ask for special patience and gentleness.

The program for alleviating vaginismus involves two parts. The first part involves generally learning to relax and focus on the enjoyable feelings of sex. You can do this by following the recommendations under SEXUAL DYSFUNCTION. You will need to go through the exercises especially slowly, being sure not to rush yourself. You should not do anything that causes you to tense your vagina *even if it's part of an exercise.* You should go so slowly that you are relaxed for each new step.

The second part of the program involves working directly on your vaginal muscles to help them relax:

• First, determine when your vaginal muscles tighten up and how big the opening is when they do. You can check this with your finger. Many women are uncomfortable doing this. If you are, you might get used to the idea slowly, putting your finger in a bit deeper each day. If you can't get comfortable with this, you will need a partner's help or a doctor's (see the next step). Once you determine how tight your muscles get, you can work to relax them by putting your fingers into your vagina and *slowly* expanding the opening.

Using a lubricating fluid (nonirritating hand or body creams are good, but don't use Vaseline), *slowly* insert your little finger into your vagina. Does it go in? If not, you may need to use a thinner object, (nothing sharp or made of glass); a toothbrush handle is often a good start (used very gently). Leave your finger (or whatever) in the vagina for a few minutes without moving it. Repeat this a few times on different days, but only when you are feeling relatively relaxed. You will begin to notice that inserting the same finger becomes easier each time as you get used to it and relax.

When it becomes very easy to insert your finger *and* you feel relaxed with it, move to a thicker finger or object. Later, as you relax even more, you can use two fingers, and so on. Be sure not to rush or force yourself in these exercises—go very slowly. (Remember, you should also be doing the other individual exercises described in SEXUAL DYS-FUNCTION as you do these relaxation exercises.)

• When you are able *comfortably* to get at least two fingers in your vagina on your own, you are ready to begin working with a partner. Before you start working on the muscles with your partner, you should have progressed with him in the caressing exercises to the point where you feel comfortable with his caressing your body, including your genitals. He will then follow the same pattern you did, except that you should work with him only after a caressing exercise. Although you will now be inserting *his* finger (remember lubrication), you should control his movement by holding his hand. Start with his little finger and do not go on until it feels comfortable and relaxed. As you become more comfortable, you can let *him* control his own hands, with the agreement that he will stop and withdraw his finger the moment you say so. Practice this signal so you can feel comfortable that *you* are in control.

• When you have progressed to two fingers with your partner, you are ready to accept insertion of his penis. Again, you should be well lubricated. Also, you should retain control: He should lie on his back while you sit over his hips. You may then *slowly* insert his penis in your vagina. This may be difficult the first time—don't force yourself to do anything you don't feel relaxed about. When you succeed in getting his penis inside you, first try sitting still. Later, if you want to you may try moving around a bit. He should be entirely still, however—you control all the movement. As you become comfortable moving with his penis inside you, you may gradually allow him more freedom of movement. Don't worry if some tightness recurs; this is normal and just needs to be relaxed in the same way. Once you have successfully mastered this problem, you should complete the program outlined for ORGASMIC DYSFUNCTION. This will help you to relax and enjoy sex even more.

By learning to relax and open up sexually by yourself and with your partner you will gain even more than sexual freedom. The ways in which we open and close to the world are all interrelated. Becoming more open and trusting in intercourse means allowing someone "into you" in emotional as well as physical ways. The success you have overcoming vaginismus will give you greater freedom and confidence in dealing with the world.

SUGGESTED READING:

Heiman, J., and Leslie and Joseph Lopiccolo. *Becoming Orgasmic: A Sexual Growth Program for Women.* Englewood Cliffs, N.J.: Prentice-Hall paperback, 1976.

Lopiccolo, Joseph and Leslie. *Handbook of Sex Therapy.* New York: Plenum Press, 1978.

See also: MASTURBATION, ORGASMIC DYSFUNCTION, SEXUAL DYSFUNCTION, SEXUAL INHIBITIONS

VASECTOMY

The problem of preventing unwanted pregnancies can be solved for men by an extremely simple surgical procedure, a vasectomy. This solution has been chosen by millions of men in recent years, and it is estimated that more men than women, worldwide, are now being sterilized.

Is this the right solution for you? To decide, you need adequate, unbiased information, and a decision-making process that suits you personally.

A vasectomy does not require hospitalization, takes only fifteen to thirty minutes, and is usually relatively painless. It involves cutting and sealing off the vas deferens, which are the tubes that conduct the pregnancy-causing sperm into the seminal fluid. One or two small incisions are made in the scrotum, through which the tubes are reached by forceps and then cut. To prevent their growing back together, the tube ends must be carefully sealed off with clips, cauterized, folded over, and tied, or covered with part of the vas sheath. The scrotum is sutured or covered with a dressing and small bandage.

Recovery involves only a few days of discomfort and a short period of avoiding heavy labor. You can resume sexual activity in about a week, but must continue using contraceptives for a few months, until tests indicate that the semen has become sperm-free. Pregnancies have resulted from carelessly done vasectomies and from failure to take precautions after the operation.

Men have vasectomies because of the risk and inconvenience of other birth control methods. Couples sometimes prefer vasectomies because they are surgically simpler, safer, and more economical than sterilization of the woman. It is a popular method of birth control with doctors. However, in spite of enthusiastic testimonials and promotional literature, this is not the whole story about vasectomy.

A vasectomy can be physically difficult for some men. Bleeding or infection can occur. A man can be out of work for up to two weeks, though this is uncommon. More important, research is still being done to determine whether there are negative side effects of trapping the sperm. Some researchers believe that when the body is forced to absorb one of its own products, in this case sperm, this may cause problems with what is known as the autoimmune system. Millions of men all over the world have had vasectomies, however, with no clearly measurable autoimmune problems.

Psychologically, lessened fears of pregnancy can be beneficial to the well-being of both men and women. On the negative side, unrealistic fears of emasculation can cause difficulties afterward, as can pre-existing problems in the love relationship.

If you are considering having a vasectomy, it is important that your choice be informed and thoughtful, rather than impulsive, coerced, or without regard for long-range life consequences. A wisely made choice, based on careful self-assessment, can open up new possibilities for freedom, self-expression, and social contribution.

• Recognize that a vasectomy means closing off a life option. Carefully weigh the reasons you do not want to have any (or more) children. Vasectomies often are performed when childbearing might endanger the wife's health, or when fear exists of Rh blood complications or possible transmission of hereditary handicaps. Some couples choose sterilization because they already have all the children they want or feel they can raise.

• Consider what might happen in the future to make you want children after all: loss of your present children through calamity or divorce; your present children growing up; your remarriage and wish to start a second family; a change in finances, geography, health, or lifestyle. Ask yourself whether you can predict your values, goals, and life situation ten years from now.

• Recognize that a vasectomy may be inadvisable if you and your wife disagree about it, if your marriage is not stable, if your life circumstances are changing, if you have emotional problems, or if you are under thirty-five and have had no children.

• Become informed on all methods of sterilization for you and your wife. Send for Pamphlet #507, "Voluntary Sterilization," from Public Affairs Pamphlets, 381 Park Avenue South, New York, New York 10016.

• Only choose vasectomy if you want permanent sterility, since reversing it is a costly and undependable new procedure. Don't count on using a sperm bank as a way to store your sperm to use later, as this procedure is still highly uncertain.

• Discuss with your partner the positive and negative impacts your vasectomy would have. Recognize that freedom from pregnancy worries may make your wife happy, but she may also have concerns about your fidelity, since sterilized men sometimes feel more free to play around.

• Consider the positive argument that vasectomy is one reliable way for you to take responsibility for contraception, rather than forcing the responsibility on the woman, as men often do.

• Recognize that choosing to remain fertile may inflict on you and your partner continuing anxiety and restricted sexual freedom. Ask yourself whether the option of having children later is worth this price.

• Face the fact that vasectomy is not always free of surgical complications and that its long-range physical side effects are not entirely certain.

• Don't let yourself be talked into vasectomy by anyone, including your wife or doctor. Psychological ill effects are more likely to occur if you are not totally committed to the operation through your free and informed choice.

• Make a general assessment of your health, energy, sense of well-being, sexuality, and marital situation. A vasectomy is not a cure for any problem except pregnancy fears.

• Explore any fantasy you may have that your masculine image is dependent on your ability to father children. Explore any fears that vasectomy will diminish your sexuality or masculinity. Are you reassured that vasectomy removes only the pregnancy-causing sperm, nothing else?

• Talk to couples who have chosen vasectomy and to doctors who perform it. Send for information from the Association for Voluntary Sterilization, Inc., 708 Third Avenue, New York, New York 10017; or Planned Parenthood Federation of America, Inc., 810 Seventh Avenue, New York, New York 10009.

• If there are many rational reasons for you to have a vasectomy but you hesitate, ask yourself whether you have other unconscious reasons, valid or invalid. Ask yourself whether you are simply resisting making a significant life decision. Explore the consequences of making that decision. What action would you then have to take and what feelings would you have to work through? Ask yourself whether you are dodging your share of responsibility for contraception and expecting your partner to risk medical problems or pregnancy.

• If you decide against vasectomy, accept and enjoy your responsibility for retaining life-giving fertility. Make sure you and your partner agree on contraceptive measures. Recognize that you are not obligated to have children later. Consider the consequences of an unplanned pregnancy.

• Understand that pregnancy can still occur following a vasectomy, for any of these reasons: inadequate contraceptive measures during the waiting period, growing back together of the tubes, existence of an undetected third (and rare) tube, or cutting of the wrong tube during the operation.

• If you decide on a vasectomy, choose a doctor who has performed many of them and is aware of all possible problems. Ask which method he uses for sealing the tubes and why he believes that's the best method.

• After the operation, follow your doctor's instructions carefully. Ask your doctor to test your seminal fluid several times during the next two years, as a precaution.

• If, after the vasectomy, you feel anxious, depressed, less sexual, or stressed in your love relationship, compare this with your earlier feelings. Don't blame the vasectomy for problems that existed before the operation or that have other causes.

• If you choose a vasectomy, be sure you have alternative plans for creative, life-giving involvement through your career, or rasing the children you already have, or adoption, or giving love to other children.

SUGGESTED READING:

Fleischman, Norman, and Peter Dixon. *Vasectomy, Sex, and Parenthood.* New York: Doubleday & Co., 1973.

Greenfield, Michael, and William Burrus. *The Complete Reference Book on Vasectomy.* New York: Avon Books, 1973.

See also: ABORTION, LIVING TOGETHER, PREMARITAL SEX, PROMISCUITY, STERILIZATION

VOYEURISM

Observing people is a natural and enjoyable pastime. We are curious to see how other people look and behave. We like looking inside our neighbors' homes and touring San Simeon and other estates. It is pleasant to walk through the bedrooms and bathrooms and imagine what it would be like to live there.

One kind of people-watching—voyeurism—refers to observing activities or acts which could be sexually provocative, such as undressing or bathing. This, too, is an aspect of human curiosity.

Society, as a whole, struggles with the desire to watch. Communities differ in their ideas about how many burlesque shows, topless bars, erotic magazines, and porno movies should be available to the public. Counties pass their own regulations in accordance with local opinion.

In itself, voyeurism is not a problem. The desire to look at nude human beings is normal and healthy for both men and women. Voyeurism is a problem when it violates the privacy of others, produces guilt in the viewer, becomes a compulsive, secret habit, or replaces normal sexual pursuits.

It is likely that a voyeur's childhood interest in sex was suppressed. He or she may have been frightened or confused by a sexual experience beyond his or her comprehension: discovering parents having intercourse, staring at the genitals of the opposite sex, or observing startling changes in mother or sister during pregnancy. As an adult, the voyeur seeks to relive the "forbidden" experience of watching without the anxiety of punishment experienced as a child.

Voyeurs may have serious conflicts about sex roles. Watching a sexual coupling, for example, may allow a voyeur to identify with both partners, safely gratifying some hidden homosexual feelings as well as heterosexual ones. Many voyeurs are in doubt about their sexual skills and attractiveness and consequently are afraid to risk a reciprocal relationship. Looking becomes a sexual turn-on and source of gratification in place of physical action.

• If you feel you have a problem with voyeurism, look for the childhood roots of your feelings about sex and about your own body. Examine your anxieties. Do you fear getting close to another person? Are you afraid to be seen because you feel unattractive? Why are you looking instead of participating? Do you feel sex is wrong? Identify the source of your fears so you can begin appropriate action, such as making yourself more attractive, learning social skills, and making a clear distinction between past problems and present opportunities.

• If you have been caught often in voyeuristic activities, look for an additional motive. Was getting caught an expression of a desire to have some interaction with the person you were watching? Did you want to be seen, and to make the person embarrassed or angry? Are you seeking punishment? (See EXHIBITIONISM, MASOCHISM.)

• Do you know the person you watch? Why are you acting out a fantasy instead of pursuing a relationship? Do you feel it is only safe to look? Review the possibilities for more direct actions and choose some that seem safe and comfortable to you.

• Does the person enjoy being watched? There are often "arrangements" between exhibitionists and voyeurs. A scantily clad housewife may leave her window shades up, subconsciously inviting passersby to peek in.

• What can you do if you are watched by a voyeur? There is no need to panic or make a fuss. Take responsibility for your part in it: Close the curtains, tell the person to leave, call the police if necessary. If you discover that you find it sexually stimulating to be observed, see EXHIBITIONISM.

• Remember that sexual curiosity is natural. We want to learn about other people to better understand ourselves. Anthropologists investigate the mating customs of remote cultures. Psychologists and sociologists study human sexuality, conduct surveys, and publish their findings. Read some books about the things which interest you to indulge this normal curiosity. Look at books and magazines that depict bodies and scenes you like.

• Realize that the "cure" to the problem of voyeurism lies in indulging rather than suppressing your curiosity. There is a rich array of socially acceptable voyeuristic activities: girl-watching on the beach, beauty pageants, fashion shows, etc.

• Go to events which offer the opportunity to watch beautiful and graceful body movement, such as ice skating, ballet, disco dancing, gymnastics, diving. Comment to your companions on the physiques you admire. You'll discover you can share the pleasure of watching with other spectators.

• Investigate hobbies or jobs which allow you to observe and express your imagination about the human body. Take a class in figure drawing, photography, sculpture, or filmmaking. Go to the museum and enjoy the grand tradition of nudes in art.

• Remember that experiencing sexual enjoyment by looking is a natural instinct and a pleasant, normal part of sexual behavior. Work at developing an intimate relationship in which looking can be integrated with touching and caring. Observing and enjoying each other's body is an enhancing part of sexual intimacy. Voyeurism is a problem only if you get stuck in it to the exclusion of other pleasures, or if you bother other people. Otherwise, it can be an exciting prelude to action.

SUGGESTED READING:

Gillan, Patricia and Richard. *Sex Therapy Today*. New York: Grove Press, 1976.

See also: COMPULSIONS, EXHIBITIONISM, SEXUAL PERVERSIONS, SHYNESS

WRITER'S BLOCK

You don't have to be an anguished would-be novelist to suffer from writer's block. You could be a businessperson writing a report, a college student doing a term paper, an applicant for a job, or anyone writing a letter. You can't get started or you can't seem to get it finished or you're plagued by the feeling "Haven't I written this before?"

The fiction writer tears up page after page of manuscript and starts over—and over and over. The free-lance magazine writer barely manages to get the copy to the editor by press time. The advertising copywriter keeps the agency waiting and loses an account. The student doesn't get the thesis in on time and can't graduate with the rest of his or her class. All profess to be "blocked" by mysterious forces within.

Sometimes finding out the cause of your block may be a useful way to find a solution. "Other writers use writer's block as an excuse not to write," asserts Academy Award-winning screenwriter Sterling Silliphant. "I use it as a challenge. I try to find out what's troubling me, why I can't get beyond FADE IN."

There are a number of things to look for. Fear of failure can keep you from your typewriter. You may not be secure enough to face the inner anguish that failure can bring. You may have too much riding on the total success of what you write, so that even the possibility of partial failure is enough to block you with anxiety and avoidance. You may have the will to write, but your conscience can't ever be satisfied that you have written *well,* so you fall back on delaying tactics, seeking merely to get by rather than triumph. Your compulsive, perfectionistic drive will find a dozen nonessential or useless chores for you to do. You overresearch and use up all your time before trying to put one word on paper.

Fear of success can be equally immobilizing. Perhaps you aren't prepared to accept the attention and obligations that success may thrust upon you. (For one thing, you'll be expected to be equally successful the next time.) You may be afraid to compete successfully with other writers or other rivals whom you fear will envy and punish you. "Misery loves company," and success can be an act of treason against your comrades in failure.

Or your block could result simply from feeling stuck with having to write something which really isn't worth the effort no matter how well you do it. Worse than being meaningless, perhaps the writing assignment is actually contrary to your deep inner convictions. The part of you that refuses to write it is trying to tell you something.

Writer's block is not unlike stage fright. Every time you show someone your writing or have it appear in print, it's a form of showing off. You're exposing yourself: "Look at me. Look at what I'm revealing about myself." You may feel guilty about being overexposed as a "ham" and want to hide. Having a writer's block "solves" this problem.

Blocked writers typically let time slip by till the last minute on a deadline assignment—all the while rationalizing that "it's easier to write under pressure"—and then stay up nights on end in a flurry of frenzied effort to slap-dash the whole thing together. The secret payoff is that you can avoid putting your real talents on the line. "I didn't have enough time."

You could be paralyzed by the impossibility of fulfilling a secret grandiose fantasy that you are destined to be a great Literary Lion. You must make either a "big splash" or no splash at all. The gap between your fantasy of lionhood and your inner suspicion of mousehood could keep you blocked forever.

If you are inwardly seething with buried resentment, you may be afraid to write for fear of being attacked by hostile critics. Since writing is an aggressive demand for attention, you may fear that your readers will roast you just as savagely as you would like to roast them. Herman Melville, the author of *Moby Dick,* felt so wounded by critics that he nurtured a writer's block for thirty years in a stubborn attempt at revenge.

You could be using your writer's block to discharge your inner resentment toward authority figures, originally Daddy but now represented by teachers, employers, editors, publishers. You soothe your sense of powerlessness by asserting your power to block, to thwart, to frustrate. You remain essentially a "naughty child" who plays at being a writer. "I won't do what they want me to do, even if I cut off my nose to spite my face."

Recognizing the inner dynamics of your block can help, but the next step is to do something.

• Fully admit up front that you are the cause, creator, and inventor of your block. Admit your own responsibility. That doesn't mean you should collapse into guilt or launch into self-flagellation. Just acknowledge that the mysterious "block" is in some way caused by you for a reason.

• Look closely within. According to Dr. Arnold Cooper, one of the better-known writers' psychiatrists: "Many writers fail to see that they aren't depressed because they're blocked; they're blocked because they're depressed." Look beyond the block; get in touch with all your feelings.

• *Become* your block in fantasy. What are you—a block of granite? Feel that immobility. As the block, talk to the helpless writer trying in vain to get past you. Switch back and forth—argue and plead with the block. What does it say to you? Does it have words of wisdom and guidance for you, as well as opposition? Gradually develop your fantasy to where the block yields or dissolves. Maybe it will even transform itself into a pile of words for you to use freely.

• Warm up your typewriter or your writing hand with a task that "doesn't count." One successful writer starts each day by typing a menu of what he plans to eat for dinner that night. Keep your ambition in check. Start things rolling by trying a short story instead of an epic novel. That's how Thomas Mann began *The Magic Mountain,* until it grew far beyond his expectations.

• Allow time for an idea to incubate. Trying to force work before you are ready is a common cause of writer's block. Relax. Sharpen pencils. Look out the window. Give your ideas time to develop. Don't expect Instant Creativity.

• On the other hand, too much waiting for inspiration is a snare and

THERE IS NO ACTING, ONLY REACTING

paraphrase of :
Walter Brennan

Richard Crenna

5-27-92

a delusion. "Do not wait for the golden moment," a professional writer advises. "It may well be worse." Go to your typewriter. Go straight to your typewriter. Do not pass through the kitchen. Do not collect junk food.

• Give yourself a designated time slot (even if only fifteen minutes) which you will devote exclusively to the writing project you're being blocked on. A famous novelist had a rule that each day he would cover at least one sheet of paper with words, whether good, bad, or indifferent. If you feel blocked from writing because you're waiting for larger chunks of free time, write a page or two a day.

• Try the Probability Theory, which holds that the more you produce by plugging away, the greater the probability that you will come up with something really good.

• If you've passed your time limit for starting your writing stint or if you've got off to some bad starts and struck out, feeling as though you've failed, go on to something else—and set an alarm clock for an hour or two later. When the alarm goes off, start all over again.

• Don't try to write something to fit a rigidly preconceived idea. Compulsive perfectionism is death to creativity. Don't begin at the beginning, necessarily. Try to write a rough draft on a nonstop basis. Cultivate your appetite, or at least tolerance, for chaos.

• If you're blocked on a structured writing task, try writing your ideas in the form of a letter to someone. When Tom Wolfe found himself blocked on his first article for *Esquire,* he gave up in despair and wrote his editor a memo on the subject instead. The editor deleted the salutation, ran the memo as the article, and a magazine writer was born.

• Force yourself to write quickly and voluminously. Garbage is good! Letting yourself go is the most difficult step and the most important.

• Don't expect polished perfection on the first draft. The whole secret of writing is rewriting. Eventually, through the method of Successive Approximation, you will be able to express yourself with clarity.

• Silence your inner critic—the chattering voice within (sounding like an angry and abusive parent)—so you can be free to be spontaneous.

• Post a conspicuous calendar on the wall above your typewriter with your due date clearly marked.

• Keep your mind steadily focused on the approval you will get if you complete the writing project on time.

• Choose a Writer's Block Buddy, who has less difficulty getting down to work and who will serve as a good role model and friendly coach for you. Call your WBB on the phone at times of blockage.

• Think of yourself as too worthwhile a person to suffer the anxiety of worrying about deadlines. People who like themselves don't punish themselves. Be nice to yourself, compliment yourself on your effort and progress, and protect yourself from the enemy within who nags about deadlines and perfectionism.

• "Sneaking up on it" sometimes helps writer Michael Crichton: "I've found I can be very productive for an hour before dinner because there isn't enough time to really do anything, so I can tell myself I'm just screwing around."

• Shake-ups are often effective. Move your typewriter to another room. Use a different lamp. Talk into a tape recorder and transcribe it. Buy some orange paper.

• Don't continually read over what you have just written in order to go back and improve it. Proceed to getting the job done. Don't stop to evaluate your work too soon before you have fully expressed yourself.

• When you are rolling along and ideas are effortlessly flowing, you might be tempted to "take five" in celebration of your victory over the blank pages. *Don't Stop!* Take full advantage of the creative flow while it's happening.

• Bribe yourself. Say that you will allow yourself to luxuriate in one of your favorite pastimes when you finish the writing assignment. If you start to block, indulge in some brief thoughts about the reward waiting for you, then get back to work.

• If you feel you have to leave your typewriter for a short period, do something by yourself. Don't seek someone to talk to. Listen to music. Walk in the garden. Do yoga. Lie down and tell each part of your body to let go.

• "Never talk about what you are going to do until after you have written it," cautions the prolific author Mario Puzo. "Never show your stuff to anybody. You can get inhibited."

• Take more risks in your writing. Get free of your habitual modes of expressing yourself. It's easier to tame down than to think up. So what's the worst that could happen? What are your "catastrophic expectations"? The fear of taking a risk on wild ideas almost guarantees blockage. Loosen up and let new kinds of words, images, and ideas flow. Be willing to be surprised, even shocked.

As you learn more about the causes of your writer's block and the solutions that work, you will end up on better terms with yourself generally. You will learn more about your destructive inner critic and its sneaky tricks. You will tap into your deeper sources of creativity and learn what it is you really want to say in writing to other people. You will discover who the authorities are—real or imagined—whom you are defying with your block. Then you will be able to move past the forced choice of submission or rebellion, and discover the joy of writing for yourself and for readers you care about.

SUGGESTED READING:

Adams, James L. *Conceptual Blockbusting: A Pleasurable Guide to Better Problem Solving.* San Francisco: San Francisco Book Co., 1976.

Kubie, L. S. *Neurotic Distortion of the Creative Process.* New York: Farrar, Straus & Giroux, 1961.

See also: FEAR OF FAILURE, FEAR OF SUCCESS, MASOCHISM, PERFECTIONISM, PROCRASTINATION, TIME-WASTING, UNDER-ACHIEVEMENT

Appendix

BEYOND SELF-HELP: THE QUESTION OF PSYCHOTHERAPY

When do we need psychotherapy? How do we know whether it will help? How do we choose a therapist? We can handle many of our problems ourselves, or with help from friends, relatives, clergy, or others. How do we know when we need expert help from a professional counselor?

We may need outside help if we feel helpless and trapped and too emotionally disturbed to see options anymore. We may need help at the very moment we become convinced that our life is such a mess that no one could possibly help us sort it out. Low self-esteem, unsatisfying personal and work relationships, and self-defeating behavior are all signs that we may need psychotherapy.

You have to make the decision for yourself. Just because you think you have problems—even disruptive and painful ones—or because someone tells you that you need psychotherapy, doesn't mean you must turn yourself over to your local head-shrinker. You have the responsibility to identify your own needs, to choose ways to handle them, to evaluate the professionals who offer to help you.

A therapist with excellent credentials who really helped your best friend may do nothing for you. Some people get considerably worse during therapy, or waste a lot of money and stay the same. Therapy is no magic cure. A great deal depends on your motivation, the relationship you and your therapist create, and the degree to which you take an active, responsible, searching role in your own change process.

• If you are already doing things to deal with the problem areas of your life and you feel good about them, stay with them. If jogging daily reduces your tension to manageable levels, keep at it. If your sex life is slowly improving because you're letting yourself enjoy a richer fantasy life, don't rush off to your business partner's newly discovered sex therapist. Ultimately, you are the best judge of whether or not you are coping. Learn what you can from other people's opinions, but don't let them do your deciding for you.

• Just because you feel the need for therapy does not mean you absolutely require it in order to change. Several recent studies have shown that people who tried to get into therapy programs but were refused because of limited therapist availability showed as much improvement after six months as the people who did enter therapy. We often seek help during a crisis, and crises do pass. Time does heal. Actually, it is our own natural self-healing processes that are at work. Therapy can strengthen and speed up those processes but they often are effective on their own.

• In our happiness- and success-oriented culture, there is a tendency to think that "normal" people do not suffer from stress, anxiety, fear, anger, frustration, depression, loneliness, despair—or anything else that is emotionally "negative." However, it is normal for human beings to suffer and be quite unhappy when sad things occur in their lives. It is normal to fear danger, feel anger, be anxious, become depressed, even give in to despair—sometimes. Accept your emotional changes. Recognize the ways they fit the circumstances of your life. Let yourself feel and experience them fully. The only real constant is change.

• If you feel comfortable with your changeable feelings and have friends or family who will offer support and care when you need it, you can probably meet the crises of your life with no more than the "normal" amount of pain. You're not crazy if you feel pain, just a suffering person. By the same token, you're not crazy if you decide that the pain isn't going away and that you want some outside help.

• Be realistic about what therapy can and cannot do for you. It involves work and commitment. It is not magic or something that someone else does *to you*. It does not merely treat symptoms. It does not barrage you with a stream of advice or put you under the control of an authority. Psychotherapy occurs in a professional—not social—relationship with a trained individual who tries to help you tap your inner resources and develop more creative ways of living. Therapy can help you let go of self-limiting forms of feeling and behaving. It focuses on you. It helps you be honest with yourself. It helps you find options and directions out of "blind alleys." It increases awareness, fosters new and productive ways to live, shows you alternatives to hopelessness, helplessness, and despair. It is growth. Sometimes it is fun. And it is hard work.

• Be aware of the variety of therapists and therapies available. Many different professions offer psychotherapy and counseling services: psychiatrists, psychoanalysts, clinical psychologists, psychiatric social workers, marriage and family counselors, some members of the clergy. There are lots of different forms of therapy to choose from, such as psychoanalytic, behavior, client-centered, humanistic, transpersonal, Gestalt, cognitive, rational-emotive, primal, bioenergetic, and Reichian. Each of these has its own theories and techniques; all of them can be successful for receptive patients. Before deciding which therapist practicing which kind of therapy might suit you, you will want to learn about the available choices. Find out what each involves. Local or county psychological associations sometimes conduct explanatory seminars for the public. What approaches fit in best with your own needs, values, and goals?

• Choose a therapist with great care if you have decided that you want to work with one. You can get information about therapists practicing in your area from local mental health associations, local or state psychological and/or medical associations, social work organizations, hospitals, your physician, your clergyman, your school counselor. Professional organizations—medical or psychological—often provide directories of members that include their educational and specialty training backgrounds as well as indicating the types of services they offer. Formal credentials are no guarantee of competence, but they do provide you with some useful information.

• It might be worth checking out a therapist who seems to have helped someone you know change in ways that you would like to change. But remember that each person is different, and each patient-therapist combination is unique.

• Investigate at least two therapists before making your choice. This will give you a basis of comparison so that you will know whether you are reacting to the therapist as an individual or to the experience of having your first therapy session. Go in with your whole list of questions: What kind of training and orientation does the therapist have? What does therapy cost? How long might it last? Discuss your needs, fears, concerns. Don't worry about appearing nervous, uncertain about your decision to begin therapy, or ignorant of psychological terms and ideas.

• Not every therapist will answer every question, sometimes on theoretical grounds. Don't be surprised by this. Watch out for evasiveness, pretentiousness, and defensiveness, however. Trust your own judgment. If you think you're being lied to, put down, or categorized, go elsewhere.

• It is usually possible to begin therapy on a trial basis. If you don't feel that the relationship is developing in helpful ways, discuss your objections and feel free to stop. Be sure you are not running away from something you need to face, however. There is no such thing as a perfect fit—you'll have some degree of conflict or disagreement even with a therapist who is well suited to you.

• Trust your own feelings and perceptions, after taking time to examine them carefully. Having faith in a theory and in a therapist can help you get off to a good start, but you need to remain skeptical and in touch with your own experience. Don't be impatient or expect change to occur in some rigidly outlined way. Learn to see yourself as an essential contributor to the process you've begun.

• A competent therapist does not tell you what you *should* be. Instead, he or she will help you explore who you are and what you wish to become. If therapy sessions repeatedly leave you feeling less adequate than when you started, or if the therapist seems to minimize your potential and narrow your options, you're in the wrong place. A good therapist will help you strengthen your sense of competence and worth at the same time you deal with whatever brought you into therapy. Needing help doesn't mean you're helpless, inadequate, or crazy, even if you sometimes feel that way. It just means that you, like many others, need help. Psychotherapy, carefully selected and responsibly used, can be a great source of that help.

• Whether or not you enter psychotherapy, you may also wish to consider joining a peer self-help group of people working together to solve difficulties similar to yours. For information about self-help groups for almost any problem, write to: National Self-Help Clearing House, 33 W. 42nd St., Suite 1227, New York, NY 10036, or consult *A Resource Guide to Self-Help Groups*, obtainable for fifty cents from *New York Magazine*, Dept. H, 755 Second Ave., New York, NY 10017.

SUGGESTED READING:

Allen, Robert D., and Marsha K. Cartier, eds. *The Mental Health Almanac.* New York: Garland STPM Press, 1978.

Barron, Jules, Benjamin Fabrikant and Jack D. Krasner. *Psychotherapy: A Psychological Perspective.* New York: Simon & Schuster, 1971. Obtainable for one dollar from Selected Academic Readings, Division of Simon & Schuster, 1 West 39th St., New York, NY 10018.

Bry, Adelaide. *Inside Psychotherapy.* New York: New American Library, 1972.

Council for the National Register of Health Service Providers in Psychology. *National Register of Health Service Providers in Psychology.* Washington, D.C.: Council for the National Register, 1978.

Fabrikant, Benjamin, Jules Barron, and Jack D. Krasner. *To Enjoy Is to Live—Psychotherapy Explained.* Chicago: Nelson-Hall, 1977.

Kiernan, Thomas. *Shrinks, Etc. A Consumer's Guide to Psychotherapies: From Freudian Analysis to Sex Therapy.* New York: Laurel, 1974.

Kovel, Joel. *A Complete Guide to Therapy: From Psychoanalysis to Behavior Modification.* New York: Pantheon Books, 1976.

National Institute of Mental Health. *Trends in Mental Health—Shopping for the Right Therapy.* Pamphlet available from the Superintendent of Documents, U.S. Government Printing Office, Washington, D.C. 20402. Stock No. 017-024-00594-1.

National Organization for Women. *A Consumer's Guide to Nonsexist Therapy; Choosing a Therapist; The Rights of Clients in Therapy.* Obtainable at $1.25 from Barbara A. Lewis, Ph.D., Coordinator Psychology Comm., NOW-N.Y. 84 Fifth Avenue, New York City, NY 10011.

Park, Clara Claiborne, and Leon N. Shapiro. *You Are Not Alone. Understanding and Dealing with Mental Illness. A Guide for Patients, Families, Doctors and Other Professionals.* Boston: Little, Brown, 1976.

Ruitenbeck, Hendrik M. *The New Group Therapies.* New York: Avon, 1970.

Smith, Adam. *Power of Mind.* New York: Ballantine Books, 1975.

Index to Common
Psychological Problems

8